Recoding World Literature

Recoding World Literature

Libraries, Print Culture, and Germany's Pact with Books

B. Venkat Mani

FORDHAM UNIVERSITY PRESS

New York 2017

Fordham University Press also publishes its books in a variety of electronic formats. Some content that appears in print may not be available in electronic books.

Visit us online at http://www.fordhampress.com.

Library of Congress Cataloging-in-Publication Data available online at http://catalog.loc.gov.

Printed in the United States of America

19 18 17 5 4 3 2 1

First edition

To

Periatte

Muniatte

Amma

and the memory of Appa

For all those stories, for all those books.

CONTENTS

Recoding World Literature

Prologue

When a citizen of a future age shall look back upon the present era of German history, he will see more books than men. . . . The meditative German nation, devoted to the exercise of its intellectual and imaginative faculties, has always time for writing. It invented the printing press for itself, and now keeps indefatigably the great machine at work.

—WOLFGANG MENZEL, "The Mass of Literature" (1828)[1]

You will certainly fancy, my dear child, that I am very fond of books. . . . But you would be quite mistaken. I am a machine, condemned to devour them and then, throw them, in a changed form, on the dunghill of history. A rather dreary task, too.

—KARL MARX, "Letter to Laura Lafargue" (1868)[2]

This is a book about books. It focuses on literary works that migrate to different parts of the world, often as books, and gain recognition as world literature. How do books travel? How do they become vessels of stories and migrate from one geographical area to another? How do they find shelf space in libraries of new readers? Why do some books travel and others do not? These questions are at the heart of the book you have in your hand, or, depending on the medium, on the screen of your electronic reading device. These questions have somehow informed my childlike curiosity about stories from elsewhere carried by books, even before I found the right words to formulate them. In many ways, this book is a result of my return to questions I asked of literature a long time ago.

Before I acquired formal training in literature and literary criticism, became acquainted with terms such as *world literature* and *history of the book*, and knew how to engage with or stage these terms—indeed long before I coined the conduit *Bibliomigrancy* to understand the movement of books—my first interaction with stories that were written down and printed (rather than told from memory or read to me) was at the point when I had acquired literacy in Hindi, my first language.

My first exposure to *viśva sāhitya* (world literature) was through a children's magazine called *Nandan*. In the early 1980s, the magazine carried a series called "Viśva kī Mahān Kritiyān" (Great creations of the world), which featured abridged versions of ancient epics as well as novels and short stories from modern literatures of the world. The first page had the title of the story and a colored illustration. On the second page, the top right column carried a short biographical blurb about the author or something about the work. As a child I was more interested in the story—the plot—than the biographical blurb, which I would read only after I had finished reading the story. At one point, slowly, I became aware that along with *Ramayana*, *Mahabharata*, and *Shakuntala*, the *Epic of Gilgamesh*, *One Thousand and One Nights*, and the *Odyssey* were great creations of the world. I realized that along with Indian classical authors (such as Valmiki, Vyasa, and Kalidasa) and modern authors (such as Rabindranath Tagore, Munshi Premchand, Mahadevi Varma, and Nirmal Varma), authors from other parts of the world (Jane Austen, Honoré de Balzac, Anton Chekhov, Daniel Defoe, Charles Dickens, Maxim Gorki, Omar Khayyam, Nasrettin Khoja, Guy de Maupassant, Sheikh Sa'adi, William Shakespeare, Leo Tolstoy among others) also belonged to the group of "great writers" of the world, who produced "great literature."

Of course, it was a very canonical exposure to world literature, but as a child, the canon was the least of my concerns. My criterion for greatness of a work was simply based on two simple factors: the plot and the characters. The fact that the works I read were translated and abridged did not matter; questions concerning why specific texts were selected for the *Nandan* series were beyond my approach. However, the interest created by the magazine continued over the years through school textbooks. English textbooks carried excerpts of works mostly from British but also from some American and Indian-English authors; Hindi textbooks, along with works of most famous Hindi authors, occasionally included translations of authors from other Indian languages. A sense of the multilingual creation of literature in various parts of India and the world was one of the greatest lessons of this early engagement with literature. This was for me the beginning of my own personal pact with books.

And then one day, in November 1984, the Soviet bookmobile—a traveling bookstore, not a lending library—arrived in Haridwar, my hometown. The off-white minibus (a Bajaj Matador) had the Soviet flag hanging from the railing of the rooftop carrier; a white banner in loud red Hindi font bearing the inscription "Soviyata Pustaka Pradarśanī" (Soviet Book Exhibition)—bracketed by hammer and sickle, also in red—hung high above the minivan, the two ends of the banner tied to bamboo poles freshly dug just for them. The table set in front of the minivan had a veritable smorgasbord for the hungry small town readers: along with colorful pop-up books with Soviet folktales, books on science and technology, and biographies of Lenin, Stalin, and Brezhnev (both in Hindi and in English), the bookmobile also carried Russian literature in Hindi and English translation. This was where I bought the first Russian novel I ever read: *Aparādha aura Daṇḍa*, a Hindi translation of Fyodor Dostoevsky's *Crime and Punishment*. I had no idea who Dostoevsky was, or what this work was about. All I could see was a beautiful book with some black-and-white illustrations and eight hundred pages available for very little money: ten rupees. In a lower-middle-class Indian household, the cost of books mattered. The Soviet bookmobile may have provided the image that led me to think about *bibliomigrancy*.

In a world without computers, the Internet, or online vendors such as Amazon, in a small town in northern India where the municipal public library only existed on paper, magazines like *Nandan* and vendors like the Soviet bookmobile and the A. H. Wheeler's book kiosk at the local train station became sources of glimpses to a larger world of literature, and a larger world per se.

My conscious interest in libraries as spaces developed perhaps during my undergraduate years at the Jawaharlal Nehru University (JNU) in New Delhi. The JNU library, a ten-story brick building that stands at the center of the campus, was my emotional refugee camp during the transitional period from my late teens to early twenties. The library introduced me to many European literary traditions in English and Hindi translation, alongside German literature in translation, and slowly, as my knowledge of German expanded, in the original. Off-campus, in the city center, the Soviet Cultural Center was no longer active (I started college in 1990). However, the British Council, the American Center, and the Max Müller Bhavan (Goethe Institute) libraries, which were all on the same street, were the prime sources of classical and contemporary literatures from the United Kingdom and Commonwealth Countries, North America, and Germany, much as the great Sahitya Akademi Library was a source of Indian literatures in approximately twenty languages. Access to literature, especially at a subsidized rate, was crucial to my formative years as a student of literature. Even with literacy in three languages and speaking competence in four more, translations into Hindi and English, and later into German, were some of the most important sources of access to literary texts from elsewhere.

Many years later, in the fall of 2008, after my first book on Turkish-German literature was published, I found myself (again) in the Staatsbibliothek zu Berlin–Preußischer Kulturbesitz (Berlin State Library–Prussian Cultural Heritage). I was looking into some sources on Indian revolutionaries in Berlin in the early twentieth century. The search term *Germany-India* led me, among other things, to the Aloys Sprenger Collection at the Staatsbibliothek, which, as I would later find out, was the largest and one of the most expensive acquisitions of Arabic, Farsi, and Hindustani books and manuscripts by a German library in the late nineteenth century. Outside of the Sprenger Collection, long catalogs of manuscripts and printed volumes of Arabic, Chinese, Japanese, Persian, and Sanskrit works in the Staatsbibliothek (and other German libraries) made me forget the research that I originally intended to conduct. Why were these books and manuscripts in Germany? How did they get there? What were they doing in German libraries? Was there a large readership for these works? After all, many of them were translated into German and published in German cities such as Leipzig, Berlin, and Munich, among others—long before Germany was unified as a nation in 1871.

As I pursued these questions, it slowly became clear to me that books are hardly innocent bearers of stories. No translation, no transmission of stories happens in a historical-political vacuum. As a reader with questions, I was as much located in a historical moment, as were the books and, more importantly, the libraries that accumulated, classified, and then dispersed them to their readers. Suddenly, the spaces where I found the materials became as interesting as the materials themselves. The role of libraries in acquiring, amassing, and circulating world literary artifacts—whether or not they were classified under that rubric—was hard to overlook.

This early research period coincided with my interest in a different kind of library: the European Digital Library. While Google Books, the Hathi Trust, and other digital collections were slowly becoming everyday research tools, I had never envisioned a transcontinental library that was a conglomeration of many "national" libraries and acted as their digital surrogate. Was the "national" library of any European nation, whose acquisitions reached far beyond the political boundaries of a nation-state, necessarily *national*? There seemed to be a clash between the materials contained within the four walls of a library and the self-image of the library in a virtual space. Material considerations seemed as important as political factors; the transformation of the book from a physical, palpable entity to a pixilated one and the recirculation of old manuscripts through digitization simply could not be overlooked.

These encounters with the material and digital circulation of books formed one important personal strand in the making of this book; the second came through an engagement with the term *world literature*. In 2007, I was offered the directorship of the Global Studies Center at the University of Wisconsin–Madison. This seemed to be the perfect opportunity to start a dialogue among colleagues and graduate students concerning discussions and debates about historical and contemporary world literature. UW–Madison was a prime center for debates on comparative and world literatures after World War II; one of the first conferences on the topic, "Teaching of World Literature," was organized here in 1959. To revive this tradition, with support and collaboration from colleagues in the departments of English, Spanish and Portuguese, and French and Italian, I organized a fiftieth anniversary conference on the topic in 2009, which culminated in the publication of "What Counts as World Literature?" a special issue of *Modern Language Quarterly* (June 2013), which I coedited with my colleague and friend Caroline Levine.

In these discussions and debates, I learned how criticisms of world literature were usually organized around the politics implicit in the formation of *conceptual collections* of world literary works: canonical European literatures, postcolonial literatures, regional and vernacular literatures, to name just a few. Little attention was paid to the actual materiality of these collections, and when it did happen, for example in criticisms of world literary anthologies in translation, the term *world literature* was considered to be a manifestation of current economic globalization, a neoliberal venture, as Emily Apter and Gayatri Chakravorty Spivak have argued.[3] Their ideas about the "power politics" of literatures in translation are illuminating, but they seemed too lodged in presentist concerns of globalization and the purported cultural homogeneity that comes with it. Using *power imbalance* as a blanket term to define all developments in the history of world literary ideas seemed as reductive as urging for a replacement of Goethe's *Weltliteratur* with Rabindranath Tagore's *Bissho Shahitto*.

How did world literature emerge as part of a globalizing power politics of the world? How did literary works circulate from one part of the world to another? Why did they circulate and under what circumstances? It seemed to me more important to pursue these questions, rather than offering another argument against reading in translation.

These two lines of inquiry—about the material circulation of books on the one hand, and world literature on the other—came together organically during my tenure as an Alexander von Humboldt Experienced Research Scholar (2011–2012) at the Leipziger Buchwissenschaft, University of Leipzig, where I learned interesting ways of looking at German book history. But it was at the Deutsche Nationalbibliothek (German National Library) and its Buch- und Schriftmuseum (Museum of Script and Writing), as well as the University of Leipzig's Bibliotheca Albertina that I had a confirmation of what Wolfgang Menzel once wrote about Germany's passion for books. It was in these libraries where it became clear how many German authors, including Marx, had devoured books like machines; how the German proclivity for books and for translating literary works from other languages created conditions for the inception and proliferation of the term *Weltliteratur*. To think of this proclivity for books merely as a love for knowledge would be entirely wrong; in the absence of a colonial empire, Germany emerged as an empire of books, at least in that period.

Even today, Germany is the world's leading publishing nation; according to UNESCO's *Index Translationum*, German has a share of 10 percent of the global translation market. This might be considered low compared to English: 55 to 60 percent of translated works in the world are originally written in English. However, only 2 to 4 percent of books published in the United States and United Kingdom are translated from other languages. Comparatively, the share of translated literature into German is rather high at 12 to 18 percent per year.[4]

But the empire of books and the empire of translation are not the only phrases that define circulation of world literature in Germany. World literature as a function of Germany's pact with books underwent many changes over the course of two centuries. It faced challenges in times of heightened nationalism, such as in the late nineteenth century and during the National Socialist period. Furthermore, the forty years of two German states witnessed a clear ideological orientation of world literature and book production. The tensions between the image of Germany as a reading nation (*Lesenation*) and a book market (*Büchermarkt*) found new manifestations in the twentieth and early twenty-first centuries. In each historical moment, world literature was coded and recoded differently, thus unfolding multiple meanings of the term. But to claim that Germany was, or is, the center for world literary production and circulation would be a mistake. Germany remains an important node in the world literary network, in spite of, and at times because of, its complicated pact with books, which in turn is fraught with the burden of its turbulent past.

In short, my initial curiosity about books and libraries became enriched with discoveries of multiple stories of creation of world literature in Germany.

The nineteenth-century British poet and grammarian William Barnes once wrote:

> Books in long dead tongues that stirred
> Loving hearts in other climes;
> Telling to my eyes, unheard,
> Glorious deeds of olden times.[5]

Writing this book has taught me that a book—whether in a tongue living or dead—must go a long way before it manages to stir a loving heart in other climes. To feel that stirring in translation is the beginning of a recoding of world literary works and their worldwide readers.

Madison
Washington DC
New Haven
New York
Tucson
Charleston
Buenos Aires
Lübeck
Cologne
Berlin
Brussels
Leipzig
London
Dresden
Paris
Prague
Frankfurt
Weimar
Belgrade
Istanbul
Sarajevo
Rome
Alcalá de Guadaira
Granada
Athens
Hattusa
Nineveh
Baghdad
Alexandria
Nippur
Isfahan
Moscow
Samarkand
Ghazni
Kurukshetra
Lucknow
New Delhi
Ayodhya
Agra
Allahabad
Macau
Calcutta
Somanatha
Bangkok
Phnom Penh
Jaffna
Colombo
Dakar
Timbuktu
Bamako
Sierra Leone

Introduction: World Literature as a Pact with Books

> The Universe (which others call a Library) is composed of an indefinite, perhaps infinite number of hexagonal galleries. . . . Like all the men of the Library, in my younger days I traveled; I have journeyed in quest of a book, perhaps the catalog of catalogs.
>
> —JORGE LUIS BORGES, "The Library of Babel" (1949)[1]

> My dazzled eyes could no longer distinguish the world that existed within the book from the book that existed within the world.
>
> —ORHAN PAMUK, *The New Life* (1998)[2]

The universe arranged like a library, the world indistinguishable from the book. Two authors from two different parts of the world: Borges, the Argentine modernist, once director of the National Public Library in Buenos Aires; Pamuk, the Turkish Nobel Laureate, founder of the Museum of Innocence in Istanbul. The former wrote in Spanish, the latter writes in Turkish; their literary careers are separated by a few decades of the twentieth century. And yet, through their penchant for material collections, they cross paths in fictionalizing two important institutions of literary circulation: the book and the library. As these authors juxtapose the fictions of the universe and the world with those of the library and the book, they pose fundamental questions about literature's relationship to the book, the library, and the world.

In "The Library of Babel," Borges recounts the narrator's journey in the quest for a "catalog of catalogs."[3] The narrator travels in the hope that such a catalog is the key to understanding the classification of the contents; that it might somehow help to make some sense of the indefinite and infinite nature of the library. In *The New Life*, the protagonist Osman ends up in a much smaller, private, "finite" library, and creates an inventory of its contents. The novel narrates the journeys of the protagonist Osman, who is in search of the author of an anonymously published book, also titled *The New Life*.[4] His quests lead him to the private library of a railroad engineer, which contains "translated works of Dante, Ib'n Arabi, and Rilke from the world classics series published by the Ministry of Education . . . translations of Jules Verne, Sherlock Holmes, Mark Twain" and many others.[5] If Borges's narrator travels in search of a single book that contains information on all books in an infinite library, Osman's journeys lead him to many books from many different parts of the world, whose translations are sponsored by the Turkish state.

I start with Borges and Pamuk not just because books and libraries are so central to their work, but also because they do not just belong to Argentina or Turkey. Through translations into many world languages, their works have traveled beyond their linguistic and cultural origins—as printed books, and more recently as e-books—and have made room for themselves on the physical bookshelves of public and private libraries and their increasingly common electronic versions around the world. Readers like me who are neither from Argentina nor Turkey might not have *inherited* Spanish or Turkish as our mother tongues. Yet we *inhabit* the worlds created by Borges and Pamuk through the act of reading, often in translation. We receive their works *recoded* in languages in which we read them; at a distance from their national locations, we assign new meanings to their works.

"The Library of Babel" and *The New Life* are much more than stories of their protagonists' journeys. They embody journeys of books, what I have come to call *bibliomigrancy*: the physical and virtual migration of literature as books from one part of the world to another. It is this migration of literature as books, this bibliomigrancy, as I want to show in this book, which contributes to the creation of a worldwide readership. Readers of translated works are not just recipients of bibliomigrancy. Along with translators, publishers, librarians, editors, booksellers, and a host of other actors, readers shape and inform bibliomigrancy. It is through bibliomigrancy that literary works that are identified—coded—as part of a national literature acquire new identities and are recoded as world literature. And this is the story of world literature that this book tries to tell: a story of coding and recoding, of transformed identities of literary works, alongside the term *world literature*.

Libraries play a special role in my story of bibliomigrancy. While scholars of world literature have begun to pay attention to material circulations of literature through booksellers and translators, there has been surprisingly little attention to libraries in recent accounts. Libraries, like books themselves, are not mere storehouses of information. They are places where texts from many places around the world can be gathered, catalogued, and known, and as such they present themselves as images of the world. The term *library* has multiple significations: a house of books, a catalog of titles, a publication series, a collection of various kinds of artifacts, including but not limited to books, papers, photographs, music, and so on. Libraries are not *merely* synonyms of the universe, as Borges implies; much as books are not *simply* replicas of the world, as Pamuk imagines. However, there is a sense of accessibility (or inaccessibility) to the world, no matter how exaggerated, that books and libraries presume to contain. Books and libraries operate on the probability of imagining the world, as a whole or in parts. They offer the possibility of encoding the universe and the world—including divisions, fragmentations, differentiations—making the world and the universe legible, interpretable, decodable, and recodable. As much as literature itself encodes the world with aural and verbal signs and promotes the pursuance of mimesis and representation—aesthetic, epistemic, political—libraries present themselves as prolific, substantial, and expansive (if not entirely all-encompassing) *texts* that rely on the collective fiction of knowledge about the world.

Libraries are located, but books can be relocated. If for a moment the library is imagined as the physical or virtual home of large and diverse collections of books, world literature begins to appear as the contents of a global bookmobile, a collection of dispersed literary texts, which are either forever homeless in the new languages in which they exist or have found new homes on the shelves of new readers beyond their points of linguistic and cultural origin. World literature becomes a mode of access to the world through books, an imagination of the world through literature, *a* literary catalog of the world, which might contain some but not all items from canonical catalogs of national literatures. World literature, however, cannot be *the* definitive literary catalog of the world. Akin to the multiple definitions of literature itself, the catalog too is dynamic and transformative and is defined differently in different literary traditions and historical moments.

At once dynamic and ever changing, a library of world literature comprises texts that migrate in the original or translation, and that are both cause and effect of bibliomigrancy. Access to world literature gives access to the literary catalog of the world and, in turn, to an imaginary global bookmobile.

The primary task of this book is to explore ways in which libraries in their multiple meanings fortify, enrich, and challenge our understanding of world literature. I am interested in exploring the affinities, proclivities, liaisons, and mutually enriching synergy of books, libraries, and world literature. I want to emphasize the dual role of books and libraries as material (*Gut*) and intellectual (*Geist*) artifacts in the circulation of literature *as* world literature, in the construction of a world literary space, and in the creation of a world literary readership. Books and libraries, I argue in this book, are crucial to bibliomigrancy and the coding and recoding of literature as world literature.

Since the moment of its documented inception in the European literary space as *Weltliteratur*—a term that gained traction after its use by Johann Wolfgang von Goethe (1827) and its immortalization by Goethe's secretary Johann Peter Eckermann (1836)[6]—world literature has promised access to literature as *Gemeingut* (shared property), implying something larger, something greater; that which is more than the sum of its parts. The term carves a space that operates in relation to—and simultaneously at a distance from—national, regional, and local arrangements of literature. World literature insinuates a mode of construction and organization of literary knowledge founded on comparison on a global scale. Like many libraries—and often assisted by literal libraries—the concept of world literature imagines the gathering, collecting, and arranging of texts that cross linguistic, national, chronological, and regional origins.

This book makes the claim that an engagement with the materiality of literary circulation sheds new light on the conceptual and ideological creation and proliferation of world literature. Three central arguments support this claim. First, the term *world literature* is a construct, and the construction of the category "world literature," especially since the early nineteenth century, has relied on an indelible connection between the book and the socio-political world. Second, libraries have served as important way stations in the collection and dissemination of world literary texts as books or manuscripts in the original and in translation; along with publishers and booksellers, libraries have contributed to the conceptualization of world literature as a literary catalog of the world. Third, and most importantly, world literature as a literary catalog of the world is far from a neutral, alphabetically organized bibliography of masterpieces translated into world languages. Translations of literary works into other languages and their circulation and reception beyond cultural or national origins do not happen in a historical, socio-cultural, or political vacuum. The proliferation of world literature in a society depends on its relationship with print culture: its pact with books.

The title of the book invokes two meanings of *coding*. One comes directly from the vocabulary of library professionals, where *coding* refers to identification and classification of an item, the act of assigning a call number. The other derives from translation studies: recoding as an act of rendering a literary work legible, accessible, and comprehensible in another language, thereby assuring a new life of the work in the new language. Coding can now also refer to the digitization of books, and certainly electronic collections are changing the nature of both libraries and access to world literature.

By discussing dual processes of coding and recoding, the identification of works of literature in the original as *national literature* and their reidentification in translation as *world literature*, I underscore the dynamic nature of world literature. What is identified as world literature undergoes transformation in different historical times and in different geographical locations and linguistic traditions. World literature is historically conditioned, culturally determined, and politically charged. A print cultural investigation of world literature in tandem with historical-political conditions assists in understanding the multiple formations, identifications, and codifications of world literature.

Scholarly works published in the last ten years ask new questions of the very institution and institutionalization of world literature. However, the walls of the classroom, the borders of the university campus, and the precincts of the conference venue have largely defined the physical and conceptual parameters of institutionality. Current debates often conflate the historic burden of the international division of literary labor with that of scholarly expertise, reducing world literature to a largely academic discipline with its foremost concerns being those of teachers and students. Scholars either focus on individual works and authors that have already gained a world literary status or critique institutions such as universities and academic publishing houses that have contributed to the proliferation of world literature as a consumable product. The intellect (*Geist*) trumps the matter (*Gut/Ware*); the imagination (*Vorstellung*) of the world somehow stays detached from the processes that defined the position (*Stellung*) of the world and world literature, now or in the past. The political, cultural, and social conditions that initiated, facilitated, even suppressed the circulation of world literature as *Gemeingut*—with all the problems that come with *shared* and *property*—are overshadowed in contemporary scholarship by an excessive attention to the conceptual. And when scholars do turn attention to institutions and material artifacts, they have most often focused on their own world—the world of academic textbooks and curricula. The larger public interaction with world literature through the circulation and collection of material books and literal collections—libraries—has remained largely invisible.

In order to make world literary studies relevant for us in the early twenty-first century, we need to relocate world literature in the public sphere where it is institutionalized in ways that are not always the same as its modes of institutionalization in the university. To this end, I discuss books and libraries in their multifaceted entities: imaginary and material, conceptual and physical, intimate and public; singular, yet connected to the multiple. Bringing these together, I propose, opens up multiple meanings of world literature: as a philosophical ideal, a mode of reading, a pedagogical strategy, a unit of aesthetic evaluation, a strategy of affiliation, and a system of classification.

Literary studies have witnessed a revitalization of interest in the term *world literature* in the first decade of the twenty-first century. It would be a fallacy to claim that such revitalization has been entirely unproblematic, or that the interest has succeeded in replacing the historically firm institutional habits of organizing literature within national political boundaries. Nonetheless, supporters and critics of world literary studies have together contributed to its reestablishment as an academic field. While this book draws on the scholarly work of world literature, it also departs from it, arguing that recent scholars of world literature have been too deeply invested in presentist concerns of economic globalization, dominance of English as a world language, and a market-driven construction of world literature. This book seeks to historicize these concerns.

By unveiling historical, cultural, and political aspects of world literature, this study is itself historical. In many ways it is a product of our current post–Cold War and post-9/11 world, where inclusive cosmopolitan affiliations continue to coexist with exclusive nationalist fervor. The necessity to develop a vocabulary for understanding the contemporary world and its power structures is exerting heretofore unforeseen influence on the humanities and social sciences. The fast pace of globalizing world economies, in tandem with developments in digital technology in the past two decades, has ushered in a new era of conceptualizing and reflecting on libraries as well as books.

The migration of books and libraries into digital space has coincided with other forms of human migration. If the second half of the twentieth century was marked by large-scale *physical* migration of human beings *from* postcolonial nations *to* metropolitan centers of Europe and North America, migration in the first decade and a half of the twenty-first century is increasingly multidirectional and multidimensional. Migration patterns within the southern hemisphere are as prolific as from the southern to the northern hemispheres. Furthermore, technological advances in the communication sector have resulted in the *virtual* migration of labor through outsourcing.[7]

In addition, as we all know, the publishing and reading landscape has drastically changed within the first decade and a half of the twenty-first century. As research in digital and electronic media is enriching the fields of library and information studies and the history of the book and print cultures, the growing field of digital humanities is reshaping the research tools as well as the critical agenda for literary studies. We are living in a time when technological innovations are, yet again, transforming the meaning of *the book* and *the library*. A book is no longer only a "portable volume consisting of a series of written, printed, or illustrated pages bound together for ease of reading,"[8] it is also a "digital file containing a body of text and images suitable for distributing electronically and displaying on-screen in a manner similar to a printed book."[9] A library is not merely a "building, room, or set of rooms, containing a collection of books for the use of the public."[10] Today it is also a virtual space, an electronic surrogate, free from the walls of the building or room, and as portable as the printed or the digital book. Search engines such as Google, electronic catalogs such as WorldCat, and numerous digital archives with open public access create the impression that we are one step closer to that idealized catalog of catalogs. Books and libraries, in other words, are migrating into the digital space, changing rules of accessibility to information and knowledge. These phenomena are also impacting readers' access to literary works: in the original languages of creation, as well as in translation.

From our current vantage point, witnessing the transformation of books and libraries and a resurgence of discussions on world literature, my book spotlights important moments in the construction of world literature over the past two centuries. I claim that beyond the author, the translator, the academic critic, or the classroom readers, a plethora of actors, institutions, and media plays an important role in the construction of world literature and its readers. These include librarians, editors, publishers, literary magazines, book fairs, special interest groups, government censors and promoters, and more recently technological innovations such as electronic reading devices and digital libraries.

In order to provide sharper focus to this precociously ambitious enterprise, this book concentrates on the German-speaking world. Germany is a case study—an instance—but one that draws attention to the relations between multiple cultural institutions and political histories in providing or limiting access to world literature. I focus on the various incarnations of "Germany"—as a conglomerate of smaller states in the early nineteenth century to a unified nation in the late nineteenth century; as a short-lived Weimar Republic and then a totalitarian state in the first half of the twentieth century, followed by two nation-states after World War II to a reunified nation-state since 1989. This is neither to fetishize the German origins of the word *Weltliteratur*, nor to underline a special path (*Sonderweg*) to bolster German particularity. Germany becomes an important case study for investigating world literature because of its turbulent historical and political transformations over the past two hundred years, which, as this book seeks to demonstrate, were intimately connected with print-cultural politics, an ever-transforming pact with books.

The proliferation of world literature in a nation, I argue in this book, is not merely the manifestation of a nation's cosmopolitan disposition. World literature can also be modified, twisted, and manipulated to serve nationalist interests, as happened in Germany, especially during the Nazi times. Circulation of world literature in a national cultural space shapes and informs national identity formation. It is my hope that the case study presented here will provide impetus for investigations of world literature as a pact with books in other linguistic, cultural, or national contexts.

Recoding World Literature asks two intertwined questions: How does our imagination of the world rely on our access to books and libraries? And conversely, how does our access to world literature shape our understanding of books and libraries? The five chapters of this book approach these core questions from multiple angles, showcasing library collections, book series, sponsored translation projects, publisher's histories, and digital libraries. First, however, I want to present how libraries in their multiple significations have paved way historically for the "worlding" of literature and sometimes even posed challenges to world literary circulation. Then, I will cover some classical articulations of the term *Weltliteratur* to show how they inform current debates. Finally, I will close with a discussion of bibliomigrancy as a way of understanding Germany's pact with books and in turn world literature.

Libraries, Books, and the Worlding of Literature

The "house of books," or *Bibliothek* (library), is far from a neutral space. Libraries are sites rife with the politics of literacy and sanctioned illiteracy, historical contingencies that condition accumulation and classification, circulation and distribution, patronage and accession, orderly organization and disorderly contention. If public libraries, like many museums, serve as major institutions of various forms of local, national, regional, or transnational representations, private libraries often represent individual collectors. If *books*, considered for a moment simply to be a publication medium for human creativity and intellect, have historically served as manifestations of the zeitgeist, libraries have served as manifestations of the *Weltbild*, the image of the world.

In moments of globalization through trade, violent conquests, imperialism, and colonialism, all the way to modern-day interaction between nation-states through multinational commerce, the worlding of peoples has initiated and facilitated the worlding of literature. *The Epic of Gilgamesh* (ca. 2600–2200 BCE) from Mesopotamia, the *Ramayana* (ca. 500 BCE) from the Indian subcontinent, *The Epic of Sunjata* (ca. 1200 CE) from West Africa, the Brothers Grimm's *Kinder- und Hausmärchen* (1812–1851) are just a few examples of narratives traveling from one part of the world to another, and in the process acquiring new forms and transforming themselves as they transform their new cultural and linguistic homes. The dissemination of literary narratives sometimes occurred through a privileging of the oral *Kanṭhastha* (in the throat) over the written *Granthastha* (in the book), as in the case of many Pali and Sanskrit texts toward the end of the first millennium BCE.[11] Memorization and recitation—either in private or in public through performances—have been at the heart of numerous oral, written, and theatrically interpreted "tellings" of the *Ramayana* in over two dozen languages from northern India to Thailand.[12] At other times, technologies of writing or visual media such as paintings played a pivotal role in the circulation, distribution, and reception of literary narratives. If clay tablets carried the first translations of the *Epic of Gilgamesh* from the Babylonians to the Hittites in the second millennium BCE,[13] a book of Mughal miniatures entitled *Razmnama* (1598–1599; The book of war) brought the text of the Sanskrit *Mahabharata* to Persia.[14] Orhan Pamuk's Turkish novel *Benim Adım Kırmızı* (1998) appropriates and translates the bimedial (writing/painting) discourse of historical documentation dating back to 1258 CE.[15] The English translation, *My Name is Red*, can be part of one's electronic library on a Kindle, Nook, or iPad.

If books have served as instruments of preservation and proliferation of cultural memory, catapulting literary works beyond their linguistic and cultural origins, libraries have acted as social and political agents of collection and dissemination of cultural power.

Moments of globalization—whether by decree, conquest, colonialism, or diplomacy—often entailed the pillaging and destroying of established libraries and sometimes the endowing and constructing of new ones. As early as 2097–2049 BCE, the Babylonian King Shulgi established the stone-tablet houses in Ur and Nippur, "in which scribes and minstrels could consult mastercopies of . . . the Sumerian songbook."[16] The collections included earlier Akkadian versions of *Bilgames*, a text that later became famous as the *Epic of Gilgamesh*. Much later, under the patronage of King Ashurbanipal (668–627 BCE), the royal libraries of Nineveh documented and stored Sumerian and Akkadian narratives "in wooden writing boards surfaced with wax, as well as on clay tablets."[17] The scriptorium is claimed to have engaged "prisoners-of-war and political hostages" as copyists.[18] These libraries become one of the first known examples of multilingual collections that promoted literature beyond local boundaries, worlding literature in the earliest moments of documented literary history.

Mahmud of Ghazni (998–1030 CE), in what is now Afghanistan, is known for his invasion of the commercial and religious center of Somanatha in the modern-day state of Gujarat in western India. Mahmud deployed multilingual state symbols and confiscated intellectual production from conquered states to establish power. On the one hand, he insisted that Ghaznavid coins carry the Koranic *Kalima* in colloquial Sanskrit, documenting his victory over Somanatha.[19] On the other hand, as the historian Romilla Thapar reports, it was important for Mahmud to establish Ghazni as a cultural center of the early Muslim world to compete with Baghdad and Alexandria. Therefore, "Persian libraries were looted, books regarded as heretical were burned, and others brought back to Ghazni and Samarqand."[20]

Tariq Ali's novel *Shadows of the Pomegranate Tree* is another example: the story starts in Al-Andalus in 1499 CE with a negotiation over the incineration of Arabic and Hebrew manuscripts. The plea to save the texts comes not from Muslims and Jews but from scholars in the service of the Catholic Church, who would rather have the manuscripts confiscated than burned. The Grand Inquisitor, Ximenes de Cisneros, agrees, at least briefly. He has plans to endow a new library in Alcalá, where he promises to house these manuscripts.[21]

The symbolic and material significance of libraries as pawns in political games continues into the late twentieth and early twenty-first centuries.[22] The Jaffna National Library was attacked by Sri Lankan soldiers in May 1981. Hundreds of thousands of books and magazines were burned, including the *Yalpanam Vaipuavama*, a historical account of Jaffna.[23] The National Library of Bosnia and Herzegovina was destroyed during the siege of Sarajevo in August 1992.[24] In April 2003, the Baghdad National Library was pillaged along with the city's museum, leading to the destruction of books and manuscripts in the thousands, spanning several centuries and many languages. One of those books was the first Arabic translation of the *Mahabharata*.[25] "Freedom is messy," was how US Secretary of Defense Donald Rumsfeld brushed off the entire incident, taking cover under the great "American" virtue that the Iraqis had supposedly internalized.[26] Most recently, one of the prime targets for Al-Qaeda and other groups in Mali were massive collections of ancient manuscripts. The brave librarians in Timbuktu—led by Abdel Kader Haidra—devised an ingenious plan of saving about three hundred thousand ancient manuscripts by smuggling them to Bamako. While it is hoped that the manuscripts will return home to Timbuktu one day, at the time of writing these lines, the fate of the manuscripts remains unclear, as many are now prone to destruction in the extremely humid conditions of Bamako.[27]

The political history of libraries certainly affects the German pact with books. In the second half of the nineteenth century, the Royal Library (Königliche Bibliothek) in Berlin was buying major collections of Oriental manuscripts as well as single items from Asia. The state library that later incorporated this royal collection—the Staatsbibliothek zu Berlin, Preußischer Kulturbesitz (Berlin State Library, Prussian Cultural Heritage)—today houses one of the largest collections in the world of items that originated thousands of miles away from Prussia. The library's holdings include 41,700 Oriental manuscripts, more than double its 18,400 occidental manuscripts.[28]

Close to home for me is an example from 1957, when the new postcolonial nation of India entered into a treaty with the United States to pay back its Wheat Loan. Under Public Law 480 1962, part of the amount to be paid back to the United States by India was earmarked for the acquisition of cultural documents by US research centers.[29] A certain number of copies of every book published in India were sent to the Library of Congress, which then distributed them to designated libraries—including Memorial Library, the primary research library of the University of Wisconsin–Madison, where research for this book began.

Libraries do not only contribute to the worlding of literatures. This book argues that they also play a very important role in nationalizing and even racializing literatures. Modern American public libraries and their self-proclaimed and state-assigned roles have both guaranteed access to texts and not infrequently withheld them from public view. Visionary librarians have fought hard to ensure readers' borrowing privileges as a civic right, as shown by Louis Robbins in *The Dismissal of Miss Ruth Brown*, and as discussed by Ethelene Whitmire in *Regina Anderson Andrews: Harlem Renaissance Librarian*. Cataloging systems often reflect the political climate of their origin, creating linguistic, regional, and also national hierarchies.

The National Bibliography section of the *Library of Congress Classification Class Z* (1898; in force 1902) devised a geolinguistic cataloging system based primarily on three factors: “Books printed and published in that country; Books by natives and residents; Books written in the language of the country by foreigners.”[30] The *Library of Congress Classification Class P* (1928), which includes philology, linguistics, and literature, extended these criteria: call letters PD–PF were assigned for Germanic philology and linguistics, including English; PJ–PL for Oriental philology and linguistics, which included everything from Indo-Iranian (PK) to African (PL) linguistics. However, two call letters, PR and PS were created for English and American literatures respectively. German, Dutch, and Scandinavian literatures received a separate call number, PT, whereas all Oriental literatures were subsumed under PX, to be further categorized following the PJ–PL (linguistic) category.[31]

Cataloguing systems and call numbers change over time, reflecting and entrenching powerful political and social values. Even more materially, the very *mediality*—the modes of creation and circulation of texts—has also changed the work of libraries over time. The cuneiform tablet depositories patronized by King Ashurbanipal in the seventh century BCE might have been meant for a few literate patrons. While ancient and medieval royal libraries were primarily intended for in-house use by select literate members of the ruling classes, monastic libraries functioned as storehouses for books as well as sites of book production through the enterprise of copying manuscripts. The print collections of the Asiatic Society Library in Calcutta (established in 1784) were largely reserved for Orientalists and officers of the British East India Company. Like university libraries with restricted use for members of the university, the early nineteenth century saw an increase in the number of private lending libraries (*Leihbibliotheken*), as well as public libraries in European capital cities that were declared national libraries, which often functioned as national archives.[32] The Library of Congress (established in 1800 in Washington, DC) is technically in the service of the US Congress, although it is open to public use. Commercial book series that packaged books into so-called libraries, such as Reclam’s Universal-Bibliothek (launched in 1867 in Leipzig), the Modern Library (launched in 1917 in New York City), Penguin Classics (launched in 1946 in London), and Heinemann’s African Writers Series (launched in 1962 in London) offer affordable editions for personal collections. The mediality of each of these libraries is defined by the media available for circulation—joining their material forms and their modes of access. Thus while borrowing privileges of members of a city or a county library may include access to music CDs, DVDs, and even video games, university or national libraries may restrict the physical access to their holdings, or conversely they may make whole sections of their holdings digitally accessible without restrictions.

The Google Book project continues to appropriate old and new published books into its database. Sales figures for Amazon's Kindle and Barnes and Nobel's Nook keep rising, even as "physical" books remain an important reading device for most readers around the world.[33] The virtual migration of books, apart from changing reading habits, reading strategies, and reader accessibility, is transforming the position, role, function, and indeed the very definition of the library as a house of books. The European Library (launched in 2005 in The Hague), the Universal Digital Library, the UNESCO-supported World Digital Library (launched in 2009 in Washington, DC), and most recently the Harvard University– and Library of Congress–sponsored Digital Public Library of America (launched in 2011 in Washington, DC) are prime examples of this change—each one of them ambitious and politically charged.[34]

As these examples show, books have constantly been on the move. Technological advances, translation enterprises, collections by libraries: all of these have allowed books to find new homes on new shelves. At the beginning of the nineteenth century, European colonialism in Asia and Africa facilitated a new kind of movement of books, a new accessibility to "the world in print." This in turn created the conditions that led to Goethe's famous usage of the term *Weltliteratur*.

Weltliteratur: *From an Empire of Books to a Reunified Nation-State*

Among German intellectuals, the idea of world literature has carried a dual valence since its inception. On the one hand, as an integral part of Enlightenment cosmopolitanism and universalism, it is positioned against national literature. On the other hand, since colonialism and Orientalism play a central role in facilitating the movement of books, world literature serves to code and classify other literatures in terms of their national origins and becomes an accomplice in "measuring the world"—offering an illusion of global knowledge and mastery to its enlightened readers.

Daniel Kehlmann's international bestseller *Die Vermessung der Welt* (2005; *Measuring the World*, 2007) documents how Enlightenment knowledge crucially served European ends.[35] He narrates the quest for knowledge through the lives of two giants of the nineteenth century: the botanist and geographer Alexander von Humboldt and the mathematician and physicist Carl Friedrich Gauss. Gauss's travels are in a virtual space of numbers. Humboldt's quest for scientific knowledge would take him to the geographical "new" world. In Kehlmann's novel, Humboldt arrives in New Amsterdam, Trinidad, in 1799 and visits a Christian mission, set up to baptize the natives. The monks cannot figure out what he and his companion Bonpland want of them; the abbot expresses his suspicion thusly: "Nobody traveled half way around the world to measure land that didn't even belong to him."[36]

Kehlmann does not give much print space to Alexander's older brother Wilhelm, but I want to comment on him briefly since he shows us the side of the Enlightenment desire to "measure the world" that depended on books and libraries. Apart from Greek and Latin, Wilhelm von Humboldt was competent in Sanskrit, Chinese, and Japanese and was working on his theories of comparative linguistics and grammatical forms. Along with his translations of Pindar's *Olympic Odes* and Aeschylus's *Agamemnon*, Wilhelm also translated the *Bhagavad-Gita* from Sanskrit into Latin, which would be published in 1820. Unlike Alexander, Wilhelm did not have to travel afar to identify certain works as world literary works. His access to literature and languages of faraway lands was made possible through libraries in Paris.

Collections like these were themselves a result of geopolitical maneuvering. French and British colonial presence in Asia and parts of northern Africa was initiating and facilitating the arrival of many works of literature to Europe—in their original languages and in translations. Along with the geographical, botanical, zoological, physical, and chemical cataloguing of the world, Europeans were developing a literary catalog of the world. Intersections of aesthetic forms, the selection of subject matters and their treatment, and affinities between modes of creative expression were already being carried out piecemeal among literatures on the European continent; the canvas was being enlarged now with increased access to literatures from other geolinguistic spaces. In other words, through acquisition of languages, translations of literary works, and constructions of rules of grammar, Wilhelm von Humboldt and others were also finding ways of "measuring" parts of the world that did not belong to them by birth or inheritance. It is in this transformative period that Germany strived to become a *Bücherreich*, an "empire of books," creating the material conditions that gave traction to the idea of *Weltliteratur*.

Goethe was not the first German intellectual to use the term *Weltliteratur*, but he certainly highlighted it, eagerly anticipating the arrival of the epoch of world literature through an engagement with that which is not one's own: the strange, the foreign. One of the first uses of the word actually occurs in 1801 when Christoph Martin Wieland located *Weltliteratur* in the urban context ("Urbanität") of ancient Rome, connecting it with character building and well-being that is derived from reading the best authors and from interactions with the most cultivated and exquisite persons in a sophisticated time period. Wieland's concept of world literature is closely tied to the world citizen, whose great familiarity with world literature cultivates his world citizenship.[37] From 1801 to 1803, August Wilhelm Schlegel used the term *Weltliteratur* in his lectures on literary history in Berlin as an idea in the service of a progressive universal poesy.[38] Herder, who attempted to construct connections between German "national" literature and other literatures in his writings on literary history, might not have commented in detail on *Nationalliteratur* or *Weltliteratur*,[39] but his thinking about a literature of humanity (*Literatur der Menschheit*) aligns him with Goethe's idea of world literature.[40]

What distinguishes Goethe's statement is its direct reference to a non-European work. In Eckermann's entry from January 31, 1827, Goethe remarks that he is currently reading a Chinese novel, whose title remains unmentioned.[41] Goethe's access to Chinese literary works reveals a larger network of works from Asia entering the European space in the eighteenth and nineteenth centuries, whereby translators, publishing houses, and libraries played a significant role. Without reference to the imperial and commercial routes that were bringing books to him, Goethe established world literature as *Gemeingut*, a philosophical, humanistic ideal, a mode of transnational arrangement of texts.

If Goethe privileges the conceptual and ideational dimension of *Weltliteratur*, Karl Marx and Friedrich Engels first acknowledge the coming of age of *Weltliteratur* by locating it in the material history of nineteenth century Europe. In *Manifest der kommunistischen Partei* (*The Manifesto of the Communist Party*), first published in German and English in London in 1848—followed since by countless translations in many world languages—Marx and Engels point to the material conditions that are hastening the approach of world literature through the spread of bourgeois capital. Not unlike Goethe, for Marx and Engels literature emerges as the *Gemeingut* of humankind. However, they highlight the *Gut* (wares, material artifacts) in *Gemeingut* and credit the emergence of the term to a rise in a "cosmopolitan consumption" through a worldwide circulation of books and literature that depends on transnational trade. Outlining the cultural consequences of the financial interdependence of nations, Marx and Engels describe the emergence of world literature out of the many national literatures.[42]

In articulating the connections between a worldwide marketplace and world literature, Marx and Engels—unlike Goethe—do not refer to a specific text that emanates outside of the European cultural space. We do know that Marx's own readings comprised literary and philosophical works from the Greek, French, Spanish, and English—many of them he had accessed at the British Library.[43]

In the second half of the nineteenth century, German discussions of world literature developed through the further establishment of Orientalist studies, exemplified among others through the founding of the German Oriental Society (Deutsche Morgenländische Gesellschaft, 1844), and the mass acquisition of non-European manuscripts and prints, such as the Aloys Sprenger Collection at the Staatsbibliothek zu Berlin in 1857. The rise of direct translations of non-European works into German—without English or French serving as intermediary languages—led to the publication of major world literary anthologies, such as Johannes Scheer's *Bildersaal der Weltliteratur* (1848). Reclam's Universal-Bibliothek series (established in 1867) expanded because of the availability of new translations, and in turn contributed to the expansion of readership of translated works. Affordable publication series like these then facilitated the growth of private libraries. This was also a period in which rising nationalism—culminating in German unification in 1871—declared world literature a penchant of Jewish intellectuals, and critiques of world literature acquired a particularly anti-Semitic character.

The first half of the twentieth century witnessed a reemergence of discussions of world literature around the mass violence caused by the two World Wars. Hermann Hesse, hitherto ignored in discussions of world literature, would be the first author to discuss world literature together with private libraries. In his essay *Eine Bibliothek der Weltliteratur* (1929), Hesse emphasizes the significance of *Weltliteratur* as one aspect of the *Bildung* (education or formation) of human beings based on love for literature and a passion for books. Drawing examples from his own library, Hesse provides his readers with an extensive guide to literatures from around the world, mentioning over four hundred works that are available in German translation. The Goethe scholar Fritz Strich would reemphasize the philosophical ideal carried by the term. In *Goethe und die Weltliteratur* (1946)—written in exile in Zurich—Strich returned to the term as part of a legacy of humanism and universalism that was relegated to the margins and trumped by National Socialist forces. Strich did not comment on the Nationalist Socialist recoding of world literature. The Nazis did not merely reject world literature for its cosmopolitan weltanschauung; they manipulated the Goethean ideal to their advantage, especially through two magazines: *Weltliteratur* and *Die Weltliteratur*. The two German states, the Federal Republic of Germany and the German Democratic Republic, favored two distinctly ideological traditions of world literature: one favoring a free market economy, the other establishing solidarity with socialist, communist, and third-world countries.

When world literature entered the US academy in the 1930s and 1940s, it was soon laden with disciplinary anxieties. What Hesse and Strich diagnosed as the general potential of world literature in the education of a human being was rejected as too general or too unhistoricized. In the US context, the meaning of world literature shifted, the philosophical ideal giving way to pedagogical discourse. In their famous book *Theory of Literature* (1942), René Wellek and Austin Warren label the term as "needlessly grandiose" and decry the necessity of studying "literature on all five continents, from New Zealand to Iceland." With their eye on "objectivity" that must be part of the theory of literature that they have set out to expound, Wellek and Warren reject world literature for the "sentimental cosmopolitanism" it apparently invokes.[44]

Their concerns found extension in the ideas of Erich Auerbach, who after writing his magnum opus, *Mimesis* (1946), in Istanbul, reflected on the term during the last station of his exilic existence in New Haven, Connecticut. In "Philologie der Weltliteratur" (1952), an essay written as a contribution to Fritz Strich's *Festschrift*, Auerbach is at best skeptical toward the idealism associated with the term *Weltliteratur*.[45] Rather than augment the idea of literature as *Gemeingut*, Auerbach operates on the pragmatics of difference. Writing in the midst of the historical sweep of decolonization in the twentieth century and the rise of a new world order immediately following World War II, Auerbach identifies a pedagogical challenge that accompanies exposure to many more new national literatures from around the world. After making the dubious claim that *Mimesis* was written in Istanbul in the absence of any libraries,[46] Auerbach seems overwhelmed by the Yale University Library. He laments the lack of *Geschichtlichkeit* (historicity)—which he specifically identifies in Goethe's age—within the philosophical consciousness of his own historical moment.[47] Auerbach's essay conveys a strong sense of restraint in the possible hastening of the approach of *Weltliteratur*, declaring its impossibility in the Goethean sense for the late twentieth century.

These years—1827, 1848, and 1952—are not the only moments when the term *Weltliteratur* surfaced and changed, but these were certainly the moments of its most prominently discussed pronouncements in theoretical discussions today. The geographical origins of these statements form a trinity of their own. Goethe's Weimar was the seat of German classicism in the nineteenth century, and it will also play home to the short-lived republic between Wilhelmine Germany and the Third Reich in the early twentieth century. Marx and Engels's London was, along with Paris, one of the most powerful commercial and colonial capitals of the world; it was also home to many political dissidents and émigrés. And Auerbach's 1950s New Haven enjoyed its prestigious status as the seat of Yale University, a racially segregated university town that became home to many Jewish intellectual exiles from Europe during the Third Reich. Due to well-funded universities and dominant languages of the production of scholarship, Germany, Great Britain, and the United States also left the marks of their commercial, political, and pedagogical hegemony on literary studies—throughout the second half of the twentieth century. Academic discussions of world literature in the late twentieth and early twenty-first centuries are cast in the shadow of this Holy Trinity—the Father: Goethe; the Son: Auerbach; and the Holy Ghost: Karl Marx.

World Literature: Historical Burdens, Contemporary Anxieties

The end of the Napoleonic wars coinciding with the rising empire of books led to Goethe's moment. The industrial revolution and the establishment of the world market led to Marx and Engels's moment. The end of World War II became central to Auerbach's uneasy relationship to world literature.

What historical conditions mark the current revival of interest in world literature? I locate these in the latest period of economic globalization, mass-migration, and a post–Cold War and post-9/11 world requiring a renewed understanding of geopolitical and transnational power structures.[48] Like the dual valence that the term *Weltliteratur* acquired in Germany at the beginning of the nineteenth century, current discussions locate world literature within the legacies of Enlightenment and cosmopolitanism, while remaining aware of uneven access to the production and consumption of literatures of the world. Recent scholars conceptualize world literature through the circulation and distribution of texts in translation, through patterns of aesthetic expression that stay local or acquire global currency, through a world system of center-peripheral economic and political relations, and through pedagogical practices in the US classroom.[49] The questions that have most concerned theorists of world literature revolve around which texts constitute world literature, the modes of access to such texts (in the original or in translation), the pedagogical aims or challenges of studying texts identified as part of world literature, and last but not least, the usability or utility of studying world literature.[50]

Most discussions of world literature today are marked by skepticism toward a restrictive nationalization of literature through traditional literary canons. They also exhibit a distinctive optimism toward literature's capacity to unsettle narrow nationalisms. Current theories try to confront the question of Euro-American cultural centers and non-Western cultural peripheries, colonial dominance and uneven playing fields of world literary circulation. In fact, some of the most heated debates—on topics ranging from the value of translations in world literary comparisons and the manifestation of the North-South divide in differential access to literary productions, to the dominance of literary works in English or French within the postcolonial canon—have revolved around the purpose, scope, and design of specific national and comparative literature departments.

Criticisms of world literature today exhibit three main trends. First, there exists an uneasy relationship with access to literature solely in translation, especially in the so-called dominant languages of European descent. Second is the question of specialized training of readers within the university. World literary studies are criticized for compromising and even obstructing or rendering superfluous literary comparison in original languages, thus entrenching the acceptance of English as the dominant language of cultural and intellectual commerce of our times.[51] And third, there is cynicism toward the growing market for literature in translation as well as scholarly publications on world literature. Most positions on world literature touch upon—without entirely engaging with—the commerce of literature itself.

In the account of recent criticism that follows, I will show how influential scholars imagine world literature in terms of networks, translations, and ideologically constructed collections of authors, texts, and titles. We can see how critics register varying degrees of attention to material, political, or socio-cultural conditions that led to circulation, translation, and collection. And most importantly, we can see how preoccupied so many scholars remain with the practices of the university—pedagogy and disciplinary methods.

It would not be an exaggeration to state that David Damrosch's *What Is World Literature?* (2003) reenergized debates on world literature. With a catalog comprised of works and authors as varied as the *Epic of Gilgamesh*, Mechtild von Magdeburg, Franz Kafka, and Rigoberta Menchu, among others, Damrosch declares that world literature is not so much an "infinite, ungraspable canon of works but rather a mode of circulation and reading"; "a form of detached engagement with worlds beyond our place and time."[52] Circulation, translation, and production are central to Damrosch's conceptualization of world literature.[53] He identifies a double process through which a work enters into world literature: "first, by being read as literature; second, by circulating out into a broader world beyond its linguistic and cultural point of origin."[54] Translation is crucial to the second step of the said double process: "world literature is writing that gains in translation,"[55] Damrosch writes. Translation serves as a vehicle for reception and circulation of a literary "work" as it becomes part of a "network" of texts that inhabit the world literary space.[56] World literature, as a network for individual works, then emerges as "an elliptical refraction of national literatures."[57]

For critics such as Gayatri Chakravorty Spivak, an engagement with worlds beyond one's place or time is anything but detached. In her Wellek Library Lectures (2000), published as *Comparative Literature: Death of a Discipline* (2003), Spivak underlines, above all, the work of literary comparison to understand the highly intense and politicized interactions between nations and regions.[58] With Jacques Derrida, Virginia Woolf, Tayeb Salih, and Mahashweta Devi on her reading list, Spivak comments on various kinds of "collectivities" that enable but also challenge comparative evaluations of economically disparate societies. If Damrosch privileges gains rather than losses in translation, Spivak laments the loss of other worlds when they are accessed solely in translation. For Spivak, world literature in translation underrecognizes a systemic linguistic hegemony that impedes the entry of certain literary works into the world literary space while assuring a red carpet welcome to others.[59] She cautions against an overinvestment in access to world literature in translation, for it erodes the linguistic and cultural differences that are woven into the fabric of literary texts. However, Spivak's rightful insistence on the reason for a less nationally frightened and more globally enthused curiosity for literary works in the "less commonly taught languages" is weakened by her overestimation of the relationship between academic and nonacademic readings of world literature. Spivak's highly critical and largely dismissive evaluation of world literature is in fact based on her idea of their purported reliance on "others" to translate difference for them, signaling her own fetishization of the original, an untranslatable original that forecloses access to any outsider. In a more recent essay, "The Stakes of a World Literature," she proposes the "loosening" of terms world and literature in order to discover the "relativistic anachronism" of the term.[60] Once again, her privileging of the original language of creation over translation becomes key to this "loosening."[61] The main political institution at stake here is the academy.

Emily Apter's critique of world literature, based primarily on a collection of words—Barbara Cassin's *Vocabulaire européen des philosophies: Dictionnaire des intradusibles* (2004)—challenges the very notion of "translatability." In *Against World Literature* (2013), Apter echoes Auerbach's and Spivak's concerns that access to world literary works solely in translation might lead to standardization and homogeneity. Apter seeks to challenge the singularity of world literature by privileging the plurality of world literature*s*,[62] cautioning at the same time against the danger posed to the diversity of comparative literature caused by a neglect of "untranslatability."[63] Criticizing pedagogical programs that compromise language acquisition, Apter denounces contemporary discussions of world literature as "an entrepreneurial, bulimic drive to anthologize and curricularize the world's cultural resources."[64] And herein lies the contradiction in her work: as she rejects the "translation assumption," she celebrates translation theory and proposes a partnering of "translation theory as Weltliteratur [which] would challenge flaccid globalisms that paid lip service to alterity while doing little more than to buttress neoliberal 'big tent' syllabi taught in English."[65] As in Spivak's work, the fears are geopolitical, but the focus of the argument most clearly targets the university.

The sense of imbalance and inequality between dominant and dominated literatures that perturbs Spivak and Apter was anticipated by Franco Moretti in his essay "Conjectures on World Literature" (2000). Drawing on the center-periphery model of Immanuel Wallerstein's "World Systems Theory," Moretti also identifies the "one and unequal" nature of world literature.[66] In order to diagnose such unity and inequality, Moretti gestures toward the materiality of literary production, arguing that literary studies have far too long concentrated on a small, select body of texts that comprise the literary canon. However, for Moretti as well, scholarly expertise and modes of production of scholarly knowledge became central to the enterprise of world literature. Characterizing world literature as a "permanent intellectual challenge to national literature," Moretti imagines a clear division between the pursuit of national and world literature in research and classroom contexts: "national literature for people who see trees; world literature for people who see waves."[67]

While most discussions of world literature have centered on pedagogical institutions and specialized, disciplinary reading strategies, there is one that breaks the mold. In her study *The World Republic of Letters* (2004), Pascale Casanova offers for consideration crucial aspects of the construction of literature as a public sphere institution, which becomes an instrument of national cultural and linguistic politics. Casanova identifies in sixteenth-century Europe the creation of an "international literary sphere" whereby literature establishes itself as a site for contestation and competition among nations, and she sets out to chart how, through the intensified processes of nation building, especially in the nineteenth century, there emerged a "world republic of letters."[68] Distinguishing the world of letters from "the received view of literature as a peaceful domain," Casanova points out that its history [of the world of letters] "is one of incessant struggle and competition on the very nature of literature itself."[69] As literature establishes itself as national cultural capital, the world of letters is increasingly marked by national rivalries; "these rivalries," she states, "are what have created world literature."[70]

The premise of Casanova's study is commendable. She aspires to wrest world literature from a purportedly humanitarian, universal, harmoniously cosmopolitan imagination and uncover the chaotic competition that splits and informs the world literary space, where many actors beyond the author acquire key roles. Paying attention to these actors makes it possible "to measure the literariness (the power, prestige, and volume of linguistic and literary capital) of a language, not in terms of the number of writers and readers it has, but in terms of the number of cosmopolitan intermediaries—publishers, editors, critics, and especially translators—who assure the circulation of texts into the language or out of it."[71]

The aim of Casanova's study seems to augment the politically charged nature of literature and its circulation as world literature.[72] However, at the center of her thinking about the world literary sphere is a sense of an aesthetic and artistic "autonomy" of the literary enterprise, a step-by-step "emancipation" that literary production must acquire from its immediate political-historical circumstances; a vague implication of the "freedom" of literature from the very politicized public sphere from which it emanates that jeopardizes an understanding of the very relationship of world literature as an institution of the international literary space.[73] While Casanova is right in pointing out that neither literary history nor literary geography can be reduced to political history, she is circumspect at best about whether the foundations of an international literary space and "the measure of literariness" could be easily dissociated from the political conditions in which these elements thrive. In other words, the generalization fails unless the complexities of the conditions of literary production within a political historical period are also given due account. Casanova cautions against the "misunderstandings and misreadings" of a "naive" conception of a "pure, dehistoricized, denationalized, and depoliticized conception of literature," warning that "misreadings . . . conferred by the leading centers . . . are evidence of the ethnocentric blindness of these centers."[74] Nonetheless, her own ethnocentric blindness becomes clear when she also states, that "literature remains relatively dependent on politics, above all in countries that are relatively under-endowed with literary resources."[75] The idea of an international public sphere that Casanova proposes is exclusively intra-European, with a projective power that far exceeds the boundaries of Europe, and reportedly applies, with manipulated flexibility, in other times and other spaces. The model of nation-building and the establishment of a nation-state that becomes the basis of Casanova's understanding of the establishment of language as a national artifact and literature as a national-cultural product is itself based on a hierarchical and progressive model:

> Renaissance Italy, fortified by its Latin heritage, was the first recognized literary power. Next came France, with the rise of the Plédidade in the mid-sixteenth century, which in challenging both the hegemony of Latin and the advance of Italian produced a first tentative sketch of a transnational literary space. Then Spain and England, followed by the rest of the countries of Europe, gradually entered into competition on the strength of their own literary "assets" and traditions. The nationalist movements that appeared in central Europe during the nineteenth century—a century that also saw the arrival of North America and Latin America on the literary scene—generated new claims to literary existence. Finally, with decolonization, countries in Africa, the Indian subcontinent, and Asia demanded access to literary legitimacy and existence as well.[76]

While the import of the Western-European nation-state onto the post-colonial political organization within decolonized African and Asian nations cannot be entirely denied, what is astounding about this passage is the not-so-subtle denial of the presence of any literary spaces within "Africa, the Indian subcontinent, and Asia" prior to, during, or even well after the nineteenth century. It is only with decolonization that a "demand" for literary legitimacy is put forth. A model of literary history that relies largely on the monolingual composition of a nation-state makes it difficult for Casanova to grasp the complexity of multilingual literary productions sometimes within, sometimes despite, the political boundaries of a given nation-state. Hindi and Serbian literatures are suddenly reduced to "small literatures," apparently due to the lack of an army of cosmopolite and polyglot intermediaries to assure the rise of their cultural stock exchange in the international literary market; Arabic, Kikuyu, Catalan, and Gaelic stand to the same "objective measures of current political and literary position" in the "median literary spaces,"[77] even though she states earlier in her book that "the most independent territories of the literary world are able to state their own law, to lay down the specific standards and principles applied by their internal hierarchies, and to evaluate works and pronounce judgements without regard for political and national divisions."[78]

In sum, a confused relationship with political history, a naive investment in a singular model of literary history, and an undifferentiated understanding of economic history compromise the larger ambition of Casanova's work. Furthermore, the projection of post-Enlightenment print-cultural developments in Western Europe to the rest of the world hardly takes into account the uneven modes of capital-dependent literary circulation, especially in Asia and Africa. For Casanova, the world literary sphere, and by inference world literature itself, become a dominion of France, "the most autonomous literary space," and Paris, its undisputed capital.[79]

To think of literature as a cultural institution that is in a constant struggle for emancipation from politics would be to think of human subjectivity itself as apolitical, as existing in an aesthetic space completely unmoored from history. This would mean a total detachment of world literature from the project of European Enlightenment, which, as I have mentioned before, expanded parallel to processes of exclusionary nation building and expansion of colonialism. It is time now to address the binaries that criticism has developed and to ask how the political and social contexts of production, circulation, and reception beyond the university might move us past rigid dichotomies. How does world literature come to be in an elliptical relationship with national literatures, as David Damrosch would like us to imagine? Is world literature in translation necessarily an erosion of cultural and linguistic particularities, as Spivak and Apter remind us? Or can looking at the materiality of translation through construction of foreign literature canons actually result in establishing better connections between world literary studies and national literary studies? Does it have to be a choice between close and distant readings, "trees" and "waves," as Moretti would like us to think? Does locating the world literary space necessarily need the identification of a singular center of literary production, a singular model of literary history? Must world literature necessarily be seen in terms of an "emancipation" from national politics, as an expression of aesthetic "autonomy," as Casanova would prefer? To move out of the impasse of conceptualizing world literature as an "imaginary" collection that belongs mostly to the university, I want to suggest that it is time to think about the concrete political, historical, and social realities that contribute to the creation of such a collection.

Recent or archaic, singular or plural, permanent or ephemeral, homogenizing or heterogenizing, disciplined or undisciplined, comparative or assimilative, universal or particular, original or in translation: world literature, as I imagine it, is not a choice between these binaries. It is in fact the productive tension between these binaries that gives world literature its many contested meanings, which in fact are in turn historically constructed, culturally located, and politically charged. It is time to part ways with the three major trends, to focus on some of the neglected, glossed over, abject, and repudiated aspects of the discussion, and to cast the terms of debate differently. It is my contention that paying attention to bibliomigrancy and attending to our pacts with books can help us to develop a new understanding of world literature.

Bibliomigrancy: Bibliothek, Bibliograph, Bibliophile, Bibliophobe

Bibliomigrancy is the term I use for the physical and virtual migration of books. It encompasses multiple modes of movement of literary narratives in original languages or translation. Bibliomigrancy contributes to the worlding of literature, the making of the catalog of the imaginary global bookmobile. The book historian Robert Darnton defines the "life-cycle" of the book in terms of the progression from author to publisher, printer, shipper, and then bookseller, before it finally reaches the reader.[80] He uses these stations to outline multiple ways of approaching the history of the book, adding, "books belong to circuits of communication that operate in consistent patterns."[81] Darnton's ideas serve as a point of departure for my thinking about bibliomigrancy. However, books do not have identical life cycles, especially if they originate in cultural-linguistic spaces in which the circulation of commercial capital follows radically different trajectories than in affluent book production centers in Europe or North America. In addition, circuits of communication are hardly ever consistent. They are also culturally determined, historically conditioned, and politically charged. Bibliomigrancy is thus a way of narrating the life cycle of books by factoring in cultural, historical, and political aspects that shape and inform such a life cycle; it is a mode of tracing and accounting for the diversity of circuits of communication to which books belong; it is a conduit for the processes that help us understand the consistencies as well as inconsistencies of book circulation patterns. The comparative literary scholar César Domínguez duly notes: "literary works do not circulate by themselves in an aesthetic vacuum. Otherwise, circulation will be at best an empty and metaphorical signifier." To illustrate his point, he offers three important factors crucial for circulation: "historical context, agency, physicality."[82] Bibliomigrancy is a term that grants insights to historical context and agency by recognizing the physicality of circulation.

Admittedly, the compound noun *bibliomigrancy* is as odd and awkward as the language of the migrant who has newly arrived in a foreign land. The term's mixed linguistic origins—*biblio* (Greek) and *migration* (Middle French and Latin)[83]—indicate code switching and free borrowing, all the while breaking grammatical rules of alliance and concord. Despite these imperfections, discordance, and defiance—and maybe even a little bit because of them—the term serves its purpose. Both halves of the word are intended in their broadest senses. *Biblio* may be opened up to acknowledge all kinds of books: written and oral, printed and handwritten, bound and unbound, stationary and portable, legible and—borrowing from Lorraine Piroux's *Moins que livres*—those which contest the ultra-legibility of the Western book form since Enlightenment. *Migrancy* takes on multiple meanings of migration, from the movement of human beings and ideas, to the "process of changing from the use of one platform, environment, IT system, etc., to another."[84]

Bibliomigrancy might seem to imply an embrace of the written word, but I want the term to be more expansive to include multiple forms of dissemination of literature. It need not imply a teleological, linear, and evolutionary progression from orality to literacy. In her insightful essay "The Great Unwritten," Caroline Levine argues that "institutions of world literature have persistently valorized literacy," and she cautions us against "the great embrace of the written word."[85] Thinking of the migration of literary narratives through multiple medialities, that is, their *coexistence* in aural, literal, and visual forms rather than the replacement of one by another, might be the best way of circumventing the valorization of the written word. After all, books existed in different forms in different cultures over different periods of time; and the traditional notion of bound books has once again been challenged by e-books. Furthermore, in the field of world literature, multiple modes of bibliomigrancy could assist with a stronger acknowledgment of bi- or multilingual, multicultural, and multilocational existences of literary works, rather than the privileging of the singularity of the original to underplay the multiplicity of translations.

On the one hand, bibliomigrancy stands for the actual *physical* movement of books from one part of the world to another through trade and travel, conquest and colonialism, donation and diplomacy, and human migration, both willed and forced. On the other hand, the term can be opened up to account for instances of *virtual* migration: through the transliteration from an oral into a written language, though the translation into a new language, through the transformation from one medium into another through recitation, illustration, illumination, installation, painting, performance, cinema, or television adaptations, and through the migration of the material book from physical into digital space. Take three different versions of bibliomigrancy in the history of *Gilgamesh*: the revision of *The Epic of Gilgamesh* from an oral tradition into an authoritative inscribed form by the Babylonian priest Sîn-lique-unnini (around 1200 BCE), the excavation of cuneiform tablets in Nineveh by Austin Henry Layard and Hormuzd Rassam (1853),[86] and then the translation of *Gilgamesh* into many modern languages. The carrying over of slave songs across the Atlantic and their translations and transformations in the North American colonies are as much a part of bibliomigrancy, as the controversial collection and annotation of *Slave Songs of the United States* during the Civil War to preserve the "relics of a state of society."[87]

Bibliomigrancy is also a way of understanding the historical valence, cultural ambition, and political charge of books and libraries. The interdiscursive connections between libraries and world literature become conspicuous when the following four terms are considered together:

Bibliothek: The material and symbolic space created and inhabited by literary artifacts; the space that conditions and shapes the pact with books.

Bibliograph: The writing of the inventory of such artifacts and objects into a catalog; the realization of the pact with books.

Bibliophile: Not merely a book lover or book collector in the traditional sense but also authors, translators, publishers, librarians, book festival organizers, and of course readers who exercise agency and imagine their subjectivities through the bibliothek and the bibliograph in multiple ways; a signatory of the pact with books.

Bibliophobe: The person, agency, cultural collective, ideological entity, or state apparatus that recognizes the power of books and libraries by impeding access by banning, burning, or censoring books, or by barring individuals or groups from having access to libraries; a manipulator or breaker of the pact with books.

In *The Order of Books*, Roger Chartier enables a rethinking of all of these terms through the concept of the inventory. In Chartier's history of the book in early modern Europe, three key features come into relief:

"the author as an organizational principle for designating the work, the dream of a universal library, real or imagined, containing all the works that have ever been written, and the emergence of a new definition of the book that made an indissoluble connection between an object, a text, and an author."[88] In his elaborations of these three points, Chartier sets up an archive that consists of affordable editions that create new communities of readers, decrees that become precursors of contemporary copyright laws, title pages that erode the exclusive anonymity of the author and establish his authority as a subject of literary discourse, and, last but not least, bibliographic catalogs that turn that author and subject into an object of epistemological organization.

The order initiated and created by the book—discursive, social, cultural, and political—comes to completion in Chartier's book through a very engaging and amusing discussion of the spats and feuds between two bibliophiles, Antoine du Verdier and La Croix de Maine, about their respective *bibliothèques*, not so much the ones between four walls but those between the covers of a folio. These folios house a tall order of titles—both real and imaginary.[89] At the source of the mutually inflicted acerbic comments of du Verdier and de Maine is not merely the question of antecedence of one work over the other, but as Chartier explains, the ordering of knowledge as it would be in a library with walls. Most importantly, the *bibliothèques* of du Verdier and de Maine inventory all discoverable titles, in anticipation of the creation of a universal library, one that contained all books. The order of books that Chartier creates for his readers ends with the invocation of extravagant happiness that accompanied the proclamation of such a library, the scale and scope of the ambition of the inventory and its implications for understanding the materiality of books, the spaces in which they are organized, and the modes of their organization: questions central to the European projects of Enlightenment and modernity.

Chartier's characters help us to see how libraries are both imaginary collections and real spaces. Michel Foucault conceptualized libraries as "heterotopias," as the "other" spaces of utopias: "effectively enacted utopias," which simultaneously represent, contest, and invert all the other real sites found in a culture.[90] Among the several heterotopias that Foucault discusses in his lecture, the library and the museum cross-reference both *topos* and *chronos*: libraries become sites of collective cultural constructs, real and imaginary, where "the pious descendents of time" conflict with "the determined inhabitants of space":[91]

> Museums and libraries have become heterotopias in which time never stops building up and topping its own summit. . . . By contrast, the idea of accumulating everything, of establishing a sort of general archive, the will to enclose in one place all times, all epochs, all forms, all tastes, the idea of constituting a place of all times that is itself outside of time and inaccessible to its ravages, the project of organizing in this way a sort of perpetual and indefinite accumulation of time in an immobile place, this whole idea belongs to our modernity.[92]

Foucault opens up the possibility of imagining museums and libraries as spaces where the cross-referencing of time and space make them collective cultural constructs, both real and imaginary. Thinking along with Chartier, world literature becomes a consciously conceived inventory of literary works. And Foucault invites us to understand how world literature comes to be shaped by concepts of simultaneity, juxtaposition, and dispersion across multiple sites, collections, and inventories in spaces that acquire meaning in reference to other geoculturally locatable sites.

The bibliothek, the bibliograph, the bibliophile, and the bibliophobe converge and depart to shape bibliomigrancy. While the chapters of this book will not explicitly list each one of them individually, these terms will inform discussions of literary propriety, systems of patronage of translation, communitarian affiliations of readers, and accessibility of literary works through translations, publications, and library acquisitions.

The book or the author as an object of study and epistemological organization, the idea of a massive collection that contains as many discoverable titles as possible, and a catalog that is universal in scope and global in scale—these are just a few ideas that have been central to the ideological conceptualization of world literature since the early nineteenth century. All of these have shaped the building and organization of real libraries. They have also sparked the creation of imaginary libraries of world literature. The inventory of world literature has been, since its inception, implicitly prospective, explicitly retrospective, and inherently interconnected with other bibliographs. It has also always carried with it an awareness—sometimes dim and sometimes sharp—of the linguistic, discursive, and material accessibility and inaccessibility that shadows the gathering of all discoverable titles from the world, classified and understood under the rubric of literature.

A Pact with Books

Rethinking world literature for the twenty-first century means changing the framework in which we ask what constitutes world literature. From the outset, the discourse of masterpieces overwhelmed the construction of world literature, and we have been struggling to get out from under this model without asking how it came to dominate the landscape in the first place. Our rethinking here will involve not only paying attention to the objects that inhabit the so-called world literary space but also constantly focusing on the nodes, the agencies, the points of transfer that become key to the construction of world literary spaces and collections and inventories. Reimagining world literature for the twenty-first century means learning lessons from the most prolific and all-encompassing discourse of our times, that of public media. And to embrace this challenge, I propose a genealogy of world literature that shifts the focus from presentist academic concerns in professionalized forms of reading and pangeographical projections of a "world republic of letters" with a single center, where one size fits all nations and publics.

I am proposing a genealogy of world literature which has at its center the notion of bibliomigrancy—the physical and virtual movement of books—which manifests itself though many material nodes: oral storytellers, authors, publishers, translators, traders, booksellers, printers, reprinters, collectors, political groups, librarians, listeners, and readers. This book uses the idea of bibliomigrancy to conceptualize the materialization of literature across multiple literary systems. In her essay "The Location of Literature," Rebecca Walkowitz writes: "[L]iterary studies will have to examine the global writing of books, in addition to their classification, design, publication, translation, anthologizing, and reception across multiple geographies. Books are no longer imagined to exist in a single literary system but may exist, now and in the future, in several literary systems, through various and uneven practices of world circulation."[93] Bibliomigrancy will help us to understand consistencies and inconsistencies in book circulation, the existence of books in multiple literary systems. I add to this an examination of what I call the *pact with books*. This phrase, as I define it, is intended to help us to understand the relations between specific publics and books, as well as the conditions in which those relations come into being in the first place and how they transform over the course of time. In particular, I seek to draw attention to the very large body of actors—beyond the author and the translator of a literary work—who determine a reader's access to literary works. If a work of literature originates in a space beyond the immediate geolinguistic location of the reader, the number of actors increases exponentially. If the author and the reader were to be tentatively imagined in a producer-consumer relationship, there is also an entire set of mediators, crossing many institutions and media, who enable the distribution and circulation of a literary artifact for a worldwide readership.

In other words, a public life of world literature exists in which various individuals and collectives come together to institutionalize world literature. And these individuals and collectives do not exist in a historical-political vacuum. In fact, the historical and political conditions for any conception of world literature often create and exert ideological pressures that emerge from within the political boundaries of a nation. One argument that emerges from my work on the German example shows that national identities and agendas do not merely shape the public life of a national literature but also the public life of world literature. The co-optation of literature as a cultural artifact in the service of the nation plays a significant role in the definition of world literature. This includes the promotion of certain authors and texts as national icons on the one hand, and the writing out of other authors and texts through censorship or other means of suppression on the other hand. The creation of a readership for literature beyond national languages and the institutionalization of world literature within a society are thus functions of the cultural politics of a society at a given historical moment. To assume, however, that a national society operates in absolute isolation from the international community would be a fallacy. The national literary space shapes itself—sometimes consciously, at other times less consciously—in relationship to the world literary space, and vice versa. Statements on national or world literature by authors, thinkers, and critics can therefore hardly be entirely dislodged from the political histories of the moments and the milieu in which they were made. World literature, if it is to find its relevance for us in the twenty-first century, needs to be understood in the larger public life of literature: beyond the university classroom, beyond the specialized community of readers.

Understanding multiple publics' pacts with books is crucial to understanding how the processes of nationalization of literature in one part of the world impacts the reception of literature from another part of the world. In other words, one needs to scrutinize ways in which the patrimony of a given national political and literary prestige actually underwrites or subsidizes the way for works from other literary spheres to enter the larger world literary space. An engagement with material conditions for public access to books helps us relearn how through habits and practices of reading, translated works become alibis for cultural nativism, cultural relativism, cultural pluralism, and, as the history of colonialism reflects, cultural subjugation. The challenge lies in unsuppressing the curiosity about new forms of reading practices that form and, in return, are informed by the multiplicity of literary spaces created and inhabited by books.

The approach I favor here focuses on the interaction of national-political histories that together create interactive cultural spaces that operate at times in alliance with, and at other times in defiance of, national political spaces. In order to understand this, we need to move beyond tracing the proliferation of world literature merely as an innocent form of reading, a "detached engagement" with literature, or as an informed discourse of academic experts in the new century. As Djelal Kadir aptly observes, "in a world marked by the systematic and meticulous capitalization of everything into a fungible commodity, literature is not immune."[94] Remaining oblivious to the commodification of literature as world literature is not a choice. We need to outline a new genealogy of world literature that helps us account for socio-political, cultural, and commercial factors that bring a vast range of readers together with a worldly variety of books.

It is the trajectory of the simultaneous making and unmaking of world literature that this book follows, unveiling institutional networks and nodes in order to draw attention to the encounters between intellectual and commercial capital that influence the circulation, distribution, and reception of world literature. If this seems like a plausible and productive line of inquiry, the next step would be to ask how local and translocal, national and transnational, provincial and cosmopolitan actors and institutions work toward the creation of a world literary space.

This examination of public pacts with books has implications for the debates about translation that have troubled world literature scholarship. Translations form the very foundations of world literature and global literary comparison and so do not always impede the idea of world literary access but do allow us to track the question of power and access. The significance of translations is not merely thinkable in terms of the task of the translator but also the power-politics of the translation industry. Production, circulation, and distribution of literature is not a given at specific points of time in history. As social capital interacts with intellectual capital, conditions arise of uneven circulation and distribution.

In some ways, the lines of inquiry that I pursue in this book intersect with those of two recently published monographs: Rebecca Walkowitz's *Born Translated* (2015), which casts translations as essential to world literary comparison, and Aamir Mufti's *Forget English!* (2016), which investigates power and access through a critical scrutiny of global English. Focusing on the contemporary novel, Walkowitz challenges the "dominant modes of literary sequencing, in which circulation always trails production," and offers for consideration "born translated works," to upset binaries of "author and translator, original and derivation, native and foreign, just to name a few of the foundational distinctions that have shaped world literature as we've known it."[95] While Walkowitz focuses primarily on Anglophone translations, Mufti questions the very status of English as the "dominant world literary language,"[96] to propose that "*the genealogy of world literature leads to Orientalism.*"[97] He pursues the relationship between "the *universal* in the 'universal library' and *world* in 'world literature'"[98] to "elucidate how 'India' has been implicated in the entanglement of Orientalism and world literature, but also, more crucially, how can it also be a site for a *critique* of this entanglement."[99]

Akin to Walkowitz, I emphasize in this book how translations into German were crucial to world literary access and comparison. In following histories of translations and publications, I suggest how these works acquired lives of their own in the German public sphere. Furthermore, through an inclusion of publication and library histories, state policies, and the book market, I underline that an entire network of social structures and institutions facilitates, and at times jeopardizes, the conditions under which a literary work can be identified as "born translated." While I concur with Mufti that the genealogy of world literature leads to Orientalism, as the case of Germany in the nineteenth century clearly reveals, our paths diverge in our investigations of the twentieth century, because of the specificity of the political contexts discussed. In the Indian context, the suppression of Indian literary traditions at the expense of English in colonial India and the rise of postcolonial Anglophone literatures on the Indian subcontinent in the late twentieth century create a genealogy of world literature that finds a continuation of historical Orientalist practices into the contemporary cultural text through the politics of language. In the case of Germany, the language of politics gains precedence over the politics of language. National Socialism, the ideological divide that characterized the two German states, the presence of a large migrant population in post–World War II (West) Germany, and the iconic fall of the Berlin Wall beg a very different set of questions to parse the relationship between the universal in the "universal library" and the world in "world literature."

The story of *Weltliteratur* within the German-speaking world is not a singular story; it both gives us models for understanding other sites and moments and itself unfolds in conjunction with other spaces around the world. The five main chapters of this book tell several stories of the construction of world literature within the German-speaking public sphere.

Instead of starting with *Weltliteratur* and looking for an inductive definition, as other critics have done, I suggest starting with one story that opens outward; following traces, bits, and shards of knowledge might help us approach the fragments that contribute to the narrative of world literature. Each chapter identifies a concern central to world literary discussions and examines it along with aspects of libraries and related print cultural institutions.

Chapter 1 focuses on canon formation in the early nineteenth century alongside the flow of Asian works in manuscript and translations that flooded German libraries in the first half of the nineteenth century. The chapter juxtaposes Goethe's celebration of non-Western literature with a statement about the supposed inferiority of non-Western literatures as proposed by Lord Thomas Babington Macaulay. This juxtaposition assists in highlighting how colonialism initiated and facilitated a climate that was fertile for the inception of the term *Weltliteratur*; furthermore, it helps in locating the comparative world literary practices that followed translations of non-European works into European languages around that time. By including a discussion of the British Oriental Translation Fund (organized in 1828) and the role of the Asiatick Society in Calcutta, I demonstrate how Germany becomes the beneficiary of British colonialism. By focusing on discussions on world literature and libraries in literary magazines like *Literarisches Conversations-Blatt* (later *Blätter für literarische Unterhaltung*), the chapter emphasizes the creation of a world literary market and a world literary readership. The chapter ends with a discussion of the public trial of Eckermann on the case he fought with his publishers over royalties for *Gespräche mit Goethe*, ultimately making it a masterpiece but rendering Eckermann the subservient slave.

Chapter 2 follows the conceptual career of the term *Weltliteratur* beyond Goethe. Central to the chapter is Heine's concept of *Welthülfsliteratur* (world-help literature) through which he accords primacy to the function of literature in the public sphere (*Öffentlichkeit*). On the one hand, in the *Communist Manifesto* (1848), Marx and Engels would unmoor the Goethean idea of world literature from *Poesie* (poesy) as the *Gemeingut* of the human race and firmly anchor it in the bourgeois production and consumption of literature. On the other hand, supporters of national literature, such as Wolfgang Menzel and Ernst Moritz Arndt, would emerge as staunch detractors of world literature and criticize it through their anticosmopolitan and at times anti-Semitic ideologies. The chapter thus presents an account of two trajectories of world literature beyond Goethe's ideas. The theorization of world literature becomes politically charged and refracted through the question of national literature. The practice of world literature—acquisition, translation, publication—becomes a niche activity, carried on almost as if it were depoliticized and disconnected from the larger social politics of the times. I discuss the publication of anthologies such as Johannes Scherr's *Bildersaal der Weltliteratur* (1848); the establishment of the library of "Die deutsche morgenländische Gesellschaft" (1844); the acquisition, by the Königliche Bibliothek in Berlin, of the Aloys Sprenger Collection, the largest acquisition of Arabic, Farsi, and Urdu works by a German library in the nineteenth century, and the launching of Reclam's Universal-Bibliothek (1867).

Chapter 3 extends the findings of chapter 2 into the twentieth century. I read Walter Benjamin's famous essay "Unpacking my Library" (1928) along with Hermann Hesse's essay "A Library of World Literature" (1929)—an important but hitherto neglected statement on world literature—to chart modes in which the early twentieth century ushers in a new relationship with books. Using Romain Rolland and Rabindranath Tagore's (failed) attempts to create a "world library" in the late 1920s as a turning point, the chapter moves to National Socialist conceptualizations of world literature as evident in the Nazi literary magazines, *Weltliteratur* and *Die Weltliteratur*. Through a detailed discussion of Nazi policies on libraries and print culture, especially translated literature, the chapter shows how direct and indirect censorship, cultural politics of intimidation, and the ethnicization of German national literature during the Nazi period radically transform the concept of world literature.

Chapter 4 has at its center the statement by Erich Auerbach (1952) on the challenges of conceptualizing world literature in the Goethean sense after World War II. Animating Auerbach's concept of historicity, the chapter considers how the cultural authorities from the United States and the former Soviet Union split the German literary market and libraries immediately following the war. By juxtaposing the state-sponsored program for publication and reception of world literature through the Leipzig Book Fair in the former German Democratic Republic with the free-market book trade led by the Frankfurt Book Fair in the Federal Republic of Germany, the chapter investigates the uneasy intimacy between history and ideology and its impact on the definition of world literature in a divided Germany. The chapter includes the first English-language discussion of the East German pedagogical program for creating a world literary readership through the publishing company Volk und Welt, which had close links to the GDR Ministries of Education and Culture.

Chapter 5 focuses on the cosmopolitan orientation of the post-1989 years and the further transformation of German national literature, first from contributions by authors of non-German ethnicities in the German language, and second through advancements in digital technologies and the establishment of pan-European literary portals like the European Library. Using the double meaning of *migration* as a point of departure, I move to the digital era of publication, and the emergence of new digital universal libraries in the early twenty-first century. I discuss the transnational construction, the cosmopolitan ambition, and the purportedly universal mission of the European Digital Library. As technology reglobalizes the "text," I account for ways in which the politics of acquisition, admission, and accumulation of digital texts impacts access to world literature.

The maps accompanying the introduction and chapters are visual depictions of accounts of bibliomigrancy narrated in the chapters. They serve a dual purpose: they illustrate the multicentric nature of world literary construction, and underline Germany's position as a node in the network of world literary circulation. The lines connecting distant spaces depict the physical circuits of bibliomigrancy and orient the readers to the geocultural spaces discussed in the chapters. But even a cursory glance would suffice to trace the transformation of patterns of bibliomigrancy over a course of two centuries, supporting the central argument of the book, that world literature is historically conditioned, culturally determined, and politically charged.

Coding/Recoding

What was world literature for Goethe, Marx, Engels, Auerbach, or even Hesse cannot exactly be the same for authors and thinkers of the second half of the twentieth century. In 1965, Mahadevi Varma—the renowned Hindi poet, essayist, and short-story writer—addressed the legislative assembly of Uttar Pradesh, a state in Northern India. In her speech, "Sāhitya, Sanskriti, aur Śāsan" (Literature, culture, and governance), Varma emphasized literature as a shared cultural heritage of humanity that breaks down barriers between nations and peoples. Juxtaposing Sanskrit and Awadhi authors such as Kalidasa and Tulasidasa with English and Russian authors such as Shakespeare and Tolstoy respectively, Varma asserted that they belonged as much to the specific linguistic and national communities of their origin as to those outside of these communities: "They belong to everyone in that they belong to each one."[100]

Forty years after Varma's remarks, in October 2003, the American author Susan Sontag addressed the audience at Frankfurt's famous Paulskirche on the occasion of receiving the German Peace Prize (Friedenspreis des deutschen Buchhandels).[101] In her acceptance speech, entitled "Literature is Freedom," Sontag reflected on "the fragile alliance" between Europe and the United States.[102] She reminisced about books—among others by German authors such as Franz Kafka and Thomas Mann—that she read growing up in Arizona and California as a third-generation American of Polish and Lithuanian decent: "To have *access to literature, world literature*, was to escape the prison of national vanity, of philistinism, of compulsory provincialism, of inane schooling, of imperfect destinies and bad luck. Literature was the passport to enter a larger life; that is, the zone of freedom."[103]

In 1999, during the 250th anniversary celebrations of Goethe in Weimar, Orhan Pamuk gave a speech, "Dünya Edebiyatı" (world literature).[104] Pamuk began with prudent uncertainty: "world literature?" he asked, calling the term at once "thought provoking" and "mysterious." By associating world literature with "a high brotherhood of those who read books" and asking if "the whole world's literature" implied a "global fraternity of literature,"[105] Pamuk at once diagnosed authority and naïveté in the term. The initial skepticism quickly gave way to a confident investment in world literature as Pamuk highlighted "influences, borrowings, and infatuations" of the last two centuries to declare, that "literature is as much a delicately constructed memory as it is a subtly constructed forgetting."[106]

The occasions on which Varma, Sontag, and Pamuk delivered their thoughts are separated by roughly forty years and the three distinct political worlds to which they belonged. And yet, their thoughts intersect in their respective understanding of literary figures and access to literature from other parts of the world in times of intense nationalization. These authors emphasize the power of engagement with literature outside of the political boundaries of a nation-state as a solution to man-made divisions, collective national narcissisms, and the consequent power hierarchies among nations. By devaluating a necessarily national arrangement of literature, these authors emancipate themselves from the overpowering burden of being "representatives" of only the nations of their origins. Their thoughts are undergirded by a cosmopolitan disposition acutely wary of a nationalistic privileging of literature. They promote world literature as an instrument of international cultural understanding, in effect, as a political and philosophical ideal.

However, their statements are hardly a continuation of earlier discussions. Unlike their German predecessors from the nineteenth and twentieth centuries, these authors cannot anticipate the arrival of world literature in the future. They can ill afford to reduce the literary activity of the twentieth century to merely a formidable pedagogical challenge for American undergraduate or graduate students. They cannot circumvent the historical sedimentation of 250 years that divides the world and literary labor into geopolitical centers and peripheries. It is therefore the present, the now- and here-ness of world literature that they must confront.

Weltliteratur, world literature, *viśva sāhitya*, *dünya edebiyatı*, *verdenslitteratur*, *literatura mundial*: No matter how limited the choice of languages—six out of at least two hundred listed in the UNESCO World Cultures Report 2010—each term for world literature carries a different inflection. If the languages represented here bear the marks of development of their own long political and cultural histories, so do their terms for world literature. While in each of these languages the term denotes something extra-local, extra-linguistic, extra-national, indeed "worldly" in scale and scope, no term is identical to the other in its import; similar, equivalent, intersecting, perhaps, but not identical. Each one of these terms derives its meaning in the relational and comparative framework that defines the position of its specific literary corpus in the world of literature. The terms and conditions of such a relation also change through time and space. In other words, the term *world literature* is from the outset relational and comparative. Such relation and comparison however do not detract from the idea of literature as a shared cultural heritage of human beings.

The story of world literature is not a single story; it comprises multiple stories of difference and comparison, of acquisition and appropriation, inhabitation and naturalization. World literature is less about ownership and expertise and more about access to and familiarity with that which is not one's own through the accident of birth and naturalness of a mother tongue. World literature is characterized by, to use another term from US library professionals, *borrowing privileges*. These privileges are defined by access: to basic literacy and the ability to read, to the production and reception of literature as a cultural artifact, to books and other media of the public dissemination of literature, and furthermore to a specific kind of linguistic and cultural literacy that readers and authors from one part of the world acquire when they access literatures from other parts of the world. This access does not necessarily have to lead to a harmonious dialogue; in fact, often it is borne out of conflicted circumstances—such as colonialism, political dominance, financial subjugation—and may very well restore the conflict in the process of reading. Thinking of world literature in terms of a pact with books helps us to understand how we as readers recode world literature, as we are recoded by reading world literary works. This dual awareness of recoding frames our understanding of the shared and the unshared in literature; it calls upon us to acknowledge ownership, usurpation, co-optation, and every other form of privileged possession through which readers associate with a literary text. Privileges, as we know, cannot be understood unless they are refracted against restriction. A careful examination of privileged and underprivileged conditions of world literary circulation can help us understand the uneven force field of literary production and circulation.

The project of world literature is fraught with tensions between local formations and global transformations, national demarcations and transnational projections, individual differentiations and universal configurations. World literature incorporates various institutions of literature, literary readings being just one of them. The act of reading is inherently connected with bibliomigrancy, of accessibility or inaccessibility to intellectual and imaginative labor of texts from elsewhere by readers from elsewhere. The space of reading—the physical and metaphorical space of the library—demands an account of the owned and the borrowed, the shared and the unshared, the agreed upon and the contestable as shelf-lives of books are created beyond their points of origin. When the act and space of reading are considered in tandem, borrowing privileges acquire new meanings. World literature ceases to remain a space encoded in infinitely accumulating time and consecutively arranged sites. It becomes recoded through multiple sites with discontinuous temporalities, each one deriving its meaning through—to use Foucault's terms—vectors of juxtaposition, dispersion, inversion, and contestation. Through this discontinuous and nonconsecutive arrangement of time and space—chronos and topos—world literature acquires its cosmochronic and cosmotopic dimensions.

To envision the intersection of the cosmochronic with the cosmotropic, I will now turn to the moment of inception of *Weltliteratur* by Goethe. Faust is waiting in his study, eager to make a pact with the devil, and, with books.

Aberdeen
Edinburgh
Oxford
London
Paris
Bonn
Hanover
Gotha
Weimar
Milan
Madrid
Rome
Sarajevo
Corfu
Athens
Tunis
Alexandria
Cairo
Tehran
Isfahan
Srinagar
Badayun
Mirzapur
Berar
Ujjain
Agra
Calcutta
Bombay
Madras
Colombo
Beijing
Tokyo
Macau
Guangzhou
Singapore
Cooperstown
New York
Lima
Rio de Janeiro

CHAPTER I

Of Masters and Masterpieces: An Empire of Books, a Mythic European Library

"But," I said, "perhaps this Chinese novel is one of their outstanding ones?" "Not at all," said Goethe, "the Chinese have them by the thousand and already had them when our ancestors were still living in the forests."

—JOHANN PETER ECKERMANN, *Conversations with Goethe* (1836)[1]

I am quite ready to take the Oriental learning at the valuation of the Orientalists themselves. I have never found one among them who could deny that a single shelf of a good European library was worth the whole native literature of India and Arabia.

—THOMAS BABINGTON MACAULAY, *Minute on Indian Education* (1835)[2]

In "Night," the opening scene of Goethe's *Faust* (Part I), Heinrich Faust sits at his desk in his study, ruminating over the usability of his erudition. Faust is restless in his dark and restrictive workspace. The study is described as a "narrow, high-vaulted Gothic chamber,"[3] a "prison," and Faust curses the "dank frowsty cabinet/Where even heaven's dear ray can pass/But murkily through tinted glass!"[4] The "lofty walls with a hundred shelves" are a domicile of moths. Faust has spent his life accumulating and studying books on philosophy, medicine, law, and theology, an enterprise that has earned him the titles of master and doctor. And yet, books become the very source of the crisis that defines Faust's world. Books are enveloped in dust, devoured by worms, and reach high up to the vault of the study; the library becomes a space "stuffed tightly with *ancestral junk*."[5]

Faust's study exemplifies the dichotomy that exists between the outer world of action and the inner world composed of mainly words, from which he longs to free himself. The passage does not only suggest a *figurative* emancipation from the world of words to a world of action but also a *physical* migration from the materiality of books to the materiality of the world outside. The crisis of the intellectual intensifies through the very crisis of the relationship between the medium of dissemination of knowledge—the books—and the place where they are stored: the intellectual's private library ("Gelehrtenbibliothek"). The pact with Mephistopheles, as is well established, assures Faust's movement from the realm of knowledge ("Erkenntnis") to experience ("Erfahrung").[6]

Through the figure of Faust, Goethe offers for consideration a pact with books in a library that is architecturally insulated, resembles a prison, and yet is the scholar's righteous abode: the space of reading, writing, and critical thinking. Faust's private library stages the collision of myth and prophecy with rational thought and enlightened discourse. After all, the master and doctor is reading *The Book of Nostradamus*. The study is also the space where the dichotomous soul of books—as material objects and intellectual artifacts—anticipates another famous duality that Faust identifies: "Two souls, alas, are dwelling in my breast,/and either would be severed from its brother."[7]

In an uncanny way, the opening scence of *Faust* brings forth the dichotomous nature of books as identified by the philosopher Immanuel Kant in the late eighteenth century. In a letter to the Berlin publisher Friedrich Nicolai written in 1798, Kant urged Nicolai to recognize the powerful social function of books as an agency of enlightenment and emphatically asked him to not give into market forces. Kant praised book production as an important line of business in a culture where reading had become common and indispensible. However, he chastised publishers for using books merely to stimulate the book market by focusing on their commodity function. The enlightening power of books rested for Kant in the restoration of their intellectual prowess, which he thought would be compromised when publishers gave in to market forces and accommodated populist ideas through mass production. The world of enlightenment that Kant wanted the readers of the book to inhabit is a world with a higher purpose, a world where rationality and intellectual discourse triumphed through a publisher's careful selection of content.[8] Kant presented the dual personalities of books: as an intellectual (*Geist*) and as a material (*Ware*) artifact; a source of knowledge as well as a commodity.

But there is another kind of pact with books that Goethe's *Faust* offers for consideration: a pact with books outside the German-speaking world.

The scope and scale of the Faustian drama has invigorated discussions on its uniqueness as a masterpiece; Goethe enters into a dialogue with the longer tradition of the Faustian myth in Europe, and in return becomes the reference point for many following discussions in the next two centuries. For its representation of the uniqueness of linguistic expression, the complexity of human thought, the conflicted nature of the human self, and the bifurcated realities of power, desire, and intellect, *Faust* is considered a masterpiece, worthy of inclusion in all major anthologies of world literature. In his essay "Goethe's Faust as a Modern Epic," Franco Moretti discusses *Faust* as a part of "world texts," highlighting the "larger geographical ambition: a global ambition, of which Faust is the unchallenged archetype." For Moretti, *Faust* becomes constitutive of "an ascending teleology—which will then end by legitimizing the dominion of the 'advanced' West over the 'backward' periphery."[9]

What is also noteworthy—and is often reduced to a footnote in many publications of *Faust*—is that *Faust* is also in dialogue with a major non-European work, whose translation and circulation in England, France, and Germany was facilitated by British colonialism in India. The publication of Georg Forster's German translation of Kalidasa's *Sakuntala* in 1791 (from William Jones's English translation of 1789) led to Goethe's addition of "Vorspiel auf dem Theater" ("Prelude in the Theater") as the second of the three prologues in his play.[10] The dialogue between the director, the "Buffoon" ("lustige Person"), and the author was inspired indeed by the prologue in Kalisada's *Sakuntala*. The prologue to *Faust* thus paves the way to thinking about the study not merely as a space of reading, writing, and critical thinking of an intellectual from which he desires to emancipate himself but as a way of connecting with another world that is political, historical, cultural, as well as literary.

Goethe is supposed to have composed the second prologue to *Faust* in the late 1790s,[11] at the same time as Kant composed his letter to Nicolai. However, it is not the chronological coincidence but rather the awareness of the split nature of books that is interesting for our discussion.

In this chapter, I want to mobilize Faust's study as a way to think about two kinds of pacts with books: the first, following Kant, reveals the duality of books as intellectual and material objects; and the second, pursuing Goethe's engagement with *Sakuntala* in his "Prologue," materializes as a pact between German (or European) and non-European literatures that marks the time when Goethe gives traction to the term *Weltliteratur*. I am interested in knowing what kind of windows open up in a mythic European library when Goethe's engagement with a growing empire of books marks a turning point in the reception of non-European works in the European cultural space. To what extent do national (or local) and world literatures find themselves in a "dual soul" relationship, a mutual conflict, waiting to be severed from each other?

Extending Moretti's thoughts beyond *Faust*, I contend that in the first half of the nineteenth century, world literature in Germany is constructed as an engagement of the European center with its non-European peripheries. This engagement is by no means unproblematic; in fact, it reveals equations of power and mastery concomitant with colonialism. On the one hand, world literature becomes an accomplice in the process of legitimizing Western domination over the Eastern periphery. On the other hand, through these processes, the "ancestral junk" ("Urväter Hausrat") of Germany and Europe undergoes scrutiny as new literary works arrive from elsewhere and national literature is posited against world literature.

Furthermore, I argue that British (and French) colonialism in Asia and Africa initiates and facilitates a specific kind of colonial bibliomigrancy: movement of Sanskrit, Chinese, Persian, and Arabic texts in the original as manuscripts and in translation. The German literary space becomes first a beneficiary and subsequently an agent of colonial bibliomigrancy. These developments prepare the intellectual climate that enables the inception and incubation of the term *Weltliteratur*. Nurturing this construction of world literature are also important local factors such as the rise in book production and magazine publications and the expansion of German libraries.

My goal is to demonstrate the connections between German constructions of *Weltliteratur* and British colonialism through three important examples. First, I compare Goethe's statement on *Weltliteratur* (first published in 1836) with Lord Thomas Babington Macaulay's "Great Minute on Indian Education" (1835). The juxtaposition of these mutually conflictual positions will help to establish the indelible mark of colonialism and Orientalism in the institutionalization of world literature. Second, I discuss August Wilhelm Schlegel's plans to publish a series on Indian classics, which he submitted as a proposal to the *Journal of the Asiatic Society* (Calcutta). Third, I offer an overview of the Oriental Translation Society (established in 1828), which served as a major globally situated translation enterprise. I end with a commentary on the afterlife of Eckermann's *Gespräche mit Goethe* in Germany, a remarkable story symptomatic of dominance and subservience.

In the rest of the discussion, I want to locate Goethe's moment within the specific tensions underlying the access to the world "in print," which also form part of the German intellectual landscape of the first half of the nineteenth century. Crucial to this section is the discussion of an intensified understanding of the dual role of the book as an intellectual and cultural artifact at the height of the German Enlightenment and the changing face of the library, especially the literal and figurative transformation of the "European library."

British colonialism and German scholarly Orientalism went hand in hand to set the stage from which Goethe and Macaulay expounded their ideas. In the midst of an international circulation of books, certain principles of global literary comparison gain currency. The literary value of a foreign text is inflated by declaring it a masterpiece, and various kinds of "masters" from a variety of institutions play their parts in the making of the masterpiece. And this is the story of world literature that this chapter unfolds: a story of relation and comparison, legislation and legitimization, masters and masterpieces.

Comparative World Literature: Goethe and Macaulay

December 31, 1827: Goethe has just finished reading a Chinese novel in translation. He shares his reflections on the novel with his editorial assistant, secretary, and, after his death, the executor of his literary will, Johann Peter Eckermann. Goethe determines the aesthetic value of the novel in comparison to a recent work he has read by the French novelist Béranger. A work from a faraway linguistic tradition that makes its way into the European literary space must be compared with something from nearby, something familiar. And to make a case for it to be read by others, it must be declared *vorzüglichst* (most outstanding).[12] The novel is *vorzüglichst*, and Goethe knows that the Chinese have "thousands of them," but he neither mentions the title of the novel nor does he possess his own copy. His extensive personal library with over 5,000 volumes has no entry for any Chinese work in translation. Goethe's library contained works from many literary traditions, including German (448), Greek (139), Latin (126), French (112), Italian (60), English (58), Oriental and Indian (32), Eastern European (25), Spanish and Portuguese (18), and Nordic (6).[13] *Goethes Bibliothek: Katalog* (1958), the comprehensive catalog of the Goethe National Library in Weimar—including holdings from Goethe's private library as well as his father's library—documents titles of literary works in twenty languages, in the original or in translation, that Goethe had acquired during his lifetime.[14] Non-European works include Georg Forster's translation of Kalidasa's *Sakontala* (1791), Wilhelm von Humboldt's *Bhagavad-Gita* (1826), and Joseph von Hammer Purgstall's translation from Persian into German of Shamsuddin Hafiz's poetic *Diwan* (1812–1813), with which Goethe engaged in his own *West-östlicher Divan* (1814–1819).[15]

The *Katalog* does not mention a single work of Chinese literature, in the original or in translation. However, the library of the Großherzogliches Haus Sachsen-Weimar (Grand Duchy of Saxony-Weimar)—today the Klassik Stiftung Weimar, a UNESCO World Heritage institution—might have enabled Goethe's access to Chinese literature. In 1797, Goethe was appointed overseer of the library by Großherzog Carl August, a position he held until his death in 1832. And although the Goethe-Schiller Archives at the Klassik Stiftung only have evidence of one borrowing card signed by Goethe (figure 1-1), as overseer and regular user he had unfettered access to the library. Akin to other well-endowed European libraries of the early nineteenth century, this library was proactively acquiring non-European works: in translations or in the original as manuscripts. From a total of 49,000 volumes in the field of literature and linguistics, many were acquired in the eighteenth and nineteenth centuries. As Jürgen Weber reports in his description of the collection, "works of world literature are in original languages, often also well represented through French translations."[16] In *Goethe als Benutzer der Weimarer Bibliothek*, Elise von Keudell documents literary works checked out by Goethe from the Anna Amalia Bibliothek. These included translations of Arabic, Persian, and Turkish works by Hammar Purgstall,[17] Chinese and Japanese manuscripts of Julius Klaproth,[18] and Horace Wilson's English translation of Kalidasa's *Megha Duta* (*The Cloud Messenger*).[19] One of the works Goethe checked out was Peter Perring Thoms's *Chinese Courtship*,[20] the English translation of a Chinese work, which probably became the immediate precursor to Goethe's most famous statement on world literature:

> I am more and more convinced that poetry is the universal possession of mankind, revealing itself everywhere and at all times. . . . But of course, if we Germans do not look beyond the narrow circle of our own environment, we all too easily fall into this kind of pedantic arrogance. I therefore like to look about me in foreign nations and advise everyone else to do so. *National literature is now rather an unmeaning term; the epoch of world literature is at hand, and everyone must strive to hasten its coming.*[21]

February 2, 1835: As Eckermann prepares the manuscript of *Gespräche* to be sent to the publisher F. A. Brockhaus in Leipzig, in another part of the world, Thomas Babington Macaulay, a British lawyer and advisor to the

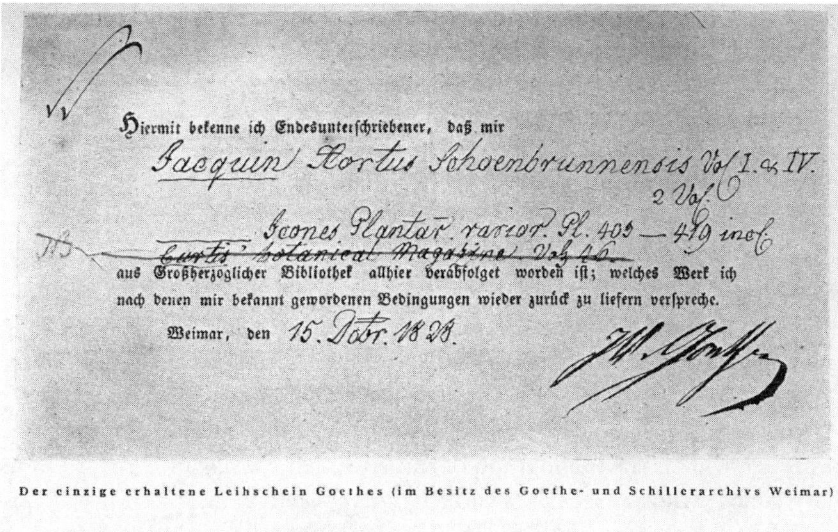

Hiermit bekenne ich Endesunterschriebener, daß mir
Jacquin Hortus Schoenbrunnensis Vol I. & IV. 2 Vol.
Icones Plantar. rarior. Pl. 405 – 419 incl.
~~Curtis' botanical Magazine Vol. 46.~~
aus Großherzoglicher Bibliothek allhier verabfolget worden ist; welches Werk ich nach denen mir bekannt gewordenen Bedingungen wieder zurück zu liefern verspreche.
Weimar, den 15. Octbr. 1828.

Der einzige erhaltene Leihschein Goethes (im Besitz des Goethe- und Schillerarchivs Weimar)

Figure 1-1. Book borrowing card with Goethe's signature, 1828. (Courtesy of Klassik Stiftung Weimar.)

Supreme Council of the British East India Company, proposes his mode of comparing world literatures. In his infamous "Great Minute on Indian Education," Macaulay simply dismisses the possibility of any work from a non-European space to ever qualify as a masterpiece or *vorzüglichst* to use Goethe's term. Macaulay is not too distant from Goethe in purpose—he is also concerned with determining the aesthetic value of a literary work from a faraway space through comparison with something familiar. Principles of aesthetic evaluation shared by the two are somewhat similar: superiority, outstanding quality, and greatness; though for Macaulay, linguistic utility will become a prime factor in privileging one kind of literature over others. Macaulay's recoding of world literature would be shaped by knowledge he claims to have borrowed from Orientalist translators. At a time when the well-oiled establishment of Orientalism is finding ever new modes of colonial patronage both for the collecting of manuscripts in Sanskrit, Arabic, Persian, Chinese, and for their translations into English, Macaulay declares, as cited in the epigraph:

> I have no knowledge of either Sanscrit or Arabic. But I have done what I could to form a correct estimate of their value. I have read translations of the most celebrated Arabic and Sanscrit works. I have

> conversed, both here and at home, with men distinguished by their proficiency in the Eastern tongues. I am quite ready to take the Oriental learning at the valuation of the Orientalists themselves. I have never found one among them who could deny that *a single shelf of a good European library was worth the whole native literature of India and Arabia*. The intrinsic superiority of the Western literature is, indeed, fully admitted by those members of the Committee who support the Oriental plan of education.[22]

Weimar and Calcutta, Goethe and Macaulay: two cities, two masters, two imaginations of a masterpiece, two moments of an emerging discourse of what David Damrosch succinctly calls "comparative world literature."[23] At the center of this comparative enterprise is the mythic European library. So what is the bibliograph of this so-called European library? Let us have a closer look at Goethe's and Macaulay's statements.

Eckermann's diary entry for Wednesday, December 31, 1827, begins, as mentioned earlier, with Goethe's discussion of an unnamed Chinese novel, which Goethe finds "im hohen Grade merkwürdig" (highly remarkable, but also strange).[24] Eckermann's first response is indeed about the strange and foreign ("fremdartig") nature of the novel, Goethe clarifies by turning to the commonalities, rather than differences, between the foreign product and the local, more familiar genre of the European novel. Remarkable here is Goethe's turning not so much to the aesthetic but more anthropological commonalities. While it is ambiguous from the passage if Goethe refers to the Chinese people in general or the characters in the novel, the premise of his establishing commonalities between a European *we* and a Chinese *they* remains grounded in modes in which human beings "think, behave, and feel" ("denken, handeln, empfinden"), which makes the *we* "like them" or "akin to them" ("ihresgleichen").[25]

The initial evaluation quickly changes from being generally anthropological to specifically aesthetic and representational. Goethe remarks how in the Chinese narration everything happens "more cleanly, lucidly, and morally," and that the representation is more "steady, and without great passion or poetic verve, and in this regard is very similar to my *Hermann and Dorothea* as well as to the English novels of Richardson."[26] Having established these commonalities between the German (or European) Self and the Chinese Other, Goethe moves to delineating differences in modes of depiction of nature, interactions between nature and human beings, and human beings and objects. More specifically, he singles out "sedan chairs" as an example of the lightness, beauty, and grace he finds in the

Chinese novel. Goethe's broader aesthetic evaluations zoom in on language as he comments on the presence of legends and proverbs woven into the narrative—with a clear eye on the morals and traditions that are part of "the Chinese culture" that Goethe receives. The story of the girl and the boy who spend hours in a room without giving into carnal pleasures becomes important to Goethe. This leads to his much larger comment on Chinese culture, which is based on "severe moderation" ("strenge Mäßigung") through which the Chinese empire has been able to exist and shall continue to do so. In other words, the unnamed Chinese novel immediately becomes the most outstanding "native informant" text. Following Goethe's critique of Béranger and his apparently insufficient motivation to engage with the cleanliness and properness that characterize the Chinese novel, Goethe turns to his most important articulation on world literature but not until Eckermann prompts him. Eckermann asks categorically if the novel Goethe mentions is one of the most outstanding ones they have; Goethe ends his discourse on the Chinese novel on an evolutionary note: "the Chinese have them by the thousands and had them when our ancestors were still living in the forests."[27]

The actual statements on world literature that follow the above-mentioned sentence grant the anthropological insinuation a more panhumanistic inflection, albeit with limitations. Goethe mentions *Poesie* as the *Gemeingut* (shared property) of humanity and confirms that the gift of poetry appears in "hundreds and hundreds" of individuals. With a curious comparison of himself with Friedrich von Matthisson—a very popular but quickly forgotten poet of the late eighteenth and early nineteenth century—Goethe moves on to state the necessity of looking beyond the individual, indeed the local. This is the crucial sentence where Goethe links the inaugural ideas about the remarkable nature of the Chinese novel and Eckermann's comment on its *fremdartig* nature to the necessity of engaging with that which is strange/foreign. The *we* here is explicitly German—"wir Deutschen" (we Germans) must look beyond in order to prevent a falling into the trap of pedantic arrogance. That is when he comments on the fact that national literature has little to say now and, in an instructive tone, adds that everyone must endeavor to hasten the coming of world literature.

The idea of world literature for Goethe in this statement, however, lies neither in the complete embrace of the foreign nor in the substitution of the foreign with the local, but rather in a historic repositioning of the foreign. Goethe comments that in evaluating the foreign, one must not cling to the particularities of, say, "the Chinese," the medieval Spanish poet Pedro Calderon, or the German medieval epic *Nibelungenlied*. But he also insists that literary works do indeed become indissoluble with a people, and vice versa. Nonetheless, for Goethe the pinnacle for the ideal "pattern" ("Muster") remains the authority of the Greeks. Greek literature, according to Goethe, is the gold standard for all literatures, especially for the German *we*: "In our need for the exemplary, we must always return to the ancient Greeks, for in their works, it is at all times man in his beauty that is depicted. Everything else we must regard mainly from a historic point of view, and adopt as much of the good in it as we can."[28]

Thus, despite the initial laudatory remarks about the Chinese and their literature, Greek literature assumes a paramount position. Following this, the conversation takes a slightly different turn and becomes more oriented to European literature. As Goethe compares works of Manzoni to his own historical fiction, Shakespeare's historical plays provide the comparative fulcrum. Shakespeare's historical figures are his interpretations of those figures, Goethe states, adding categorically that Egmont is "my Egmont" ("mein Egmont"). As Goethe moves between text-internal and text-external comparisons, between a collective (the Chinese) and an individual (Béranger), aesthetic comparison paves way for a peculiar anthropological conjecturing. And through this, the primacy of the outstanding—the best and the most representative—is established.

Based on this discussion, the bibliograph of the European library that Goethe presents to Eckermann is the following: the Greeks (Aeschylus, Euripides, Sophocles); the medieval epics and epic poets: *Nibelungenlied* and Calderon; the British classical dramatists: Shakespeare; his contemporaries: Béranger, Manzoni, and of course himself. The Chinese might have had thousands of novels akin to what Goethe has read, but, despite all their narrative and moralistic qualities, along with the Serbs and Calderon, they remain merely a historical reference point to Goethe's idea of world literature.

For Macaulay, the Greeks form the most important part of the inventory of the European library, if only to declare non-European literatures bereft of any quality. Macaulay's mode of literary comparison is based on the usability of literature, and in that sense, compared to Goethe, he is less aesthetically driven. Macaulay privileges the material (*Ware*) over the intellectual (*Geist*) value of books, albeit in the service of Western-style enlightenment for his colonial subjects.

The purpose of Macaulay's statement was the distribution of resources and allocation of funds to educational establishments in India funded by the British East India Company. Through an act of Parliament in 1813, the British had set aside funds for the education of local pupils in Sanskrit, Farsi, and, in the case of Egypt, Arabic; funding was supported until 1835, the year Macaulay arrived in India. This act was considered to be part of the British responsibility to educate the natives in their own languages. Macaulay's plan was to steer the funding toward education in English. Macaulay's ideas are also full of internal ambiguities and built-in contradictions. While Goethe insinuates the superiority of Chinese literature, only to quickly marginalize it, Macaulay rejects the possibility of any non-European works to be a model altogether. And he couches his concerns by vouching for the ability of non-Europeans in acquiring training and education in English. The text is therefore more cryptic than it first appears to be, because it actually highlights an enlightenment function in order to include the colonial subjects into the project of modernity, without their languages or literatures:

> We have a fund to be employed as Government shall direct for the intellectual improvement of the people of this country. The simple question is, what is the most useful way of employing it? All parties seem to be agreed on one point, that the dialects commonly spoken among the natives of this part of India contain neither literary or scientific information, and are, moreover, so poor and rude that, until they are enriched from some other quarter it will not be easy to translate any valuable work to them.[29]

One of the first tasks that Macaulay has upon his arrival is to radically redesign the medium of education and dissemination of knowledge among the subjects of the British Empire. His argument is categorically against the education of the natives in their native languages. Indeed Macaulay starts his argument by accusing the members of the Committee of Public Instruction that they "never would have given the honorable appellation of 'a learned native' to a native who was familiar with the poetry of Milton, the Metaphysics of Locke, and the Physics of Newton."[30] Much like Goethe, Macaulay's literary evaluation is also evolutionary. However, unlike Goethe, who privileges the Chinese in their literary evolution, Macaulay rejects the Indians for only developing knowledge about "all the uses of the cusa-grass" and the Egyptians for "hieroglyphics . . . all the doctrines disguised under the fable of Osiris . . . [and] the rituals with which cats were anciently adorned."[31] Macaulay presents English and French as languages that bear the keys to modern science, prophesizing that Sanskrit, Arabic, and other languages may one day "become useless."[32] Dismissing Indian languages as "poor and rude" dialects, Macaulay declares the impossibility of any Western work that could be translated into them due to the lack of a necessary correspondent vocabulary.

In his discussion of the Chinese novel, Goethe is quick to identify a piece of furniture—sedan chairs—that never receive any representation in Western literature. Macaulay also chooses a piece of furniture: a book shelf. Goethe picks his French contemporary and moves to Greek and Latin classics; Macaulay starts with Greek and Latin classics and then moves to contemporary English literature. Macaulay and Goethe make their statements in the light of "access" to literatures from various parts of the world; Macaulay privileges the total suppression of non-Western literatures through his stringent "aesthetic" evaluation, Goethe momentarily accepts the significance of reading non-Western literatures by identifying poetry as the shared property of humankind, even if to eventually establish the primacy of Western literatures.

Macaulay's statement sparks curiosity about the orderly composition of "a good European library"; it draws attention, through comparison, to the unruly heap on which Macaulay throws literatures from India and Arabia. Indeed, Macaulay prompts an investigation of the transcultural and transcontinental principles of evaluating literature through which he grants a superior space to Western literatures. Goethe, with a perspective radically different from Macaulay, further inspires an investigation of how the European library was indeed changing around the time when he pronounces the arrival of the epoch of world literature.

There is one crucial difference between Goethe and Macaulay. While Goethe is perfectly at ease with reading the Chinese novel in translation—even though he does not mention if he reads it in English or French translation—Macaulay passes a judgment on literature based on language. Speaking against the support of publications in Arabic, Farsi, and Sanskrit, Macaulay makes his grand bid to usurp the funds allocated for such tasks and to divert them to the support of education in English, categorically declaring: "The intrinsic superiority of the Western literature is, indeed, fully admitted by those members of the Committee who support the Oriental plan of education."[33] The inventory of this "good European library" is based on the comparison of superlative works. While Macaulay hails "Eastern writers" for their "highest stand in poetry," he states, "when we pass from works of imagination to works in which facts are recorded, and general principles investigated, the superiority of Europeans becomes absolutely immeasurable." Historical writing in Sanskrit becomes comparable to "paltry abridgments used in preparatory schools in England."[34] English emerges as the supreme language of commerce and intellect, fact and fiction, "a pre-eminent language of the West" which "abounds with works of imagination not inferior to the noblest which Greece has bequeathed to us."[35] Macaulay is in fact most explicit in his mention of Greek lineages of European literatures. English is indeed the new Latin and Greek, as Macaulay establishes in his evaluation of the development of vernaculars within English. He also wants Indians to engage with the foreign. "Let us teach them a foreign language" he says, referring to the teaching of English, which apparently will assist in overcoming the ignorance and backwardness of native languages.[36]

Macaulay's "Minute on Indian Education" inaugurated the systematic institutionalization of English as a medium of education on the Indian subcontinent and has acquired the status of a classic document of intellectual and creative colonization. Through its ideological implication, the document singles out and expels literary traditions in Sanskrit and Arabic from the larger literary landscape of the world. But by implication, he dismisses many unnamed languages and literatures that populated the vast terrains owned and managed by the British. Through its legislative conviction, the document executes the scientific and philosophical hegemony of the colonial metropolis in the management of languages and literatures of the colony (and in the colony). Most importantly, through its discursive ambition, Macaulay's minute signifies the colonial epistemic violence that forever transforms the medium of dominant literary production on the Indian subcontinent as well as in other colonies for centuries to come.

In short, Goethe had one person in his intellectual apprenticeship, Macaulay was about to gain millions more.

Macaulay's concerns are pecuniary, and this is where the idea of the book as a material artifact becomes most pronounced. Macaulay laments the waste of money on the publication of Sanskrit and Arabic books: "Twenty-three thousand volumes, most of them in folios and quartos, fill the libraries, or rather the lumber rooms."[37] The "lumber rooms" must be replaced with one good shelf of a European library. The mythic European library would become one with books by Milton, Newton, the Greeks, and maybe some French literature.

This juxtaposition of Macaulay and Goethe serves well not just to think through literature in the abstract but also through its materiality: the medium of literary dissemination—in translation or in the original, as books or as other print cultural artifacts. At the center of Macaulay's and Goethe's statements are their visions of a "European library"—which through the historical forces of colonialism is transforming in unprecedented ways. In other words, Goethe's moment of *Weltliteratur* is concurrent with the moment when a particular colonialist stance on Western literatures would inaugurate an entire set of comparative literary approaches, which will project—for most of the nineteenth and well into the late twentieth century—the political power structures of European superiority onto literatures and languages from non-European parts of the world. Through these strategies, many images of the world in binary oppositions would emerge: dominant and dominated, civilized and savage, developed and underdeveloped—in other words, important and unimportant. These worlds will clash eternally and struggle with each other in literary and political recognition, creating many divisions between literary centers and peripheries, empiricisms and theories, and major and minor literatures. With this juxtaposition in mind, let us move to see how despite Macaulay's efforts in India, an empire of books was already on the rise elsewhere, namely in Germany, and acknowledged as such.

Beyond Scholarly Orientalism

The most familiar retelling of the story of Goethe's pronouncement of the dawning of the epoch of world literature is one in which Goethe is at the center, standing, looking down at Eckermann, who sits with his head buried in a stack of pages in which he is industriously recording every word said by his master. The only interruptions occur when Eckermann looks up to ask a question, only to bow his head into the paper again when the master responds.

This mode of discussion is particularly characteristic of the German tradition. Goethe is the hero of Fritz Strich's foundational study *Goethe und die Weltliteratur* (1946). Written in exile in Switzerland during the height of the National Socialist takeover of Germany and published after the end of World War II, Strich's *Goethe* is the embodiment of the humanistic tradition represented by German thought, which was forgotten by the Nazis as they committed crimes against humanity. When Erich Auerbach publishes his essay "Philologie und die Weltliteratur" (1952) in the *Festschrift* for Strich, the two images of Goethe are somewhat aligned. Writing, once again, under the shadow of recent history, Auerbach declares the impossibility of world literature in the Goethean sense, primarily due to the lack of a kind of historicity associated with the appreciation of world literature that he sees during Goethe's era.[38] In more recent interpretations, the grandeur of Goethe returns. "Goethe verkündet bei Tisch eine neue Idee" (Goethe announces a new idea at the dinner table) is the opening chapter of Dieter

Lamping's *Die Idee der Weltliteratur: Ein Konzept Goethes und seine Karriere* (2010): an evolutionary history of the idea of world literature as developed by Goethe.[39] Anchored around the word *verkünden*—to announce, but also to foretell or prophesy (as in to herald a new epoch)—Lamping's Goethe of the twenty-first century is a perfect silhouette of the romantic genius.

This is one mode of evaluating Goethe. The second is to link the very idea of *Weltliteratur* to the birth of the *Weltmarkt*, as Antoine Berman aptly proposes in *The Experience of the Foreign: Culture and Translation in Romantic Germany* (1992). Berman accentuates Goethe's investment in reading translations of German works by himself and his contemporaries, and the significance Goethe accords to the translator.

The third mode of reading extends this idea into Pascale Casanova's proclamation of a *World Republic of Letters*, of which Paris is the unquestioned capital, and Goethe, though a German, a permanent resident if not a citizen. For Casanova, "Goethe elaborates the notion of *Weltliteratur* precisely at the moment of Germany's entry into the international literary space."[40] Let it be clear that with this "entry," Casanova implies a one-way traffic, of German literary works acquiring readerships elsewhere, and not the entry of non-German works into Germany. However, Goethe's foreign exchange brokerage seems limited to that of mostly Western European literatures within the European literary space. So here is Goethe, the harbinger of the age of *Weltliteratur*, the great cosmopolitan spirit, the reader, translator, and interpreter of works from Latin, Greek, Italian, French, and English, the quintessential European literary embodiment, who in a stroke of genius pronounces an idea that shall transform perception of literature for centuries to come!

Apart from the centrality of the figure of Goethe, these modes of interpretation share a few other lines of argumentation. First, the immitigable primacy of literary traditions in languages such as French, English, German, and Italian, with some references to peninsular Spanish, that set the standards for literary evaluations. Second, an established, and seemingly insular intra-European network of translations, which co-opt classical Greek and Latin texts. This itself is a hierarchical network, with London, Paris, Weimar, and Florence forming the first tier of centers of literary and cultural exchange, and northern European cities such as Copenhagen, Christiania, Uppsala, Lund, or southern European such as Madrid and Lisbon as the second-tier, and therefore insignificant, centers. And third, an arbitrary, almost insignificant discursive space granted to literary works from non-European languages in the nineteenth-century construction of world literature. This fact is particularly jarring when one reads an almost unquestioned significance bestowed upon Asian and African literatures (mostly in English or French) in the late twentieth century. Lamping performs it under the pretext of postcolonial migration to Europe; Casanova traces postcolonial literary developments all the way back to Paris to dismiss other "vernaculars": Hindi, Serbian, Turkish—to name just a few—as "small literatures."

As an alternative line of thought to the above-mentioned modes of argumentation, let us consider a slightly different conceptual prehistory of world literature. In *A Critique of Postcolonial Reason* (1999), Gayatri Chakravorty Spivak characterizes late eighteenth-century Germany as a place of "self-styled difference," a space that is yet to organize itself as a homogenous, unified nation-state, a space that defines itself through the act of comparison. Spivak identifies in this period the birth of several comparative disciplines—comparative religion, comparative linguistics, and eventually comparative literature—which result in the "'scientific' fabrication of new representations of self and world that would provide alibis for the domination, exploitation, and epistemic violation entailed by colony and empire."[41] Through these brief introductory insights on German engagements with India, Spivak modifies and qualifies Edward Said's claim in his influential work *Orientalism*, specifically his assertion that in the absence of colonies, "[the] German Orient was almost exclusively a scholarly, or at least a classical, Orient. . . . Yet what German Orientalism had in common with Anglo-French and later American Orientalism was a kind of intellectual authority over the Orient within Western culture."[42]

Said's own statement proves that there is no such thing as an "exclusively, scholarly" Orient. I should mention here that a number of scholars in German studies—including Vanessa Agnew, Nina Berman, Todd Kontje, Suzanne Marchand, Kamakshi Murti, and Georg Steinmetz—have successfully challenged Said's proposition and revealed the nexus between Orientalism and German philosophical, literary, historical, and cultural anthropological discourses about the non-Western Other. Focusing on a variety of disciplinary and interdisciplinary investigations in musicology, sociology, literary studies, philosophy, historiography, science, and art history, these scholars have shown the construction of a non-European Other in the German cultural tradition was embedded in the larger hegemonic European discourse of the European Self.[43] However, print cultural institutions, especially in conjunction with the proliferation of the term *Weltliteratur*, have remained outside the critical spectrum of this rich body of scholarship. What is important for our discussion here, is how the scholarly, classical Orient was not entirely exclusive in the fundamental manipulation of Oriental knowledge, it in fact, benefited from it. What is more important is how this scholarly, classical Orient becomes both the harbinger of a self-styled difference and an alibi of colonial dominance and subjugation through the conduit of world literature.

Preparations for Goethe's and Macaulay's statements begin in the early nineteenth century with a new idea of the world and a new idea of the world-in-print that one can access in Europe. Not yet a unified nation (like Britain and France) and not an established colonial power (such as Britain, France, Spain, or Portugal), Germany becomes a major beneficiary of continued physical access to faraway societies and cultures opened through colonialisms in Asia and Africa. There is an unprecedented mass acquisition of knowledge and sources of knowledge as well as a systematic accumulation and collation of these sources in royal, university, and private libraries (of intellectuals). In addition, there occurs a major change in print-cultural production and dissemination: the mass production of books, the rise of multiple publication houses, the proliferation of literary magazines and catalogues, and the establishment of lending libraries create an atmosphere whereby discussions on "the book"—the quintessential medium for access of printed matter—must consider both its intellectual as well as its material aspects.

Goethe did not announce or prophesize his idea on world literature in a historical vacuum. The stage was already set for the master to be in the spotlight and say the dialogue in front of his understudy and apprentice Eckermann. The stage was also set for Macaulay to denounce any usability for Oriental literatures. Apart from Goethe and Macaulay's centrality in their spheres of influence—literary and political—there was another element that would play out in curious ways in the lives of their famous texts: the very stature of "the book" as an institution and its bifurcated nature as intellect (*Geist*) and material object (*Ware*), an idea that would take central stage in both Germany and British India in the first half of the nineteenth century. A massive force field—generated by structures of political governance, organized and sponsored through translation enterprises, print cultural institutions (such as literary magazines) and collection or distribution mechanisms (such as libraries)—builds up before the decade in which Goethe reflects on *Weltliteratur*. Drawing attention to this force field, I want to suggest, might assist in understanding the inauguration of comparative world literature with a mythic European library at its center.

Works and Networks in an Empire of Books

The idea of a mythic European library as underlined by Goethe and Macaulay must be evaluated against the radical change in its face value in the early nineteenth century as non-European works, through manuscripts and translations, acquired their assigned places on bookshelves and treasure chambers across Europe. A century and a half before the migration of individuals from Asia and Africa to parts of Europe and North America happened on a large scale, a different kind of migration of ideas from these continents was already taking place.

The early nineteenth century is the time when a very particular kind of bibliomigrancy—in print and in manuscript form—mostly from South, Central, and East Asia as well as Northern Africa to Europe happens on an unprecedented scale. The idea of the "New World," in its history and contemporaneity, becomes an object of fascination and exploration. The travelogue, which had long served as a major source of knowledge about the world in past centuries, still found validation. What was new was the privileging of a different kind of travel narrative that was not merely about impressions but about knowledge: evaluated, tested, and scientifically *exact* knowledge. The world, be it in its metaphysical, epistemological, ontological, or physical form, was now being accessed through scientific treatises, documents, and maps. New developments in the sciences and technology exemplify the vital energy that characterized the dawn of a speedier age.[44] The launching of several encyclopedias—Diderot's *Encyclopédie* (1751), *Encyclopedia Britannica* (1768), which expanded to twenty volumes by 1810, and Renatus Gotthelf Löbel and Christian Wilhelm Franke's *Conversations-Lexicon* (1796), which became the *Brockhaus Enzyklopedie* in 1808—were part of the collection, collation, and classification of knowledge about the world. In other words, in the late eighteenth and early nineteenth centuries, textual knowledge becomes key to grasping a world beyond one's physical reach. Accessibility to the world was not merely a function of travel; the world was fast becoming accessible *in print*.

It would be a fallacy indeed to assume that the growth of knowledge and the support to quench the curiosity about the world happened in a vacuum. The growing trade between Asian and European nations gave birth to the idea of world trade (*Welthandel*) and world market (*Weltmarkt*) to designate international exchange of goods and international traffic of capital.[45] This growing mercantilism, which led eventually to the establishment of colonial regimes, facilitated access to geographical and historical knowledge about distant parts of the world.[46] A sense of comparative world history was developing. Leading intellectuals and thinkers, especially in Germany—such as Immanuel Kant, Johann Gottfried Herder, and Georg Wilhelm Friedrich Hegel—were all developing comparative modalities of world history (*Weltgeschichte*).[47]

However, this growing sense of "worldliness" in the German-speaking world was in competition with a sense of "national" community, which, in the absence of a nation-state, was largely shaped around the idea of language and literature. On the one hand, as the translator and scholar Susan Bernofsky outlines in *Foreign Words* (2005), there is a massive proliferation of translations in Germany in the early nineteenth century. On the other hand, the Napoleonic Wars create a concentrated interest in German as a national language and literature—exemplified among others by the Brothers Grimm's ascription of a specific "German" nature to their curation and publication of fairy tales (1812–1851), as well as the *Deutsches Wörterbuch* (launched in 1838). As Lynne Tatlock notes in the introduction to the anthology *Publishing Culture and the Reading Nation* (2010), expansion of book production in Germany in the early decades of the nineteenth century doubles from the last half of the eighteenth century.[48] Tatlock identifies an emerging sense of a national reading public, whereby books create a "national" reading community—even in the absence of a nation-state—as much as readers augment and affirm their national communitarian affiliations through reading.[49] Andrew Piper, in his authoritative study *Dreaming in Books* (2009), elaborates on the "bibliographic imagination" of the German romantic period. Documenting the publishing strategies around the 1820s, Piper lists how novellas, keepsakes, collected works, but also translations led to a surplus of books in the German-speaking world.

It is in this important and transformative period in German literary and political history that the "bibliographic imagination" slowly but surely starts to include works from non-German, non-European spaces. The surplus of books goes beyond local creative production; it starts acquiring a worldly dimension as well. The "reading nation" reads the national and that which is extranational. While an intra-European circulation of literature in translation and original languages was already in place, an extra-European traffic of books was growing at an unprecedented rate. Germany at that point in time was more than just a "republic of letters"; there is a recognition of the expansion of the empire of books ("die Vermehrung des Bücherreichs").[50] This empire of books creates the conditions for Goethe's pronouncement of the term *Weltliteratur*. Books were delivered, literally, to one's doorstep, including Goethe's.

Consider the example of *Sakuntala*. In 1791, Johann Georg Adam Forster, a young German migrant living in London, acquired a copy of *Sakontala*, the English translation of the Sanskrit play *Abhigyana Sakuntalam* (ca. 500–600 CE) by Kalidasa. The play was translated into English by Sir William Jones, Orientalist, comparative linguist, and judge of the supreme court at the seat of the British East India Company in Calcutta. Forster, who had been living in England since the age of seven, had just returned from a long trip; he and his father, Johann Reinhold Forster, had accompanied Captain James Cook on his second voyage around the world (1772–1775). Georg had published the journals of his father, first in English as *A Voyage Towards the South Pole and Round the World* (1777), and then in German as *Reise um die Welt* (1778–1780), which had already found him critical appreciation from German literary figures and thinkers such as Johann Gottfried Herder and Goethe. Fascinated by what he had read, Forster decided to translate *Sakontala* into German, giving it the title *Sakontala oder der entscheidende Ring, ein indisches Schauspiel von Kalidasa*. He then sent the translation to Herder, who received it with enthusiasm. It is this particular translation that Goethe receives with the following reaction:

> Will ich die Blumen des frühen, die Früchte des späteren Jahres,
> Will ich, was reizt und erquickt, will ich was sättigt und nährt,
> Will ich den Himmel, die Erde, mit einem Worte begreifen,
> Nenn' ich Sakontala dich, und so ist alles gesagt.[51]

The English translation of this verse by Georg Forster was referenced by Rabindranath Tagore in his Bengali essay "Shakuntala" (1902):

> Shall I embrace the blossoms of spring, the fruits of the autumn,
> All that enchants and that charms, all that nurtures and fills?
> Shall I embrace in a name all heaven and all of the earth,
> Call I, Shakuntala, thee—all is comprised in one name.[52]

Calling Goethe "the wise master in the line of European Poets," Tagore stated, "Goethe's observation is not a hyperbolic expression of delight; it is the considered judgment of a connoisseur."[53] An act of translation that originated in the British Empire initiated an entire tradition of translations—both literally and figuratively. More importantly, it facilitated a new organization of knowledge in Germany through the very idea of comparison. *Sakontala* will be subsequently translated for the German stage by William Gerhard in 1820, and published by F. A. Brockhaus in Leipzig, the first publishers of Eckermann's *Gespräche mit Goethe*.

Goethe's evaluation of non-European literatures in superlative terms became central to his many writings on world literature published before and after 1827. In an essay, "Indian Poetry" ("Indische Dichtungen"), written around the end of 1821 and published only after his death, Goethe stated that we (Germans) would be "most ungrateful, if we were not to mention Indian poetry also in glowing terms." He found Indian poetry admirable for its ability to manage the "conflict with the most abstruse philosophy on the one side and the most monstrous religion on the other in a most happy temperament."[54] Kalidasa's *Sakuntala* and *Megha-Duta*, as well as Jayadeva's *Gita-Govinda* belonged for him to this category of works. Calling William Jones "incomparable," Goethe praises him for his understanding of his "western islanders," for he was apparently able to hold the limits of European propriety and yet was daring enough to present all innuendos contained in the text. In a set of writings on Asian literatures, Goethe praised Carl Jakob Ludwig Iken's German translation (*Das Papageienbuch*, published 1822) of Muhammad Khudavand Kadiri's version (ca. 1600) of Ziya-al-din Nakshabi's *Tuti Nameh* (Tales of a parrot, ca. 1329), for "with every line one is lead over the whole world, through allegories and tropes, through the amassing and showering of related subjects."[55] After reading Hagen's translation of *One Thousand and One Nights* Goethe wrote: "The subject matter [is] real, absolutely contemporary, through its inestimable richness often oppressive, but never irritating. . . . With this in mind there will be hardly be more meaningful work to be found."[56]

While Goethe was mostly concerned with the reception of Indian or Asian literature, there was another German intellectual who had exacted plans to publish Indian literature, even before Goethe. In 1823, the German philologist, critic, and poet August Wilhelm Schlegel submitted a "Prospectus" for publishing Oriental literature in Europe to the Royal Asiatic Society in London. Schlegel was an honorary member of the Royal Asiatic Society; the "Prospectus" was published (in English) in the January 1824 issue of *The Asiatic Journal*.[57] In the "Prospectus," Schlegel announced his plans to "publish a series of editions of some works, selected from the most distinguished production of the ancient and original literatures of the Brahmins."[58] After presenting his credentials as the translator of the *Bhagvad-Gita* into Latin,[59] Schlegel proposes the translation and publication of "the complete edition of the epic poem Ramayana, or *The Exploits of Rama*."[60] Akin to his brother Friedrich Schlegel's positioning of Sanskrit literature in his *Über die Sprache und Weisheit der Indier* (*On the Language and Wisdom of Indians*, 1808), August Wilhelm Schlegel also underlines the uniqueness, originality, and, most importantly, the comparability of Sanskrit texts to those from classical Greek and Latin literatures:

> The literature of ancient Greece was still in existence at Constantinople, when, in the 15th Century, some Greek fugitives taught their languages in Western Europe. These Greeks were undoubtedly very learned; but they laboured under certain prejudices, and were grown old in certain habits; and if the task of editing the classic authors had been left to them alone, we should never had had any text so correct, nor any comments so satisfactory, as those of which we are now in possession.[61]

In fact, August Wilhelm Schlegel is the first German intellectual to explicitly locate the necessity of translation of (Sanskrit) literary works into European languages for the development of comparative scientific knowledge:

> The admirable structure of that language, its surprising affinity with the Persian, the Greek, the Latin, and the Teutonic languages makes it a leading object of a science, which may be called quite new, *viz.* comparative grammar, a science which, being upheld by facts, will advance with a progressive and sure step; while conjectural etymology, treated as it has been, had led to nothing but chimerical systems. Moreover, the ancient religion, the mythology . . . throw the greatest light on similar objects . . . especially among the Egyptians. The written monuments of a literature . . . make us acquainted with the source of their manners and customs, of their notions and prejudices. . . . In one word, it may be affirmed that a thorough knowledge of ancient India is the only key to the state of modern India.[62]

However, August Wilhelm Schlegel's "Prospectus" distinguishes itself through its main focus, which is less on the content and more on material sources of literary works that he proposes to publish. He expands his plans to publish voluminous Latin translations of Sanskrit epics. The prerequisite for such a mammoth task, he declares, is the evaluation of "genuineness and correctness" of available Sanskrit manuscripts, a task he claims necessitates the acquisition and comparison of as many manuscripts as possible from different parts of India. In addition to promising explanatory footnotes along with annotated commentaries on the texts in his edition, Schlegel lays out a plan whereby the Sanskrit manuscripts would be transformed into printed books. They would be published in Paris in the Devanagari script, "of which the types were cut and cast, under my [Schlegel's] direction, by order of the Prussian government."[63] Furthermore, he promises institutional libraries and private collectors a high quality of paper and exactitude of typographical execution and projects the publication of eight volumes of the *Ramayana*, to be delivered in 1825 at the retail price of four pounds. A Latin translation of Valmiki's *Ramayana* by Schlegel was indeed published in 1829—four years after the projected date of publication—as *Rāmāyana, id est, carmen epicum de Ramæ rebus gestis poetæ antiquissimi Valmicis opus* (The Ramayana, the epic song of Rama, the great work of the ancient poet Valmiki). In many ways, the "Prospectus" extends some of the ideas that Schlegel published in the foreword to the first volume of the periodical *Die indische Bibliothek* (1820), which specialized in translations of Sanskrit literature into German.

Schlegel was not alone in his desire to establish a journal called "indische Bibliothek" or publish Sanskrit works in Europe. In 1826, Othmar Frank, Professor Ordinarius at the Königlich Bayerische Ludwig Maximilians Universität, München—also an honorary member of the Royal Asiatic Society—published the first volume of the journal *Vjāsa: über Philosophie, Mythologie, Literatur und Sprache der Hindu*, which was dedicated to the idea of proliferating Sanskrit literature in the German academy. The *Vorrede* (preface) to the first volume acknowledges Maximilian I and Ludwig I as "the first princes of Germany to understand the value of knowledge of ancient India . . . who, in this endeavor, [were able to] imitate the royal government of Prussia."[64] In addition, he states that "in Germany, Bavaria was also the first place where for the first time the suggestion for a Sanskrit-typeset press was made, the first Sanskrit script was printed (with the help of lithograph), and the first elementary Sanskrit works were edited."[65] As Frank reports, the journal was printed by the university press of the Ludwig Maximilians Universität, with the Sanskrit typeface provided by the Mayer foundry in Nuremberg. It was the second place to publish Devanagari in Germany after Berlin (with the typeface designed in Bonn, also known as the Bonner Schrift).[66]

Frank positions himself as a collector and mediator of the knowledge imparted by the "written monuments" ("schriftliche Denkmäler") of ancient India. And for this reason, he states, the journal is named after "*Vjāsa*, also known as *Vædavjāsa* (collector and organizer of Vedas) . . . who is considered to be the inaugural and the focal point of all Indian literature, mythology, and philosophy."[67] Having established himself as the modern-day equivalent of Vyasa, Frank moves to the actual act of collecting, collating, editing, and publishing: through his journal, but also through the library.

A comparison of statements by Schlegel and Frank with regard to lavishing praise on their royal patrons for the acquisition of manuscripts and the setting up of prototypes for the Devanagari script reveals how non-European manuscripts, positioned as "masterpieces," were also sources of competition for prestige between Prussia and Bavaria. In his preface, Frank reports with a fair degree of lament that he had already planned the journal in 1817, but, unbeknownst to him, was superseded by the earlier publication of another "indische Bibliothek"—explicitly leaving the editor's name unmentioned—while emphasizing immediately that given the extensive nature and the significance of Sanskrit literature, and the difference in content, perspective, and treatment, there would be many libraries with similar names published in the following years.

Beyond this internal rivalry, what is most striking is Frank's detailed account of the number of Sanskrit manuscripts with origins spanning a wide period that are available in London at the British Library and in many private collections, with whom he sees himself in competition. In his opening essay on the "Scientific Content of Sanskrit Literature" in the journal,[68] Frank comments on the collection of H. T. Colebrooke, director of the Royal Asiatic Society of Great Britain and Ireland, who acquired his collection carefully ("sorgfältig") and assiduously ("mit Eifer") during his various positions of authority in Mirzapur and Berar in Eastern India, and who was assisted in his collecting by the most thorough experts and critics ("gründlichsten Kenner und Kritiker").[69] Frank lists 57 medical, 67 mathematical and astronomical, 136 grammatical, 61 lexical, 239 puranic, mythic, and saga-related, and 200 nonreligious poetic works, and many more as being part of Colebrooke's collection. In addition, he sends clear signals to his royal patrons encouraging them to acquire some of them by stating the richness of the 1807 catalogue of the Royal Library of Paris and the unknown number of works that exist in the Propaganda Library in Rome.[70]

While royal libraries in Germany were engaged in their own feuds about manuscripts, the availability of translated works in print was enabling literary magazines to build a wider readership interested in world literature. As already mentioned, Wieland and Schlegel were precursors to Goethe's discussion of the term *Weltliteratur* in the German-speaking world. But beyond these well-known figures, there were others, publishing anonymously in literary magazines, identifying the rise of access to a "world-in-print" through books and literature, examining the connections between a changing geopolitical world order in an era of colonialism to the east and the south and the establishment of the United States to the west of the European continent, seeing *Weltliteratur* both as a catalyst and a product of an "empire of books."

The literary magazine *Literarisches Conversations-Blatt* (1820–1825), later entitled *Blätter für literarische Unterhaltung* (1826–1898)—published in Leipzig by F. A. Brockhaus—became an important platform for these anonymous voices. As Heinrich Eduard Brockhaus discusses in his history of the publishing company, *Die Firma F. A. Brockhaus* (1905), the magazine was acquired by Friedrich Arnold Brockhaus in 1820 from August von Kotzbue in Weimar, who published it as *Literarisches-Wochenblatt* (1818–1820). The change of names came about due to two separate instances of the magazine's banning in Prussia, the first because of the publication of a piece about König Friedrich Wilhelm and his wife from the perspective of a French diplomat (1820), after which the magazine acquired the new name *Literarisches Conversations-Blatt*. And a second time due to the publication of the Prussian calendar without the official endorsement of König Friedrich Wilhelm (1825), after which the magazine changed its name to *Blätter für literarische Unterhaltung*.[71] The magazine was published daily (except Sundays), thus amounting to three hundred issues a year. Neither the subscription numbers nor the print run of the magazine can be reproduced exactly, especially since the Brockhaus Archives were destroyed during World War II; one can only speculate that the readership must have included an educated elite as well as a discerning bourgeois readership. Just between 1826 and 1828, so roughly two years before Goethe's pronouncement of *Weltliteratur*, the magazine published around two hundred major feature articles, advertisements, or publication news on literary works primarily from European languages other than German and on works from Asia, the United States, and occasionally from South America, which were translated into English, French, and German. The magazine regularly carried news features on acquisitions of major European libraries, such as the Propaganda Library in Italy, the Bibliothèque nationale de France in Paris, the British Museum, as well as libraries in Asia, such as the collections of the Asiatick Society in Calcutta, or British plans to acquire new libraries *en masse*, such as the Tibetan library in Lhasa. In sum, the magazine profiled local (German) and world literatures, with a keen eye on the transformation in the book market. Two articles in particular, published prior to Goethe's pronouncement of *Weltliteratur*, merit attention for my discussion.

On November 27, 1822, the *Conversations-Blatt* published an article, "Betrachtungen über Bücher und Büchervermehrung" (Reflections on books and the growth of books). The article begins with a discussion of a "wealthy, mercantile England" ("reiche, kaufmännische England") complaining about the rising poverty and declining gold and silver reserves in Europe. Against these products that decline by overuse, the author locates in Europe one product that increases by its use, namely, literary products ("literarische Erzeugnisse"), a sector in which other parts of the world lag behind the comparatively smaller continent of Europe. Crediting the current stock of books ("Büchervorrath") to the history of increased book production in Europe since the invention of Gutenberg's printing press, the anonymous author moves quickly to articulate the problem of this ever-growing stock of books as a problem of "librarians and litterateurs, whose duty it is to recognize and order this stock" ("Bibliothekare und Literatoren, deren Pflicht es ist, diese Masse zu erkennen und zu ordnen"). Fortified by the idealism of the immortality of books and the supremacy of the European share in book production, the author declares:

> One can say, most certainly, that all the current large book-collections do not have the required space, and that in a shorter or longer period of time, they will not be able to make space for the surging treasures of books. In the coming centuries this surge will become stronger and richer, depending upon how *the culture* spreads on all parts of the globe. For a long time, Europe will have the largest share in the growth of the *empire of books*. But the literature of North America is already not entirely insignificant, and the hard-fought freedom and independence of the present European colonies in those parts of the world will add to a flourishing literature. (The Europeans must either give those colonies a constitution concurrent with the demands of the Zeitgeist and the rising culture, or they will sooner or later be lost for Europe). Books are written and published in Asia as well. European literature itself can perhaps expect a significant expansion in the future; because in the old fatherland of classical writings in Attica, as in the rest of Greece, after a successful struggle for freedom, a born-again empire of writing will certainly arise. . . . Such happy prospects for the literature as a whole, or for a world-literature, might have, as per the above-mentioned perspective, something disturbing for librarians and literati; but only apparently so.[72] (Italics added)

This long quotation encapsulates several mutually conflicting and yet mutually fortifying thoughts. The increased awareness of a growing "empire of books" directs the author's attention to worlds outside of Europe where book production is on the rise: Asia must be acknowledged for its literary productions; the new access to North American writings can no longer be ignored. However—no different than Goethe or Macaulay—the vested interest in a purported European supremacy over literary production and the book market will trace the roots of European literature squarely in Attica and the rest of Greece. Furthermore, these tensions add to a very mono-dimensional implication of "culture" as European culture, which the colonial regimes must deploy—in service of a Hegelian manifestation of the Zeitgeist—to manage the colonies through the dissemination of European culture. By setting up the opposition between commodities such as gold and silver and books, the author implicitly establishes the German-speaking world (through Europe) as the foundational force behind the empire of books. England is reduced to a mercantile nation as opposed to the cultural and intellectual dimensions that set apart the German-speaking world. I will soon turn to the role of England in establishing a global network of production of world literature in translation, which will also feature German intellectuals. Suffice it to say now that there is a strong implication of a German *Kulturnation*, which becomes part of the discussions of world literature in early nineteenth-century Germany.[73]

The anonymous author emphasizes the role of the library as the central agency, whose work it is to collect both old and new books, from Europe and abroad. And yet this library remains necessarily Eurocentric. In other words, the positive outlook on the expansion of the book market and the new rising "empire of books" is expressed along with uncertainties and anxieties about the unknown aspects of that expanding empire.

These anxieties, mixed with skepticism toward growing readerships of European works outside of Europe, are articulated in a much stronger register in another article, published on August 4, 1827—just a few months before Goethe's famous pronouncement of the term—in the *Blätter für literarische Unterhaltung*. Entitled "Weltliteratur: Cooper's neuster Roman," the article was a damning review of the German translation of James Fenimore Cooper's *The Prairie* (1827). The opening section of the review is worthy of a lengthy citation:

> World literature and yet ephemeral literature [*Tagesliteratur*]! We want to talk not of the old immortals whose continued worth, resembled the growing currents that fulfilled every long century, and which, like those currents, conducted by the ever powerful rampaging education, are carried over from their motherland over the big seas to Asia, Africa, and America. May the old Homer boast to the immortals up there that he is read on the borders of the Hottentots, the Burmese, and the Sioux; what more is it, than what the editor of the "British Chronicle" can prove with his works published here below, after it is merely a few

> months old. Isn't the king [*Kaiser*] of Brazil its first subscriber? Is it not published in Gotha and New York, does it not circulate in Rio de Janeiro and Petersburg, in Vienna and Washington, in London and Paris, in Berlin and Calcutta, not to mention Weimar and Lima? Who knows, what would become of the cabinet library of German classics, if the petty guilds of booksellers in Leipzig and Berlin were in the position to consider the excellent plan of the Bibliographic Institute in Gotha and New York, which certainly went from the premise to introduce Schiller's, Goethe's and Jean Paul's great works in the capital cities of the Burmese, the Californians, and the Kaffirs. . . . The prospects, which are opening up in similar undertakings for world literature, are so big and vast, that they can make one dizzy. We shall refrain from them and turn to the latest novel by the North American Walter Scott, who in short would be called Cooper and who, in comparison to the book-list of the Bibliographic Institutes in Gotha and New York only has a moderate world public. Because that novel, "The Prairie," entitled *Die Prairie* in German, has appeared, as announced, at most in four countries and three languages simultaneously, in the original language in London and New York, in French in Paris, and in German in Berlin with Duncker and Humblot.[74]

Comparable to, but also differing from Goethe and Macaulay, the author of this article establishes several sets of hierarchies: of circulated materials, trajectories of circulation, as well the recipients of circulation—all as distinguishing features of the category of world literature. *Tagesliteratur* is a term used for regionally or locally circulated writings. The inauguration of the article with a distinction between world literature (*Weltliteratur*) and ephemeral literature (*Tagesliteratur*) is particularly instructive to understand the set of hierarchies—composed of binary opposites—that the author of the article would create and then pursue in order to situate his reading of Cooper's novel. The immediate following of a reference to the German poet Friedrich Gottlieb Klopstock's first poem "Der Lehrling der Griechen" (1747; The apprentice to the Greeks)—a poem that is supposed to reintroduce classical lyric meter into German poetry—further substantiates the distinction between the two: world literature is Greek, i.e., of timeless value, whereas a purportedly badly written novel such as *The Prairie* might be published in several languages simultaneously, and although it may acquire some readership beyond its point of origin, it will remain the flavor of the day (*Tagesgeschmack*) and therefore ephemeral. With a sarcastic tone, the geographies of literary circulation acquire varied statuses. The rampaging power of education (*Bildung*) might carry a Homer to natives in West Africa, South East Asia, or the American Midwest; a phenomenon that would be no more and no less than the readership of the *British Chronicle* in places as distant as Lima and St. Petersburg. The suspicion that follows—about the fate of German classics with a reference to the "Miniatur Bibliothek" of the Bibliographic Institute of Gotha and New York (established in 1826)—is equally uncharitable. When read in context, the use of German literature by the Burmese, Californians, the Sioux, or even the Kaffirs—then and until the end of Apartheid a pejorative term for Blacks in South Africa—remains questionable for the author. The "dizzying" prospect of world literature thus becomes the immediate precursor to the circulation trajectory of a North American author, who, the author declares later in the essay, is by no means an American Walter Scott.

These are two examples, selected from hundreds published in *Die Blätter*, become symptomatic of the tensions and anxieties that are ascribed to the term *Weltliteratur* in the early nineteenth-century German literary sphere. Along with English-language works published in the United States, available traditionally through England but now being translated into German and French, there was a growing awareness of *Weltliteratur* that was in full swing parallel to—and not merely as a consequence of—the famous statement by Goethe. In addition to the acquisition of manuscripts by royal and university libraries, and the publication of translations into German, the period also saw the organization and establishment of some of the first worldwide-sponsored translation funds, the most prominent of them being the Oriental Translation Fund, to which I now turn.

The Oriental Translation Fund and the Unnamed Chinese "Novel"

The Oriental Translation Fund was set up by the Oriental Translation Committee in London in 1828, with the "Plan for translating and publishing such interesting and valuable Works on Eastern History, Science, and Belles-Lettres as are still in M[anu]S[cript] in the Libraries of the Universities, the British Museum, and the East-India House, and in other Collections, in Asia and Africa, as well as in Europe, and for providing Funds to carry this object into execution."[75] The committee's connections to German-speaking Europe were first through royalty: the main patron was King George IV of Great Britain and Ireland and King of Hanover; one of the first vice-patrons included Royal Highness Prince Leopold I of Saxe-Coburg, who had his roots in modern day Thuringia; later German universities became subscribers to their publications. The administrative structure of the committee reflected the nexus between aristocratic, academic, and colonial elites; it also embodied the global scale and scope of the plan. The vice-patrons included the Dukes of Clarence, Sussex, and Wellington, the Archbishop of Canterbury, and the chancellors of the universities of Oxford and Cambridge. Overseas vice-patrons included Lord William Bentinck (at the time, the Governor-General of India), governors of the presidencies of Bombay, Ceylon, and Madras, and H. T. Colebrook (who at the time was the director of the Royal Asiatic Society of Great Britain and Ireland). The committee itself was globally constituted, with representation from professors of Hebrew, Arabic, Sanskrit, Hindustani, and "Oriental Languages, and History" both in England and in cities as far flung as Aberdeen, Alexandria, Colombo, Calcutta, Corfu, Bombay, Madras, Tehran, Tunis, and Singapore, to name just a few.[76] The first report lists about one hundred subscribers, ranging from individuals—mostly nobility—to all major libraries in England, as well as literary societies of major cities in the British colonies and the Asiatic society in Calcutta.[77] Even by today's standards, the endeavor was impressively multinational.

However, it is not merely the globality of the enterprise but its aim and scope that makes it worthy of consideration even in the contemporary context. The organization's task was to acquire manuscripts, commision translations, and subsidize the production of Oriental texts in European languages. The network of trajectories of manuscripts and books thus becomes more complex than one can imagine. The committee positioned itself transnationally—promising to act as a liaison between British centers of learning with those in the colonies—and appointed itself to make Eastern literature accessible to the public. The Prospectus of the Committee from 1828 explicitly mentions the significance of public accessibility to literary and scholarly works. The very first point of the prospectus underscores how the committee's goal is to explore ways through which "the public may be put in possession of all that is valuable in Eastern literature, and an opportunity be presented for shewing that this country is not at present backward in contributing to the advancement of Oriental learning, which she has long held the foremost rank."[78] The agenda of publications reflects this spirit: the committee identifies several works in Arabic, Persian, Syrian, Sanskrit, and Hindustani, in fields as diverse as geography, statistics, history, law, and literature. The results of this endeavor are consequently promised for both "England and its Eastern possessions . . . productive for the good of both the governors and the governed."[79] The legislative source and the executive force of the last quotes attest the power of the Oriental discourse as described by Edward Said and the numerous publications thereafter. What is equally remarkable, and must be noted, is the idea of the *Gemeingut*—the common or shared property—which appears in the prospectus to qualify literary works. Texts, when converted from manuscripts to mass-published books—in the original and in translation—acquire their dual role as intellectual and material artifacts.

Which works were first identified as worthy of translation and publication? The annotated bibliography of the Second Report of the Oriental Translation Fund attests the multilingual nature and the historical range of these texts. The bibliography groups works under three rubrics: "Theology, Ethics, and Metaphysics," "History, Geography, and Travels," and "Belles Lettres." Richard Clarke's translation from Tamil of Thiruvalluvar's *Thirukkural* (2 BCE to 8 CE), H. T. Colebrooke's translation from Sanskrit of Gauḍapāda's *Sānkhyakārikā* (400–500 CE), and James Ross's translation from Farsi of Sheikh Sa'adi's *Bostān* (1257 CE) fall under the first category; Henderson's translation from Arabic of Ibn Khaldun's *Kitab-ul-Ibar* (ca. 1400 CE) and Joseph von Hammer-Purgstall's translation from Turkish of Evliya Çelebi's *Seyāhatnāme* form part of the second group. The "Belles Lettres" category lists three works, all originally in Persian: the popular poem *Meher va Mushteri*, the accounts of *Hātim Tāi*, and the love story of *Shirin and Ferhād*. This list would expand considerably in the next years. The second report includes translations of two literary works (classified as romances) from Chinese;[80] the third report lists over fifty works in three categories in six languages.[81]

The Oriental Translation Fund provides an important link in juxtaposing Goethe's and Macaulay's statements on the literary evaluation of non-European works. While Macaulay's reliance on the "translations by Orientalists" can be linked easily to the Oriental Translation Fund, a brief discussion of the story of Goethe's "unnamed" Chinese novel helps to make further connections.

Since the late nineteenth century, speculative discussions about the exact title of the novel have abounded among members of the subfield of "Goethe-Philology" within German studies (*Germanistik*), establishing *Hau-qiu zhuan* (German: *Haoh Kjöh Tschwen*) as the most likely title.[82] Not all scholarly sources agree with this speculation. Hanns Eppelsheimer's authoritative *Handbuch der Weltliteratur* annotates *Yu Jiaoli* (German: *Yu Giaoli oder die Beiden Basen*) with the remark that this humble story of manners ("diese bescheidene Sittengeschichte") is being included in the handbook only because of its European fame ("europäischen Rufes"); the readers are directed to Eckermann's *Gespräche*.[83] U. C. Fischer links *Chin Ku Chi' Kuan* (German: *Kin-ku-ki-kuan*) with Goethe's *Chinesisch-Deutsche Jahre- und Tageszeiten* (1827), claiming that an English translation of the novel was present in Goethe's library in Weimar.[84] In most of these discussions, details of the content of the Chinese novel provided by Goethe—his mention of the moon, goldfish, "Rohrstühle" (sedan chairs), a couple in love, Chinese legends, and most importantly the specific comparative reference to his own novel *Hermann und Dorothea* (1797)—become conclusive evidence for detecting the title of the novel. Underlying these discoveries are expectations of exactitude from Eckermann who, in the foreword to *Gespräche*, categorically defies such anticipations by stating that his book portrays "*mein Goethe*" (*my Goethe*; italics in the original), to the extent that he (Eckermann) "was able to perceive and depict him."[85]

Such expectations notwithstanding, Goethe's access to Chinese literary works reveals a larger network of works from Asia entering the European space in the eighteenth and nineteenth centuries, whereby translators, publishing houses, and libraries play a significant role. *Hao-qiu zhuan* was first translated into English by James Wilkinson (later edited by Thomas Percy) as *The Pleasing History* (1761); its translation into German by Christoph Gottlieb von Murr, *Haoh Kjöh Tschwen d. i. die angenehme Geschichte des Haoh Kjöh. Ein chinesischer Roman* (1766) references the English title and was published by the famous Johann Friedrich Junius Verlag. Wilhelm Grimm, in a letter to his brother Jakob, mentioned that Goethe read from the novel in Heidelberg in 1815.[86] In the early twentieth century, a new German translation of *Hao-qiu zhuan* by the philologist Franz Kuhn was published by Insel Verlag. The long title, *Eisherz und Edeljaspis oder Die Geschichte einer glücklichen Gattenwahl: ein Roman aus der Ming-Zeit* (literal translation: "Ice-Heart and the royal Jasper or the story of a happy choice of spouse: A novel from the Ming-times") was perhaps meant to signal an improvement over von Murr's translation from English; Kuhn had translated the Chinese work into German. However, the translation bears no mention of von Murr. In his afterword to the translation, Kuhn cites the passage on the Chinese novel from *Gespräche* to affirm the superiority of his translation over the inadequate ("unzulänglich") French translation of the novel by Abel Rémusat that was purportedly available to Goethe in 1827.[87] Rémusat's translation of *Yu Jiaoli* as *Ju-kiao-li, ou les deux cousines: Roman chinois* from Chinese into French was published in Paris by Moutardier in 1826, and was indeed available at the Großherzogliche Bibliothek in Weimar. A German translation, *Ju-kiao-li, oder die beiden Basen: ein chinesischer Roman* (translator unknown) was published by Franckh in Stuttgart in 1827. As for *Chin Ku Chi' Kuan*, Eduard Griesbach's German translation was first published in 1880 as *Kin-ku-ki-kuan: neue und alte Novellen der chinesischen 1001 Nacht*, thus positioning the novel as the Chinese *Alif Laila wa Laila* for German readers. Unlike von Murr's reliance on Percy's English translation of *Hao-qiu zhuan*, Griesbach's translation did not rely on the first English translation of *Chin Ku Chi' Kuan*.

In 1820, Peter Perring Thoms, an employee of the British East India Company stationed in Macau, had published *The Affectionate Pair, or The History of Sung-kin: A Chinese Tale* with the London-based publisher Black, Kingsbury, Parbury, and Allen (BKPA). In the early nineteenth century BKPA was the leading publishing house of books about and translations from the British colonies. Next to Perring's translation, BKPA published John B. Gilchrist's *The Stranger's Infallible East-Indian Guide* (1820) and Charles Mills's *History of Mohammedanism* (1817), and held publishing rights to Daniel Defoe's *Robinson Crusoe* (1818 edition). In 1829, John Francis Davis published a new English translation of *Hao-qiu zhuan* as *The Fortunate Union: A Romance* with BKPA, who then were also the official printers for the Oriental Translation Fund. Thoms also published the work *Chinese Courtship* (BKPA, 1824), which Goethe had access to in 1827.[88] Bookended by *The Pleasing History* (1761) and *The Fortunate Union* (1829), Goethe's moment of giving traction to the term *Weltliteratur* from 1827 becomes part of a larger network of literary works that made their way to Europe in translation.

Goethe was aware of this growing traffic of works in the age of faster book publication. In his address to the "Gesellschaft für ausländische schöne Literatur" (Society for foreign beautiful literature) founded on the occasion of his birthday on August 28, 1829, Goethe encouraged their endeavors and their mission, stating that in the quick-acting contemporary book market, one was able to refer to any work in haste, but he also warned that it is no small task to be able to penetrate literature of the latest times.[89] From asking everyone to hasten the approach of world literature in 1827, two years later Goethe thinks of world literature as an extension of national literature: "When such a world literature, which is inevitable in the case of the growing speed of traffic, forms next time, we may no longer and not otherwise expect from it than what they can afford and guarantee. The vast world, as extended it may be, is always only an expanded homeland, and strictly speaking, does not give us more than what was awarded by the native soil."[90]

Goethe's sentiment about the world as an expanded homeland will be echoed by Erich Auerbach after World War II, as I will discuss in detail in chapter 4. Suffice it to say that the growing traffic of literature in translation granted Eckermann's *Gespräche mit Goethe* new homelands in many languages. David Damrosch has wonderfully sketched the many lives of Eckermann's book in English in the introduction to *What Is World Literature?*[91] But there is another story of Eckermann's book, one that further reveals the dual nature of books through a legal battle in which Eckermann was involved with his publisher. While *Conversations with Goethe* gained in translation, *Gespräche mit Goethe* caused Eckermann to lose a few battles of his own. After a long walk through print cultural developments contributing to the primacy of masters and masterpieces, I will next cast a final glance at another pact: the one between master Goethe and his apprentice Eckermann.

Eckermann after Goethe

Eckermann is duly credited with bringing to public light Goethe's famous statement about world literature through his *Gespräche*. However, the story of the making of this masterpiece is also a story of Eckermann's subservience and total dedication that occurs through his exploitation at Goethe's hands and ultimately his betrayal by Goethe's descendants. It is also a story of legal intrigue through copyright law at a time of transition in the book market of the German-speaking world. The story of world literature is incomplete without the story of Eckermann.

"Bei Goethe zu Tisch" (Dinner with Goethe), so begins Eckermann's entry for December 31, 1827, in *Gespräche mit Goethe in letzten Jahren seines Lebens*. Eckermann might not have realized that this was a fateful New Year's Eve dinner, and Goethe's conversations with him, especially his dictum on *Weltliteratur*, would contribute to the making of Eckermann's book into his most, and sadly only, notable work. Eckermann also did not know that this work was the beginning of the end of his literary career, and he would pay dearly for his service and his many conversations with Goethe until the end of his life. By 1827 Eckermann had been in Weimar for a good four years, documenting and reconstructing his meetings with the larger-than-life literary figure—the reigning master of literature and the arts, not only in Germany, but in all of Europe at the time. His subservience vis-à-vis Goethe was self-generated and self-confessed: "My relationship to him was of a peculiar kind and [of] a very delicate nature. It was that of a pupil to his master, a son to the father, of someone needy of education to the erudite."[92] That Goethe hugely benefited from Eckermann's taking up residence in Weimar would be an understatement. Apart from providing editorial supervision for the publication of *Faust II*, *Dichtung und Wahrheit IV*, and a forty-volume collected works—all unpaid—Eckermann was living on a meager income of less than three hundred thaler a year, earned mostly by providing German lessons to young Englishmen spending time in Weimar.[93] He had been instructed by Goethe—who earned three thousand thaler a year just from the court of Weimar and thousands more through his royalties—to do so. Eckermann was obliged to be in Goethe's company. He started humbly as the son of a door-to-door cloth merchant in Winsen an der Lühe near Hamburg, as he also states in the preface to *Gespräche*. His childhood interest in becoming a painter was denied because the villagers could not imagine that he wanted to be a painter of art, and not a house painter, and since Hamburg had buildings over five stories high, painting was declared a dangerous profession and so off-limits for him. After serving in the Franco-Prussian wars and then managing to study for two years at the University of Göttingen on a stipend, Eckermann felt that he had finally arrived when he met with Goethe for the first time in Weimar in June 1823. Eckermann had sent his treatise on Goethe's poetry to him prior to his arrival and was hoping that his own poetry would one day be blessed by Goethe. But Goethe had other plans. Goethe was more than obliged to have a young man both as an acolyte to archive his ideas in the last stages of his life and as a secretary and editor until his death in 1832.

Three years after Goethe's death, in December 1835, Eckermann sent the manuscript of the first volume of *Gespräche mit Goethe* to the publishing house F. A. Brockhaus in Leipzig. Eckermann's pitch was no less grandiose than Goethe's actual following: in his initial letter to Friederick Brockhaus, Eckermann stated how the book would be of immense interest to English, French, Italian, and Spanish reading publics. The proposal was approved with some important negotiations and the first two parts were set to be released as a book at the Ostermesse in Leipzig (today the annual Leipziger Buchmesse) in June 1836.[94]

Eckermann's publication of the volume happens around the same time when the definition of copyright law was being transformed due to the change in the primary employment of authors. Unlike Goethe, an employee of the court of Weimar, a new generation of authors with professions ranging from medicine, law, and university teaching was on the rise. The rising number of authors wanting to make their living through writing and demanding more control over their works also challenged publishers and by extension the copyright law. The dissemination of works now took place through intermediary book dealers (*Zwischenbuchhändler*), which basically meant that books were bought by bookstores and prices paid and accounts settled at the end of the year.

Eckermann, who, on Goethe's instructions, had funded himself primarily as a German teacher for the English who came to Weimar, was left with no pecuniary resources after Goethe's death. His sole source of income through writing was focused on *Gespräche*, and in 1843 he realized that something might be wrong with the figures provided by the accounting department of Brockhaus. In his bid to correct the error, he wrote to Brockhaus, noting that he had heard many praises about his book and expected more copies to be sold than was projected. Heinrich Brockhaus wrote to him personally, first assuring him that he would look into the matter, pretending all the same that there might not be an error, as all copies sold were yet to be accounted for. However, upon finding out that there was indeed an error in the payment of manuscripts, he immediately sent more money. But the errors and misunderstandings continued, and a spate of correspondence followed—first between Eckermann and Brockhaus, and then between Eckermann's lawyer, Dr. Wydenbrygk, and Brockhaus's lawyer, Dr. Schreckenberg. The trial ran for three years. Brockhaus, who himself was a prominent politician apart from being a member of the Dresden parliament, decided to fight tooth and nail and won the political and the print-cultural battle. Eckermann was left to fend for himself. He suggested a reconciliation with Brockhaus and wanted to publish the last volume of *Gespräche*. Brockhaus wrote back in utmost disgust and denial, declaring that his interactions with Eckermann were the most disgusting ("erwidrigste") experience in his life. The proposed volume was never published.

It is hardly a surprise that the drama between Eckermann and Goethe that plays out in *Gespräche* would lend itself to the theatrical form. Martin Walser's play *In Goethes Hand* (1982) and Jan Decker's theatrical monologue *Eckermann oder die Geburt der modernen Psychologie* (2012) depict Goethe's exploitation of Eckermann and Eckermann's own moral masochism with amazing facility. At the core of these plays are Goethe's instruction and Eckermann's dedication; Goethe's sexual and erotic prowess even at the very end of his life and Eckermann's asexual existence as he serves Goethe. The pact between the book, the author, and the author's assistant gets depicted in two poignant scenes, with which I will end this chapter.

In Decker's monologue, Eckermann lies on a chaise longue in a room full of bird cages in front of Dr. Johann Christian August Heinroth, professor of psychotherapy at the University of Leipzig. Eckermann's initial description of Goethe attests to and critiques Goethe's stature in the world of literature: “We had a god in Weimar, who was called Goethe. His life comprised childish pleasures, otherwise he tended towards melancholia.”[95] Eckermann sums up his contributions to Goethe’s life in the following way: “What I gave Goethe, was my life. What I got for it, you can see laying in front of you: a classically minded soul. And a doctorate, for which I can buy nothing . . . Not a good deal, you would say.”[96] The wonderful illustrations by the Jena-based artist Kay Voigtmann in the limited edition publication of the play illustrate Goethe’s power over Eckermann: Goethe carries a book by its spine over his erect penis, his semen ejaculating; the dripping pen is replaced by a dripping penis.

While Decker’s Eckermann is seeking to finally distinguish his ego from the Goethean super-ego, Walser’s Eckermann is exploited by Goethe on the one hand and the court culture of Weimar on the other. As a slew of painters wait for one of Goethe’s “sittings” to paint him, Eckermann briefs them: “How does one represent Goethe? I would say . . . Beautifully.”[97]

The second act of Walser’s play is set in November 1848, sixteen years after Goethe’s death. Eckermann lives in a tiny apartment on the Brauhausgasse in Weimar; he is poor and sick. Unlike his former master Goethe, Eckermann does not own a well-organized library. “More cage-birds than books. We are at Eckermann’s” comments Gustchen, a character in the play.[98] Someone knocks on the door, it is the poet Ferdinand Freiligrath, who has come to “interview the author of *Conversations with Goethe*.” Eckermann greets Freiligrath with praise for his poems, Freiligrath wittily responds that one of his poems landed him in jail; it is the time of the revolution and the censorship of writings against the establishment. Freiligrath tells Eckermann of Karl Marx, who asked him to work for *NRZ* (*Die neurheinische Zeitung*), adding that Marx was initially skeptical about the idea for the interview because “Weimar represents for him temple ghetto, senior bureaucrats, and memorial swindle.”[99] Eckermann does not know the editor; Freiligrath assists: “Marx, you know him, right?” Eckermann responds warily: “Poet?”[100]

Karl Marx might not have become famous for what Eckermann was taught to understand under the term poetry. However, the same year in which the fictitious scene takes place, together with his collaborator Friedrich Engels, Marx publishes the *Communist Manifesto*, a text that would revolutionize political thought for over a century to come and would provide an extension of Goethe’s idea of world literature by locating it squarely in the commerce between nations, when the empire of books would undergo further expansion.

Masters and Masterpieces

"Masterpieces of world literature," "world classics," "great books," "great works of world literature," "Great Works series"—these are just some of the labels that publishers, authors, translators, but also librarians, critics, academics, and nonprofessional readers around the world have used for at least the past two centuries to designate specific texts. Especially in the context of something as grand sounding as world literature, these terms appear as categorical notations: on covers of book series and anthologies, card catalogs, online search portals, course titles, and syllabi. From John Macy's *The Story of the World's Literature* (1932) to Paul Wiegler's *Geschichte der fremdsprachigen Weltliteratur* (1933) to Harold Bloom's *The Western Canon* (1994) and more recently *Where Shall Wisdom Be Found?* (2004), the aforementioned labels are inescapable. The reader's reception, conditioned by such an elaborate publication and distribution apparatus therefore reaffirms these categories. The best, the most representative of a linguistic, cultural, or national narrative tradition, the foremost, the outstanding, the larger-than-life, the timeless—these are consequently some of the first, if not the only associations that informed readers often ascribe to world literature.

A literary work is hailed as a masterpiece when it exhibits uniqueness of poetic expression, complexity of aesthetic representation, a large scale and scope, or a search for reflections of an indefatigable human spirit with or without divine intervention; indeed, a sense of mastery of the human being on the human self has traditionally determined the definition of a "great work" of literature. Through comparison on a local and a transnational scale—a specific kind of vetting—a process of value judgment is carried out whereby masterpieces are constructed and propagated as such. In the case of multiauthored works or where authors are speculatively identifiable, mastery is either collectively ascribed to a civilization and its inhabitants: the Sumerians (*The Epic of Gilgamesh*), the Egyptians (*The Egyptian Book of the Dead*), or the Indians (*Vedas*). When the author is identifiable (in some cases) the masterpiece becomes a function of the craftsmanship of single authors, the masters: Aeschylus, Plato, Dante, Shakespeare, Goethe, Dickens, Tolstoy, Strindberg, Ibsen, Mann, Nexø, Premchand, Pamuk, and so on. In the university classroom, where language as the medium of instruction plays a significant role, mastery acquires a different meaning: the masterpiece must in turn be mastered—in the original or in translation—by the teacher who mediates the superiority of the text and the student who must then emulate the teacher. A translated work itself is seen as a product of someone having mastered the original language in order to render the work masterfully in the target language, thus further attesting to the primacy of a masterpiece.

The masterpiece is today a debatable category. Like many other grand narratives, the narrative of the masterpiece is slowly being un-written. It is being punctured, eroded, unraveled, because it has come to represent the burden of dominant eurocentrism that has been an inimitable feature of our cultural histories. In the light of the multiple canon debates—classical, modern, feminist, national, postcolonial, multicultural—one either witnesses a careful surpassing of the issue of great works at a safe distance or a circumvention of the same by declaring the literary field as composed of major and minor literary traditions with major and minor contributions to world literature.[101] Amidst the resurgence in discussions of world literature in the early twenty-first century, a neat line is often drawn between "Old World" and "New World" literatures, insinuating the grand canon of world literature versus the seemingly more democratic category of literatures of the world. However, the transition to the more subaltern impactful, influential, significant, and therefore the "must-read" does not always guarantee an absolute overcoming of nineteenth-century principles of evaluation: aesthetic and political representation and mastery.

The *Oxford English Dictionary* defines masterpiece as a "work of outstanding artistry or skill, specially the greatest work of a particular artist, writer, etc.; a consummate example of some skill or other kind of excellence. Also: a piece of work produced by a craftsman in order to be admitted to a guild as an acknowledged master."[102] German splits the different usages into two words: *Meisterstück* and *Meisterwerk*. *Trübners Deutsches Wörterbuch* defines the *Meisterstück* as "die Probearbeit eines Gesellen, mit der er die Meisterwürde erringen will" a definition that corresponds with the second meaning listed in the *OED*.[103] *Meisterwerk*, "was der Meister anfertigt," is captured by the first meaning in English.[104] *Trübners* also claims that the "English Masterpiece is the oldest calque (loan-translation) of a low-High German word into English."[105] The juxtaposition of these lexical definitions thus serves more than to merely present the nuanced linguistic differences between English and German usages of the term *masterpiece*. In fact, this juxtaposition energizes the inquiry into the establishment of the masterpiece as an evaluative principle of world literary comparison, especially around the time of its most well-known conceptualization in the European literary space by Goethe, captured in his statement on *Weltliteratur* (1827).[106]

As this chapter has shown, starting with the first documentations of its inception in the European literary space, world literature became a guild where a foreign literary work or an author had to pass a test of standards to become a member. World literature started as a hierarchical system to classify literary works from around the world; the cosmopolitan spirit of Goethe's statement was from the very beginning fractured through dominance and subjugation. The idea of mastery and the establishment of the discourse of masterpieces shaped and informed this ideational space. Comparison and relation were manipulated in the public sphere—among common readers—to give world literature its categorical designation of aesthetic superiority.

The empire of books, as well as the mythic European library, were constructed through multiple processes of legislation and legitimization of masters and masterpieces. The dual nature of the pact with books—as material and cultural artifacts as well as between European and non-European sources—had a tremendous effect on literary comparison and relation in the early nineteenth century. From Goethe's engagement with *Sakuntala* in the "Prologue" to *Faust*, all the way to the story of his unnamed Chinese novel, the circulation and reception of literary works as *world* literary works went through the colonial highway. The establishment of the Oriental Translation Fund, the celebration of Sanskrit masterpieces by August Wilhelm Schlegel, the desire to acquire more manuscripts for the royal library in Munich as presented by Othmar Frank, the anxiety about the growing empire of books that will create unknown results when European works are read by the Burmese, the positing of world literature not just against national but also "ephemeral" literature—all signify ways in which the "ancestral junk" of Europe, to use Goethe's term, was slowly being challenged through the availability of literary works from elsewhere. And this availability did not create an instant, harmonious dialogue between European and non-European works, nor did it lead to an immediate acceptance of non-European works as those at par with the purportedly superior Greek works.

The best, the greatest, the most representative works must have their others—the good, the average, the worst. The unique prerequisites the common, the superior prerequisites the imagined inferior, the dominant prerequisites the potential subservient, the timeless prerequisites the would-be ephemeral. A prerequisite must be legitimized and legislated in order for it to sustain its existence as a prerequisite. Every masterpiece needs a master, every master needs an apprentice, and sometimes, the apprentice is in fact enslaved. The beginnings of the discourse of *Weltliteratur* around Goethe's time attests to this legislation and legitimization of world literary masterpieces. Any attempt to overcome eurocentrism within discourses of world literature will have to confront the beginnings of this itinerary. *Vorzüglichst* or not, as we will soon discover, the burden of the masters would weigh heavy on the shoulders of the enslaved apprentices.

Göttingen
Oslo
Leiden
Weimar
Berlin
Oxford
Leipzig
London
Dresden
Paris
Vienna
Tübingen
Istanbul
Rome
Washington
Boston
Madrid
Athens
Beirut
Rhodes
Baghdad
Khorasan
Cairo
Isfahan
Amman
Damascus
Delhi
Lucknow
Calcutta
Madras
Cochin

CHAPTER 2

Half Epic, Half Drastic: From a Parliament of Letters to a National Library

The bourgeoisie has through its exploitation of the World Market given a cosmopolitan character to production and consumption in every country. . . . And as in material, so also in intellectual production. The intellectual creations of individual nations become common property. National one-sidedness and narrow-mindedness become more and more impossible, and from the numerous national and local literatures, there arises world literature.

—KARL MARX AND FRIEDRICH ENGELS, *The Communist Manifesto* (1848)[1]

Oriental nations are no longer able to take care of their own literary treasures . . . they allow their books to rot, to be devoured by insects and destroyed by neglect, though a Muslim never willfully tears up a book. . . . Under these circumstances the duty of taking care of the patrimony of our eastern brethren devolves upon the enlightened public of Europe, and every man who finds an opportunity ought to secure as many books as he can.

—ALOYS SPRENGER, *Bibliotheca Orientalis* (1857)[2]

Heinrich Heine's *Deutschland: Ein Wintermärchen* (1844; *Germany: A Winter's Tale*) begins at the political border between France and Germany. On a windy morning in the "dreary month of November," the lyrical "I" returns home from exile.[3] The opening stanzas capture the returnee's sensory perceptions as he refamiliarizes himself with a place he once called home. His eyes try to capture the expansive pastoral landscape; his mind recalls the words of a folk song sung by a local village girl. Before he can realize, the exilic subject is pulled away from nostalgia and romanticism to return to face the logistics of border control. It is the time of political upheaval and dissent, and freedom of speech is compromised. Heine belonged to the group of authors who were identified as Junges Deutschland (Young Germany)—champions of political liberalism, free speech, and the emancipation of individuals, women, and Jews, and supporters of a cosmopolitan perspective on life—whose ideas against convention, orthodoxy, absolutism, and feudalism led to the banning of their writings by the German Convention of 1835. As Prussian soldiers rummage through Heine's belongings, checking for contraband objects, Heine responds:

And I carry many books in my head—
Solemnly I state it:
My head is a bird's nest twittering
With books to be confiscated.[4]

He calls the Prussian customs officers "fools," stating that "the contraband that journeys with me/I've stuck away in my mind."[5] He assures them that the books he carries in his head are more dangerous than those that can be found in Satan's library.[6]

Heine's defiance of censorship and authority, his proclamation of carrying dangerous books, indeed an entire library worse than that of Satan, acquires a special meaning a few verses later when the lyrical "I" is addressed by a fellow traveler, for whom a customs union ("Zollverein") "will be our true foundation,/and bind the dismembered fatherland/Into one great nation."[7] But that customs union, explains the fellow traveler, will only provide external unity; the spiritual unity will come from the censors. Censorship, which forces a unity of thought, a unity that is built on the grave of any semblance of diversity or dissent, becomes the agency of unity among a people that is in urgent need of it—from the inside, and the outside![8]

"Germany: A Winter's Tale" contains one of the most amazing literary depictions of an ideologically charged bibliomigrancy. With astounding wit, seasoned with sharp sarcasm, Heine pits the financial union against the suppression of ideational diversity; he places the library—at once physical and virtual, material and mnemonic—at the border between two political territories. Books appear as both palpable (material) and invisible (intellectual) artifacts. They are the kind of contraband that can be carried in one's head, which—as he accepts—are his weapons as he crosses the border. Heine thus undergirds the remarkable role of print-cultural artifacts and their promotion, or suppression in determining the self-image of a nation as performance and pedagogy. The political state is scared of the printed word; it is so concerned about sustaining its power that it will allow no unwanted book or pamphlet to penetrate its political boundaries.

Heine's imagination of the power of books and printed material was reanimated, albeit in very different terms, on a global scale by Karl Marx and Friedrich Engels. In *The Communist Manifesto* (1848), Marx and Engels point toward a very different kind of border crossing of literary works, as cited in the epigraph of this chapter.[9] It is in this text that Marx and Engels unmoor the Goethean idea of world literature from *Poesie* (poesy) as the *Gemeingut* (shared property) of the human race and firmly anchor it in the bourgeois production and consumption of literature. If Goethe establishes world literature as a poetic-aesthetic ideal, Marx and Engels recognize the commercial and material networks across national political boundaries that lead to the establishment of such an ideal. Marx and Engels chime with Goethe in augmenting the cosmopolitan and transnational nature of world literature; and yet, instead of referring to *Poesie* as the universal shared entity among peoples of the world, they provide a whole new meaning to the term *Gemeingut*, thereby enhancing the material and commercial aspects of world literature. While Goethe anticipates the idea of *Weltliteratur* and asks everyone to hasten its approach, for Marx and Engels the commercial interdependence of nations has already hastened the approach of *Weltliteratur*. World literature appears as a parliament of letters, a conglomeration of local and national literatures.

The beginning of Heine's *Wintermärchen* and the passage from the *Communist Manifesto* serve as apt points of departure to imagine the trajectory of world literature through books and libraries in Germany beyond Goethe. Censorship remains a crucial defining element in the period around the March Revolution of 1848, following which a starker nationalism paves way for an even more conservative nationalization of literature. Between Goethe's pronouncement of *Weltliteratur* (1827) and Marx and Engel's statement (1848), some critics of world literature and cosmopolitanism call for a hastening of *Nationalliteratur* rather than *Weltliteratur*. This trend resurfaces in the second half of the nineteenth century, especially after German unification in 1871. "German" surfaces ever more prominently as a national, rather than merely a linguistic, qualifier for literature written and produced within the political boundaries of Germany. The national, the worldly, and the universal at some times clash and at other times lead parallel existences.

To be sure, these processes do not completely impede public access to world literature. If the story of world literature as it unfolds in the first half of the nineteenth century in Germany is a story of comparison through relation, then in the second half of the nineteenth century it is largely a story of comparison through domestication, through national integration. There are two particular trajectories of development. Publications of anthologies and new book series, discussions in literary magazines, acquisition of world literary manuscripts and printed volumes in public libraries, in other words, the *practice* of world literary circulation and dissemination continues, even though it sometimes appears as a niche activity, carried out along with, and sometimes despite, the larger social politics of the times. However, in *theoretical* conceptualizations after Goethe, world literature becomes more politically charged, increasingly more contrasted with the space of national political representation through literature. Within the course of a few decades, world literature simultaneously experiences idealization on the one hand and total negation in the larger political sphere on the other. In the academic sphere, the connections but also tensions between national and world literature start becoming conspicuous. And in the print-cultural field, one witnesses a combination of these trends, whereby world literature undergoes further commercialization and institutionalization. What will qualify as the best and foremost would be those works favored by political critics in support of a particular kind of ethnic German nation. Jewish authors and critics play a prominent role in the construction of world literary anthologies, only to be shunned by conservative nationalist critics for their purported rootlessness and antipatriotic disposition. In other words, world literature and national literature become contested fields of cosmopolitanism and patriotism. German national literature itself would gain prominence as a "hall of fame," a space to recognize the achievements of the nation, and in relation to it, of other nations; something that would prominently figure in a petition for the foundation of an imperial library (*Reichsbibliothek*) that the German Writers' Association would submit to Chancellor Otto von Bismarck in 1881.

How does the conceptualization of world literature change from a humanitarian philosophical idea to one that gains a sharper political edge and a material dimension in Germany after Goethe? What was the nature of the literary landscape: a "nationalized" civic space or a more internationally oriented, cosmopolitan space? How was the idea of the most outstanding (*vorzüglichst*) literary quality expanded and challenged in the second half of the nineteenth century towards the creation of a world literary readership? What role did anthologies, libraries, and book series play in the propagation of world literature? How did the proliferation of German Orientalist scholarship contribute to the expansion of the inventory of world literature?

To find answers to these questions, we must step out of Goethe's Juno Room, the stage for the theater of Eckermann's subservience; out of the office of Lord William Babington Macaulay in Calcutta, where the contract of subservience of local literary traditions over colonial languages has been sealed. From the mass-acquisition of manuscripts, translations, and adaptations of works from non-European literatures into European languages, we must turn to a historical moment in which public affordability of printed books becomes a key access to world literature, a period that is marked by the expansion of lending and public libraries (*Leih- und Volksbibliotheken*) and the establishment of affordable book series such as the Reclam Universal-Bibliothek.

This chapter follows the cultural consequences of the worldwide distribution and consumption of books that Marx and Engels mention in the *Communist Manifesto*. However, instead of naively searching for a potential revolution caused by public access to literary works from other parts of the world, this chapter traces how the very project of world literature in the second half of the nineteenth century becomes more closely linked to a more anthologized collection and acquisition, as it is simultaneously co-opted by the institution of national literature. It is in this space that world literature emerges as an institution of a particular kind of middle-class education (*bildungspolitische Institution*), whereby the internationalization of the literary market will proceed along with, and sometimes in spite of, the nationalization of public institutions in the face of German unification of 1871. In addition, this period is marked by the acquisition of one of the largest consignment of books in non-European languages by a European library in the nineteenth century. The story of Aloys Sprenger, a native Austrian who later became an important British East India Company official, and the controversy surrounding the Prussian Reichsbibliothek's acquisition of the "Bibliotheca Sprengeriana" will form the last part of this chapter, to see how the idea of shared property was also misused to propagate a particular European prerogative over non-European literary traditions.

Let us turn our attention to some other voices from around Goethe's time to understand how the tensions between the national and the worldly slowly come to a point of culmination.

A Parliament of Letters: Heine's Welthülfsliteratur

In extant scholarship, the pre- and post-1848 discourse of world literature in the German sphere has been widely discussed as a contestation between cosmopolitan world literary ideals and rising nationalist tendencies. Heine, as well as Marx and Engels, have served as important figures in this discussion. For John Pizer, Heine becomes the "mediator of *Weltliteratur* as understood by Goethe."[10] In his study of Heine and Young Germany, Pizer chooses to focus on the term's "temporally limiting and fixed aspects in its subsequent mediation and reception in Germany until 1848."[11] The post-1848 period for Pizer is the actual period of "Nationalism and Revival," with Marx and Engels serving as a turning point. For Peter Goßens, Marx and Engels's statement marks the end of a political appropriation of the term and the beginning of a "purely literary historical and canonizing engagement" with the "object" that is world literature.[12] In the discussion that follows, I want to argue that the story is much more complicated than a mere mediation of Goethe's concept by Heine or a complete aestheticization of the term in the second half of the nineteenth century. I will start with Heine, who, as I want to show, is not simply a mediator but also a modifier and, in his own right, a challenger of the Goethean idea of world literature. Heine's awareness of material, intellectual, and political aspects of books and libraries, captured in his many witty remarks, might be a good place to start.

"The library and the town-hall pub are ruining me," Heine wrote to his friend Moses Moser on February 25, 1824.[13] Heine was at the time a student of law at the University of Göttingen. He mentions in his letter that the "Corpus Juris is my pillow, but I also undertake other things, among them reading chronicles and drinking beer."[14] As Walter Kanowsky notes, in the 1820s, the library of the University of Göttingen was the most-used library in Europe. Around 200 books were checked out everyday from a collection that was roughly 240,000 volumes strong. The services of the library made it unique: complete collections of international literature, model displays, and good catalogues, among others.[15] However, in his letter, Heine is least concerned about tabulating these immense achievements of the Göttingen university library. He simply confesses that he is a "monotheist" neither in drinking nor in love—he drinks "double beer" and is in love with the statue of the Medican Venus at the library as well as the cook of his landlord, Hofrath Bayer. But unsuccessfully so—one of them is made of plaster of Paris ("Gyps") and the other is too "venerable." The Göttingen university library finds a mention again in Heine's *Harzreise* (1824), where he describes Göttingen as the city famous for its "sausages and the university, a library and a town-hall pub where the beer is good."[16] Furthermore, he mentions that he is delighted to have left Göttingen early in the morning when "the intellectual certainly lay in bed and dreamed habitually that he turns into a beautiful garden, on whose beds grow numerous white papers with quotes."[17]

Heine's profound suspicion of institutionalized intellectualism, its self-referential nature, and its tendency to take itself seriously is most evident at the beginning of his essay "Concerning History of Religion and Philosophy in Germany":

> I am not a scholar, I am one of the people myself. I am not a scholar, I am not among the seven hundred wise men of Germany. I stand with the great multitude before portals of their wisdom, and if any bit of truth has slipped through, and if this truth has gotten as far as to me, then it has gone far enough;—I write it on paper in pretty lettering and give it to the compositor; he sets it in lead and gives it to the printer; the latter prints it, and then it belongs to the whole world.[18]

The dissemination process of an idea from its genesis to its distribution in print is hard to miss in this quote. What is equally prominent is a parallel combination of attachment and detachment, reverence and irreverence that marks the unique openness and playfulness that characterizes Heine's relationship with libraries. It is also this double-love, this dual-edged approach that will define Heine's relationship with literary/intellectual production in general and with world literature in particular.

In *Der Tannhäuser* (1836), a witty interpretation of the legendary figure, Heine famously makes fun of Weimar, calling it the "home of the widowed muses" ("Musenwitwensitz") where people are wailing over the death of Goethe as Eckermann lives on.[19] Eckermann was for Heine nothing more than Goethe's parrot.[20] Heine also had a unique way of engaging with world literature. In theory and in practice, both aesthetically and politically, Heine situated himself at a distance from the poetic ideal set up by Goethe.

As early as 1828, the same year Goethe made his famous statement but before it saw public light, Heine came up with the term *Welthülfsliteratur* (world-help literature). In a note to the *English Fragments* (1828), Heine commented on the French magazine *Le Globe*, which Goethe also referenced in conjunction with his works and his idea of world literature. Heine refers to an intellectual revolution in France, which, according to him, goes beyond well-known names. Focusing on the innovations that mark the content of *Le Globe*, Heine privileges in world literature the possibility of sharing what is usable from various parts of the world and is made available to the readers:

> World-Help Literature: At the mention of this intellectual revolution in France one thinks certainly of the beautiful names: Cousin, Jouffroy, Guizot, Batante, Thiérry, Thiérs, Mignet etc.; but I have much more in sight the youth of the new France, whose organ I consider the *Globe*, a journal appearing in Paris for many years now, in which young democrats of the sciences, unanimous in purpose and bereft of vanity, publish the results of their research, often the researching itself, in that

> they clearly articulate the most important questions of the human race, *l'ordre du jour*, or better stated *l'ordre du siècle*, and exactly dictate world-help literature, make the preparatory work of all nations usable, and simultaneously facilitate the collective studying of a whole generation in a wonderful way.[21]

Heine does not explain in this passage what exactly he means by the "usable" literature from various parts of the world; he could be using "literature" to mean not just fiction but also other forms of scientific writing. However, the "usability"—or more clearly stated, the purposiveness—of world literature becomes central to his discussion. To arrive at an understanding of Heine's "world-help" literature, it might be useful to think about his interventions in literature—German and French, but also other languages that range from ancient Greek and Sanskrit to medieval Spanish and modern English—exemplified in his work as an author and poet, a translator, a critic, and a "user" of literature within and beyond his national boundaries. What binds all these facets of Heine's personality and his work is ultimately his disregard for iconicity and cult worship, especially the kind that is constantly in the service of the nation. Heine's iconoclastic approach is evident in another letter to his friend Moser, in which he declares himself a Persian poet:

> Actually, I am also no German, as you know . . . there are only three educated, and civilized people: the French, the Chinese, and the Persians. I am proud to be a Persian. That I write poetry in German has its own reasons. The beautiful Gulnar heard from a sheep's head that German is related to my mother tongue Persian, and now the beautiful girl sits in Isfahan and studies the German language from my songs . . . I miss the minarets and the fragrant gardens . . . it is a horrendous fate for a Persian poet that he should toil with your dastardly jolty language and your equally jolty post wagons, your bad weather, your dumb tobacco faces, your Roman pandects and your philosophical cants, and the rest of your lumpen existence. O Firdausi, O Jami, O Hafiz, how sad is your brother![22]

This passage from a personal letter to a friend is just another example of Heine's witty and imaginative engagement with world literature, which continues in *Die Romantische Schule* (1833), with which Heine attempted to transform the discourse about contemporary German literature in France as expounded by the figures made famous in France by Germaine de Staël through her book *De l'Allmagne* (1813). Here one sees Heine's suspicion of a fetishized nationalism, first, through a dual engagement with a national and international literature, and second, through his critique of the stalwarts of German literature, including Goethe and the brothers Schlegel. By questioning the stature of Mme. de Staël's book as the prime source of information for the French "concerning the intellectual life of Germany," Heine also wanted to interrogate whether Goethe's death should be the most important historical marker in contemporary German literature—if "with Goethe's death a new literary period began in Germany, that the old Germany went to the grave with him, that the aristocratic period of literature came to an end and the democratic began."[23] Heine's own engagement with Goethe in this text is worth considering, because he focuses both on Goethe's suppression of talented new voices in the national sphere as he amplified his stature on the national and the world literary scene. Heine compares Goethe to "Louis XI who oppressed the nobility and exalted the *tiers état*,"[24] and he considered him to be a "centennial oak whose branches towered far above them [new poets] and overshadowed them . . . The general public, however, revered the tree just because it was so magnificent in its independence."[25] To this end, Heine engages with Goethe's critics and with those whom he calls his "apologists"—Eckermann among them. However, instead of regurgitating their ideas, Heine presents his own evaluations of Goethe's engagement with world literary works. Especially significant here is his discussion of Goethe's *West-östlicher Divan* (1819), whereby Heine extols the book but also pans it in the same playful tone in which he declares Hafiz, Jami, and Firdausi his brothers:

> It [*West-östlicher Divan*] contains, in its bright lyrics and pithy gnomic poems, the Oriental manner of thought and feeling; and there is a fragrance and glow in the book like a harem full of odalisks with black, rouged, gazelle-like eyes and passionate white arms. . . . Sometimes the reader even seems to be stretched out comfortably on a Persian carpet, smoking the golden tobacco of Turkistan from a long-stemmed water pipe, while a black slave woman cools him with a colorful fan of peacock feathers and a handsome lad reaches him a cup of genuine mocha coffee . . . and while doing so Goethe is always smiling serenely and is as innocent as a child and full of wisdom as an old man. . . . The magic of the book defies description, it is a salaam sent by the Occident to the Orient.[26]

At a distance from Goethe's adulation for *Sakuntala* (discussed in chapter 1), Heine detected in Goethe an apparent "repugnance for India," which he thought "may have arisen because he [Goethe] suspected Catholic vile in the Sanskrit studies of the Schlegels and their friends."[27] Heine locates Goethe's affinity for Persian and Arabic literatures in the peculiar way in which "these gentlemen [the Schlegel brothers] regarded Hindustan as the cradle of the Catholic world order," where they found their "trinity, their incarnation, their penance . . . and all their other beloved manias."[28]

Goethe's essay on Indian literature (mentioned in chapter 1) was published posthumously, and Heine may not have had access to the essay. Nonetheless, his opinion of the Schlegels' responsibility for Goethe's repugnance of India is worth a pause. Heine's criticism is based on the evaluation of literary translations by the Schlegels, which he considers to be ideologically appropriated. He presents strategies of comparative literary evaluation that focus on difference rather than mere similarities between texts and textual traditions.

Heine's comments on the Sanskrit translations by the Schlegel brothers are particularly illustrative of these observations. He starts with telegraphically communicating an intellectual outline of the differences as he sees between Germany and France and moves quickly to an evaluation of the Schlegel brothers' work in Sanskrit. Heine foregrounds his thoughts on Friedrich Schlegel by criticizing the novel *Lucinde*, which he considers a work that decidedly espouses Catholic values. Calling religion and hypocrisy twin sisters, "with the same figure, clothing and speech" Heine ascribes hypocrisy to the ability to use the word *love* more than religion, only to declare: "I am speaking of Germany; in France the one sister has died, and we see the other still in deepest mourning."[29]

With these comparative intra-European "national" worlds in tow, Heine turns to the extra-European world of comparison through Friedrich Schlegel, calling his works *Die Sprache und Weisheit der Indier* (1808) and *Vorlesungen über die Geschichte der Literatur* (1810) his best and therefore most famous. Heine praises Friedrich Schlegel for his efforts in educating himself in Sanskrit and for establishing Sanskrit studies in Germany; for Heine, Schlegel is for Germany what William Jones was for England. Heine commends Friedrich Schlegel for his perspectival depth ("tiefes Anschauungsvermögen") that grants him access to the "Shloka," the epic verse-form from India. Nonetheless, Heine finds his brother August Wilhelm Schlegel petty ("kleinlich") with his translations of "Sanskrit verses in Hexameters" whereby he (August Wilhelm) merely ends up carving some tricks from Alexandrian poetry. He also deducts a level of appropriation of the otherness through translation when he diagnoses in the work of Friedrich Schlegel a rediscovery of Catholicism:

> My only criticism is the ulterior motive behind the book. It was written in the interests of Catholicism. These people had rediscovered in the

> Indian poems not merely the mysteries of Catholicism, but the whole Catholic hierarchy as well as its struggles with secular authority. In the *Mahabharata* and the *Ramayana* they saw, as it were, the elephantine middle ages. As a matter of fact, when in the latter epic King Vishwamitra quarrels with the priest Vashishtha, this quarrel concerns the same interests about which the Emperor quarreled with the Pope, although here in Europe the point in dispute was called investiture and there in India it was called the cow Sabala.[30]

The specificity and authority with which Heine comments on these translations stem from his own training in Sanskrit literature with the Indologist Franz Bopp (1791–1867) at the University of Berlin when Heine attended his seminar on Comparative Grammar in 1822. Heine was familiar with Bopp's translations of Sanskrit works, especially episodes from the *Mahabharata*.[31] But it is not just Heine's familiarity with Sanskrit that reveals itself in his critique of the Schlegels' translations. Heine shows a special eye for the localization of world literature, a proclivity to detect personal, political, and religious projections, as evidenced in his criticism. Living up to his own reputation as *enfant terrible* of German literature, he also had a special disposition for mocking trendsetters and their acolytes, as registered in his critique of Goethe. In a poem, "Oestliche Poeten" (Eastern poets) published in *Romanzero* (1851), his final collection of poems, Heine described the Persian poet Sheikh Saadi (1215–1292) as the Pied Piper of Hamlin, who is ready to be followed by all the "small singers." Ridiculing the trend to "coo in the manner of Saadi," Heine adds that for him it hardly makes a difference if one puts about in water like a poodle in an Eastern or Western way; there is no difference between the Persian bird Bulbul or Ovid's Philomela turned into a nightingale. The desire to "worship the cows of pious Indians," he notes wittily, is based on the desire to "find Mount Olympus [or a mount of dung] in the cowshed." For him, such poets "steal fruits from the garden of Shiraz" and end up regurgitating Ghazals.[32]

If the Schlegel brothers and Goethe turn world literature into a sacrosanct ideal, Heine comes and punctures it without being a jingoist or a nationalist. He does not pretend to have imaginative conversations with foreign poets and yet he is able to declare himself one with them, challenging his own Germanness. While Goethe sees himself as the epitome of a German author, Heine sees the exact opposite. And in that move away from the narcissism of a collective that will contest his deserved space, Heine becomes the most flamboyant and perhaps also the most political practitioner of world literature.

Heine's uneasy relationship with the dominance of a nationalist discourse and the cooptation of literature as a national artifact is central to his itinerary as an author and a political figure. As someone associated with the Young Germany movement—although he himself never explicitly avowed this connection—Heine was involved in the mobilization of the public against the tyranny of monarchy through his writings, expressed in his support of the weavers' uprising in Silesia in 1844 and best represented in his poem *Die schlesischen Weber* (1844), first published in Karl Marx's newspaper *Vorwärts!* (Forward!). *Deutschland: Ein Wintermärchen* (1844)—whose subtitle carries a direct reference to Shakespeare's *The Winter's Tale* (1623)—was conceived during Heine's years in exile in France. In this work, Heine had critically engaged with the text of the German "nation" as a cultural and a political-geographical unit much before Germany unified as a nation in 1871. The democratizing spirit of situating literature politically is reflected in Heine's accordance of primacy to the function of literature in the public sphere. Heine's writings lay the groundwork on which the tensions between national literature and world literature, indeed a national literary public sphere and a world literary public sphere emerge. At the center of Heine's thought is his profound belief in the transformative role of literature but also his deep suspicion of the institutionalization of literature through genial figures and their acolytes. Furthermore, Heine had a deep understanding of the materiality of literary production and its instrumentalization. It is this public-sphere figure of Heine as a philosophical idealist and a print-cultural pragmatist that makes him a useful figure to start thinking about the transformations in the materiality of print-cultural influences and the institutionalization of world literature in the second half of the nineteenth century.

Heine's concept of *Welthülfsliteratur*, his cosmopolitanism, his attempts to add new dimensions to the discourse of world literature, and his attitude toward the institution of the nation and national literature make him unique in many ways. No one understood the fetishization of national and world literatures better than Heine, who intervenes most uniquely in the parallel textuality of national and world literatures. Through his stringent critique of earlier propagators of world literature, such as Goethe and the Schlegel brothers, through his avant-garde approach to the enterprise of literary history as necessarily transnational and therefore comparative, and through his political commitment to the cosmopolitan dimension of world literature—through the term *Welthülfsliteratur*—Heine in many ways clears the way for Marx and Engels's explicit mention of world literature as a product of transnational cosmopolitan consumption. As I discuss in the following sections, Heine's *Welthülfsliteratur* and Marx and Engels's "circulated" world literature provide keys to understanding detractors of world literature as well as practitioners who contribute to its construction through anthologies, library acquisitions, book series, and translation enterprises.

Against Cosmopolitanism: Critics of Weltliteratur

If Goethe declared the meaninglessness of national literature, Heine called for a world-help literature, and Marx and Engels conceived the formation of world literature through many local and national literatures, there were many other voices in Germany in the nineteenth century for whom world literature was not an emancipation from national literature but in fact dependent on it. For others still, world literature was an impediment to the construction of national literature, indeed a threat to nationalism itself.

In the essay "Über Goethe im Wendepunkt zweier Jahrhunderte" (1835), the author Karl Gutzkow (1811–1878) addressed the question of world literature. Locating Goethe at the turn of two centuries, Gutzkow decidedly expresses the fortification of national literature through world literature. The term *national* for Gutzkow serves as a ring around the perspectives of an author that brings all of the images and thoughts to a central point. "The nation wants to be reflected in the literature," Gutzkow wrote, underlining that the will of the nation is that literature becomes the means of expression for its political, religious, and moral conditions. The idea of world literature is for him not opposed to but in the service of the nation:

> World literature does not suppress nationality. It does not demand that one gives up one's native hills and valleys to get used to cosmopolitan images and foreign landscapes. World literature, on the contrary, is the guarantee of nationality. At least it will make possible certain things in front of a European forum, which still seems inadmissible at home. Nationality is not canceled by the world literary state, but rather justified by it. The evaluation and the birth of domestic literature is facilitated by it [the world literary state].[33]

Gutzkow found the idea of national self-reliance in literature and the criticism of world literature "quarrelsome" ("zänkisch") and "hypochondriac," and he called for an examination of the "outer physiognomy" of world literature to understand its nature. And for him, world literature was "everything that is worthy of translation in a foreign language, so that all discoveries, through which the sciences can be enriched, and all phenomena, which appear to devise a new law in the arts and which destroy the rules of old aesthetic."[34] While Gutzkow's definition of world literature includes scientific works—thus intersecting with Heine's ideas of *Welthülfsliteratur*—the value of aesthetic works remains central to his understanding of the term. Gutzkow sees in the growth of world literature a possibility of infusing a higher purpose to fields of intellectual inquiry as an alternative to mediocrity and its decoration with "false laurels." His sharpest critique is against the philologist and poet Ludwig Uhland—author of *Vaterländische Gedichte* (1815)—in whose poetry Gutzkow sees a festive and yet placid "Sunday mood" ("Sonntagsstimmung"). Such poetry, according to Gutzkow, becomes symptomatic as a German genre, "a collection of national costumes, which an Englishman buys for himself when he returns home."[35] Gutzkow criticizes the patriotic coquetterie and vanity that he thinks comes to rescue the justification of the purportedly higher quality of German writings against French or English in the German literary scene. According to him, "The so-called real German products of our literature are surely the most mediocre."[36]

Goethe's suggestion of world literature is for Gutzkow an attempt to "flee the so-called [mediocre] contemporary poetry."[37] He sees in Goethe's suggestion a means to regulate the internal values of Germans through an exposure to the foreign. Gutzkow's explicit pronouncement for the guaranteeing of national literature through world literature might seem to be in opposition to the otherwise cosmopolitan idea of world literature *per se*; for John Pizer, Gutzkow seems to be taking a "defensive posture."[38] However, Gutzkow goes a great distance to criticize the mediocrity of homegrown "real German" products. Gutzkow's own political leanings and his intellectual and creative engagement with the world outside of Germany and Europe—exemplified at the very beginning of his career in a sociophilosophical satire on the Dalai Lama as a human god in *Maha Guru* (1833)—leave room for such speculations. In his own words, "anyone who wants to partake in foreign life, should gamble his own first."[39]

However, there were other critics, harsher and more uncharitable than Gutzkow, for whom partaking in foreign life through world literature was an unworthy gamble. Premier among them is the historical and social critic Wolfgang Menzel (1798–1873). Menzel was the editor of the literary journal *Literatur-Blatt* (published by Goethe's publisher, Cotta, in Stuttgart) from 1825–1849 and the author of the four-volume *Die deutsche Literatur* (1828, expanded revised edition 1835). Menzel, who had brought Gutzkow to Stuttgart and acted as his mentor, quickly became his staunchest critic.

While Gutzkow saw the possibility of a guarantee of national literature through world literature, Menzel was critical of German engagements with foreign literatures. In his essay, "Influence of Foreign Literature," Menzel detects a special "imitative propensity of the Germans [which] prevails to a very great extent in their literature."[40] He classifies Germans as either "imitators" or "purists" and identifies a sense of self-loathing within these groups. On the one hand, Menzel is pragmatic in his evaluation of the inevitability of foreign influences. Anticipating Marx and Engels's famous proclamation by a good decade, Menzel states that as much as the commercial connections between nations lead to circulation of material products, literature has the potential of becoming the agent of a larger dissemination of the "intellectual treasures of a nation."[41] On the other hand, he also thinks that the "extraordinary predilection for what is foreign, and a rare ability for imitation" have led the Germans to "an unnatural forgetfulness of their own worth."[42] Menzel considers Germans to be "thorough cosmopolitans," ready to "substitute for our national individuality something applicable to the whole human race."[43]

Menzel's views on engagement with the foreign are guided by a purposiveness and utility. He is open to the idea of adapting to that which serves national progress, culture, and civilization; an unreflective appropriation, he states however, leads to two kinds of faults: "that of a blind slavish devotion to everything foreign, and that of blindly undervaluing ourselves."[44] Such an undervaluation of the German Self becomes crucial to Menzel's identification of various kinds of "mania" for foreign trends, which he claims, in the end, balance themselves out due to the sheer diversity among themselves: "Thus the ultra-refinement of the Gallomania has been counterbalanced by the blunt humor of the Anglomania, the cold and regular classicality of Grecomania, by the luxuriant riches of Orientalism, the superficial Rationalism by the mystic Romanticism."[45]

The manifestation of German proclivity for the foreign, Menzel notes, is evident in the abundance of translations into German. He states that Germans translate notoriously, thereby turning Germany into a factory of translated works. Referencing a whole array of multiple translations from Greek, Latin, French, Italian, Spanish, and other languages into German in the first decades of the nineteenth century, Menzel curiously claims that this appropriation of the foreign is slowly coming to an end: "we have now returned home for a while, and we are meditating."[46] This imagined return becomes central to the last section of his essay, where he cites at length his own review of Heinrich Stieglitz's *Bilder des Orients*, crucifying him for wandering in other nations and indulging in a slavish fascination for the foreign. Here the idea of the native-born versus the foreign imitation, the original versus the translation takes precedence. Menzel locates Stieglitz among the many Gallo-, Anglo-, Turko-, Indo-, Perso- and other maniacs, holding him and others of his ilk responsible for turning German literature into "a madhouse, in which hundreds of fools are aping the costume and habits, the language and ideas of a hundred different nations of ancient and modern times."[47] Criticizing Stieglitz for his "affected imitations" of Hafiz, Firdausi, Jami, and Kalidasa, Menzel completes a full circle by bemoaning the German propensity for foreign imitation.

Menzel's stringent critique of foreign influence on German literature, couched in an otherwise appealing criticism of affective imitations, acquires a much stronger, anti–world literature stance in his other essays. The idea of "foreign-mania" would be picked up again by Menzel in two essays with which he ends the fourth volume of the *Die Deutsche Literatur*: "The New Anglo-Mania" and "The New Gallo-Mania." The latter would also become central to his critique of the authors of Young Germany, whom he considered unpatriotic, anti-German, and pro-France:

> The coterie took the name of Young Germans [das junge Deutschland], only, however, as an emancipation from Young Europe, for they expressly declared that patriotism was nothing but "an animal impulse of the blood," that, therefore, a man must not devote himself to one nation, but to all mankind, which, however, was deduced from France; and that, therefore, all national literature must be done away with, and a "world literature" put in its place. . . . In Germany they were much applauded by Jews, who had long before deified their Heine.[48]

Clearly for Menzel, world literature is a product of antipatriotic thought as despicable as other ideas and movements emanating from Paris. Read through Menzel, world literature appears not as a humanitarian, philosophical ideal but as an agency that inspires commitments away from those to the national public, as a force that disintegrates a nation and disrespects its own literature. Menzel calls "young Paris" a conglomerating point of fugitives from the rest of Europe, a space that initiates movements such as Young Italy and Young Germany. These fugitives, he adds, work heavily under the influence of French literature and work with French sources, like a number of Heine followers in Germany. He suggests that the Young Germans are influenced by the new French free spiriters who fight against religion and morality and have launched a war of destruction against it. In his vicious polemic against writers of Young Germany, he finds Heine to be the degenerate and misguided leader of the Francophile crowd.

Heine stays at the center of Menzel's critique of world literature. Heine becomes the instrument and the product, the cause and the effect of Menzel's critique. Menzel first praises Heine; for him, Heine is not only a humorist in prose writings but also the first one to introduce irony in lyrical form, the one who had the capability of combining the most daring frivolity and the most cutting wit with the tenderest sentimentality.[49] Menzel considers Heine's *Französische Zustände* (1833) his best prose work. But he also sees the book as the cause of his being derailed from his poetic track, causing his turn to the political, critical, historical, and philosophical writings.[50]

Menzel's thoughts were not limited to his literary history; as the editor of the *Literatur-Blatt*, with a much larger nonspecialized audience, Menzel used his position to influence public opinion against the authors associated with Young Germany and also against world literature. As Peter Goßens points out in his study, a slightly modified version of his ideas in *Die deutsche Literatur* was published as part of a series of articles in the *Literatur-Blatt* (1836), in which he explicitly used the word *staatsgefährdend* (dangerous for the state) for the authors of Young Germany. His anti-Semitic and anti-French stance becomes even more explicit. Citing long passages from an anonymous publication against authors connected with Young Germany, Menzel mobilizes hate speech to privilege the cause of German nationality over French and Jewish influences. According to him, the French and the Jews "stir up the unholy fire that saps our best juices, that poisons the calm patrimony of our inner nationality."[51]

By pitching patriotism against cosmopolitanism, national literature against world literature, by calling world literature essentially French and Jewish, Menzel actually extends a line of thought that systematically excludes German-Jewish subjects from the mainstream of the German nation.

Menzel represents one of the most prominent voices for whom the nation must look inward in order to define its exteriority. The basis of comparison for Menzel remains French literature. But there were critics for whom the interactive tension between the national and the foreign stayed at the center of the conceptualization of world literature. World literature for them did emerge as an international parliament of letters where national literature must acquire a prominent place. It also emerges as a hall of fame where works of other nations enter and acquire their prominent places. Ludolf Wienbarg, for example, in an essay entitled "Goethe und die Weltliteratur" (1835) sensed a positive transformation in the position of German national literature within world literature. For him, while German literature was traditionally a recipient of literary ideas from England

and France, it was now ready to leave its mark on those literatures, largely due to increased interactions between people of various nations: "This much is for sure, the mutual effect between the literature of the earth can only grow and become intimate, with the continuously growing brotherly band of nations."[52] Wienbarg's ideas were challenged by Michael Enk von der Burg (1835), who considered the idea of world literature to be something that extends beyond the literary, warning that the attractive idea of world literature should not lead to the forgetting of national particularity and the feeling of (a national) self.[53] Theodor Mundt remained skeptical of the Goethean idea; for him *Weltliteratur* was more a "beautiful word or a great dream rather than a true idea."[54]

One of the strongest reactions against a world literary cosmopolitanism came from Ernst Moritz Arndt (1769–1860). Arndt considered world literature a kind of seduction away from the nation and national literature. In his essay, "Lasset Euch nicht verführen, oder die Weltliteratur" (1842; Do not let yourself be seduced, or world literature), Arndt insinuates that many a statement that Goethe made in the last stages of his life have become more significant than they ought to have. Arndt considers Goethe's ideas in the last years of his life a product of the "tired and sleeping time, when the power of the creator and the doer are also stalked by a tired slumber."[55] Arndt further contends that Goethe had also become comfortable, affable, and talkative in the last years of his life, and his engagements with the foreign are to be seen in this light: "In his later years, Goethe is said to have sampled all periods and peoples and ways, many even strange to himself . . . Indians, Chinese, Arabs and Mongols and Tartars with their structures and possible and actual customs and views and feelings are said to have given the younger entrants and trackers much material. How cute! As the saying goes: What does the German not do for money?"[56]

Goethe's use of the term *Weltliteratur* is for Arndt the result of this state of being comfortable and affable, a state in which Goethe took the latest findings and products from works of all foreign peoples, and it is in this context that he also created a few "casual and agreeable" ("gelegentlich und gefällig") terms which came about through his "soft and flattering" friendships with Italians and Englishmen (insinuating Manzoni and Carlyle) and his "light and thin conversations" (insinuating the ones with Eckermann). Arndt blames younger authors of according undue significance to Goethe's term, for receiving it with "huge gaiety and intensity" ("großer Lustigkeit und Heftigkeit") and for applying and exploiting it in ways that even "the great master" ("der große Meister") would have never intentioned.[57] His advice to the younger generation is simple: "Dwell in the land and you shall be fed!"[58] Arndt states that he does want Germans to learn the best from every country that there is, but he also insists that "[a German] should follow this beautiful desire with wisdom and moderation and use it with reason."[59] By this he means a local orientation of intellect, which he claimed could never ever be attained in full. Pursuing a nativist politics, Arndt thinks that the only thing one ever has access to, one can ever enjoy in totality, is what one was born into: "Do you believe then, you German, also you very learned and educated Germans, that when you read your Aristophanes, Sophocles, that you read like an Athenian, when you read Shakespeare, you read like an Englishman, when you read Racine and Béranger, that you can feel and taste them like a Parisian, in sum, that you can entirely and fully enjoy them? No! No!"[60] Arndt believes the native language to be like the mother's milk: the most natural, and therefore the most accessible. Arndt also accredits the accessibility to literatures other than German and the growing market of *Allerweltliteratur* (literature of the whole world) in the German intellectual and educated class's desire to engage with world literature. But he also warns that from this *Allerweltliteratur* one cannot hope for the approach of *Weltliteratur*.

While this is by no means an exhaustive list of all voices from the German-speaking world, suffice it to say that the tensions between belonging to a national community and the understanding of the national self were at the heart of debates on nationalism's world literary cosmopolitanism. These tensions informed conceptualizations of world literature as a collection, as exemplified in the first published anthology of world literature in Germany.

Anthologizing World Literature

In the midst of the loud contestation for the value of national and world literatures, between the suppression of free speech, restrictions laid upon literary productivity, and the proposed insularity of German-language literature, the first ever anthology of world literature was printed in Germany in 1848. The editor was Johannes Scherr (1817–1886), a critic and cultural historian educated in Zürich and Tübingen, whose name was also associated with the Young Germany movement. Scherr called his anthology *Bildersaal der Weltliteratur* (Portrait gallery of world literature). In this volume that spans over twelve hundred pages, Scherr utilized regional, national, and linguistic categories to organize world literary works in ten sections, each divided into five to seven subsections. Book 1 covers the Orient (*Morgenland*) and consisted of translated works from Sanskrit, Chinese,

Hebrew, Turkish, Persian, and Arabic languages; Book 2 samples ancient Greek and Latin literatures; Book 3 is dedicated to Troubadors and literatures in European languages; and the last book ends with writings from Slavic nations. Most of the shorter works were published in whole, and some works are excerpted in their German translations; each category is preceded by a small essay about the regional or national work whose examples the reader is about to examine.

In the epilogue to the anthology, Scherr quotes three authors: the Indologist and Sanskrit translator Friedrich Rückert, Ludolf Wienbarg, and, of course, Goethe.[61] The first quote by Rückert, the translator of Sanskrit poetry into German, invites those readers who like to befriend the coaxing habitation ("schmeichelnde Gewöhnung") with foreign accents, asking them to recognize that world poesy ("Weltpoesie") is world reconciliation ("Weltversöhnung"). The last quote by Ludolf Wienbarg (1802–1872)—a *Vormärz* author who also wrote aesthetic theory—provides the means to access world poesy through the plethora of various national forms of poesy; the "German" becomes the collector, who goes around the world and gathers from holy streams of various national *poesies* with a crystal begging bowl ("Opferschale") of humanity. Between Rückert and Wienbarg, the quote by Goethe reminds the readers that the world is an extended fatherland.

The epilogue thus frames the significance of world literature for the reader politically and aesthetically. The relationship between national and world literature in the context of (world) historical developments is particularly noticeable in the preface. Scherr begins by calling the February Revolution in France (1848) a signal for Germany to "impede its literary activity in the service of history."[62] He is of the point of view that Germans have learned nothing from recent history, and that the enthusiastic embrace of the principles of revolution has been rendered stagnant by the fact that the revolution has been co-opted by enthusiastic bureaucrats. According to Scherr, the liberals are now playing with democracy much as they did with absolutism; that the French and Swiss borders of Germany are full of banished people. Those who were for the revolution, he claims, are not denying it, such are the autumnal winds of despair that come after the hope of a revolutionary spring. The tone of the preface changes when Scherr turns from commenting on politics to focusing on his work. Scherr asks his readers for forgiveness and turns then to the topic of world literature. Three factors gain primacy: the space of the production of the work (Germany), the mediators (translators), and the receivers (the German reading public).[63] Scherr categorically states that the target readership for the book is the larger public. He adds that along with the purpose of teaching ("Belehrung"), the book is also meant for the entertainment ("Unterhaltung") of its reading public, a certain kind of "poetic pleasure."[64]

By suturing his comments on the contemporary political situation in Germany with those on the compendium, Scherr most directly lets the national confront the worldly, thereby illuminating many questions about the relationship of world and national literatures around the time that Scherr published the compendium and also for the coming years.

"A book such as the one in hand is only possible in Germany,"[65] Scherr notes, expanding immediately on the reasons for such a specifically German facility for world literature. First, he credits the "universality of the German intellect and the inexhaustibility of German sciences," which have led to an understanding of the "intellectual products of all peoples and times" to a degree that no other group could afford. Second, he mentions the abundance of "masterful translations, which no other nation has," and which has made the literary treasures of foreign nations into Germany's shared property. Finally, Scherr goes to the extent of calling Germans "owners" of the Goethean term *Weltliteratur*.[66]

Scherr situates his compendium within this "German ownership" of world literature. He characterizes his collection as one that contains everything from the "fantastic darkness of the Indian ages" to Greek antiquity, from the Middle Ages to the modern times, from folksongs to tragedies. The aim and scope of his anthology, he insists, is to provide a complete picture of the poetic creativity of humanity ("Gesamtbild des dichterischen Schaffens der Menschheit").[67] He promises a comprehensive history of poetic literature from various nations in a chronological order. This is precisely where the Goethean idea of the "Vorzüglischste"—the most superior example of aesthetic expression—gains currency to distinguish *Weltliteratur* from *Allerweltliteratur*. Aesthetic representation ("Darstellung") becomes part of cultural and political representation ("Vertretung"). The Indians are credited with "fantastic darkness," the Orient becomes the source of rich imagery and profoundness ("Bilderpracht und Tiefsinn"), the Greek antiquity is the site for sculptural plasticity and wisdom ("Plastik und Weisheit"), the Romans have warm passion and blazing fantasy ("heisse Leidenschaft und lodernde Phantasie"), the Germanic people are seen as possessing intellectual majesty, power, and soul-purposiveness ("Geisteshoheit, Kraft, und Gemütsinnigkeit") and the Slavs are the owners of a melodious melancholy ("melodienreiche Schwermuth").[68] Scherr states that the inclusion of German poetry in great numbers requires no justification and should not alienate anyone; neither would the inclusion of old Germanic poetry in new German translations. The reason, he states, is because the book is meant for the larger public. Scherr ends his preface with a few notes on what he perceives as some shortcomings of the anthology: among other things, a rearrangement of certain texts or reframing of certain excerpts. He wishes the publication of a second edition but quickly expresses the impossibility of his wish, bringing the readers back to contemporary times. He mentions that as politics take over aesthetic concerns in the German-speaking world, the primacy accorded to literature and authors faces a decline. Nonetheless, he ends on an upbeat note, stating that the idea of beauty is as immortal as the thought of freedom, and a short period of darkness and barbarism does not entirely compromise its future.[69]

Scherr highlights not just intellectual but also consumerist aspects of literature. Cashing in on the abundance of translations from world literature into German in the first three decades of the nineteenth century, he showcases them—even if to declare a very specific German "ownership" of world literature. And last, but not least, through his long commentary on contemporary German politics, Scherr immediately situates world literature within the sociopolitical reality of Germany. Scherr embeds world literature in the political and ideological climate in which it is conceived. Its conceptualization remains an inimitable feature of the society in which it develops. Scherr made his statement, as noted before, in 1848, a year in which the most well-known statement by Marx and Engels would appear in the *Communist Manifesto*. Scherr is not too distant from Marx and Engels. Like them, he would use the term *geistige Produkte* to determine the intellectual production of a particular nation and also present books as the *Gemeingut* (shared wares) of humanity. This idea of shared property would undergo further transformation. The formal organization of the German Orientalist Society institutionalized world literature in many different ways. Aloys Sprenger, world-traveled cataloger and book collector, played a central role in this process.

The German Oriental Society and Aloys Sprenger

What Scherr institutionalized in his anthology, especially with regard to non-Western literatures, is part of a continuation of a tradition of translation. If the first half of the nineteenth century witnesses a selective albeit concentrated effort in the entry of literatures from non-European languages into the German-speaking sphere, by the second half of the nineteenth century these efforts systematize themselves. First, there is an increase in the number of translations into German directly from languages such as Sanskrit, Arabic, Chinese, Persian (and later, Japanese). English and French slowly lose their status as "intermediary" languages. Second, there is a concerted effort to institutionalize acquisition, collection, translation, publication, research, and education in non-European languages and literatures, exemplified among other things by the foundation and efforts of the Deutsche Morgenländische Gesellschaft (German Oriental Society) in 1844, a society that also establishes the first specialized library for non-European manuscripts and printed books.[70]

From October 1 to 4, 1844, a conference of German Orientalists took place in Dresden.[71] The conference, the first of its kind in Germany, was a sign of the growing institutionalization of Oriental studies in Germany. The participants came from various principalities in Germany but also universities of the Austro-Hungarian Empire. Although the group was first called the Deutsche Gesellschaft für Kunde des Morgenlandes (German Society for the Study of the Orient), the participants decided in 1845 that they were going to change the name to Morgenländische Gesellschaft für Deutschland (Orientalist Society for Germany). The prominence of Orientalists from Middle-Germany (Mittel-Deutschland) such as Dr. Fleischer (Professor, University of Leipzig), and Dr. Brockhaus (University of Leipzig) is particularly notable, because it was not in Berlin (Prussia) or in Munich (Bavaria) but in smaller cities that an institutionalization of non-European literatures would take place. Leipzig had long since established its status as the "book city" (Buchstadt Leipzig). It was also the city where Hermann Brockhaus, heir to the Brockhaus print empire and professor of Sanskrit at the University of Leipzig would find his seat and would make the first suggestions for printing non-European works, especially those from Sanskrit, Pali, and Hindi Zend in the Latin script. The opening statement of *Ueber den Druck sanskritischer Werke mit Lateinischen Buchstaben*—Brockhaus's prospectus to publish literary works in original and translation, as well as textbooks and grammar books for students—captures the print cultural realization of Orientalist condescension and world literary institutionalization:

> Everyday the Orient moves closer to us. Europe now has the high assignment of breathing new life into the ossifying East. But for the Orient to not be a merely external shell copy of the West, rather regenerate itself from its own inner cores, stimulated by our [Europe's] higher and more developed intelligence, it needs to be researched and recognized from its own sources. Herein lies the true meaning and value of Oriental studies. In order to understand and grasp the monuments of

> Oriental spirit, one must open the way to the languages of the Orient through grammars and dictionaries, and by domesticating its most important and significant literary products of the same by publishing the originals, by translations and adaptations.[72]

Brockhaus's message of recognition, organization, and domestication of the orient in order to breathe new life into it and save it from becoming rigid was echoed in the guidelines of the Orientalist Society. The organization's purpose was to promote knowledge of Asia and a stronger relationship with Asian countries. However, the organization was not only concerned about Oriental antiquity but also wished to engage with "recent history and the contemporary conditions" in these countries.[73] The fulfillment of these objectives was proposed through the following means:

> Through the collection of Oriental natural and cultural products, print and manuscripts.
> Through the publication, translation, and exploitation (output) of Oriental literary works.
> Through the publication of a journal.
> Through the encouragement, privileging, and support for undertakings (enterprises) for the promotion of knowledge about Asia.
> Through the maintenance of relations with similar societies and intellectuals within the nation and abroad.[74]

The foundational guidelines of the society further emphasize the establishment of a library and the appointment of the second secretary of the society as the group's librarian. His responsibilities included the ordering, numbering, marking, and preservation of materials acquired by the library through purchase or through gifts. The librarian's responsibilities also included the opening and closing of the library, the distribution and collection of materials from the members, as well as the preparation of a yearly report for the annual conference. The society's reports from the first years of its founding make frequent mentions of the libraries in Leiden, Berlin, Paris, and London, which were prominently acquiring books and manuscripts from Asia. The curious connection that one sees here is the dependence on diplomatic missions in Jordan, Turkey, Lebanon, and other Middle-Eastern places for the acquisition of manuscripts and printed books in Arabic, Persian, Chughtai Turkish, and Ottoman Turkish, and the close ties with the Christian religious missionaries in Halle (who in turn were connected with Danish missionaries) to acquire manuscripts and printed books from the Indian subcontinent, especially southern India.

A report published by the society's journal, the *Zeitschrift der Deutschen Morgenländischen Gesellshaft* (*ZDMG*) in 1847 listed about ten manuscripts and over twenty printed works acquired from India by the University of Tübingen. These works are in addition to the gifts to the university by missionaries in Kerala and Karnataka in Southern India. They include copies of *Keralā Utpatti*, *Hari Vanshā*, and *Sarva Sidhhantā Sangraha*, in palm leaves and written in the Tamil script; titles which were also to be found in the McKenzie Manuscripts at the Madras Christian College.[75]

The interest of this organization in systematically fortifying Oriental studies in Germany, its desire to acquire new manuscripts and translations, and its reports on print-cultural developments in other countries are well illustrated by three documents published in the very first years of its foundation.

In 1849, the *ZDMG* published a short note about an Oriental library in Rhodes (Greece). Sent by authors traveling in the region in 1842, the brief note reports that the library was founded in 1792 by Turbend Amasi Ahmed Aga and contains about one thousand Oriental works. The travelers had a nice conversation with the librarian, Haji Mehmed Effendi, and found him to be a "real bookworm, buried under manuscripts and folios." The report further states: "May traveling Orientalists follow this pointed finger and try to send us a catalog of this library."[76]

This report is followed by a letter from Dr. Friedrich Max Müller from Oxford University, considered to be the preeminent translator and interlocutor of Sanskrit religious texts in the late nineteenth century. Müller writes about the progress on his planned publication of the *Rig Veda*; seventy pages in Sanskrit, he reports, have already been printed, and he is working with proofs now. Mentioning the English translation of the *Rig Veda* by Dr. Wilson, Müller adds comments on his own ongoing translation of the work. In addition, Max Müller reports on the developments on the Veda in India: Dr. Roer has published two chapters from the Sayan's commentary on the *Rig Veda* in *Biblioteca Orientalis* and is about to publish the *Brihad-Araṇya-Upanishad* with commentary and translation.[77] Max Müller then lists a number of works of Sanskrit literature: *Tatva Bodhini*, *Tatva Kaumudi*, *Rusamanjali*—all of them newly republished in India from existing manuscripts. He adds that Dr. Wilson is done with his *History of India*, and that his next project would be a lexicon of native expressions from Arabic, Persian, Sanskrit, and new Indian languages, which are now common practice in India. Dr. Wilson would also publish a catalog of the Sanskrit manuscripts at the India House in London, where new Vedic commentaries are to be expected.

That the society was part of an international network of scholars and librarians is evident from its members list. The society included translators such as Joseph von Hammer-Pursgstall and Friedrich Rückert. Among its corresponding members was also Aloys Sprenger, the Austrian Orientalist who, with his student Aly Akbar of Delhi College, cataloged the Farsi, Arabic, and Urdu collections of the libraries of the Kingdom of Oudh (archaic spelling of Awadh).

In 1849, Aloys Sprenger sent a letter from India reporting on the state of literature. Entitled "Literaturbericht aus Ostindien," the letter, written on November 5, 1848, reports on the developments in Indian magazines and books during the mid-nineteenth century. Sprenger starts his letter with a historical acknowledgment: "It has been almost one hundred years since the British, the locomotors of European education in its developments outside, have been ruling India and working on the intellectual rebirth of this wonderful country. Their efforts and the creative power of the conditions, in which India has entered through English rule, has already had great effects."[78] Sprenger lists among these the immense number of magazines that are now being published in India in indigenous languages. Delhi, he reports, has six political magazines, published weekly, two of which have a section on literature, and one that is a literary monthly. He lists the languages in which these and other magazines are pubished (Farsi, Hindi, Urdu) and the originating cities (Calcutta, Bombay, Agra, Bareilley, Ghazipur, and Benaras). Crediting the British for this achievement, Sprenger notes that the government is not distrustful of its own child: englightenment. He mentions schoolbooks, medicinal publications, scholarly works, and illustrated works, and notes that these are in lithography and typeset. Sprenger then lists about two dozen publications in Persian and Arabic, including textbooks. Praising the Asiatic company for its commitment to knowledge and learning, Sprenger mentions a "learning expedition" that the British government had sent to Tibet, and then discusses his primary assignment: the compilation of a bibliography of the collections in Lucknow, a major center for Islamic Studies in India. Sprenger promises to send reports of his findings to the *ZDMG* and ends his letter abruptly on the note: "my history of Mohammad is currently in press."[79] Sprenger's contributions to this volume went beyond the literary report. He published an essay on the *Kitáb Tabaqát al-Kabyr* (ca. 1318), which he called the most important codex he had ever seen in India.[80] The journal itself celebrated Sprenger by stating: "Our compatriot and correspondent Dr. A. Sprenger, head of a scholarly institution in Delhi, seems to have been appointed to that post by science itself, to redeem the Oriental school studies from its one-sidedness and uniformity and to revive the exploitation of the rich treasure trove of Arabic and Persian literature."[81]

The journal was not exaggerating. Sprenger merits special discussion, because he becomes one of the most important agents of acquisition, collation, and then transportation of the largest collection of literary and scientific works in Urdu, Farsi, Arabic, and Hindustani to a European nation. Sprenger was born in 1813 in the Austro-Hungarian Empire, in a small village of Nassereith near Innsbruck in Tirol. His father was a toll-tax collector. He studied Arabic, Persian, and Turkish at the University of Vienna (1832–1836) with the leading translator Joseph von Hammer-Purgstall (1774–1856), whose translations of Hafiz were read by Goethe. Despite Hammer-Purgstall's support, Sprenger was denied a university position at the Viennese Oriental Academy, so he went to England and is supposed to have helped the Earl of Munster (1749–1842), president of the Royal Asiatic Society, with his project on the history of Mongol invasions in India.

Sprenger became a British citizen in 1838, and then—it is not clear whether through the sponsorship of the Earl of Munster—he went to Leiden (Netherlands) to study medicine and wrote his dissertation on medical history in the Arab world. As a doctor of medicine, Sprenger had the necessary qualifications to be sent to India as an assistant surgeon in the service of the British East India Company, and he arrived at Fort William (Calcutta) on September 2, 1843.[82] Sprenger's expertise in fields beyond medicine opened new avenues for him to pursue his primary interest in Oriental literatures. On March 6, 1845, he was appointed the principal of Delhi College, a premier institution that had its beginnings in the late seventeenth or early eighteenth century as a Madrasa with Persian and Arabic as languages of instruction. Starting in 1825, it was established as a British college with classes offered in English as well.[83]

Delhi College, which some historians consider modern and advanced for its time due to its pedagogical innovations (especially in Farsi literature) and its strong Vernacular Translation Society (since 1827), seems to have been a good fit for Sprenger, who introduced *One Thousand and One Nights* and *Kalilā-wa-Dimnā* to the college's Arabic syllabus. Within two years of his principalship, Sprenger was appointed as a temporary "extra-assistant" to the British resident of Lucknow for the purpose of preparing a catalog of the royal libraries of Awadh. Sprenger had several other important positions with the East India company, including principal of the Calcutta Madrasa (1850) and Persian translator of the Government of India (1850). But it is his position as the official cataloger of the libraries of Awadh that makes him an important and passionate bibliophile, albeit, as I am about to show, with suspicious intentions—the creator of a world literary bibliograph of Arabic, Persian, and Hindustani texts *and* a dubious agent of bibliomigrancy.

The first volume of Sprenger's *Catalogue* was published in Calcutta in 1854. As Sprenger writes in the preface, he worked on cataloging the libraries of Awadh for two years (1848–1850). During this time, he examined ten thousand volumes.[84] In the preface to the *Catalogue*, Sprenger gives a historical account of the libraries in Awadh, their upkeep, and the modes of their maintenance. He mentions that many of the works are in duplicate, because the librarians (*daroghas* or custodians) are concerned more with maintaining numbers and not the content of the books. He discusses the establishment of lithographic presses and the transformation from rote learning to learning through texts that underwent an expansion in India. The annotated bibliography he provides consists of twelve chapters, with a few thousand major and minor poets and scholars from the entire Persian- and Arabic-speaking world as well as poets of Rekhtah—a hybrid language with Persian, Arabic, and various forms of Hindi developing alongside Urdu in India—spanning over six hundred pages in the volume. This is an important document of world literature that evidences the circulation of literary texts from Baghdad, Isphahan, Ghazni, Khorasan, Cairo, and many others to—in this case—Lucknow. However, a European city with no direct colonial administrative relationship to India becomes added to this list of cities, and it must be discussed, because it is through Sprenger that an entire contingent of world literary artifacts finds a new home in another royal library—in Berlin.

Following the publication of the *Catalogue* in 1854, Sprenger traveled to various countries in the Middle East. Upon his return to India in July 1856, he was charged with dishonoring a financial commitment made to Boutros, the former principal of the Delhi College, and removed from all his civil appointments,[85] forcing Sprenger to return to Germany—but not empty-handed.

In 1857, upon his return to Germany, Sprenger published *Bibliotheca Orientalis Sprengeriana*,[86] a catalogue of his personal collection of about two thousand manuscripts. The preface to this volume is much harsher and bitterer than the one to the *Catalogue* (1854). In it Sprenger mentions his years of service in India and his travels to Egypt, Syria, and Iraq during which he "visited every library, public or private, to which [he] could obtain access, [he] examined every book [he] could lay hold of, [he] spared no expense to secure a good manuscript," and claims even to have agents who acquired books for him from the holy centers of Mecca and Medinah

(*CBOS*, iii). Sprenger declares that he collected books not out of a "childish bibliomania" but out of "a sense of duty" (*CBOS*, iv). Akin to Macaulay, he states: "I admit that the literature of the East has no intrinsic value . . . it contains few facts, if any . . . even in poetry and philosophy, Oriental works contain few sentiments and ideas which we can admire or would like to adopt. Nevertheless it deserves to be cultivated" (*CBOS*, iv). The reasons for the cultivation of this literature, Sprenger states, lie in its history, which is longer than that of European literature, and its ability to help one expand beyond the "narrow limits of European prejudices and associations" (*CBOS*, iv). Sprenger swings like a pendulum between his praise of Oriental literature—which belongs to his collection—and his disgust for the Oriental destruction of books. On the one hand, Sprenger praises the veneration of knowledge—especially in the case of religious texts—which he witnessed in his travels through the East. On the other hand, it is not a lack of veneration but the "apathy and imbicility" of the Orientals that he claims is the reason for the neglect and disrespect of books by the general population in the East. Sprenger blames the Orientals for "an erroneous view of their own literature," for their inability to recognize the significance of "bags and bags of old leaves of the most valuable volumes" (*CBOS*, iv). From India, all the way to Lebanon, he mentions the existence of books not on bookshelves but in large heaps or in trunks where they coexist with rats. Under these circumstances, he declares, "the duty of taking care of the patrimony of our eastern brethren devolves upon the enlightened public of Europe, and every man who finds an opportunity ought to secure as many good books as he can" (*CBOS*, iii). Having made a case for his mass acquisition of books, Sprenger highlights the features of his collection, which he claims contains the "complete knowledge of habits, life, and literature of Asia," represented through "manuscripts, but also books that have been issued through Musulman presses" (*CBOS*, iv). In sum, he claims that his is the most complete of all collections, and his private library is equivalent to the best collections in Europe.

Sprenger was not exaggerating. The two thousand volumes he had managed to bring with him included many rare manuscripts, such as Yaqut al-Hamawi's part geographical dictionary, part literary history, *Mu'jam al-buldan* (ca. 1228), and copies of works of some of the most well-known authors, including the Indian Sufi Amir Khusrow (1253–1325). The works listed in the *Bibliotheca Orientalis Sprengeriana* included 267 works of Arabic poetry and prose (*CBOS*, 69–77), 165 works of Persian poetry (*CBOS*, 77–84), 11 translations of Sanksrit works into Persian and Hindustani (*CBOS*, 90–91), 96 works of Hindustani literature (*CBOS*, 91–96), and several hundred aesthetic, grammatical, logical, medical, geographical, historical, astronomical, and encyclopedic volumes in Arabic, Persian, Urdu, and Chaghatai Turkish. As Hars Kurio aptly notes in his brief but insightful analysis of the Arabic Manuscripts of the *Bibliotheca Orientalis Sprengeriana*: "The emergence of the 'Bibliotheca Orientalis Sprengeriana' is embedded in a specific historical situation in Europe; both intellectual history—the rise of Oriental studies, romanticism—as well as political and economic factors are relevant here. The creation of this collection is incomprehensible without the intellectual-historical and political developments, in which it is woven."[87] Kurio does not provide information on the political conditions in which Sprenger "acquired" his collection. Were all these volumes acquired through legal and legitimate means? Or was Sprenger a book thief? One cannot say for sure, even when Sprenger takes for granted his borrowing privileges in the libraries that he visited. His acquisition process does not seem to disturb his employers in India or, for that matter, the purchasers of his collection in Berlin. However, the story of the acquisition of the *Bibliotheca Orientalis Sprengeriana* by the Reichsbibliothek in Berlin was itself not free of controversy. As documented in the files "Sprenger, Seine Sammlung" (Sprenger Collection files; figure 2-1) housed today at the Staatsbibliothek zu Berlin, the long-drawn process of acquisition

Figure 2-1. Cover of the Sprenger Collection files of Oriental manuscripts: "Sprenger, Seine Sammlung," Acta III B 49, 1857. (Courtesy of Staatsbibliothek zu Berlin.)

reveals the same competition for Oriental manuscripts between the Munich and Berlin royal libraries as seen in the description of Othmar Frank in chapter 1.

As Dr. Karl Halm, director of the Staatsbibliothek in Munich reported, his correspondence with Sprenger began around the time the news of Sprenger's collection was published—on February 9, 1857—in a newspaper based in Weinheim. Halm wrote to him on February 13 expressing interest in buying his collection; he also offered him a position at the library, thinking that someone who acquired this collection with so much love would hardly be ready to part with it.[88] In his own *Denkschrift* against Halm, Sprenger claimed that he did not want to sell it before it arrived in Hamburg, because he had yet to decide where he would finally settle.[89] Sprenger asked for fifty thousand Dutch gulden for his collection, to which Halm agreed on the condition of the collection's appraisal upon its arrival in Hamburg. Both parties agreed to these terms in principle, as also documented by Sprenger. A sum of money was advanced by the library in Munich, but a series of misunderstandings and accusations started in April 1857 when Sprenger was approached by Dr. Pinder, director of the Reichsbibliothek in Berlin. Halm claimed that Sprenger's collection did not tally with the inventory of items he had provided; Sprenger claimed otherwise, stating that Berlin was ready to offer him the asked price for his collection. The case was brought to an arbitration tribunal in Heidelberg that decided in favor of Sprenger, and the collection was bought by the Reichsbibliothek. The news of acquisition of the Sprenger Collection—1,515 manuscripts, 558 lithohraphs, and 2 stone tablets with cuneiform script—was published in the *Preussische Staatsanzeiger* on September 2, 1857, on the same page that carried the news of the "Indian Revolt" of 1857.[90]

The huge number of foreign works acquired by the Reichsbibliothek in the form of *Bibliotheca Sprengeriana* was not immediately open to the public. However, not far from Berlin, in the book city of Leipzig, another development was taking place, which would heavily emphasize the access of world literature in translation to its readers in affordable editions, a development that would change the face of world literary circulation in Germany far beyond the nineteenth century.

Hall of Fame: Reclam's Universal-Bibliothek

In 1828, a young man of twenty-one years called Anton Phillip Reclam (1807–1896) borrowed three thousand thaler from his father and bought a lending library called Literarisches Museum on the Grimmaische Strasse in Leipzig. The libray contained "the latest in German, French, English, and Italian literature" and had a reading room with about seventy-eight newspapers and magazines.[91] Reclam sold the Literarisches Museum in 1837 and founded the Philipp Reclam jun. Verlag with the plan to publish contemporary and classical literature, entertainment literature, as well as left-liberal political writings, which would continue for the next decade, especially around the political turmoil of 1848.[92] The turning point came in 1858 when Reclam published a twelve-volume *Complete Works of Shakespeare*—by twelve different translators—at half the price (1.5 thaler for the collected works) of other available editions. The edition was so popular that it went into fifth and sixth editions within the second year of its publication and turned Reclam into a major player within the publishing landscape of the German-speaking world.[93] To continue the marketing success of these translations, Reclam introduced individual dramas of Shakespeare in paperback in 1865 at a price of two groschen apiece.[94]

Reclam's rise to the ranks of a leading publisher came at a time of landmark change within the German publishing industry. German-language publishers had fully accepted the benefits of the free trade enterprise introduced in 1810, and technological innovations in typesetting and binding had opened up new possibilities for the publishing industry. The growth of literacy had created new markets of readership that resulted in the expansion of booksellers and publishers: between 1840 and 1865 the number of firms trading in books (publishing and sale) had doubled. Starting in 1867, the *Börsenblatt für den deutschen Buchhandel*, the most important trade paper for the book industry, was published on all business days. Most importanly, on November 9, 1867, works of German authors who died before 1837 went out of copyright and became the "common property of the nation" ("Gemeingut der Nation").[95] Many publishers were preparing for the upcoming change and so was Reclam.

The commercial success of the Shakespeare edition gave birth to the idea of a series that would be universal in scope—it would include titles from German literature and from other national literatures in German translations—and reach; the editions would be cheap and therefore affordable to interested readers from all classes of society. And so on November 10, 1867, Reclam's Universal-Bibliothek series was launched with Goethe's *Faust. Eine Tragödie* (*Faust Part I*) as the first title. Along with German translations of Shakespeare, Reclam published canonical German authors such as Gotthold Ephraim Lessing, Friedrich Schiller, and Jean Paul. The publishing house was cashing in on the growing reading public with its volumes priced so low that Anton Philipp acquired the nickname "Groschenreclam" in the publishing industry.[96]

Anton Philipp's vision was energized further when his son Hans Heinrich Reclam joined the firm. While the commerical nature of the venture can hardly be denied, the intellectual impetus came from left-liberal rebels of Young Germany. As the Reclam historian Dietrich Bode notes, Universal-Bibliothek was geared toward an "enormous construction of a library of world literature,"[97] each with a uniquely assigned Reclam Universal-Bibliothek (RUB) number. Drama became the preferred genre in the first steps toward building this library. Along with Shakespeare, Spanish (Agustín Moreto y Cavana's *Donna Diana*, Pedro Calderón's *La Vida es Sueño*) and French (Racine's *Phèdre*, Moliére's *L'École des Maris*) dramas were the first to be published by Reclam.[98]

Reclam thus very much relied on the idea of "masterpieces." There is no doubt that the Universal-Bibliothek was a world literary library of already established national canons. While the editions were cheap, the purpose was loftier. There was a growing sense of educating the public through national and world literatures. As Bode observes, ancient Greek and Latin authors, philosophers, and historians, along with the German classical works, came to and continue to embody the "humanist educational ideal," and therefore the centerpiece of Universal-Bibliothek's publication agenda.[99] Johann Heinrich Voss's translations of Virgil's *Aeneid* and Homer's *Illiad* and *Odyssee* were some of the first works to be published in the year leading up to German unification.[100] On the one hand, Reclam's program for non-European "Oriental" literatures relied on the name recognition of famous works and authors. On the other hand, it also benefited from the growing number of translations into German, partially also due to the activities of the Deutsche Morgenländische Gesellschaft. These included Ludwig Fritzes's translations of Kalidasa's *Vikramorvashiyam* and *Mālavikāgnimitra*, and Bhavabhuti's *Mālatimādhava*.[101] Kalidasa's *Sakuntala* was published twice: once as Alfred von Wolzogen's "free" interpretation for stage to mark Reclam's inaugural publication of Indian literature,[102] and then as Hermann Camillo Kellner's new translation of *Sakuntala*,[103] released to mark the centennial of Georg Forster's German translation of the play.

Parallel to—or in spite of—the rise of significance of national literature after 1871, Reclam continued to expand its publication of non-German works in translation. And the publishing agenda was slowly turning from canonical works from antiquity or early modern periods to translations of contemporary literatures. Henry Wadsworth Longfellow's *The Song of Hiawatha* became the first American work to be published in the

Universal-Bibliothek series,[104] followed by Pushkin's *Prisoner of the Causasus* and *Eugene Onegin*.[105] In fact, Russian and Scandinavian literatures signified Universal-Bibliothek's most sustained engagement with world literary contemporaneity. Alexander Turgenev's works, such as *King Lear of the Steppe* and *Fathers and Sons*,[106] were published in the 1880s, probably also because of his connections with German authors such as Theodor Storm and Heyse. These were followed by works of Gogol, Tolstoi, Gorki, and Chekhov in quick succession.[107] Henrik Ibsen's *Pillars of Society* marked the beginning of Reclam's publication of his plays;[108] by 1893 Reclam had published eighteen plays by Ibsen, gaining the status of "Ibsen-publishers."[109]

While Reclam's unique contribution to the expansion of the circulation of world literature cannot be denied, especially in the unified Germany at the end of the nineteenth century, there is no doubt that a growing body of readership already existed. Reclam contributed to increasing that readership in a time when national literature was regaining importance. One last example will suffice to illustrate this change from the first to the second half of the nineteenth century.

In 1832, the year Goethe died, a literary journal called *Das Magazin für die Literatur des Auslandes* was founded in Berlin by Joseph Lehmann.[110] Much like the *Blätter für literarische Unterhaltung*, *Das Magazin* identified the larger public as its target readership and was published three times a week. The articles were organized under geolinguistic rubrics covering all major European literatures as well as literatures from East-India, North America, the Orient (China, Japan, and Korea) and Egypt (mostly covering literatures in Arabic). In addition, every issue featured a section on "German Literature Abroad" ("Deutsche Literatur im Auslande"), highlighting the publication of German-language fiction, drama, newspapers, but also lexicons and dictionaries in migrant communities such as the United States.

With its fiftieth anniversary issue (January 1881), the magazine changed its name. From a journal dedicated primarily to literatures in foreign languages, it included domestic literature in its title and became *Das Magazin für die Literatur des In- und Auslandes: Kritisches Organ der Weltliteratur*.[111] Eduard Engel—literary critic, linguist, and later editor of an anthology on world literature—became the new editor.[112] While all the other historical features were retained, a new expanded section on Germany titled "Deutschland" was added to the journal. The editorial foreword promised that the magazine was "not in service of any political party"[113] and was meant to provide all readers access to "all significant phenomena and currents of all literatures,"[114] including German literature: "The magazine vouches that the educated reader should have knowledge of that which is meaningful, created in literary nations on both sides of the ocean. That the literary movement in Germany and the neighboring countries will be given special attention, needs no explanation."[115]

The lead article, "Weltliteratur und Humanität," was authored by well-known German-Jewish poet and writer Berthold Auerbach (Moyses Baruch Auerbach, 1812–1882).[116] Auerbach starts the article by stating that the idea of humanity as proposed by Lessing and Herder was appended by Goethe through his idea of world literature but laments what he sees as a dwindling in the currency of the word *humanity* ("Humanität") in the late nineteenth century. Humanity, he reports, has been transformed in the late nineteenth century by extreme spirits ("Starkgeister") into an expression of softness ("Weichlichkeit"), sweetness ("Süsslichkeit"), and sentimentality ("Sentimentalität").[117] Speaking in the context of a rising materialist thought within the society on the one hand and realpolitik on the other, Auerbach identifies the question of power ("Machtfrage") as it has acquired central stage in individual as well as social lives. It is in this rise of the question of power that Auerbach gives currency to the word *human*, describing it as an act of putting oneself in other conditions of existence ("sich in andere Daseinsbedingungen zu versetzen").[118] Identifying language as the main distinguishing element between humans and other animals, Auerbach states that "the division of human beings through languages does not dissolve the unity of human beings, it is given much more life-content through it."[119] It is in this context of a power-infested and divisive politics—between a borderless humanity and a nationally defined public based on language—that Auerbach presents his understanding of world literature: "World literature! It would be unfair if it were named together with the utopia of a world empire and a world language. For world literature already exists and is growing more and more, regardless that in our time peoples are collecting themselves even more strongly within [themselves] and perhaps because of that."[120] Underlining the significance of nationally and historically conditioned forms of expression ("Erscheinungsformen"), Auerbach declares the unity of world literature in its diversity: "The truth is the united, but the truthfulness is the diversity of its appearance. The innermost being of the genius is truthfulness—subjective, national, timely—and what emanates from truthfulness, that lives and has an effect later."[121]

Auerbach was aware that it would be erroneous to expect from world literature to give expression to something that is universally human ("allgemein menschlich"), that a work does not carry a signature of its spatial or temporal origin. Instead, he argues that the more physignomically recognizable the appearance is, the purer the diversity of the countenance, and more willingly is it understood by foreign nations and other times. Calling Shakespeare and Walter Scott national authors who were received by all nations and referring to *Faust*, *Nathan the Wise*, and *Wilhelm Tell* as the greatest works of German literature that are becoming a "property of the world" ("Weltbesitz"), Auerbach ends his essay with the coda: "The essence and concept of world literature is not uniformity, but rather the accord of different notes towards world harmony."[122]

It is this particular story of world literature that unfolds in the German-speaking space in the second half of the nineteenth century: marked by a growing consciousness in materialist conceptions of class relations and society on the one hand, and a growing understanding of the materialist dimensions of the intellectual market on the other. In addition, the forces of nation building, the advent of the unified German nation, and a growing sense of national self-recognition give rise to a complicated but very interesting text in which world literature ceases to be merely a philosophical ideal emanating from the Enlightenment concept of a universal humanity but, in fact, aligns itself more with the national in its examination of the universal. World literature thus acquires a more public and more political appearance. Both within the theory and in practice, world literature now emerges as a space where the universally human is staged through the national, where the universal unity is imagined only through national particularity. This ideational composition of world literature is evident—even when it cannot always be called a direct consequence of it—in the practice of publishing world literature in German translation as the "national" literature of foreign countries. The effort to augment and forefront the national also comes in the form of the first efforts to establish a national library.

The May 21, 1881, issue of *Das Magazin* published a petition by the executive council (Vorstand) of the Association of German Authors (Allgemeine Deutsche Schriftstellerband). Signed in Leipzig on March 30, 1881, the petition was addressed to the Reich's Chancellor Otto von Bismarck, asking for the establishment of a German Imperial Library (Deutsche Reichsbibliothek) as a hall of fame (*Ruhmeshalle*) of German intellectual achievements.[123]

In its prefactory note to the petition, the magazine refered to an "evil" which should have been long removed in the land of authors and thinkers if the government's concern about the intellectual superpower-standing of Germany were to become even just a miniscule part of the protection of the material outlook of the country.[124] The petition itself starts by underlining the significance of libraries for the intellectual culture of the German people and then moves quickly to outline a print-cultural portrayal of Germany. The signatories go a bit overboard in declaring "every writing that has appeared in print: from the most encompassing scientific work to the smallest of an ephemeral pamphlet" as representative of the expression of the intellectual life of the nation and as a cultural-historical witness of the moment.[125] To illustrate their point, the signatories mention the donation by Kaiser Wilhelm I of all documents related to the Franco-Prussian war to the Royal Library in Berlin.

The petitioners make a case for a change in the perception of libraries and their function as they also present a review of how libraries functioned in the past. They ask for a change in the agenda of libraries, specifically, a freedom from the intellectual bias of librarians. The acquisition and collection within a library was a function of the decisions made by the librarians; they collected what they thought was the best. The petitioners want this process to be replaced by an objective one. They ask for change by mentioning that a library should not just acquire objects according to what is readable but also that which is produced. A library was so far a workshop where specific tools were stored in order to produce specific things. But it was never the purpose to produce the knowledge of the national spirit ("Volksgeist") and its history, and no one needed the means for it. Now the literary production of a time becomes its intellectual consciousness.[126]

The petitioners further compare the cultural significance of this library project with other state-funded German projects, such as the archeological project in Rome and the excavation in Olympia, among others. As role models for such a library they list the national libraries in Paris and Washington, DC, and the English libraries, whereby every theater brochure, every ticket, every little piece concerning Shakespeare can be consulted if one were doing research on it. In addition, they also mention libraries in England, Italy, Austria, and the United States, where free copies of every publication by law must be sent to the national library for its collection.

This particular petition demonstrates the acceptance of the changing role of books and of libraries that was manifest in Germany by the end of the nineteenth century. Fueling this growing consciousness was the self-image of the nation—now unified—as a nation of thinkers and authors. There was also an added value attached to the institution of national literature, especially *belles lettres*, which, according to the petitioners, had not been given the all-encompassing attention that it deserved.

If public libraries, meaning university or research libraries (*Gelehrten Bibliotheken*) during the first half of the nineteenth century bore marks of the individual niche that the library or its patrons had created for themselves, by the end of the nineteenth century it was about to change to depict literature on a national level. In addition, a close look at the petition reveals that all printed matter—everything that appears in print—rather than as manuscript, is now promoted as the witness to or evidence of national intellectual life. Books become the victorious trophies of a nation, deserving their own hall of fame. They cease to be tools from which other products can be generated. Consequently, libraries cease to be workshops where other products are manufactured through the existing tools; libraries become the showcases of a workshop, the display cabinet for national memory. In short, through both anthologizing and the development of academic societies, the acquisition, distribution, and circulation of non-German literatures continues. Sometimes this activity is categorically labeled world literature and, at other times, merely as literatures from the world. That this period is marked also by censorship and impediments to the circulation of local and national literature makes it even more interesting: the second half of the nineteenth century in Germany is a time when the forces of nation-building exert their influence on the construction of both national and world literature.

Half Epic, Half Drastic: From Cosmopolitanism to Nationalism

The picture of world literature in the German-speaking world in the post-Goethean age is very complex. Nationalist sentiments coexist with cosmopolitan ideas. Anti-Semitism, as well as an out-and-open racial stereotyping of the Orientals and their literature, their reading habits and their sheer ignorance of book culture punctuate the larger text of world literature. While Heine, Marx, and Engels, and later proponents of the programmatic publications of world literature like Reclam's Universal-Bibliothek, promote a cosmopolitan view of literature, there are "birthers" in the business of national literature who deem anything foreign as dangerous to the national, and anything non-Christian and critical of the nation as unpatriotic and worthy of being written out of the text of the nation. The concept of the "national" library that is constructed is the library primarily of works by white Christian authors.

The empire of books that started taking shape in the German-speaking world in the early nineteenth century found its competitor in a national parliament of letters in a united German nation. The anti-Semitic nationalism of Arndt and others would acquire a much stronger form in the twentieth century. The *Lebensraum* concept would fuel the way to an empire built on military might and assumed racial superiority. Step by step, the Jewish dimension of German culture would be annihilated; and book collection would be replaced by book burning.

No one understood this better than Heinrich Heine. Unlike Aloys Sprenger, who considered that the destruction of books or engaging in their willful neglect was a special prerogative of non-European, Eastern brethren, Heine had a different opinion. In *Wintermärchen*, he could declare that his ideas, his books, the library he carried in his head, was the most dangerous item he had when he crossed borders. On the other hand, he also knew that the European Christian brethren had the equal pleasure of destroying books when it came to political and intellectual occupation.

This chapter started with a discussion of the homecoming of an exiled subject in Heine's *Wintermärchen*. In closing, I turn to one of his earliest works, *Almansor: Eine Tragödie* (1823). Set in 1492, the play refracts the question of assimilation into the majority culture through the issue of religious conversion; the Christianization of Islamic and Jewish subjects is part of the administrative mission of the Conquistadors. The prologue introduces the play as "half epic, half drastic."[127] Almansor, son of an Arab exile, returns to his homeland Granada to witness the cultural horror initiated by the Spaniards. As Almansor examines his abandoned house, he runs into his childhood friend Hassan, who reports to him about the burning of books in Andalusia. The tyranny of monocultural solidarity expresses its wrath upon books—copies of the Holy Koran are being burned, Hassan explains to him, adding, "it was just a foreplay, there, where one burns books, in the end human beings are burned."[128]

When the Jewish-German author Berthold Auerbach pleaded for the diversity of perspective in the time of nationalist power and asked for looking at world literature as a way of understanding "other conditions of existence," he did not know what was in store in the next century. What happens in the field of world literature, books, and libraries in the second half of the nineteenth century could indeed be considered a half epic, half drastic foreplay for many things to come. First books, and in the end, human beings would be burned, demanding a new meaning of the world and world literature.

Oslo
Stockholm
St. Petersberg
Copenhagen
Klaipeda
Weimar
Berlin
Warsaw
London
Munich
Nuremberg
Zurich
Budapest
Montagnola
Belgrade
Madrid
Zagreb
Ljubljana
Tucson
Calcutta
Thalassery
Bamako
Canberra

CHAPTER 3

The Shadow of Empty Shelves: Two World Wars and the Rise and Fall of World Literature

Before the masterworks seek to prove their worth to us, we must have proven our worth to them.

—HERMANN HESSE, "A Library of World Literature" (1929)[1]

To pursue world literature is to honor the masters. To honor the masters is to mobilize that which is most powerful in the world for oneself.

—LIEUTENANT SIGMUND GRAFF, "Germanness and World Literature" (1940)[2]

In Thomas Mann's novella *Tonio Kröger* (1903), the protagonist Tonio Kröger, son of a wealthy industrialist northern German father and a mother of "foreign origins" decides to move to Italy, away from the stifling lifestyle of his bourgeois family in northern Germany. Later in life, as a successful author, he is overcome by the desire to travel back to his hometown. Upon his arrival, Kröger finds his way to his parents' home. He enters the house, walks up the once familiar staircase, and then stops on the landing, because he sees a sign that says "Public Library." He is astonished, for he feels "that neither the public nor literature had any business being here."[3] Kröger's interaction with the librarian amplifies his bewilderment: "'So this is the public library? Would you permit me to have a look at the collection?' . . . 'Certainly; it is open to everyone.'"[4]

Tonio Kröger was published at the beginning of the twentieth century when Germany, united as a nation-state in 1871, had already experienced two decades of the Second Reich. At the time of the story's publication, the Third Reich—one of the darkest hours of human history—was still thirty years away. While power imbalances in Europe had already rendered the political fabric of Europe fragile in the late nineteenth century, the idea of the world coming together and being divided and destroyed under the aegis of war—not once, but twice, in which Germany would play a central role—might have appeared unthinkable even to the most stringent *Realpolitiker*. And no one had imagined that a return to one's home, not just for an author, but for anyone forced into exile—not for art, but for race, ethnicity, religion, politics, or sexual orientation—would be a return to a drastically transformed space. Through a culture of political domination and control, what was once intimate and private would turn into a public spectacle. The manipulation of books and other print media, as well as libraries, to serve the ideological purposes of a totalitarian regime would turn the returnee's former life into a public space "open to everyone."

The homecoming scene from Mann's *Tonio Kröger* captures the time around 1900, when book culture in Germany undergoes a renewal: book production, magazine and newspaper publishing, and the establishment of public libraries is on the rise. Further advancements in print technology, the cheap availability of paper, and the rise of literacy rates during a period of political and financial stability reinvigorate a culture of reading whereby the printed material becomes the creator and facilitator of many cultural movements.[5] The thriving book culture was also instrumental in the increase in the number of private libraries, not only among the intellectual elite but also among the bourgeoisie. In addition, the Kaiserreich's investment in public access to knowledge resulted in the rise of the public libraries (*Volksbibliotheken*).

This scene also uncannily anticipates the time when the word *Volk* would cease to signify collective residents of a national terrain; it would move closer to meaning a discriminating collective defined primarily by race and religion. This would be a time when the term *Volksbibliothek* would be fractured, when Germany would become a space where the association of the public with a library, or the public with literature, would be subject to extreme state scrutiny. There would be no unsupervised room for people or literature; the idea of the world and world literature would be appropriated by the Nazis in the shadow of the *Lebensraum*, massive book burnings would be organized to destroy the culture of books, and the stature of the political nation would assume new meaning in the compound noun *Büchernation*.

What was the face of world literature in Germany during the first half of the twentieth century? How did the pre- and interwar periods correspond to an awareness of books and world literature? What was the effect of the establishment of the Nobel Prize on the perception of world literature in Europe in general, and Germany in particular? How did National Socialist literary politics mobilize the concept of world literature to promote its own agenda? To what extent was literature and literary recognition renationalized by the Nazis? What role did the Nazi policies on institutions of disseminating world literature—books, libraries, publishers, and the translation enterprise—play in transforming the shape of world literature from the beginning of the twentieth century to the third and fourth decades?

These questions are central to this chapter and would be best approached if located within the following historical markers: the period of internal stability and prosperity in the unified nation-state of Germany, which also leads to the establishment of a German national library (Die deutsche Bücherei) in Leipzig in 1913; the inflation and insecurity during the Weimar Republic, which does not necessarily prevent efforts to internationalize the literary space, especially beyond the borders of Europe; and the rise of National Socialism, which reinstates a nationalism of German literature with the censoring of ideas and the burning of books, especially by German-Jewish authors. Before we arrive at an examination of the idea of world literature, it would be beneficial to look at how the very mediality of the book is constructed and perceived in the German-speaking world in the early twentieth century. Walter Benjamin, who apart from being a journalist and essayist was a translator and book collector, serves as an excellent interlocutor.

Order and Chaos: Walter Benjamin on Books and Libraries

Walter Benjamin's writings on the many new media in the twentieth century covered a wide range of topics: film, advertisement, radio plays, newspapers, magazines, and even the telephone. But it is in his writings on books that his understanding of the medium appears with quintessential wit and playfulness. From commentaries on bestsellers and masterpieces, to renowned French authors such as Charles Baudelaire and André Gide, to classical European authors from Cervantes to Goethe, Benjamin was very aware of the media through which literature is accessed. Especially in the last years of the Weimar Republic (1928–1932), he published several essays on books. Apart from his essays on the dime novels of the nineteenth century, children's books, and reading trends among Germans during the time of the writing of German classics, Benjamin wrote two very intimate reflections on books: "No. 13: Books and Prostitutes" (1928) and the better-known essay "Unpacking My Library" (1931).[6]

"Books and Prostitutes" is a collection of thirteen "theses"—provocations would be the best word to describe them, due to their satirical and playful nature. Benjamin starts with citations from Marcel Proust and Stéphane Mallarmé and proceeds to establish relationships among three sets of entities: the book and its reader, the prostitute and the customer, and books and prostitutes. The opening thesis: "One can take books and prostitutes in bed" (1) illustrates this intimacy; books and prostitutes become agents of the shrinkage of time (2); they have an unfortunate relationship with each other (due to the lack of literacy) (4); they have their own specific (male) clientele (5); they live in public houses for students (6); they tend to disappear before they are over (7); they love to turn their backs toward their readers or customers (9); they rejuvenate their users (10); they carry their trials and tribulations in public (12); and what is a footnote for one, is a money bill in the stocking for the other (13).[7] Thesis 8, the longest of all, explains the narrative qualities of books and prostitutes: "Books and prostitutes narrate as eagerly and insincerely, as [eager and insincere] they have become. In fact, they often do not notice it all. One follows them for years 'out of love' and one day one stands like a large body in the red-light district, which, 'for the purpose of studying' hangs about only for that [love]."[8] With the personification of books and their comparison to prostitutes, Benjamin establishes the transactional nature of book acquisition and reading: the cost of entertainment, the possibility of addiction, a predilection for falling in love, and a guaranteed self-manipulation of the reader or client through surrender to the object of his desire. Yet, it is not merely the subject that chooses the object of his entertainment who defines the objectivity and utility of the object. The object itself exerts pressure and influence over the subject to transform the subject's subjectivity. The material and the intellectual dimensions of the object of desire thus inform a reader's relationship to the book, much as a client's to a prostitute; and although for the prostitute or book, the interaction with the client or reader might not always be a matter of choice, for the client or reader it is.

Benjamin's playful reflections on books and prostitutes acquire a more serious intimacy in his essay "Unpacking My Library." Written on the occasion of moving into a new, partially furnished apartment due to his divorce from his wife Dora,[9] Benjamin's essay on the library extends the spirit of mutual transformation of the consumer and the consumed, the subject and the object, the collector and the collected. And Benjamin locates such transformative forces between the tedious agony of organization and collation, and the euphoric ecstasy of acquiring books. Benjamin begins his essay with a declaration of an act: the act of unpacking his books before they find their places on bookshelves. He invites his readers to join the chaos of a library that is dispersed in crates and on the floor, a library that has not taken the form of what is associated with the word: an orderly arrangement of books on display. Benjamin associates this dispersed, strewn about disorderliness with the chaotic energy of the passion for book collecting. Benjamin's essay is thus not about the collection itself; he states: "Would it not be presumptuous of me if, in order to appear convincingly objective and down-to-earth, I enumerated for you the main sections or the prize pieces of a library, if I presented you with their history or even their usefulness to a writer? . . . ; what I am really concerned with is giving you some insight into the relationship of a book collector to his possessions, to collecting, rather than the collection."[10]

Arbitrary modes, rather than exact knowledge, randomness of passion, rather than the programmatic energy of rationalism thus set the tone for Benjamin's reflections. Citing Anatole France, Benjamin attests that the "only exact knowledge there is, is the knowledge of the date of publication and the format of the books." The collector exists in a "dialectical tension between the poles of order and disorder." What informs his own text, his own recounting of the act of collecting books, as they stay strewn around in his apartment, is a distinct dialectical tension between "fate" and "freedom." Counterbalancing this tension, as Benjamin further proposes, is the torque of "memory" that resounds in the very act of collecting. Benjamin draws a direct connection between remembering and book collecting: "Every passion borders on the chaotic, but the collector's passion borders on the chaos of memories." Immediately following this line is a comment on fate: "More than that, the chance, the fate that has suffused the past before my eyes is conspicuously present in the accustomed confusion of these books." To collect is to reconstruct the past, "to renew the old age." But that renewal is dependent on the fate of an object as it is taken from one's collection and becomes part of someone else's. The person who acquires it accumulates a sense of freedom in receiving, borrowing, or even purloining a work from someone else's collection, in order to give a new meaning to the object in the new collection. This is where the art of collecting books becomes a question of accessibility to them, which Benjamin further connects with the act of writing. Having declared earlier that "Collectors are physiognomists of objects,"[11] Benjamin states—drawing on the example of Jean Paul's protagonist in *Schulmeisterlein Wutz* (1790), who wrote books that he could not afford—"Writers are really people who write books not because they are poor, but because they are dissatisfied with books they could buy but do not like."[12] This is a remarkable shift in Benjamin's essay. His recollection of cities where he acquired specific books, catalogues that informed him of particular books, and memories of coming across those catalogues all become part of the action of collection. In the specific kind of physiognomic exercise carried out by collectors, many moments of chance are involved: the chance of coming across a particularly treasured object, the chance of having that object available for purchase, the chance that the object will actually be acquired by the collector. Benjamin's reflections on fate and memory culminate in a sense of a peculiar kind of freedom that for him is associated with the act of collecting: "One of the finest memories of a collector is the moment when he rescued a book to which he might never have given a thought, much less a wishful look, because he found it lonely and abandoned on the market place and bought it and gave it its freedom—the way the prince bought a beautiful slave-girl in the Arabian Nights. To a book collector, you see, the true freedom of all books is somewhere on his shelf."[13]

It is hard to miss the gendered political tension that is part of Benjamin's imagination of the freedom that involves the particular "rescuing" of books. The personal library—a confined space—can hardly be seen as a site of freedom from the openness of a market; the condescension invoked by the emancipation of a beautiful slave girl by a prince similarly implies a further exploitation of sexualized labor. Acknowledging these tensions actually helps in identifying the ineluctable power dynamic that is an essential part of any library, private or public. Libraries are founded upon the collector's sense of an epistemic privilege, a desire to grant an object a new meaning, function, and ambition. It is hardly a surprise that in Benjamin's essay, the thrill of collecting, the excitement of acquiring a new and less-circulated item, the heroic sense of purchasing "freedom" for an "enslaved" book and granting it emancipation on one's own shelf, is also accompanied toward the end by the sense that a collector's work might never really be recognized during his lifetime, "but, as Hegel put it, only when it is dark does the owl of Minerva begin its flight, only in extinction is the collector comprehended."[14]

Benjamin's essay calls upon its readers to focus on many issues, especially on the dialectical relationship between order and chaos. But what the reader cannot miss is the dialectical tension between dissemination (*Zerstreuung*) and accumulation (*Sammlung*). The entire act of collection simultaneously becomes an act of de-collection, of anticipating a collection. At the center of Benjamin's essay is a personal library, which becomes a reflection of the collector's inclinations, proclivities, and even idiosyncrasies. And the freedom of books, as well as the freedom of the collector, lies precisely in the personal nature of this collection.

What Benjamin does for a book collector of precious and rare volumes is what Hermann Hesse would do for a potential collector of world literary works. While there are differences in the aim and scope of these essays, considering the two together provide wonderful insights into the culture of books as medium, as well as world literature as a collection and recollection. Before discussing Hesse's essay, however, it might be worthwhile to start with the establishment of the Nobel Prize and the popularization of world literature through literary magazines. This will assist in charting the networks of ideas that contributed to the proliferation of world literature in Europe and help to locate Hesse's essay within this network.

The Nobel Prize and the Failed World Library

As is well known, the Nobel Prize in Literature was the fourth of the prize categories established by Alfred Nobel in his will (1895). Nobel intended the award for someone who "had produced the most outstanding work in an ideal direction."[15] While a circulation of literary works from the non-European world into Europe—mostly from antiquity to the early modern period—was already in place, the task of evaluating contemporary non-European literatures became a source of anxiety for the Nobel Committee set up in Stockholm. The committee found itself woefully inadequate to judge literatures from around the world; two members of the Swedish Academy reportedly "spoke strongly against accepting Nobel's legacy, for fear that the obligation would detract from the Academy's proper concerns and turn it into 'a cosmopolitan tribunal of literature.'"[16] Nonetheless, the Committee was indeed convinced, following the intervention of the Permanent Secretary Carl David af Wirsén, who commented that working against Nobel's will would deny recognition to "the great figures of continental literature" and asked the committee to "acquire an influential position in world literature."[17] And the committee did acquire an influential position in world literature, even if its beginnings were largely limited to "continental literature."

With two Scandinavian, one Spanish, one Italian, one English, and one German author as Nobel Prize recipients for the first decade of the twentieth century, the watershed event came in 1913 when Rabindranath Tagore became the first non-European Nobel Laureate for literature. Admittedly, Tagore's reception of world literature cannot be seen as having provoked an instant surge of interest in Bengali or other contemporary Indian literatures; Tagore was as much a British Indian subject as Rudyard Kipling—who was also born and brought up in India—the recipient of the Nobel Prize for Literature in 1907. Nonetheless, the recognition of *Gitanjali* in Tagore's own English translation by the Swedish academy was in fact an acknowledgment of a writer from a geoculturally distant space.

The Academy's prize motivation for Tagore reinscribed Goethe's idea of poetry as the shared property of humans: "[Tagore receives the prize] because of his profoundly sensitive, fresh and beautiful verse, by which, with consummate skill, he has made his poetic thought, expressed in his own English words, a part of the literature of the West."[18] While this statement could easily be criticized for its inherent Orientalism or for its lack of recognition of Tagore's writings as part of the literature of the East, what is more important here is the recognition of Tagore's English words as his own: the first recognition of creation of English verse by a person of non-European ethnic origin, who nonetheless was a British subject. In his "Banquet Speech"—a telegraphically sent message that was read by Robert Clive, the British Charges d'Affaires in Sweden—Tagore reciprocated with cosmopolitan humanism: "I beg to convey to the Swedish Academy my grateful appreciation of the breadth of understanding which has brought the distant near, and has made a stranger a brother."[19]

The overcoming of distances toward a creation of intimacy and fraternity through literature soon found resonances within European literary circles, especially through the renowned French novelist and 1915 Nobel Laureate, Romain Rolland. Along with Tagore, Rolland, with his Zürich- and Leipzig-based German-language publisher Rotapfel Verlag, had an important albeit unfulfilled role in the proposed establishment of a *Weltbibliothek* (world library).

As the first exercise in mass destruction that had repercussions on a global scale, World War I becomes the harbinger of a new idea of understanding the world and worldliness. The fragile alliances between nations, Germany's ambitions of territorial and political dominance, and a world that was no longer held by the rules of the nineteenth century all come to a head in 1914. The idea of a collection of knowledge sources about the world in the form of subject-headed, cross-listed bibliographies and catalogs—think of it as the print equivalent of Google, housed today in the Mundaneum in Mons, Belgium—was already conceived by Paul Otlet and Henri de la Fontain during their collaboration from 1895–1934.[20] The idea of a world library focusing on world literature, which would bring together knowledge from the East and the West, was conceived for the first time by Rolland.[21] As an established public intellectual and artist, Rolland was well connected with many important literary figures in Europe and kept a keen eye on political developments in Asia. When approached by Emil Roniger, owner of the Rotapfel Verlag, Rolland translated his biographical essay on Mahatma Gandhi from French to German, which was then published by Rotapfel in 1923. Rolland was well acquainted with the Bern-based Hermann Hesse, whose *Siddhartha* had become a best seller in 1922; Hesse even dedicated the first section of *Siddhartha*, "Der Sohn des Brahmanen," to Rolland.[22] In 1923, Rolland came upon the idea of a world library—a collection of the most important literary works from the Orient as well as the Occident—as well as a "House of Friendship" (*Haus der Freundschaft*), which would serve as a meeting space for the exchange of ideas among influential intellectuals from around the world. The inspiration for the "House of Friendship" was reportedly Santiniketan,[23] the university outside of Calcutta that Tagore founded in 1918 with the motto: "Yatra Vishwam Bhavatekyanidam" (where the world becomes home in one nest).

While the spirit and grand ambition of the plan was commendable, several factors made its execution impossible. If Roniger's overcommitment to many projects—including his publication house—made fundraising an issue, the hyperinflation in Germany during the early Weimar Republic added further complications to the plan. Despite initial difficulties, Rolland and Roniger's plan enjoyed a brief period of optimism when it found resonance with Tagore, who visited Rolland in 1926, and with Mahatma Gandhi, whose visit followed in 1931. To show support, Tagore and Gandhi gave German translation rights for their works to Rotapfel Verlag.[24] However, Rolland's own lack of confidence in Roniger to execute the project as a collaboration and a lack of understanding between Ganesa Publishing House, Calcutta, and Rotapfel Verlag led to the slow death of the project. By the beginning of the 1930s, with the changed financial realities and the political climate of Europe, the world library with the best works of East and West proved to be a pipe dream. As Jean-Pierre Meylan aptly comments in his essay, "When seen retrospectively, their [Rolland and Roniger's] plan of an Indo-European bridging was visionary, they just came half a century and a world war too early."[25]

The *Weltbibliothek* was a failed idea. Political instability, hyperinflation, and a sinking book market characterized the new German Republic, especially in the first five years of the 1920s. However, around World War I, there was massive rise in publications on world literature. Book series like Reclam's Universal-Bibliothek and a literary magazine called *Die Welt-Literatur* played an important role in creating world literary readership and personal world libraries.

Book Series, Anthologies, and Die Welt-Literatur

As discussed in the previous chapter, on November 9, 1867, Reclam's Universal-Bibliothek series was launched with Goethe's *Faust: Eine Tragödie*

(*Faust Part I*).[26] From translations of first Spanish, then Scandinavian and Russian literatures in the 1870s—Henrik Ibsen, Jens Peter Jacobsen, August Strindberg, Ivan Turgenev, and Fyodor Dostoevsky—the Universal-Bibliothek quickly moved into publishing translations of classical Sanskrit, Chinese, and Japanese texts. The Reclam catalog from 1904 contains over fifty titles of works from *Altisländisch* (Old Icelandic) to *Ungarisch* (Hungarian). By 1917, Reclam officially declared an agenda of publishing world literature, "wie sie Goethe gehofft hat" ("as hoped for by Goethe").[27]

While the philosophical idealism that informed Goethe's concept might have inspired this declaration, market realities facilitated them. Between 1852 and 1900, German book production had tripled: from 8,857 works to 24,792 works respectively.[28] In addition, the establishment of the Nobel Prize in Literature in 1901 further energized the circulation of world literature. Many handbooks and anthologies were published right at the beginning of the twentieth century and in the period leading up to World War I. Apart from Alexander Baumgartner's four-volume anthology that showcased literary works in German translations from antiquity,[29] many important, multivolume works were being published, such as Eduard Naschér's *Handbuch der Geschichte der Weltliteratur* (1900), Carl Busse's *Die Geschichte der Weltliteratur* (1910), Eduard Bertz's *Spemanns goldenes Buch der Weltliteratur* (1912), Karl Holtermann's *Kurze Geschichte der Weltliteratur: Mit 82 Bildern* (1912), Adolf Bartels' *Einführung in die Weltliteratur* (1913), and Paul Wiegler's *Geschichte der Weltliteratur: Dichtung fremder Völker* (1920).

In addition, between 1912 and 1920, Diedrichs Verlag in Jena brought to fruition its ambitious plan of publishing multiple volumes of folk- and fairy tales from Europe, Asia, Africa, North and South America, and the South Pacific/Oceania.[30] As Meike Werner points out in her essay on modern Jena, "Influenced by Goethe's understanding of the relationship between world literature and world culture, Diedrichs especially after 1910 buttressed his phalanx of books with broadly conceived publication series."[31]

During this high tide of world literature and activity among the publishing industry, the first-ever dissertation on the subject was submitted to the University of Leipzig by a student called Else Beil (1886–1965), who as Else Ulich-Beil would go on to become one of the most important political activists for women's rights. In *Zur Entwicklung des Begriffs der Weltliteratur*, Beil credits the rise in the discussion and use of the term *Weltliteratur* as the main reason for writing her dissertation. She traces the history of the concept from the early to late nineteenth century, drawing a genealogy of the term through discussions of the world and world cultures by Kant,

Herder, Schlegel, and Humboldt, bringing her dissertation to focus on the literary and translation activities of Goethe, which prepare the ground for the construction of the term *Weltliteratur*. Beil ends with the resistance to world literature in the mid-nineteenth century with Ernst Moritz Arndt. While Beil's study remains fairly centered on European literary connections, and she makes no attempt to connect the massive amounts of translations from non-European languages into German or other European languages, the dissertation remains one of the first in the field.

In addition to the publication of anthologies before and after World War I, the very first magazine dedicated to world literature (in the twentieth century) was established during the war in 1915. The magazine is significant for a number of reasons: first, because it gives an account of the reception and circulation of world literature, to which Hesse pays attention in his essay; second, because the publication history of the magazine, including its pricing and location, is symptomatic of the financially volatile period in Germany during the war and the Weimar Republic; and third, because the magazine would be revived, in a drastically transformed way, by the Nazi Ministry for Public Enlightenment and Propaganda (Ministerium für Volksaufklärung und Propaganda) in 1935, becoming an important historical document on the Nazi definition of world literature.

Entitled *Die Welt-Literatur: Die besten Romane und Novellen aller Zeiten und Völker*, the magazine was published by Verlag Die Weltliteratur in Munich, in folio format with around sixteen pages per issue; its banner promised its readers "a work every Saturday" (changed in 1917 to "a work every week").[32] Costing 10 pfennig per issue or 1.20 mark for a quarterly subscription, the magazine aimed to provide world literary works at a reasonable price for its readers. The works published were rarely commissioned especially for the magazine; they were reprinted with permission from major publishers in Munich, Leipzig, Berlin, Stuttgart, and other cities. Each issue was published with a very brief introduction to the author and his or her intellectual biography and contained short prose, poems, or excerpts from novels.

Primarily showcasing works by German authors such as Kleist (1/1915, 4/1916), Eichendorff (2/1915, 1/1916), Hoffmann (3/1915, 1/1916), Goethe (2/1916), Heine (6/1916), and Schiller (10/1916), the magazine initially included three foreign authors: the Russians Turgenev (9/1916) and Dostoevsky (15/1916), and the American Edgar Allen Poe (13/1916). With a few issues dedicated to classic authors such as Shakespeare (27/1916), Cervantes (31/1916), and Cellini (21/1921), the magazine mostly published eighteenth- and nineteenth-century authors from Europe, such as

Voltaire, Balzac, Gogol, Maupassant, Andersen, Flaubert, Chekhov, Gorki, Björnson, Pushkin, Strindberg, Merimeé, Tolstoy, Zola, Jokai, and many more. It would be impossible to list here the large number of German authors published in the magazine. Suffice it to say that most of the canonical authors from the nineteenth century as well as contemporary authors such as Thomas Mann (250th issue) and Heinrich Mann were published in the magazine. Nobel Laureates did not go unnoticed by the magazine; Knut Hamsun (3/1917, 50/1919), Selma Lagerlöff (7/1917), and Rudyard Kipling (39/1919) also featured in the magazine, and so did Rabindranath Tagore (49/1920), who became the first non-European author to be featured in the magazine.

But it is not merely the number of authors, languages, or regions covered that made *Die Welt-Literatur* important. While there is no explicit editorial statement in the issues of the magazine available today (starting with 13/1916),[33] the brief introductions to authors and their works and the advertisements published in the magazine provide a rich picture of the magazine's purpose and its clientele. Together they provide information on the kind of readers and reading habits that *Die Welt-Literatur* aimed to create. The repeated publication of advertisements, such as "Send 'Die Welt-Literatur' to the field: It brings the best novels and short-stories of all times and peoples" or "Die Welt-Literatur: As Present for Soldiers and Officers"[34]—along with many other advertisements for war bonds (*Kriegsanleihe*) as well as donations for the submarine war (*U-Boot Kampf*)—clearly demonstrate that the magazine was directed to both civil and military readerships. An advertisement inviting private subscriptions to the magazine states its purpose:

> "Die Welt-Literatur" wants to work against pulp fiction and the easy, but often really expensive light-fiction. "Die Welt-Literatur" appeals to the entire nation! By building enjoyment, "Die Welt-Literatur" wants to work to educate without [a sense of] school-mastery. Because of its inexpensive price, "Die Welt-Literatur" stays open to all classes of the German people! All hotels, cafés, pensions, sanatoria should display "Die Welt-Literatur"; for all of those living in the countryside it is a valuable diversion and stimulation. During travels it is the favorite and the most inexpensive reading, and for our soldiers in the trenches as well as in the communications zones it is a welcome greeting from the homeland![35]

Such a program for the creation of a world literature readership—one that pitched itself beyond hierarchies in the civil and military spheres of society, in urban and rural areas and in all institutions of rest and recovery, and that made the idea of world literature through the magazine a greeting from the homeland—is truly unique and ambitious. But the magazine derived its unique character and appeal not merely through its all-encompassing target readership but also through a specific take on reading habits. While the advertisement promises an educational experience beyond a pedantic, formal pedagogy, the sections introducing the authors carried explicit, and sometimes indirect, modes of educating the audience. They provided tips to connect authors and works across periods and languages, the vocabulary to express one's understanding of a particular reader or work, and through a comparative aesthetic evaluation, they made a case for their choice of literary materials to be published in the magazine. Introductions to authors often contained comments on the universal values, cosmopolitan stature, and global humanity that were to find expression through their writings—thus framing the texts and the authors for the readers in a language of Enlightenment and Universalism. For example, in the introduction to E. T. A. Hoffmann (37/1916), the biographical notes about the author are interrupted by a detour to the content of the magazine, working in the spirit of both improving the taste of the masses through a magazine such as *Die Welt-Literatur* as well as decrying any criticism of the selection of demanding prose:

> One would suggest to "Die Welt-Literatur" to not publish such valuable and serious works. They are (supposedly) not for the masses. Their instincts demand easier goods. We believe this is a mistake. For the masses, even here the best appears good enough to us. And to anyone with an unspoiled taste, so we hope, E. T. A Hoffmann and Kleist will not only appear as more pleasant than the diet of our oh-how-modern light-fiction writers, but they will also appear as more lively and exciting. Yes, they will perhaps even be capable of captivating the reader more than some odd family saga.[36]

A year later, in a special issue on François Gayot de Pitaval, the introduction cites Schiller's praise for Pitaval in times of what he (Schiller) saw as the effect of "mediocre writings and profit-oriented publishers" on the cultures and manners of the people, to state that precisely this awareness of mediocrity led to the rise of the idea within *Die Welt-Literatur* "to counter the mediocre with the valuable and to offer the people [*Volk*] none of the diluted or harmful surrogate, but only the best for intellectual nourishment."[37]

But was the magazine consistent with its idea of world literature as a philosophical ideal and a pedagogical tool for the aesthetic education of its readers? An analysis of the available issues of the magazine suggests the following: (1) the decision regarding what counted as world literature was culturally determined and historically based, meaning the most important German-language authors from the late eighteenth to the early twentieth century were featured in the magazine; (2) the magazine did not discriminate against authors from nations against whom Germany was fighting during World War I, and Russian and French authors continue to be published repeatedly during the war (one can say, however, that British authors are, by comparison, underrepresented); (3) while the magazine never really worked in tandem with any "official" program of presenting world literature—something that would categorically take place when the Nazis revived the magazine in 1935—there is no doubt that in the selection of works to publish, the magazine pitched texts that might have been interesting to soldiers: Goethe's *Kampagne in Frankreich 1792* (2/1916); Turgenev's *Das Abenteuer des Leutnants Jergunow* and *Der Brigadier* (9/1916); Flaubert's *Oberst Chabert* (18/1916); Schiller's *Prozess und Hinrichtung der Grafen Egmont und von Hoorne* and *Belagerung von Antwerpen* (28/1916) to name just a few from the first full year of its publication. That the effort was also focused on establishing German authors within the larger world literary canon is evident not merely in the selection of iconic authors such as Goethe, Heine, Schiller, among others, but also those who today are considered lesser known among the general reading public, even in Germany. Notable names among them would be Karl Immerman (8/1918), William Blumenhagen (37/1918), Joseph Ruederer (14/1918), and Paul Scheerbart (28/1919). Keeping in mind their military readership, the magazine published stories pertaining to military cultures, but they also included many love stories (Dostoevksy's *Die fremde Frau und der Mann unter dem Bett*, 13/1917), those with women at the center (Cervantes, *Die beiden Mädchen* 3/1918) or, starting in 1919, those authored by women. While Selma Lagerlöff was published as early as 1917, Lena Christ becomes the first German-language woman author (23/1919), followed by Isolde Kurz (34/1919), Clara Viebig (37/1919), Elisabeth Dauthendey (20/1920), and Sophie Hoechstaetter (29/1920), among others. The gender targeting of the magazine was also reflected in the advertisement section: starting in 1917, in advertisements for personal effects, leather accessories, cosmetic products, procedures for skin-improvement, and sewing machines for women increased. World literature is thus also institutionalized through a middle-class consumership. In addition, the magazine creates a sexualized body of readers, who, during the height of the war, seek contacts for pen-friendships or even marriages. These include soldiers seeking contacts with women and vice versa or, in rare cases, even men seeking friendship with other men. In addition, advertisements for the growing market for target-driven readerships—self-help books, "teach yourself" foreign language books (especially English and French), books on (hetero)sexuality and sex—reveal that by 1917, the magazine had indeed established itself and was generating revenue.[38] Praise for the magazine came from regional and urban presses in Germany, which hailed it as one of the most important contributions to readership.[39]

Important changes come to the magazine in the year 1920. On the one hand, the magazine publishes its first issue on a non-European author, Tagore. On the other hand, the pressures of an increasingly hyperinflating economy are clearly reflected in the magazine too. In January 1920, the magazine moved its office to Berlin, and then moved back to Munich in June 1921.[40] While the price had been increasing over the years, from 10 pfennig per issue from 1915 to 1917 to 25 pfennig in 1919, and then 80 pfennig in 1920, the magazine declared in 1921 that it would no longer be published weekly but only biweekly.[41] The price went up to 1.50 mark per issue, and, in a quick succession of a few months, to 6 marks (16/1922), then to 9 marks (18/1922), and finally to 30 marks an issue (22/1922). From 1921, the magazine also demonstrated a theme-based, rather than an author-based approach to world literature, with special issues on African Folktales (26/1921), India (30/1921), and Hungary (12/1922), all the way to "Exotische Frauen" (Exotic women, 1/1922), "Heilige Legenden" (Holy legends, 8/1922), and even "Wilde Völker" (Savage nations, 11/1922). Despite its new bi-chrome cover, the magazine showed signs of decline. The advertisements became few and far between, and with a combined issue (23/24 1922) on new German writers, the magazine published its last biweekly edition.

The magazine was revived by the Regensburg-based (and later Regensburg and Leipzig–based) Habbel und Naumann Verlag. Published under the new imprint "Verlag der Weltliteratur," the magazine was relaunched in 1923 under its old name: *Die Welt-Literatur: Die besten Romane und Novellen aller Zeiten und Völker* (figure 3-1). With a special issue on "Spanische Novellen," which included E. T. A. Hoffmann's translation of Don Juan Manuel's *Der Graf Lucanor* and Ludwig Tieck's translation of Miguel de Cervantes's *Die Novelle von der unziemlichen Neugier*.[42] In the foreword to the issue, the publishers address their potential readers and ask them to help with publicizing the new series, thus constructing new readers from

Figure 3-1. Poster for *Die Welt-Literatur* magazine, 1923. (Courtesy of Deutsche Nationalbibliothek and Buch- und Schriftmuseum Leipzig.)

old to help with the survival of the series.[43] The first series was followed by others including “Ungarische Erzähler,” “Orientalische Novellen: indische Liebesgeschichten,” and “Arabische Erzählungen.”[44] These issues were published biweekly and priced at one mark each (or a *Buchmark*: a prepaid “forever stamp” costing sixty pfennig). In December 1924, the series published Hugo von Hoffmanthal’s *Augenblicke in Griechenland* and declared the discontinuation of the biweekly, small-book format publication to be replaced by large novels. The explanation provided some interesting insights into the changing market for volumes of world literature:

> We took over *Die Welt-Literatur* two years ago to create a German Home Library with it, and therefore gave it a handy book-format. Literary developments and the desires of the circle of readers prevail upon us to execute a fundamental and meaningful change in the design and publication form of *Die Welt-Literatur* starting with the new year. . . . Since the necessary splitting of long works in half-monthly issues leads to a lot of disadvantages, and since the unprotected name "Weltliteratur" has often come to be used so varyingly in recent times, starting January 1, 1925, out of our magazine, we are forming: *Die Sammlung: New Sequel to Die Welt-Literatur*.[45]

It is in this transformative book market in which world literature is used by many series and an affordable small-format book, rather than a magazine, is privileged by readers, that Reclam tries to pitch its Universal-Bibliothek. And it does so with Hesse's name recognition. The geographical and linguistic expansion of world literature in Reclam's publishing agenda in 1904—three years after the establishment of the Nobel Prize in Literature—or its categorical revitalization in 1917, during World War I, can hardly be read as a mere coincidence. The programmatic publication of "masterpieces" from the gamut of world literary works—not just by Reclam but by other publishers—is very much in line with the phrasing of the award's purpose in Alfred Nobel's will. *Die Welt-Literatur* (1915–1919) already published advertisements from many publishing houses (Kurt Wolff, Langenscheidtische Bibliothek, Diederiechs, etc.) for collected works on world literature. Slowly but surely, the evaluation and recognition of an author's work on a global scale was influencing publishers' agendas, and Reclam did not remain untouched.

Hesse and the Private Library of World Literature

In 1927, on its sixtieth anniversary, the Universal-Bibliothek commissioned Hermann Hesse to write a short essay on book collection for smaller, private libraries for their *Lexikon des praktischen Wissens* (Lexicon of practical knowledge, 1927). Reclam had vested financial interests in publishing this essay. In 1925, Germany led the list of the top five publishing nations in the world (Britain, France, the United States, and Italy were the other four) with 31,595 titles; of these, 6,338 were classified under "belles lettres."[46] Hesse could not have been a better choice of an author for this essay; he enjoyed wide name recognition as the best-selling German author of novels such as *Demian* (1919) and *Siddhartha* (1922). From Hermann Gundert, his maternal grandfather—a publisher and a Christian missionary in Kerala, India, in the mid-nineteenth century—Hesse had inherited a huge private library. This library contained over 3,000 works of German and European literature, many of them priceless first editions as well as scores of English and German translations of Sanskrit, Chinese, Sinhali, Persian, and Arabic texts that Hesse himself had added to the library. As a book-lover, collector, author, and reader, Hesse himself wanted his essay to be a medium of propaganda (*Propagandamittel*) for the book and discussed it with Reclam. In a letter to Hesse written on July 8, 1929, Ernst Reclam agreed to Hesse's vision, asking him to expand the manuscript by at least thirty pages in order to be published as a Reclam Universal-Bibliothek volume.[47] If Walter Benjamin emphasized the significance of books as a medium of knowledge and as an object for personal collectors, Hermann Hesse took book collection for private libraries to the next level by linking it directly to world literature. Spending some time with this essay is fruitful, because it not only democratizes world literature for a public interested in engaging with literature but also marks a moment of transition after which literature will soon become a prerogative of a totalitarian state. In the years following the publication of the essay, a strong sense of the book as one of the most important media in state propaganda and as a weapon of war will develop. Personal libraries will be destroyed, the fate of public libraries will be decided by book bannings and book burnings, and a grim era for world literature will begin.

Hesse also deserves a special mention because he has been entirely overlooked in genealogies of theories of world literature, which generally skip from Goethe and Marx to Erich Auerbach or René Wellek and Austin Warren, to the publishing and pedagogical ventures of the twentieth century. Hesse is important to the theorization of the library as a mediator of world literature: he is the first author to discuss world literature as a problem of libraries. And he is somehow the one who makes Rolland's idea of a world library accessible for a general reader in the privacy of his or her home.

Hesse's conceptualization of a library of world literature draws its inspiration from a private collection rather than the public library and most strongly emphasizes purchasing rather than borrowing. Yet it is by no means an elite venture. Hesse imagines an accessibility that crosses classes and income levels, and he thinks carefully about how an ordinary person should amass a library of world literature. He urges readers to create individualized collections, choosing for themselves what counts as world literature. In this way he democratizes the practice of making libraries, suggesting that every reader can create such a collection. He emphasizes borrowing from distant traditions while endorsing ownership as a way to forge an intimate relationship with the abstraction of world literature.

Hesse's essay, *Eine Bibliothek der Weltliteratur*, was in fact partly a response to the success of European publishers printing inexpensive series of classic literature from around the world, many in translation. If the essay had immediate ties to the book market, Hesse had also been consistently engaged in bridging the gap between national literatures and world literature. In 1913, he was commissioned by Die deutsche Bibliothek—a prominent publishing house in Leipzig that produced well-designed and affordable hardcovers—to edit an anthology of German texts from 1700 to 1900. In his afterword to the anthology, he refers to Goethe's term *Weltliteratur* to endorse world literature's mass accessibility, which was growing in the German-speaking world through the translation, editing, and popularization of world-literary works.[48]

In *Eine Bibliothek der Weltliteratur*, the library becomes an agent of the idea of world literature, which it in turn both contains and disseminates. What counts as world literature for Hesse is not a quick list of authors, titles, and their linguistic, geographic, or, as in his case, "national" (*völkisch*) origins—in the essay Hesse lists roughly seven hundred works from nearly twenty languages—but the basic tenets of human existence that find aesthetic expression through language. The study of world literature becomes a process, a slow familiarization ("allmählich sich vertrautmachen") with such thoughts, experiences, symbols, and so on.[49] The first definition of world literature that Hesse offers is the "enormous treasure of thoughts, experiences, symbols, fantasies, and desired images, which the past has left in the works of authors and thinkers of numerous peoples" (*BW*, 3).[50] "Real education," for Hesse, is a consistent state of itinerancy toward the unending and timeless universe. The purpose of such a *Bildung*, therefore, lies not in the advancement of specific capabilities or achievements but in the granting of meaning to life, which in turn is to "explain the past and to stay open to the future with fearless readiness" (*BW*, 3).[51] Given that it is difficult enough to undertake an in-depth study of literary works of one people, Hesse states that the study of literature of the "whole of humanity" seems impossible. However, highlighting the enabling prospect of this otherwise intimidating, even debilitating challenge, Hesse asserts that it is precisely because of the impossible, unreachable nature of this enterprise that every single engagement with a literary work or an author becomes a mode of realizing genuine *Bildung*, a joyous experience. What counts as world literature for him is the extensiveness ("Weite") and the abundance

("Fülle") of what humanity has thought and what it strives for (*BW*, 4). In short, world literature surfaces as the totality of human aesthetic, experiential, and intellectual expression; it then becomes the source of a reader's personal formation. While this fulfillment seems to locate Hesse among the idealists and the sentimentalists, the essay is distinguished by its emphasis on democratization. Hesse quickly undoes the burden of implying that world literature means access to works of literature in the original languages; in the context of the library, he displays sympathies to readers' varied financial backgrounds, busting the myth that acquiring books is all about commodified objects and therefore necessitates obtaining the most expensive editions (*BW*, 7–8). While Hesse often imagines the vastness of world literature, he also theorizes *a* library ("eine Bibliothek") and not *the* library ("die Bibliothek"). And the narrative of such a collection remains directive rather than instructive; suggestive rather than prescriptive; indeed, democratic rather than pedantic.

In turning to the model of a personal library, Hesse dramatically individualizes the ideal of world literature. What counts as world literature will be a matter of individual choices and preferences, of time restrictions that govern the business of everyday life, and, naturally, of pecuniary concerns (*BW*, 4, 8). In listing these challenges and restrictions, what remains important for Hesse is a lively relationship ("lebendiges Verständnis") with the idea of world literature, in which a reader lets a particular work have an effect on him or her rather than acquiescing to the master status of a particular work (*BW*, 5). In a mode very different from the university courses and anthologies that were emerging around the same time, Hesse does not encourage his readers to undertake a *Bildungsprogramm*. "The key to a living relationship with world literature on the reader's part is . . . to follow the way of love, not of duty" (*BW*, 5–6).[52] In fact, Hesse categorically rejects a forced reading of a masterpiece based on its fame or on the reader's sense of shame of not having read it. There is no single library, Hesse tells us; rather, there are a thousand ways of collecting books ("der Wege sind tausend") (*BW*, 6). Hesse draws attention to the multifaceted nature of the book as a material-cultural artifact, encouraging readers to think about how they choose among books. He provides details on distinguishing between editions and on the various modes of acquiring books so that one might build a library of world literature even on a limited budget (*BW*, 8–10). Hesse accepts that there is no simple recipe for selecting editions—which works by which publishers are best and therefore worth acquiring. Some acquisitions, he states, stem from the love of a particular work or author; others, from admiration for the format or the layout of the edition;

and still others, from a penchant for price or binding (*BW*, 9). There are many ways to decide which books count as world literature: from luxurious gold-embossed and leather-bound special editions that might fire one's imagination, to reasonably priced editions for readers on a tight budget. Books thus become much more than vessels of texts dispersed ("zerstreut") around the world; they become the instruments of collecting ("sammeln") these texts (*BW*, 10). While the context may remain the same, the medium that grants a reader access to that text can acquire different forms.

In a similarly democratic fashion, Hesse welcomes texts in translation as integral to the act of collecting. He recognizes the culturally embedded nature of a literary work, the special character that it acquires by virtue of its creation in a specific language. Instead of fetishizing the original, however, Hesse celebrates the idea of translation, because only in translation does a work of literature become accessible to readers who are ignorant of the original language. He defines translation as approximation ("Annäherung") and highlights the significance not just of translations of foreign works but also of multiple translations of works in a particular language (*BW*, 11). In another novel moment in the European literary space, Hesse transforms the perception of world literature when he champions the inclusion of works from Farsi, Arabic, Chinese, Sanskrit, Tibetan, and Pali literatures (*BW*, 12). But he does not claim complete access to them (*BW*, 30–31, 40), decrying a kind of idealization of these works expected of him after the publication of *Siddhartha*. Hesse thus redefines the European bourgeois library. He embraces the ordinary reader, the cheap edition, the material artifact of the book, the act of reading in translation, and, most of all, the democratizing of the act of selection. For him, a library of world literature will always already be incomplete ("unvollkommen"): distinct from a university education, it must reflect the collector's desire for reading ("Lesetrieb") and the pleasure of engaging with books ("Bücherfreude") (*BW*, 34). Finally, Hesse democratizes world literature by noting that it would acquire different meanings in different historical moments: "What appears to me today as the embodiment of world literature will one day appear as one-sided and insufficient to my sons as it would have appeared laughable to my father or grandfather" (*BW*, 43).[53] World literature in the Goethean sense is thus *aufgehoben*—preserved but also canceled.

What Hesse implied with the changing definition of world literature for each epoch came to fruition very quickly in Germany, in fact, within four years of the first publication of Hesse's essay. The epochal change came about with the Nazi ascension to power in 1933. The Ministry for Public Enlightenment and Propaganda (Reichsministerium für Volksaufklärung und Propaganda), headed by Joseph Goebbels, was established on March 13, 1933, and on July 30, 1933, through a special ordinance, all cultural institutions, including the German National Library (Die Deutsche Bücherei) in Leipzig and the entire book industry was brought under its precinct.[54] On September 22, 1933, a special plan was announced to set up a Cultural Chamber (Reichskulturkammer),[55] which would lay the groundwork for the management of all cultural institutions, including literature. This chamber would oversee not just belletristic works but all kinds of published works, including professional manuals and help books. To understand the drastic redefinition that world literature went through in Germany between 1933 and 1945, it would be best to situate the world literary politics of the Nazis within their literary politics, which in turn are strongly connected to their vision of books, libraries, and translations.

National Socialist Book Politics

As Dietrich Strothmann underlines in his groundbreaking study *Nationalsozialistische Literaturpolitik* (1960; National-Socialist literary politics), the Nazi strategy of controlling and reorientating the book market was not merely due to the success of Adolf Hitler's *Mein Kampf* (1925) but also due to a very early acceptance of the book as an important social medium, therefore making it worthy of scrutiny and control to achieve political goals. While radio and film really emerged as the favored media for propaganda, "the book" was nonetheless acknowledged by the Nazis as an essential medium to establish a totalitarian system of publicity.[56] Following Hitler's pronouncement of hygienic requirements ("hygienischen Erfordernissen") and a sanitization of the public/national corpus ("Sanierung des Völkerkörpers") at the Nuremberg Rally in 1933,[57] the idea of mobilizing all cultural products in the interest of ideology was fast taking shape. In order to instrumentalize culture in the life-essential self-assertion and self-realization ("lebensnotwendige Selbstbehauptung und Selbstverwirklichung") of the nation, on March 23, 1933, in front of the Reichstag, Hitler took away the right to control the domains of culture and education from the states and entrusted the federal government (Reichsregierung) with the "highest leadership and management of German cultural life."[58]

The cultural policy of domination through discrimination and elimination became manifest on November 15, 1935, when Goebbels declared the completion of the two-year process of establishing the Reichskulturkammer and the founding of the cultural senate (*Kultursenat*), which consisted of representatives of all artistic media. In his inaugural speech, Goebbels stated: "The Reichskulturkammer is today free of Jews. In the cultural life of our people no Jew is employed any more. A Jew can therefore not be a member of the chamber."[59] To promote such a "Jew-Free" cultural life of the nation, Goebbels also announced "practical, political measures" for all the arts. In the field of literature, prize money for 250,000 reichsmarks per year, a financial support fund for authors with the sum of 100,000 reichsmarks, and another fund for 500,000 reichsmarks for promotion and publicity were established.[60]

Such "practical and political measures" were not limited to the establishment of funds and prizes. The Supervising Offices (*Aufsichtsämter*) of the Reichskulturkammer and the Chamber of Literature (*Reichsschrifttumkammer*) included close surveillance of authors, publishers, libraries, literary societies, literary publicity, and book reviews.[61] While a detailed discussion of all these institutions is impossible, suffice it to say that the foremost form of discrimination was against authors of Jewish origins and affiliations. The "Juden" section of the *Handbuch der Reichsschrifttumskammer* listed the citizenship law (Reichsbürgergesetz) and the Law of the Protection of German Blood and Honor (Gesetz zum Schutz des deutschen Blutes und der deutschen Ehre) of September 15, 1935, as the preface to all the other ordinances related to treatment of books by publishers, booksellers, and librarians.[62] The following four groups were earmarked for discrimination:

1. Jews and "privileged non-Aryans."
2. Those related to Jews by marriage.
3. Cronies of Jews ("Judengenossen") or "Jews in spirit," to which also belonged the "Salon Bolshevists."
4. Among religious writers, those who constantly lived in the past ("ewig Gestrigen") and world citizens ("Weltbürger").[63]

There were 2,634 publishing houses in Germany in 1933, a number that had drastically decreased from the 3,380 in 1925; this number would go up again to 3,253 in 1939, just around the onset of the war. These publishing houses were considered to be in the service of the state and were scrutinized as needed. Apart from financial control, there were measures taken for the "cleansing of the state of the book trade from unsuitable elements," as declared by Goebbels at the annual conference of the German book trader's association in Leipzig (1936).[64] The policies for public libraries, therefore, were in the service of the cleansing (*Säuberung*) and the state-controlled propagandistic measures. After shutting down union libraries (*Gewerkschaftsbibliotheken*), the bid to expand control over state-run public libraries became central to library management. The Nazis established public libraries in the thousands; their numbers rose from 6,000 in 1933, to 10,000 in 1938, and by 1942 there were 25,000 public libraries in Germany. There were also plans to have a Deutsche Bücherei in every big city.[65] The idea behind these libraries was education (*Bildung*), albeit of a very special kind. Walter Rumpf, one of the members of the Verband deutscher Bibliothekare e.V. considered libraries the "bearers, realizers, and protectors of the idea of National Socialism." Their main purpose was not just knowledge, but the "construction of a political will."[66] For libraries who would not comply to these policies and guidelines, the idea was to set up a weapons chamber ("Waffenkammer") that would dismantle them as a burden ("Ballast"), or even as a devil's workshop ("Giftküche").[67] According to the guidelines published in the journal *Die Bücherei* (1935), the official magazine of the Office of Public Libraries, the following kinds of works were to be exterminated:

- Works by people who commit treason, emigrants, and authors of foreign countries who believe in fighting the new Germany and disparaging the new Germany (e.g., works by H. G. Wells and Romain Rolland).
- Marxist, Communist, and Bolshevist literature.
- Pacifist literature.
- Literature of a liberal democratic tendency and attitude, and works by the propagandists of the Weimar state (e.g., works by Walther Rathenau and Heinrich Mann).
- All historical works that are structured toward disparaging the origin, existence, and culture of the German people, toward the dissolution of the order of the German people, toward denying the power and meaning of great leading figures in the favor of the masses in the wake of egalitarian thought, and [in favor of] casting a slur on their greatness (e.g., works by Emil Ludwig).
- Writings that communicate a world-view (*weltanschaulich*) and life skills (*lebenskundlich*) whose content are the false natural scientific enlightenment of primitive Darwinism and Monism (e.g., works by Haeckel).
- Books on the arts, whose representatives consider degenerate, bloodless, pure constructive art positively as "art."
- Writings about sexual pedagogy and sexual enlightenment that take a position in the service of pleasurable egotism and thus greatly appear as disturbing to race and nation.

Decadent, subversive, and publically harmful literature of "civilizational literati."
Literature by Jewish authors, regardless of field or genre.
Social- or entertainment literature, in which life and the purpose of life are represented in a superficial, untrue, and ingratiating way on the basis of a bourgeois or a feudal point of view.[68]

Translated literature was to be handled with special care, out of fear of wrongly influencing German youth and those vulnerable to a liberal-democratic propaganda.[69] With such absolutist policies, control over the book market, the authors, the booksellers, the libraries, indeed the entire existence of book publishing, a decided discrimination against not just German-Jewish authors, but also German authors of "foreign-sounding names," not to mention all the content-based objections listed in the directives against books, the idea of a world literature with the Nazis sounds like an absolute impossibility. And yet, it existed, once again, as we shall see, in line with the larger controlling and state-oriented agenda of the Ministry for Culture and Public Enlightenment. The irony with the Nazis—who denounced literature written by *Weltbürger* with a *Weltanschauung*—is that instead of completely denouncing world literature, they redefined, redesigned, and reinvented it to fit their ideological program. Much as they appropriated books and libraries as "weapons" in the service of state ideology, so did they deploy world literature in the creation of a very specific political world for the German reader. The manifestation of this weapon came in the form of two magazines, *Weltliteratur* (1935–1939), and *Die Weltliteratur* (1940–1944).

Against Weltanschauung: *Nazi Appropriations of Goethe's* Weltliteratur

As discussed earlier, in the first two decades of the twentieth century, there was a proliferation of publications on world literary works in German translations. In 1934, Franz Ludwig Habbel merged Habbel und Naumann into the Wiking Verlag in Berlin, and in October 1935, under the editorial leadership of Hellmuth Langenbucher, the magazine *Weltliteratur: Romane, Erzählungen und Gedichte aller Zeiten und Völker* (Weltliteratur: Novels, stories, and poems of all times and peoples) was launched.[70] Langenbucher's Nazi sympathies had assisted him in becoming the most famous Nazi Germanist; he was even mocked as a self-appointed "pope" for literature during the Nazi era. Hellmuth, along with his younger brother Erich, had important positions in the Nazi administration.[71] Hellmuth

Langenbucher became a member of the Nazi party in 1929 while he was finishing his dissertation on the German Minnesang at the University of Heidelberg. His entry into the upper echelons of the National Socialist Party was made possible by his friendship with Gerhard Schumann at the University of Tübingen, where he had enrolled after Heidelberg. Schumann was already active within the cultural politics of the Nazi party, and through this friendship emerged Langenbucher's first anti-Semitic writings in 1930. From here, after a short stint with the Hanseatische Verlagsanstalt (HAVA) in Hamburg (1931–1932) followed by his association with Alfred Rosenberg's "Kampfbund für deutsche Kultur" (War-League for German Culture), Langenbucher quickly rose through the ranks; within a month of the famous book burning on May 10, 1934, Langenbucher was appointed editor-in-chief (*Chefredakteur*) of the *Börsenblatt für den deutschen Buchhandel*,[72] the most important trade magazine for the publishing industry, a position he used to publish many pieces declaring books as cultural objects that provide meaning to the German folk, as weapons that can be used in the process of German renaissance and rejuvenation, as commercial commodities that are vulnerable to be manipulated by those intending to do harm to the German public (implying Jews, British, and French), and as a "public" medium with a very strong potential for manipulative capacities.[73] Langenbucher was also behind the idea of "volkhafte Dichtung"—a seemingly "people-oriented" but actually politically nationalist/race-based literature, populist (*volkstümlich*), though not described as such—which he presented in his third monograph, *Volkhafte Dichtung der Zeit* (1933). Locating his idea of the *Volk* between that of Wilhelm Grimm's (the *Volk* as "highest form of intellectual life") and Richard Wagner's ("the epitome of all that feel the same hardship"), Langenbucher proposed: "We call people-oriented writing [*volkhafte Dichtung*] every literary statement which stays in the life-space [*Lebensraum*] of the German people, which arises out of its reality, the reason of its being, its fate . . . the depth of an inner connection of the author with the life of its people is a natural requirement, which only humans of our blood, the knowers of our being, the designers of our fate, the makers of our people can aspire to be."[74]

With a well worked-out position that would credit him with literary and cultural offices, Langenbucher became the person of choice to spearhead the Nazi appropriation of world literature: as an idea, a phenomenon, a pedagogical plan, and most importantly, an ideological tool. To understand the direction that the idea of world literature will take in the magazine *Weltliteratur* under his direction, it might be worthwile to cast a glimpse at the following quote from his foreword to the second, expanded edition of *Volkhafte Dichtung* (1935):

> At that time [in 1933] it was valid to work one's way out of the big trends of a new evaluation and representation of the phenomenon of literary lives; it was valid to clearly mark the non-German phenomenon of a bygone time, which claimed an improper dominance in the intellectual lives of the German people, and it came in the first place through a general understanding to prepare the way for those writers, in whose work the lives of German people became the symbol and metaphor in all its radiance. . . . This development, for which we thank the unstoppable progression and what has today become the definitive purging of German cultural life from all uncharacteristic distortions, has also managed clear, healthy conditions in the area of literary life, which will again enable meaningful work for those who work creatively or with the media.[75]

The definitive purging of German cultural life from all uncharacteristic distortions becomes central to the Nazi construction and dissemination of world literature, and Langenbucher becomes the foremost purveyor of this idea through the magazine *Weltliteratur*. The magazine reveals a story of circulation, reception, and creation of world literature for a public that was militantly nationalized through every propaganda tool available. The very first issue (October 1935) carries the spirit of the times: it evinces a world literature that is strategically inserted within the ethnic, religious, and border politics that was central to the Nazi government after Hitler's Nuremberg rally of 1933. The October 1935 issue had as its leading piece a short excerpt from an anti-Semitic novel, *Kamraden an der Memel* (Comrades at the Memel) by Heinz Gerhard. Set in Memelland—the part of northern East Prussia over which Germany lost control between 1920 and 1939 to Lithuania—the novel emphasizes the yearning of the German ethnic group settled by the river Memel to be one with mainland Germany. The introduction to the excerpt, published under the title "Schicksal an der Memel" (Fate at the Memel) begins with an explanation of the Führer's position on the situation in Lithuania, especially against the mishandling of the "Memeldeutschen" by the local administration.[76] Through the use of strong language, the introduction makes the *Reichsdeutsche* (those residing within the boundaries of the Third Reich) aware of the "hate-psychosis" ("Haß-Psychose") instigated by Lithuanian bureaucrats against that German ethnic group ("Volksgruppe") in Lithuania and other borderlands of

Germany.[77] The "novel" is therefore not merely a work of fiction, as the introduction states:

> There appears at the right moment a book, in which the fate of the Memel-Germans has found a horrifying form, especially horrifying because from every line of this book, which the author calls a "novel," and even more from what we experience from what we read between the lines, that only the naked report of cruel facts is present here. . . . The entire book is a tremendous denunciation of the system of Versailles, which in the end is also at fault for the innocent fate of the Memelland.[78]

The introduction ends by outlining the plot of the novel: the story of the (German) farmer Feldmann and a Jewish businessman, "who has no relationship to the soil and is only obsessed with his greed for money" and tries to bring him (Feldmann) down.[79] The general tone of world literature is established with the idea of an ever-expanding *Lebensraum* and explicit anti-Semitism. Langenbucher's note following the novel excerpt, entitled "Zwischen zwei Völkern" (In-between two peoples), extends and reemphasizes the border-politics, this time in the context of the reading interests of Germans, which lie increasingly, Langenbucher observes, in the writings of Germans living abroad and in German borderlands. The current (and future) borders of a potentially expansive Germany become the borders of world literature. Langenbucher cites at length Heinz Kindermann's essay "Von den Toren des Reichs" (1835; From the gates of the Reich)—published in the special issue of the journal *Buch und Volk*—to underline that the "Germans in border- and foreign lands are our bridges to other nations and races . . . if we win them for our perspectives, we will be successful in convincing other nations and races of the greatness and unfolding power of the new Germany. . . . Here it is about values that go far beyond the literary into the people's political [sphere]."[80] Langenbucher ends with stating the need for a united Germany and German people ("Volk"), asking for a disavowal of the division carried out in 1923.

The readers of the magazine would have to wait a few months for an overview of the program and purpose of the magazine. In the "News from the Publisher," Langenbucher briefly reports on the success of the magazine and promises—in line with his "volkhafte Dichtung"—that the purpose of the magazine is to give its readers works that are of a high literary value and high entertainment power and to accomplish that, in the new year, the magazine will switch between German and foreign authors.[81] This section also announces a publication of special focus on Poland and England in the coming months. The publishing agenda of *Weltliteratur* thus extends the foreign policy of Nazi Germany with regards to its neighbors. Polish literature becomes the focus of the March 1936 issue ("Polnische Literatur"), Southern Slavic literature is featured in June 1936 ("Südslavisches Schrifttum"), with excerpts from writers from Croatia, Serbia, Southern Serbia, and Slovenia, and an essay on Yugoslavian literature, and Hungarian literature is the focus of the March 1937 issue ("Ungarische Dichtung"). The March 1938 issue is dedicated to Benito Mussolini, with a long excerpt from his book *Vita di Arnaldo* accompanied by an essay on contemporary Italian literature.[82] The April 1938 issue has as one of its lead articles an essay on "German-French Intersections" in the contemporary novel;[83] the May and June 1938 issues ("Deutsche Dichtung in Österreich 1" and "Deutsche Dichtung in Österreich 2") focus on "German writings in Austria" (and not Austrian literature); and the August 1938 issue ("Sudetendeutsche Dichtung") on Sudeten-German Writings. April 1939 is a special issue on Robinson Crusoe.

German writers were also exploited and appropriated, especially with the assistance of the beautiful woodcut illustrations that were printed on the covers of the magazine. The May 1939 issue features excerpts from Grillparzer's *Der arme Spielmann* (1848), a story set in the provincial Brigittenau near Vienna. The lead article on Grillparzer, authored by Robert Hohlbaum, ends with a plea for "Großes Deutschland" and the need to recognize the spirit of an expanded Germany through the works of Grillparzer. The September 1939 issue features an excerpt from Herybert Menzel's "Umstrittene Erde" (Divided earth). The woodcut by Alfred Zacharias depicts a borderland with barbed wires around wooden poles and a solder in a helmet in the foreground. In the introduction, Menzel is described as writer of the German Eastland ("Dichter des deutschen Ostlands").

Through its strategically timed special foci on significant languages and literatures, the magazine acted as an organ of the Ministry for Public Enlightenment and Propaganda. But was there a specific position on world literature or the politics of the world literary enterprise, which also found space in *Weltliteratur*? Three articles in particular—two specifically on world literature and one on the alleged Anglo-American invasion of Scandinavia through translated works—deserve special discussion.

The June 1936 issue on Southern Slavic literatures carries an editorial note about foreign issues of *Die Weltliteratur* titled "Zu den Auslandsheften der *Weltliteratur*." Identifying this issue as the third issue (after the Norwegian and Polish literature ones) that deals with the literature of another people ("Dichtung eines anderen Volkes"), the editor underlines that the issue will once again acquaint its readers with the folklore (*Volkstum*) of the peoples of Yugoslavia:

> With these issues, *Weltliteratur* fulfills an essential part of its purpose. It offers people-oriented [*volkhaftes*] intellectual goods of other nations and should contribute thereby to the understanding of national life [*völkisches Leben*] of other kinds. It is natural that such literature requires a different consideration than works of our own German literature. It is not so readily accessible and often not immediately "appealing." Because *Weltliteratur* can after all select little from foreign commodity as compared to German writings, something of an easy, internationally accessible caliber, like the social novels that are to be found everywhere. It [*Weltliteratur*] will only draw from sources of real literature.[84]

In opposition to the program of the previous version, *Die Welt-Literatur*, which tried to bring the best literature to the readers, the Nazi magazine redefines world literature for its readers. It is no longer the most famous and well-known works of the "high" canon, but popular works, selected on the basis of their ability to provide glimpses into the lives of other societies. However, to speculate that this was some kind of a move for the democratization of the canon would be an obvious fallacy. Much like in Hesse's conception, for the Nazis too (via Langenbucher), world literature appears as the source of understanding the customs, traditions, indeed the intellectual wealth of other nations. But world literature is no longer defined by language; it is now also ethnically and racially defined. It is another source of the *Völkerkunde* (race studies) that the Nazis so actively promoted. Admittedly, even here, the particularity of literatures from elsewhere, the reader's limited access to such literature, and, last but not least, a different reading experience that does not render the work of literature immediately accessible do become part of *Weltliteratur*'s framing of other literatures for its German readers. However, there is an underlying political urgency to understand other nations, especially those in which the current political ideology is most directly invested. Moreover, it is not the poetry, but social novels in different languages, that become the sources of real literature; only they would offer a picture of the everyday lives of the people. World literature, in other words, acquires a sociological and anthropological function. This was reflected by the choice of texts, which swung between the popular and the canonical. While the Sudeten-German and Slavic literature issues focus on lesser-known authors, the German issues swing between Nazi-sympathizing, nationalist authors, or classical authors such as Goethe (October 1937) and Heinrich von Kleist (October 1938).

An extension of the above-mentioned idea: reader's accessibility, foreignness of world literature, and a sense of communication of national particularities characterizes Langenbucher's further engagement with the term, especially in the twenty-fifth issue of *Weltliteratur* (October 1937), which was dedicated to Goethe. In that issue the magazine made the first explicit reference to Goethe's concept of world literature. Langenbucher's editorial "Weltliteratur?" bears the interrogative tone of the title and appears as a public clarification of the magazine's task, as if the magazine had been reprimanded for its focus on foreign works. The article starts by directly addressing the readers and, in an uncanny fashion, bears the same sentiment about a common reader's fear of world literature that Hesse refers to in his essay, albeit by referring to food consumption: "It is likely that some people have not been able to win access to our magazine, because they are afraid of the term *world literature*. They confuse [*verwechseln*] the term with the case [of] 'literature of the entire world' [*Allerweltsliteratur*] and believe that in this magazine they will be offered a literary salad, which could have no other effect than upsetting their stomachs."[85]

The piece further provides comparative numbers for issues on German and foreign literatures; the former by far outweighs the latter. The article also states that the non-German literatures featured in the magazine are from nations with Germanic heritages (Nordic and Flemish) or of nations with whom Germany enjoys good diplomatic relationships (Spain, Hungary, Poland, and Yugoslavia). The editorial distinguishes its idea of *Weltliteratur* from *Allerweltsliteratur*:

> We nurture world literature not as literature of the entire world, to restate our position, but as literature which is a characteristic expression of its people, from whom it has developed. We do not want a literary world language, rather we are more concerned with getting to know nations [*Völker*] as they really are, and with that no international literary hodgepodge can help us, but only the literature that grows from the life-soil of its people. . . . Only in this way and shape do we promote the mutual understanding of individual peoples. The name of Goethe, with whom we and the whole world . . . associate everlastingly valid accomplishment . . . , should grant us the duty to carry out our work in such a way, that it is in the service of a relationship of cultural collaboration between nations that is determined by mutual respect.[86]

Apart from the distinction between "world literature" and "literature of the entire world," what is remarkable about Langenbucher's position is the rejection of any common, or even intersecting, deployment of language in the creation of world literature. The outright aversion to a "literary world language" stands in exact opposition to the sense in which Goethe was trying to conceptualize poesy as the *Gemeingut*, as the shared property of human beings. That sense of shared property is of no concern to the magazine, for it purportedly creates a literary hodgepodge ("literarischer Kauderwelsch") and prevents the acquisition of knowledge of individual nations and peoples, a knowledge that undoubtedly has its own social purpose and political goals. Despite the invocation of Goethe's name and the lavish praise bestowed on him, the idea of "cultural collaboration between peoples" remains bound to the life-soil ("Lebensboden") of nations. The translation of works from foreign languages and literatures into German for the German reading public is hardly a concern here. What is of utmost importance is the rootedness of works of literature. Once again, the cosmopolitan notion of world literature, one that transcends literary boundaries, one that renders national literatures meaningless (Goethe), one that emerges out of the literatures of many nations (Marx and Engels), or one that gives us a glimpse of the intersection of one society with the rest of the world (Hesse), is rejected. What works, what functions best, is world literature as a tree rooted in German soil, a notion that will continue as the magazine changes its name and its editorial leadership after 1939.

Wiking Verlag's *Weltliteratur*, edited by Langenbucher, lasted until 1939. In 1940, Schwerter Verlag with Friedhelm Kaiser as editor took over and gave the magazine a new name, *Die Weltliteratur: Berichte, Leseproben und Wertung* (World literature: Reports, excerpts, and evaluation") and a new font, Antiqua (figure 3-2).[87] As Strothmann contends, with the new editorial leadership, the magazine passed from the Ministry for Culture and Propaganda into the hands of the SS, and the funding for the magazine now came from the extreme right-wing Ahnenerbe Stiftung.[88] As Kater mentions in his study, starting in 1940, the magazine was to become a cultural-political organ of the SS.[89]

In his first editorial to *Die Weltliteratur*, "Die Waffen des Geistes" (The weapons of the intellect), Kaiser set the tone for the magazine: nationalist, jingoistic, selectively and strategically worldly, and in the service of the dominant Nazi ideology. The editorial extends the values of the magazine's predecessor, albeit with an amplified urgency of the decisive year ("Jahr der Entscheidung") of the English War in which Germany found itself since 1939. There is no exception for literature in this deciding moment for Germany, Kaiser states: "In this moment we experience again that also in the domain of the 'literary,' there is no space that stands outside of this: the Decision."[90] Along with weapons of steel and iron, there are "weapons

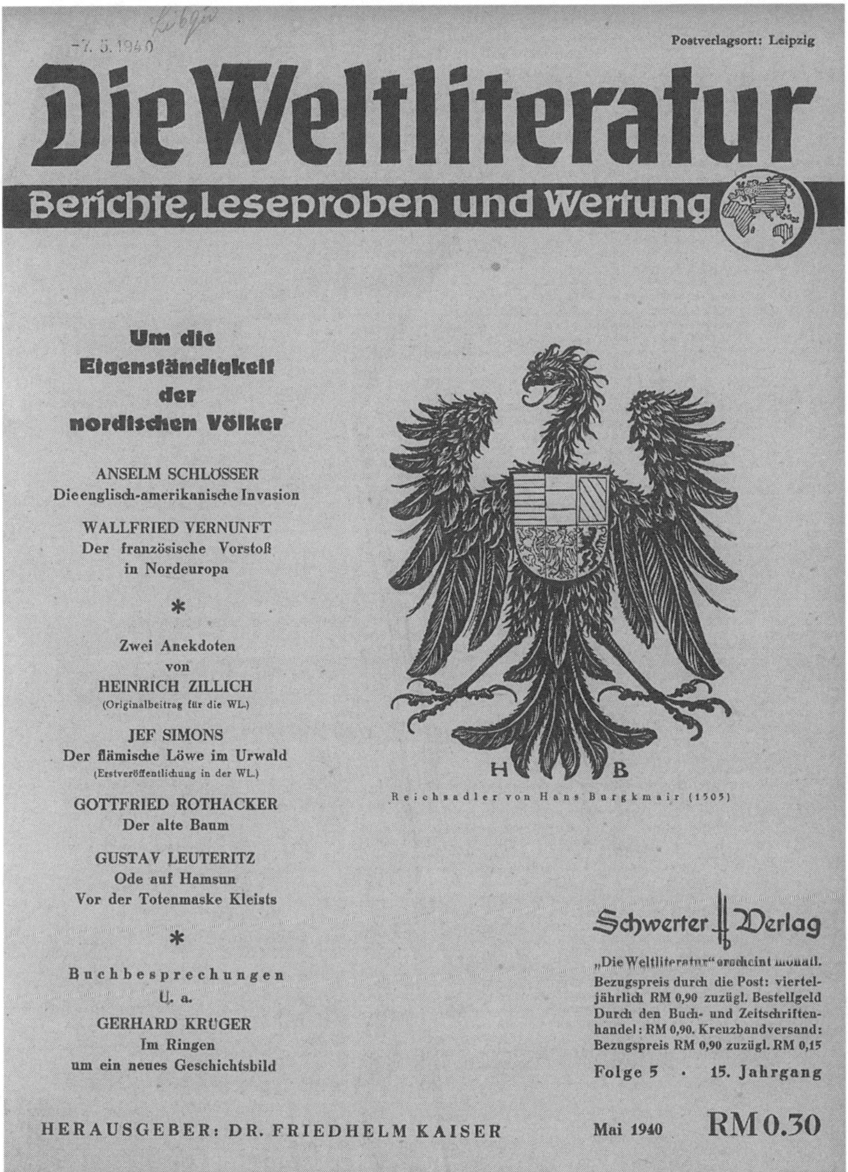

Postverlagsort: Leipzig

Die Weltliteratur

Berichte, Leseproben und Wertung

Um die Eigenständigkeit der nordischen Völker

ANSELM SCHLÖSSER
Die englisch-amerikanische Invasion

WALLFRIED VERNUNFT
Der französische Vorstoß in Nordeuropa

*

Zwei Anekdoten von
HEINRICH ZILLICH
(Originalbeitrag für die WL.)

JEF SIMONS
Der flämische Löwe im Urwald
(Erstveröffentlichung in der WL.)

GOTTFRIED ROTHACKER
Der alte Baum

GUSTAV LEUTERITZ
Ode auf Hamsun
Vor der Totenmaske Kleists

*

Buchbesprechungen
U. a.
GERHARD KRÜGER
Im Ringen um ein neues Geschichtsbild

H B
Reichsadler von Hans Burgkmair (1505)

Schwerter Verlag

„Die Weltliteratur“ erscheint monatl.
Bezugspreis durch die Post: vierteljährlich RM 0,90 zuzügl. Bestellgeld
Durch den Buch- und Zeitschriftenhandel: RM 0,90. Kreuzbandversand: Bezugspreis RM 0,90 zuzügl. RM 0,15

Folge 5 · 15. Jahrgang

HERAUSGEBER: DR. FRIEDHELM KAISER

Mai 1940 RM 0.30

Figure 3-2. Cover of *Die Weltliteratur* magazine, May 1940. (Courtesy of Deutsche Nationalbibliothek and Buch- und Schriftmuseum Leipzig.)

of the intellect," and the humanities (*Geisteswissenschaften*) are part of the weapons that strengthen the soul and the feelings ("Seele und Gemüt") of the people. This despite the global struggle in which Germany—a nation of Western culture with Indo-Germanic imprint ("abendländische Kultur indogermanischer Prägung")—reportedly finds itself in; it remains true to its predicament: to collect and to radiate ("zu sammeln und auszustrahlen"). The establishment of the new Faculty of Foreign Studies ("Auslandswissenschaftliche Fakultät") at the University of Berlin thus becomes a symptom of this collection and dissemination of knowledge about the world. It is in this context that Kaiser locates the concept of world literature and the new (version of the) magazine, which includes the most important reader: the soldier. Glossing over the complicated history of the magazine, Kaiser establishes a direct link between the current magazine and its first predecessor, *Die Weltliteratur* (1915–1924), a magazine that "emanated during the war" and brought novels, novellas, and stories to the soldiers on the front.[91] The purpose of the current magazine as the "old and new" voice of world literature is thus twofold, states Kaiser: "first to acknowledge from German literature and to represent what was made with a worldwide approach; something that found a 'world' format, and next, to bring literature of the world to the German readers, which is useful or even necessary for them."[92] The key to this statement is of course the mention of the "useful" or the "necessary" works of world literature for the German people, the authority for which rests with the editors of the magazine as well as the officials of the Ministry for Culture and Propaganda and the SS.

According to Kaiser, the condition of war unfolded a new problem of a German engagement with the world, the world spirit (*Weltgeist*), and world literature. To illustrate his point about the "useful" and the "necessary" world literature, Kaiser quickly mentions his own piece on the flood of translations ("Übersetzungsflut") in the *Nationalsozialistische Bibliographie* (1939). His self-citation is telling of his own position on the selective engagement with foreign literatures but also on the shape that the magazine will take under his leadership. At its core is the struggle between national and foreign literatures. He warns against newspapers that continue to direct readers to foreign literature by discussing them in great detail while the advancement of German literature falls behind. Criticizing such "Weltblätter" and their satellites, Kaiser complains that these papers nurture the "ill-fated German tendency to consider all that is foreign already as good and refined, and the engagement with it [the foreign] to be 'intellectual,' 'cosmopolitan,' and splendid."[93] Distancing the current magazine from such news media, Kaiser states categorically: "One would notice in this that for us nothing is more distant than to 'foreignize' [the readers]. In the spirit consonant with the intellectual exchange between peoples, the magazine considers world literature as a 'conversation beyond the borders,' to include all the 'great and meaningful' literature."[94] However, Kaiser also warms that it must be taken for granted that the place for such conversations is a "national socialist Germany," and "for us there is no other 'literary' world view than the political [view] of Adolf Hitler, according to which the collective arrangement of peoples can only be based on the arrangement of specific peoples [*Einzelvolk*] as per their individuality." Ultimately, world literature becomes an "intellectual weapon," that provides a perspective on the world and, in turn, gives the world a perspective on Germany. Kaiser promises to "take it to the battle field" as the "German Volk marches in the double step of world history."[95]

An extension of this militarized form of world literature, as a weapon in the service of a nation at war, is reiterated in a statement on world literature from the battlefield. Despite its brevity, Lieutenant Siegmund Graff's note "Deutschheit und Weltliteratur" (Germanness and world literature) offers one of the most potent manipulations of Goethe's idea of world literature and a complete reversal of Hermann Hesse's notion of a masterpiece. The interrogative note that marked the beginning of Langenbucher's article from *Weltliteratur*, October 1937, is now replaced with a confident exclamation mark: "World literature! Goethe coined the word."[96] Graff sets out to establish the connection between Goethe's concept of world literature and Adolf Hitler's notion of Germany. Having credited Goethe at the beginning of the essay with the coinage of the term, Graff briefly explains the difference between the term and its use by Goethe, which for him is "something that we became used to understanding . . . the concept and sum of those literary creations of all peoples and languages, which through their human reality and their artistic form and—not in the least—their national fundamental content have become worthy for the entire world of the educated."[97] Almost as if in a rushed bid to change "what one became used to understanding," Graff reminds his readers that for Goethe, the concept of the valid was one that was timelessly worthy and influential. Goethe, according to Graff, was not interested in school-level ("schulmäßige") rubrics. Paraphrasing and selectively citing Eckermann, Graff goes on to claim that for Goethe, it made no difference if poetry were classified as romantic or classical, as long as it was through and through ("durch und durch") literature. Graff then presents his interpretation of Goethe's understanding of the classical, something that is complete and perfected ("vollendet"). If Goethe's conceptualization of the term world literature had any value in a country during World War II, it is through the fact that perfection is a value typical of Germans, it is a German conceptualization.[98] Graff moves to emphasize the significance and justification of Goethe's concept for his contemporaries. Graff references the most difficult deciding battle ("schwerste Entscheidungskampf") in which Germany finds itself at the time, where a concept such as Goethe's leads to knowledge of the spirit that recognizes the spirit of others, out of which emanates a transnational power that becomes beneficial for all. This militarization of Goethe's concept of world literature comes to completion with Graff's establishment of a direct connection between Hitler and Goethe: "Adolf Hitler once used the beautiful image of the tree that stretches out its branches farthest in all sides, because it is most deeply rooted in the mother-ground of one's own earth. This image expresses most meaningfully, what we—in Goethe's sense—despite struggle and war, understand under *Weltliteratur*."[99] The last section of the short article illustrates this extension of the ever-expanding tree in all directions through the example of Shakespeare. Despite the war against England, Graff claims, Shakespeare would remain the most respected figure for Germans. Shakespeare becomes part of the German "idea" of perfection that must be protected, as much as the cathedral in Cologne or the statue of the Bamberg Rider. Graff's essay ends with the proclamation that masters and masterpieces ought to be honored for one's own good, as stated in the lines that form the epigraph to this chapter.

One cannot find an explicit reference to Goethe's concept of world literature even in the many writings of Goebbels, considered to be the most well-read of all Nazi officials. However, the discussion of the magazines *Weltliteratur* and *Die Weltliteratur* reveals the appropriation of Goethe's concept, as well as the figure of Goethe himself, for serving the political ideology of the Nazis. While the conceptualization of world literature at the beginning of the nineteenth century relies heavily on the circulation of literatures from Asia and Africa, there is hardly any discussion of non-European literatures in the two magazines. World literature remains either literature written by Germans in foreign countries or in the borderlands of Germany, or literature written by authors in countries most beneficial to Germany in its politics of the *Lebensraum*. The *Lebensraum* of Germany becomes the *Lebensraum* of *Weltliteratur*, stifled under the politics of tyranny, one-sidedness, discrimination, and, if the article by Graff bears any testimony, to populism. During the Nazi era, world literature becomes a conduit in the larger militarization of the Nazi polity. A smug sense of ownership—not borrowing—prevails, whereby the Nazis show openness to all masterpieces and all worldly cultural heritage, only if to indulge in the strengthening of their own prowess over literature. Even in the selection and showcasing of national literatures, it is none of the German Nobel Laureates—Theodor Mommsen (1902), Gerhart Hauptmann (1912), or Thomas Mann (1929)—but as per the guidelines, a host of Nazi-sympathizing nationalists, or at best provincially domestic and locally acclaimed jingoistic authors, who would be presented as if they were in dialogue with the larger world of literature beyond the borders of Germany. Classic German authors such as Heinrich von Kleist or Goethe, or Austrian authors such as Grillparzer, would be exploited for obvious reasons. However, in this undulating focus on what is populist (*volkshaft*) and has a transnational appeal, the ultimate authority would rest with the Nazis and their idea of which literatures might be allowed for circulation.

The significance of books and other forms of printed materials to the propaganda machine was clear to the Nazis. However, it is not as if a systematic effort to translate German literature into other European languages was necessarily part of the Nazi strategy for winning "soft" power. Their aim was militaristic expansion, and through that it seems that the expansion of German language as the dominating language even for literature had been taken for granted by the Nazis. While the Ministry for Public Enlightenment and Propaganda kept a keen eye on the use of books for the ideologization of the masses, as for German literature—populist or high—the effect tended more in the direction of banning rather than publishing new texts, especially in translation. The use of literary translations as a weapon of war, and potentially as a medium for anti-German propaganda, came as a revelation to the Nazis, especially in the first year of the war and in the case of non-German-speaking "Germanic" territories in Scandinavia.

The May 1940 issue of *Die Weltliteratur* carried a three-page article (about five thousand words) titled "Die englisch-amerikanische Invasion" (The English-American invasion) of Scandinavian countries through translated literature. Kaiser's introductory editorial note to the article carries the following banner:

> About the Self-Sufficiency of Nordic Countries
>
> English, American, and French Cultural Propaganda in Scandinavia / Preparation for War through Books / Translated literature stronger than Scandinavia's own Production[100]

The urgency and sensationalism of the banner is carried through the highly ideologized register of the introduction. Kaiser frames the popularity of

English and American authors in translation as a problem of the "neutrality of Scandinavian countries." He presents the entry of Hitler's army in Denmark and Norway on April 1, 1940, as a question of the "security and neutrality" of these countries, and calls the move essential due to the situation of the war ("Kriegslage"). He is quick to justify the military action as an offering from the Germans "against the brutality and scrupulousness of the English and the French." The great Germanic commonality ("Gemeinsamkeit") is thus supposed to have realized itself selflessly. It is in this historical framework that Kaiser situates the article by Schlösser, which reveals how cultural propaganda had gained firm ground in Scandinavia, and, until the German entry, which cultural-political direction the Scandinavian countries were either taking or "let themselves be taken in." Kaiser describes the overview of conditions of the book market and the "deep-seated" precursors to the event (i.e., popularity of translations) as two among the greatest contributions to the intellectual struggles of Europe and of humanity! As an attestation of superior German capabilities in protecting and promoting Scandinavian literature, Kaiser cites the Icelandic author Gunnar Gunnarson: "There is no other country in the world in which one finds more knowledge and a fine understanding of Nordic literatures as in Germany. There exists a feeling for Nordic literary treasures in Germany, which lies in the disposition [*Gemüt*] of the people, and that naturally has not been changed by what is happening in Europe politically."[101]

The article by Schlösser illustrates the overwhelming number of translations abundant in the Scandinavian book market in three ways: (1) through facts from the book market; (2) through trends in popular authors; and (3) through warnings about a forthcoming cultural political disaster if these translations and their readers are not held in check. The language of the entire article is stark and bombastic. Schlösser starts with stressing that "not much that is meaningful [*bedeutendes*] [in literature]" was published in the Nordic countries in 1939, and even book production declined; the growing number of English and American translations is turning Nordic countries into a "cultural dominion" of England and the United States. Schlösser mentiones over ninety books from England and over one hundred from American literature translated almost simultaneously in all three Nordic languages, with Sweden serving as the center for publications.

Citing bestseller lists in the *Swenska Dagblatt*—the leading national daily in Sweden—which are primarily led by English and American authors, Schlösser complains that the rise of foreign influence is the reason for a disproportionate decrease in national productivity. While Kaiser couches his arguments against translations in the spirit of protecting Scandinavian national and linguistic particularities and the spirit of Germanic commonality, for Schlösser, the availability of translations from another country thus becomes a reason for a lack of national cultural production, a reason for national cultural decline. What Schlösser draws is an interesting picture of the reception of English and American novels in Scandinavia, especially in the interwar period. British authors such as John Galsworthy and A. J. Cronin led the bestseller lists; Americans such as Edna Ferber (Schlösser makes sure that he uses the word *Jüdin* as a qualifier for this author), Hervey Allen, and John Steinbeck reportedly found great resonance in Scandinavia. The reasons for the grandiose success of these authors lies for Schlösser in the general fashionable trends in Europe, which do not have much explanation, the comfort ("Bequemlichkeit") of publishing houses in publishing these works, and the rise of "Literatursnobs" who then encourage the uncritical reception of any work produced in England or America. While Schlösser acknowledges the cultural connections between Scandinavia and the United States due to the mass-migration of Scandinavians, he categorically states that contemporary literature produced in America is "not based on the national [*völkisch*] relationship between Scandinavia and the US, and does not promote [*fortsetzt*] any real traditions, but rather it is overwhelmingly in the service of a Western democratic propaganda against Germany."[102] As for English dominance, the British Council emerges as the supreme agent of English imperialism; not only did council members change the patterns of the old relationships between Norway, Sweden, and England—which were primarily economic—according to Schlösser they also forged relationships with the "Anglophiles" and influenced the reform of the foreign-langauge classroom. As a consequence, English is the most common second language in Norway and enjoys an increase in Sweden. So in the entire business of world literature and English imperialism around the world, the countries that become of most sensitive concern are Norway and Sweden. Through the foreign-langauge classroom, the British and the Americans are supposedly making their way into the publishing industry, duping the publishers and the reading publics into printing and reading books about a "barbaric" Germany. Schlösser names the "Jewish publicist and sociologist" Walter Lippman as one of those who advances the anti-German agenda.

Apart from more famous authors such as Galsworthy or Steinbeck, the article mentions a series of authors of popular thrillers, which Schlösser claims are decidedly anti-German. These include Leon G. Torrou and Joseph Gallomb (*Armies of Spies*), pamphleteers such as Hendrik van Loon

("Our Battle"), Pierre van Passen's *Days of our Years* and Conrad Heiden's *The Eleventh Hour*. Books by Chamberlain, Churchill, and Eden translated into Norwegian are reportedly part of the conspiracy for the preparation of war, and so are the many criminal novels as well as English novels set in various British colonies around the world. Schlösser compares the impoverished state of German translations, especially historical novels that were published in Germany, which stand in no competition with British novels. From Graham Greene, James Hilton, P. G. Wodehouse, J. B. Priestly, Richard Hughes, all the way to D. H. Lawrence, the Nazi position on this circulating world literature in Scandinavia is that it is allegedly leading to the decline of traditional Scandinavian values.

As a coda to this long article, the author reports on the uneven playing field of literary translation that is affecting the course of European politics. Apart from explicitly political books, such as biographies of Churchill, world circulation of literature, especially in translation, has become a siren of Western democratic propaganda, jeopardizing the beautiful spirit of Scandinavian home-grown fiction. The article ends on a hopeful note: "Maybe one day a new political constellation in Europe and the world will reconstruct the balance destroyed through no fault of the North, and this will lead to a cultural healing in Scandinavia."[103] The inset to the article, a poem with the title "Ode auf Hamsun" (Ode to Hamsun) seals this hope.

The concern for the domination of an intellectually "sick" Scandinavia through translated books from England and the United States was in fact part of a well worked-out control of translations through National Socialist policies. What Kaiser, and then Schlösser, refer to in 1940 was part of a larger process that had started in 1939. The Nazi control of translations of literary works into German is particularly important in the context of world literature, as it operated parallel to, and often through, magazines such as *Die Weltliteratur*. A complete control of translations of works into German from the enemy states ("Feindstaaten") was impossible, simply considering the translation contracts that were signed before the beginning of the war. Already in May 1938 the Nazis had issued an ordinance requiring prior approval to publish works in translation.[104] However, a memo from the Ministry of People's Enlightenment and Propaganda on September 20, 1939, instructed the newspapers "preferably not to touch upon the topic of translation."[105] A close scrutiny of translated literature was to become an important part of the Nazi policy on books, especially after 1941.[106] Friedhelm Kaiser himself suggested the establishment of an agency that would examine and control the influx of foreign-language literature in Germany (Prüfstelle zur Einfuhr ausländischer Literatur in Deutschland). As mentioned earlier, Kaiser was concerned about what he saw as the flooding ("Überflut") of the book market with translated works. Kaiser's concerns were not directly pitched against the ideological influence of the works, rather, on the neglect of homegrown writing through the consumption of foreign literature. The control of translations fell under the propriety of the Reichsschrifttumskammer (RSK). As Goebbels brought all the offices of the book market under his control in 1938, it became mandatory for publishing houses to inform the officer-in-charge at the RSK of their translation plans ahead of the proposed date of publication.[107]

Given the detailed list of the various categories of books banned for public circulation, the publishers were already aware of the financial losses they might have to suffer if they invested money in the production of a questionable book by an author of non-Aryan, Jewish, foreign, or even foreign-sounding name. Slowly but surely, the number of translated works published in German declined. Already in September 1939, through the language ordinance (Sprachreglung 20, September 1939), about 60 to 70 percent of the translation contracts were declared invalid.[108] Starting in 1941 with the state rationing of paper allotments to publishing companies, more publishers came under pressure to select translated works judiciously. Nonetheless, through various clauses and subclauses the control of translated literatures was brought to fruition: classical Russian literature was banned in 1941, North-American literature was banned in 1942, and in both cases, the rules followed those that were behind the ban of English and French literatures. Holland, Belgium, and the Scandinavian countries were the only "translation-free" states, although even here the works of some authors were permitted in translation on a case-by-case basis. For example, Shakespeare and Bernard Shaw could continue to exist on the German stage; Heinrich Heine's "Lorelei" was included as a poem by an "unknown" author in a collection of poems, and so on. Works by foreign authors that were critical of their contemporary societies or were anti-Semitic were beyond the restrictions of the ban. Archibald Joseph Cronin's *The Stars Look Down* (1935)—a critique of the medical profession in England—could be published as *Die Sterne blicken herab*;[109] Henry Ford's four-volume *The International Jew* (1920–1922) was published as *Der internationale Jude* (1935); Sinclar Lewis's *Babbitt* (1922), a tale of the pressure to conform in American society, was accepted, and John Steinbeck's *Grapes of Wrath* (1939) was published as *Früchte des Zorns* (1940). Among the most favored Nordic literatures, Sigrid Undset, who openly criticized the entry of the German Wehrmacht into Norway, was banned from circulation in libraries.[110] From German literature, the effort was directed toward translating pro-Nazi German writings into foreign languages, in order to break the hegemony of emigrated authors.[111]

In addition to various categories established by the RSK, the Buchkommision (Book Commission) worked in tandem with Alfred Rosenberg's war against ideological ("weltanschauliche") writings. Thus works were to be tested on the basis of their ideological ("politisch-weltanschaulich"), artistic ("künstlerisch"), and national-educational ("volkserzieherischen") qualities. The evaluation system followed the following criteria:

1. positive
2. negative
3. restricted circle of interest
4. irrelevant
5. outdated—with limitations
6. qualified positive
7. qualified negative

These categories were often arbitrary and depended upon Germany's relationship with the country at the time of the specific ordinance's passing. In the case of British and American writings, for example, according to an ordinance from 1940, works by authors who died before 1904 were allowed to be published, but in 1942, they were completely banned, at least for the duration of the war.[112] Such authors included Bacon, Carlyle, Chaucer, Defoe, Dickens, Marlowe, Milton, Macpherson, Shakespeare, Swift, and Wilde. In addition, the handbook of the Reichsschrifttumskammer included Chesterton, Conrad, Forster, Maugham, Maurier, Mansfield, and Woolf among those who could not be published anymore. Among American authors, Emerson, Longfellow, Melville, Poe, and Whitman were published, while Bromfield, Buck, Disney, Faulkner, Fitzgerald, Saroyan, Wilder, and Wolfe were banned.

For a government that outlawed its own most famous authors, including Heine, it could hardly be expected that foreign authors would be allowed. Nexö, Balzac, Boccaccio, Diderot, Huxley, Proust, and Zola were all among the banned authors. And so were the two that were dreaming of a world library in the 1920s: Romain Rolland (all works) and Rabindranath Tagore (one work). The classified communications to the book industry from the Reichskulturkammer—*Liste verbotener und nicht erwünschter Schriften* (1934–1943; List of banned and unwanted books), which was published monthly;[113] *Jahresliste des schädlichen und unerwünschten Schrifttums* (1939–1943; Annual list of harmful and unwanted books), complied annually;[114] *Liste der in der Deutschen Bücherei unter Verschluß gestellten Druckschriften*

(1939–1943; List of locked case books in the German national library), published monthly;[115] and *Vertrauliche Mitteilungen der Fachschaft Verlag* (1935–1943; Confidential reports of the department of publishing)[116]—stipulated organizations, institutions, and individuals who were one by one being banned by the Nazis.

In 1941, Hans Ernst Schneider took over as editor-in-chief of *Die Weltliteratur*. The last years of the magazine (1941–1944) reflect the slow emptying out of shelves from all German libraries. The issues reveal an emptiness, a lack of agenda, a "why bother at all" attitude. The magazine loses its militant defense of world literature, or even German literature. The contributions are now almost exclusively focused on the idea of the Reich, and the magazine turns into a platform for justifying and explaning all the policies that were communicated through the confidential reports and lists of unwanted and harmful books. Literary works published in the magazine are mostly poems written by soldiers, either about the Vaterland or odes to the Führer. The essay section becomes limited to a few authors such as Hans Hagen, Bernhard Pyr, and the editor Schneider; most of the essays are about the glory of the Reich. In addition, the magazine started publishing citations from Hitler, Himmler, and Goebbels in big insets, as if to cover space. With most of the German authors and non-German authors in translation banned, the idea of world literature becomes either regional within territories occupied or "reclaimed" by Germany (such as Swabia, Silesia, Lorraine) or Eastern Europe, with a few features on Bulgarian, Romanian, and Croatian literatures. British and American novels are reduced to one article each, only to highlight the social discrepancies within the respective nations.[117] The Netherlands, Belgium, and the Scandinavian countries receive the most coverage. The entire business of world literature—in the original language or in translation—is cast in the vocabulary of enemies and friends, allies and opposers, or just racial kinship. An article about translations of Nordic literatures succinctly communicates the party's stand on translation. Explaining the wider accessibility of Nordic literatures in German translations, when compared to other (unnamed) literatures, the author states:

> The purpose of translated literature lies in that it shows other people in their deepest and most characteristic particularity. . . . And especially the countries of the North are especially close to us in this respect, because from the racial and people-oriented [*volkhaft*] kinship or similarity certain connections must arise, which are stronger than those with any other people, understandings that are necessary in the

> Germanic space. . . . And it is not only of significance for us, rather for this greater decision, who is with us or against us. To be sure this is no more an artistic decision . . . than when a victim invites his robber to dinner, and therefore we do not want any feasts for our enemies; even if we have to renounce artistic values because of this, so for us the larger assignment is more important than a concession that is not essential to life. . . . We reject authors who work against us.[118]

This passage precisely captures the militarization of the magazine and in some ways also its further compromise of artistic values. The division of the world into allies and enemies of the German nation, long established by Langenbucher in the founding of the magazine, acquires a specifically distinct character here. The magazine seems less and less interested in any contributions to the world outside what is deemed "friendly" by the National Socialists. What receives amplification is race. The Germanic connection, that is, the racial kinship and similarity, acquires a specifically Aryan/Indo-Germanic dimension in another piece, especially in the context of literary accomplishments. A long article on "Indo-German Confessions" ("Indogermanische Bekenntnisse")—an excerpt from a book by Walther Wüst—establishes a "glorious" geneology of Aryan achievements from emperors Asoka to Harsha in India, to Kaiser Maximilian in Germany, to the philosophers Plato and Kant; he then states:

> It is no false arrogance, but a certainty stemming from the sharpest awareness for distinctive independence and unique valency, when we detect that it is hard to find a Kalidasa, Firdausi, Goethe, Dante or Shakespeare among the Eskimos or the [American] Indians, to establish proof of a music of the highest rank from a Johann Sebastian Bach, Beethoven, Bruckner, or Richard Wagner among the Negros, or to track down a Dürer, Rembrandt, or Phidias among the Jews. There is only one Indo-German symphony, one Indo-German tragedy, one Indo-German Epic.[119]

Thus very clearly the magazine—by virtue of providing a platform to a pro-Aryan, anti-Semitic, and racist writer—establishes world literature as a prerogative of the Indo-Germanic race. The history of world literature, world music, world art is reduced to the history of a handful of names, all Aryans. No wonder, that *Die Weltliteratur* ran out of steam in March 1944!

The Nazis knew what they were doing to world literature and to the world of books. With over five hundred authors on the list of "Schädliche und unerwünschte Bücher," a rationing of paper supplies to publishing companies, and the increasing investment in the war, which was depleting the nation of its resources—not to mention the closing of all the Jewish-owned publishing companies—the effect on the book market was devastating. In "Ein Blick in den Buchhandel" (1943), Gottfried Lindener accepted the lack of books in book stores and the fact that many titles were out of print ("vergriffen"). In the article he blamed it on the high-demand of books and printed materials in the great nation of readers (*Lesenation*) and promised that the book publishers, binders, and sellers were doing their best in the service of the "German book."[120] But the reality, as would be clear, was very different. Hermann Hesse's essay from 1929, a call for the democratization of world literature and a pamphlet for the medium of the book, had become completely insignificant within a few years.

Following the Nazi ascension to power in 1933, editions of *Eine Bibliothek der Weltliteratur* disappeared from the market.[121] Like most publishers, Reclam was increasingly nationalistic and propagandistic, assuring its existence by acceding to the Nazi discrimination against Jewish authors. Hesse was pressured to release a "contemporized" version of his essay from which the works of Jewish authors such as Martin Buber were deleted. Hesse's essay thus witnessed its own prophecy of the changing definition of world literature. On December 13, 1934, Hesse informed Reclam that he would not honor its request for a new edition. Using the dimunitive, Hesse characterizes his little book ("Büchlein") as a confession ("Bekenntnis") of what has grown from his own reading experience ("Lese-Erlebnis und Lese-Erfahrung") during his fifty-seven years. Asserting that *Eine Bibliothek der Weltliteratur* is no objective or study guide ("schulmäßiger Führer") to literature, he categorically states that he will make "no other changes, such as the deletion of Jewish authors." He gives Reclam two options: give back his publication rights or publish the essay as is, unchanged.[122] He received a vituperative response on his sixtieth birthday in 1937. Within weeks the Nazi Ministry of Public Enlightenment and Propaganda released a sham document asking for "no more future assaults on Hermann Hesse"; however, the 1937 essay "Hermann Hesse und der deutsche Buchhandel," published in *Der Buchhändler* (The booktrader), the journal of the German Book Trader's Association, declared that Hesse had proved to be "someone who did not belong to the German Reich but was merely Swiss."[123]

Hesse understood very well the dangerous game that the Nazis were playing with literature and libraries—real and imaginary. Writing from Montagnola in 1945 for the 1946 edition of *Eine Bibliothek der Weltliteratur* (published by Werner Classen in Zürich), Hesse reminds his readers of the recent destruction of book culture and private libraries through terror and war and puts great hope in the idea that a few public libraries will give people access to world literature, which he now simply designates as the world of books ("Bücherwelt"):

> This attempt at an introduction to world literature was written at a time when procuring a book was easy and less expensive. Meanwhile, terror and war have done away with the world of books, especially German books: there is almost nothing left. Much of what has been destroyed will stay destroyed forever, or at least for a long time. When my little book first appeared, anyone who was interested could order the books it recommended at any bookstore. That will not happen for a good while now. But at least in our country, public libraries have stayed intact, and our publishers are rapidly issuing new editions. However, to a large extent they are only first editions. Nonetheless, even today serious readers will find the books that are most important to them.[124]

Shadows of Empty Shelves

In 1913, the German scholar Richard Meyer published an important volume, *Die Weltliteratur im zwanzigsten Jahrhundert: Vom deutschen Standpunkt aus betrachtet* (World literature in the twentieth century: from the German perspective). Meyer, too, distinguished between *Weltliteratur* and "Literatur aus aller Welt," favoring the best and the most representative of all literary traditions. Citing Goethe's words from the magazine *Kunst und Altertum*, Meyer explored the possibility of building "a general world literature, in which the Germans have an honorable role reserved for themselves."[125] The first half of the twentieth century displays both the claiming of that honorable role, not merely through reception of the works of some of the best German authors in the international literary space but also through the recognition of international authors in the German-speaking space through translations. During World War I, magazines like *Die Welt-Literatur*, publishing houses, translators, and the proliferation of cheap editions, as well as the formation of private libraries of world literature all contributed to the semblance of an important role that Germany might have played in the construction of world literature. And yet this role transformed at an alarming rate as the nation completely insulated itself from all foreign influences, purged its own cultural heritage, and marched to a racist beat into the darkest hour of history. As a philosophical ideal, world literature became an instrument of pedantic arrogance rather than a way out of it. As a pedagogical strategy, world literature became an instrument of political propaganda. As a strategy of affiliation, world literature turned into a mode of affiliation with nations subservient to, conquered by, or about to be captured by the Nazis. As a unit of aesthetic evaluation, world literature changes from the best and most representative, to the mediocre and therefore the most accessible: from *vorzüglichst* to *volkhaft*. From an acquired world literature, the picture switched to an inherited world literature, where the world was only formed by those related by blood or race.

One of the most disconcerting memorials to the destruction of books and libraries in the world is the Monument in Memory of the Burning of Books (Denkmal zur Erinnerung an Bücherverbrennung) in Berlin. Designed by the famous Israeli sculptor Micha Ullman, the monument is just off the popular boulevard Unter den Linden, in the middle of Bebelplatz—named after the famous German Social Democrat August Bebel (1840–1913)—in front of what used to be the Alte Bibliothek (old library) of the Humoldt Universität. A stone's throw from the Museum Insel and Alexanderplatz, the memorial occupies a central spot in the heart of Berlin's tourist center.

The momument is empty! It commemorates the Nazi book burnings of works by Jewish intellectuals, liberals, and communists on May 10, 1933, and consists of a glass lid on top of subterranean pit (of about 175 cubic feet) lined with empty bookshelves painted white—the emptiness exacerbated by the naked rods of glowing fluorescent light. The viewer has a top-down perspective of the bookshelves through the glass lid—there is no other form of access. All one sees are stark empty bookshelves, inviting the visitor to imagine the names of authors and titles of books—national and foreign—included on the yearly lists of "unwanted books" that might have filled this pit of a library. But it is hard to imagine a book on a shelf from where it was forcefully removed and burned. As Heine had already reminded us in *Almansor*, "where one burns books, in the end human beings are burned." Akin to the experience of Mann's Tonio Kröger, the monument reminds of a space where the intimate has gone public; and yet there is a total disconnect between public and literature. As Hesse reminds us, the library of world literature remains a dream and an idea, it exists in the imagination. And no ownership or private libraries, or even the staying intact of public libraries, will provide an easy recourse. Because the rest of history will not forget, that five years after the book burnings, by a special order of the Reichsschrifttumskammer on November 1, 1938, Jews were banned from all public libraries and robbed of their borrowing privileges.

Frankfurt
Amsterdam
Leipzig
Berlin
Moscow
Dublin
Warsaw
London
Prague
Budapest
Paris
Belgrade
Madison
Stuttgart
Bucharest
New Haven
Sarajevo
Sofia
Washington DC
New York
Madrid
Rome
Istanbul
Beijing
Tirana
Athens
Tokyo
Haifa
Shanghai
Cairo
New Delhi
Varanasi
Havana
Calcutta
Mexico City
Hanoi
Guatemala City
Dakar
Caracas
Ibadan
Douala
Campala
Jakarta
Lima
Luanda
Rio de Janeiro
Johannesberg
Santiago de Chile
Montevideo
Buenos Aires
Canberra

CHAPTER 4

Windows on the Berlin Wall: Unfinished Histories of World Literature in a Divided Germany

By token of this, our conception of *Weltliteratur* and its philology is no less human, no less humanistic, than its antecedent; the implicit comprehension of history—which underlies this conception of *Weltliteratur*—is not the same as the former one, yet it is a development of it and unthinkable without it.

—ERICH AUERBACH, "Philology and *Weltliteratur*" (1952)[1]

You would not consider [it] book burning, a rather vicious thing, if we insist that you do not have the works of Communist authors on your shelves to indoctrinate the German people?

—SENATOR JOSEPH R. MCCARTHY, "Senate Appropriations Committee Hearings" (1953)[2]

The East German author Volker Braun's novel *Unvollendete Geschichte* (Unfinished story/history, 1975) is regarded as one of the most controversial and widely discussed literary works critiquing social life in the former German Democratic Republic (GDR). The novel sutures individual and collective stories and histories. The protagonist Frank, thirty-two years old and socially isolated, is chastised by the parents of his girlfriend, Karin, for his connections to the West and is later reported to the state. Karin's father, a state official and member of the ruling socialist party, is dismayed by her relationship with Frank. During one of her visits home, the father decides to read a poem to her. Karin finds it strange, because her father never showed any interest in literature. Literature had a utilitarian function for the party, and it could be referenced through "official praise or a semi-official critique": "The reason for this was that authors write in unfocused ways about all possible things, almost as it occurred to them, instead of agreeing on the essential, current question, and preferably writing that *one*, necessary book instead of so many confusing ones. Moreover, as a trained historian with statistical leanings he [the father] had an aversion to the belletristic mode of representation."[3] As an example of clear and focused writing with a purpose, Karin's father reads a poem about political commitment by Johannes R. Becher, the GDR's first cultural minister. The poem extols the "real" socialism of a *Menschen-Staat*, a state built on the foundations of humanity.

Karin's disconnect with her father's beliefs and ideas on literature take a turn at Frank's place; in his personal library she discovers the novel *Die neuen Leiden des jungen W.* (1976; *The New Sorrows of Young W.*), an equally controversial social commentary on East Germany by Ulrich Plenzdorf, who rose to fame with the publication of this work. The novel, a late twentieth-century treatment of Goethe's *Leiden des jungen Werthers* (1776), documents the coming of age of the teenager Edgar Wiebeau, a young man growing up in East Germany. Edgar is fascinated by Werther's resistance to imposed social norms and his obsession with Charlotte. However, unlike Werther's penchant for painting and the Scottish author James McPharsen's *Ossian* (1760), Edgar is enamored by American jeans, beat music, and two books that he almost knows by heart: Daniel Defoe's *Robinson Crusoe* and J. D. Salinger's *The Catcher in the Rye*. Edgar's attitude towards books makes his appreciation of Defoe and Salinger particularly interesting:

> My opinion on books was: no human being can read all books, not even all the very good ones. Consequently, I concentrated on two. Anyway, in my opinion, in every book there are almost *all* the books. I do not know if anyone understands me. I mean, in order to write a book, one must have read a couple of thousand other pieces. . . . My two favorite books were: Robinson Crusoe . . . the other one was from that Salinger. And I got hold of it by pure chance. I mean, no one recommended them or so. . . . My experience with prescribed books was mightily miserable.[4]

Braun's *Unvollendete Geschichte* draws attention to the function of literature as a utilitarian tool to support a system or a state ideology. The father, a state official for whom history is curiously statistical, displays aversion to literature and privileges singularity of opinion over the multiplicity of narratives. Plenzdorf's *Die neuen Leiden des jungen W.* offers for consideration the question of individual and collective readership by setting up a contrast between "prescribed" and "self-discovered" titles. The two books that quell the sorrows of young Edgar originate from and are set in other worlds and other times. As Edgar reports, these books are not part of prescribed texts; they are his favorite precisely because they help him escape a programmatic social conformation.

Braun and Plenzdorf's novels criticize the use of literature as an ideological tool in the GDR. They can easily be read, as has been done before, as examples of a nation in which a purportedly "liberal" censorship—one that was on its face extremely tolerant, even open to many world literary traditions—worked within the parameters of a tightly defined, purportedly pro-worker and pro-citizen state ideology. However, it would be historically biased and in line with the widespread pro-market opinion, if the GDR were declared to be nothing but an ideologized, completely totalitarian, closed state with no connections to the rest of the world. It would be as naive to think of world literary circulation in the Federal Republic of Germany (FRG) as independent of any ideological pressures, where any and every work was accessible to a reader through the virtues of a free-market press. To circumvent the simplistic bifurcation that would draw a straight line from Nazi censorship to East German censorship—portraying West Germany as the haven of unbiased publishing and reading (a picture in which world literature in Germany finally receives emancipation through the fall of the Berlin Wall in 1989)—I propose to take a closer look at some of the defining moments pertaining to books, libraries, and world literature in the GDR and the FRG. This will allow us to view how ideological forces shaped the construction of the idea of the world, and in turn world literature, in the two German states.

There is no doubt that in a divided German public sphere, two rather different collections of texts came to be understood under the rubric of world literature. While the state apparatus's involvement in the promotion of world literature in the GDR was much more active than in the FRG, the procapitalist agenda of the FRG was also clearly visible in the orientation of the book market. Considering these two states in tandem will provide a far better picture of how world literature, through the politics of books, becomes instrumental to and an instrument of political ideology in a divided Germany. The two states differed not merely in their reception of literatures from other parts of the world but also in their production of a concept of world literature for their respective readerships. This story of two distinct modes of the institutionalization of world literature in a divided Germany, a story that was framed around the iconicity of the Berlin Wall, is the focus of this chapter.

How were books and literature politicized in the occupation zones (1945–1949)? How did this politicization shape and define the course of world literature in the two German states (1949–1989)? To what extent did the United States and the Soviet Union—as primary funders and subsidizers of the initial phase of cultural politics in the two respective German states—influence book production, translations, and library acquisition and circulation? Did the ideological division impede or facilitate the translation and reception of literatures from newly decolonized nations in Asia and Africa? What role was played by the postwar migration programs of the two German states in the introduction of newer literatures from Asia and Africa? These questions are central to this chapter, and to answer them we must first consider the question of world literature in conjunction with the predicament of history in a new world order after World War II. To approach these questions, I begin with the German exiled scholar Erich Auerbach. His seminal essay "Philologie der Weltliteratur" (1952) was written in the United States during his professorship at Yale. The moment and the milieu of the essay's origin make it an excellent document for the construction of world literary debates after World War II.

Auerbach and the Impossibility of World Literature

Auerbach's "Philology and *Weltliteratur*" is often cited in current debates in world literary studies.[5] In his comparative reading of Auerbach and the Danish intellectual Georg Brandes, Peter Madsen identifies "variegation, unification, and the idea of inner history" as key terms in Auerbach's essay, proposing that the central question for Auerbach was "whether a similar set of terms made sense in his [Auerbach's] own time, in a situation that seemed to be entirely determined by the process of modernization."[6] Aamir Mufti parses Auerbach through filters of nationalism and Orientalism on the one hand, and exile and diversification on the other. Mufti forcefully argues that "Auerbach's essay, while seeking to refashion the concept of Weltliteratur in the light of the contemporary turning point in the history of the West, in effect absolves the Goethean tradition of its involvement with the modern imperial process and remains itself ambivalent about the emerging postcolonial contours of the postwar world."[7]

The following discussion takes the insights of these scholars into consideration. However, in my reading of the text I want to demonstrate that Auerbach's ambivalence is not merely historical and theoretical but also political and pedagogical, and these multiple levels of ambivalence impact his imagination of world literature. The title of the English translation of the German text foregrounds such ambivalence in interesting ways.

The German original, published under the title "Philologie der Weltliteratur" in the *Festschrift* for Fritz Strich (1952), insinuates an investigation of the philology *of* world literature. However, in their translation, published seventeen years after the original, Maire and Edward Said chose to replace the genitive possessive in the title with a conjunction. They also decided in favor of not translating the term *Weltliteratur*:

> In our translation of Auerbach's article we have chosen not to put *Weltliteratur* into English. An expedient such as "world literature" betrays the rather unique tradition behind the German word. It is, of course, Goethe's own word [*sic*] which he used increasingly after 1827 for universal literature, or literature which expresses *Humanität*, humanity, and this expression is literature's ultimate purpose. *Weltliteratur* is therefore a visionary concept, for it transcends national literatures without, at the same time, destroying their individualities. Moreover, *Weltliteratur* is not to be understood as a selective collection of world classics or great books—although Goethe seemed often to be implying this—but rather as a concert among all the literature produced by man about man. (*PaW*, 1)

Notwithstanding the fact that *Weltliteratur* was not exclusively Goethe's term, with this particular framing of the text, the translators project in a way their own imagination of world literature onto Auerbach's. They locate Goethean *Weltliteratur* in a history of ideas whose proponents include "Herder, Grimm, Schlegel, and especially in Auerbach's case, Giambattista Vico" (*PaW*, 1). The Saids extrapolate from Auerbach the meaning of philology as "all, or most of human verbal activity," intimately connected to and even dominated by the discipline of history, and they thus locate Auerbach's ideas in the "German idealist tradition of historiography" (*PaW*, 2; *PdW*, 39). The translators' privileging of the German *Weltliteratur* over world literature is symptomatic of the visionary aspect of world literature that they aim to underline in Auerbach's essay. Although, as we are about to see, Auerbach is prudently skeptical, even anxious about the term. To understand Auerbach's skepticism and anxiety, it might be productive to briefly review some of the foundational moments of his essay.

"It is time to ask what meaning the word *Weltliteratur* can still have if we relate it, as Goethe did, both to the past and to the future" (*PaW*, 2; *PdW*, 39), thus begins Auerbach's inquiry on the meaning of the term. The simultaneously prospective and retrospective nature of this beginning has its origins in a transitional period of history—a point that both Madsen and Mufti also register in their readings. The essay is thus the product *and* witness of its historical moment, a revisitation of the legacies of the European philological tradition at an important world historical and intellectual juncture. Having experienced a period when traditions of historiography and philology were completely usurped by fascist ideology, and living in a period where national reconstruction and the revival of civic life is manifesting itself in diverse ways in Europe but also in the newly decolonized nations of Asia and Africa, Auerbach is not concerned with a simplistic revival of the German idealist tradition. His central focus is on the imminent threat that he sees in the "imposed uniformity . . . of individual traditions" (*PaW*, 2; *PdW*, 39). Seeing the world polarized through "European-American" or "Russian-Bolshevist" modes of human activity, Auerbach is quick to point out that the "differences between these two patterns are comparatively minimal when they are both contrasted with the basic patterns underlying the Islamic, Indian, or Chinese traditions" (*PaW*, 3; *PdW*, 39).

With this curious mixture of continental, ideological, religious, and linguistic/cultural grouping of the peoples of the world, Auerbach spells out two phenomena that challenge "relating" to the Goethean concept in the new world order: standardization and radical diversification. However, without quite resolving the tension between the two, he anticipates a world in which "a single literary culture, only a few literary languages, and perhaps even a single literary language" would gain precedence, and the Goethean concept would be "at once realized and destroyed" (*PaW*, 3; *PdW*, 39). Having started on a historical note, he now turns to a "*sense* of historicism" (italics added) that for him "permitted the formation of the concept of *Weltliteratur*" (*PaW*, 3; *PdW*, 40).

The unresolved tension between Auerbach's anticipation of simultaneous standardization and diversification permeates the rest of the essay. A derivative historicism forms the force field of this tension. On the one hand, Auerbach's concerns are directed toward a possible intellectual exchange between peoples and nations through literature. On the other hand, he also recognizes the limitations of such a hope in the select nature of these kinds of exchanges. Literature seems to be the perfect vehicle for cultural dialogue and mutual understanding, possibly even reconciliation between people. However, in light of his perceived standardization of "world culture," he sees more challenges than opportunities in placing hope in world literature as the great conciliator and mediator of humanity. And this is the point when history reenters the discourse, because despite the politicized difference that polarizes people (but curiously standardizes world culture), for Auerbach history is what apparently becomes the agent of difference, of particularity, thus rendering world literature in the twentieth century as human—and as humanistic—as the Goethean concept. Auerbach presupposes an "implicit comprehension of history" (*PaW*, 7; *PdW*, 43) for an individual to achieve "a scholarly and synthesizing philology of *Weltliteratur*" (*PaW*, 9; *PdW*, 44).

Auerbach's conceptualization of world literature sways between the historical and the contemporary, the (localized) literary and the (worldly) cultural, the political and the aesthetic, but ultimately it moves to the practical. The ambivalence that Mufti points out actually manifests itself not so much in Auerbach's nuanced understanding or even presentation of pressing current historical concerns. The ambivalence in fact is couched in a negotiation of the distance between a theoretical understanding of world literature and its political utility for the mid-twentieth century. And in a bid to negotiate this distance, Auerbach turns away from history to zoom into the relatively selective field of literature and literary pedagogy. For him, the question of an individual's command and mastery over world literary material remains as crucial as the ability of an individual to process this material through a sense of historicism, which he mentions earlier on in the essay. This also pervades his understanding of cultures; the anxiety about the standardization of the world is the anxiety of the commingling of diverse cultures, which—although he does not explicitly admit it—seems to come from a particular perception of culture.

In remembering the historicism of Goethe's period with a sense of profound loss, Auerbach forgets the inherent hybridity that has long informed the formation of cultures, not just in the current moment of his writing about world literature but also within the historical time of Goethe. A monolingual and monocultural—unmixed and therefore unadulterated—perception of both history and culture informs his anxiety about the linguistic and literary training required to deepen a scholarly understanding of world literature. Despite his curiosity about the larger public interaction through literature, world literature remains, for Auerbach, too, an exchange between literary works representative of those cultures. And the mediators of such a world literature will be the trained experts in specific literary fields, trained, one may add, in a particular synthesis of philology. As the Saids were quick to pick up in their introduction, philology emerges as a field where "foreign, nonphilological, or scientific methods begin to be felt" (*PaW*, 8; *PdW*, 43). The task of philology seems to be the assimilation and ordering of these methods and concepts. What Auerbach seems to be encouraging is a way out of specialization, while promoting it all the same. His invocation of "a commanding overview of the European material," as a special trait of the "generation that matured before the two World Wars," is particularly illustrative of this point: "These scholars cannot be replaced very easily, for since their generation the academic study of Greek, Latin, and the Bible—which was a mainstay of the late period of the bourgeois humanistic culture—has collapsed nearly everywhere. If I may draw conclusions from my own experiences in Turkey, then it is easy to note corresponding changes in non-European, but equally ancient, cultures" (*PaW*, 9; *PdW*, 44).

This point is debatable on several counts. First, as we have already seen in the course of the nineteenth century, even for the generation before the two world wars, non-European cultures became part of a bourgeois humanistic ideal through the concept of world literature. Second, the European bourgeois humanistic ideal was itself not formed without the political and ideological contradictions of the nineteenth century, in fact it developed parallel to, and in spite of, the politics of dominance and subjugation that were challenged by many in the nineteenth century—Heine and Marx being just two among them. Third, and this relates directly to the immediate context of training for a world literary, synthesizing philology: note how the "academic training" in Greek and Latin is conveniently pitted against Auerbach's "experiences" in Turkey. While an engagement with the *textual traditions* of Europe is essential to arrive at a philology of world literature, *life experiences* in other cultures will suffice as the basis of knowledge.

It is precisely this asymmetry that makes its way into Auerbach's call for a "history-from-within," (which Madsen refers to as "inner history"). That "history-from-within" is also decidedly Eurocentric; for Auerbach, history itself is "the genos of the *European* tradition of literary art" (*PaW*, 12, italics added; *PdW*, 46). Buried in this sentence is a century of ideas about the disconnect between history and literary narrative in the non-European world. So it is not really standardization (through colonialism and, in the twentieth century, the nation-state imperialism in Europe) that Auerbach cannot seem to resolve. This difference between history and literature is at the root of Auerbach's practical and pedagogical anxiety, which in his opinion the Western academy is woefully underprepared to process in order to train its subjects in newly circulating literatures of the "Islamic, Indian, and . . . Chinese" worlds. Auerbach's evaluation of world literature is thus very close to Goethe's own momentary celebration of the Chinese novel, only to then present Greek antiquity as the model of all Western literary works, as has already been discussed.

In sum, the Saids' choice to retain the German *Weltliteratur* was right, although for all the wrong reasons. In the distance from "Philologie der Weltliteratur" to "Philology and *Weltliteratur*," from the genitive possessive (*der*) to the coordinating conjunction (and), what remains unchanged is the understanding of *Weltliteratur* itself. Unlike the translators' projection that for Auerbach world literature emerges as a "concert between literatures," Auerbachian world literature remains a primarily European "collection of texts"; the harmony of the concert seems to be threatened by the cacophony of literatures from the Islamic, Indian, and Chinese worlds. Auerbach thus emerges as the model nonsanguine son and inheritor of Goethe—a twentieth-century version of Eckermann.

Despite Auerbach's lopsided view of culture and non-European literatures, the necessity for a multiplicity of points of departures ("Ansatzpunkte") that he presents as essential to developing a world literary philology remain singularly helpful. On the one hand, his ideas about the lack of intellectual preparation (in the West) for the entry and reception of non-Western literatures serve well to capture the state of literary circulation in the historical moment following World War II. On the other hand, the essay exudes a sense of uneasiness between the historical moment and the sense of historicism that Auerbach promotes, an uneasiness that makes world literature in the Goethean sense impossible for the twentieth century. It is precisely this uneasiness that, when harnessed, can shed new light on the correspondences between historical forces that shape the idea of the world and of world literature.

Auerbach starts his essay by pointing out that "the presupposition of world literature is a *felix culpa*: mankind's division into many cultures" (*PaW*, 2; *PdW*, 93). In a slight reformulation of Goethe's idea of the world as an extended homeland, Auerbach ends his essay by stating that the earth, not the nation, is our philological home. Nonetheless, in line with Goethe, he still points out, that "the most priceless and indispensable part of a philologist's heritage is still his own nation's culture and language. Only when he is separated from this heritage, however, and then transcends it does it become truly effective" (*PaW*, 17). Somewhere between the happy fault or sin (*felix culpa*) and the philological home, the nation and its separation, new definitions of world literature in practice, not just in theory, would start to emerge in the twentieth century. And some of the most dramatic manifestations of this division and separation would be visible in the materiality of the literary world in a place that Auerbach once called home—a Germany that would be taken over by forces of history from within and from without.

Split Bibliographs: The German Book Industry after World War II

The revival of the book market in postwar Germany is an uncanny repetition of historical circumstances. As early as the mid-seventeenth century, immediately following the Thirty Years' War (1618–1648), the East German city of Leipzig replaced the monopoly of Frankfurt am Main as the main center of the German book trade. Since the early nineteenth century, Leipzig was not only the prime site for book production and publication but also book trade through its Buchhändler Messe (book fair). In the aftermath of World War II, Frankfurt would regain its status as the most important German city for book trade (if not for book production).[8]

Following World War II, the German publishing industry split. Leipzig was under US control until April 16, 1945, but in line with the horse-trading at the Yalta Conference (1945), US forces had to pull out of middle Germany. At the instigation of the headquarters of the Allies, Major Douglas Waplas—in his civil life a professor of the Graduate Library School at the University of Chicago—asked a slew of German publishers such as Brockhaus, Georg Thieme, Dietrich'sche Verlagsbuchhandlung, and Insel to "transfer" to Wiesbaden with a US army convoy.[9] Within months, Georg Kurt Schauer—publisher and book historian—was given the license for the West German edition of the *Börsenblatt für den deutschen Buchhandel*.

The division of the book fair was not far. When the Leipzig Book Fair was revived in 1946 as the "First Leipzig Peace Book Fair," the representation was mostly local; at the second Book Fair in 1947, the representation was overwhelmingly from publishing houses from the Soviet occupation zone: seventy, as compared to twenty from the other zones. Notably present were publishers from Venezuela and Uruguay. But a number of Western publishers and all American publishers declined to participate.[10] The Americans were already planning to found a new German National Library in Frankfurt. On February 16, 1946, the representatives of the book trade in Frankfurt signed a contract according to which all works published since May 6, 1945, would be sent in trust to the library of the University of Frankfurt, the Deutsche Bücherei in Leipzig (today the German National Library), and the future (West) German National Library in Frankfurt. The British occupation forces supported the plan, and through a contract signed on March 24, 1947, the new publishing house of the Börsenverein in West Germany was authorized to publish the national bibliography in Frankfurt.[11] The political division of the country was reflected in the splitting of the national bibliography.

It was in these two terrains of ideologically divided "national" bibliographies that two different—albeit at times intersecting—"bibliographs" of world literature came into being. In the FRG, the Frankfurt Book Fair would play a major role in capitalizing on world literary goods, thus becoming a point of dissemination for literatures from around the world and establishing an international book market (*Büchermarkt*). In the GDR, the state apparatus, in opposition to a *Büchermarkt*, would strive to create a "reading nation" (*Leseland*). While the impact of the Leipziger Buchmesse on the larger German-language book market would be somewhat curtailed, publishing houses such as Reclam and Volk und Buch—especially designated for the publication of international literature—would bring world literary works to the reading public.

Books and Libraries in East Germany

To understand the picture of world literature in the former GDR, it might be best to return to Plenzdorf's Edgar and ask if there was indeed a prescribed list of foreign literary works—was world literature indeed part of the socialist government's pedagogical plan? Crucial to understanding this would be the cultural orientation of the state under the Soviet occupation zone, which reveals a new politics of libraries and books and a top-down, quick renunciation of recent history.

The rebuilding of libraries following World War II had three main concerns: the extraction ("Aussonderung") of National Socialist literature; the construction of a new antifascist library collection; and the winning of new classes of readers for the library.[12] Within a month of the end of World War II, on September 15, 1945, Marshall G. Shukov, commander-in-chief of the Soviet military government in the eastern zone released an order directed to all individuals, university, school, public, and private libraries, as well as bookstores, publishers, and wholesale book suppliers to hand over "all books, brochures, magazines, albums, and other literature containing fascist propaganda, race theory, literature about forceful acquisition of foreign nations, furthermore *all kinds of literature directed against the Soviet Union and other united nations*."[13] The deadline for turning in the banned materials was set for October 1, 1945, which obviously was too soon. So a slightly modified version of this order—with the deletion of "Soviet Union"—was released by the Allied Board of Control (Alliierten Kontrolrate) on May 13, 1946, allowing a period of two months for the submission of such materials.[14]

Prior to the second order, on February 1, 1946, a document entitled "Satzung für Volksbücherein" set the foundational framework for the renewal of public libraries in the Soviet occupation zone. The central purpose of the libraries was spelled out as "leading the people to the valuable classical and progressive literature of Germany and of other nations, and through that to found a humane and democratic Weltanschauung of the German people."[15] The idea of world literature was at the center of the development of this "humane and democratic Weltanschauung." Erich Schröter, director of the Leipzig School of Library Science, understood the cultural and political work that lay in front of German libraries. Privileging an open, transparent system of public libraries to replace the centrally controlled system during the NS era, Schröter argued:

> The public library should come out of the kingdom of sleeping beauty, in which it has often stood. It belongs to the pulsating streets of our lives. It should circulate the treasures of literature before us, it should place works of our classic authors and of world literature next to books about contemporary politics in front of us. It [the library] should urge us to take a position on the intellectual and political problems of our times, it should avail material pertaining to that and should not bury [this material] as in a holy shrine, far away from the reality of everyday life.[16]

An extension of Schröter's ideas can be found in a statement of Ernst Adler, who, along with Schröter, was a leading figure in library sciences as well as one of the editors of the journal *Der Volksbibliothekar*. Adler underlined that the libraries should not merely serve as "the memory of the nation" but also "as the conscience of the nation."[17]

The distinction between the library as the "memory" versus the "conscience" of the nation—privileging one function over the other—is a problematic one. In order to promote the role of the library as a conscience to the nation, the first task was to dismantle any recent memory of substantial central control and mass destruction. For this reason, any books that propagated Nazi ideology and propaganda, supported racist theories, instigated people to war, or in general opposed the political values represented by the Allies were promptly removed. Already in 1946 the Central Authority of Public Education in the Soviet occupation zone released a list of books to be eliminated from libraries.[18] In addition, the Deutsche Bücherei (Leipzig) also followed the order of the Allied headquarters from May 13, 1946, to facilitate the process of de-Nazification in the libraries. Books authored by Hitler, Himmler, Goebbels, and other NS officials were pulled off the shelves. After 1948, upon the completed political division of Germany, the GDR developed its own rules for the design and development of private libraries. With the political orientation of the GDR toward a new socialist state, the acquisition policies for open, public libraries were designed and shaped accordingly. On February 4, 1949, the parliament of Saxony passed the Law for Democratization of the Book Industry.[19] Libraries now went beyond the negative measures of crossing out and removing fascist literature and moved to a positive phase of identifying works that would orient the new public libraries to its working-class reading public.

But to assume that this democratization happened without a glitch would be a fallacy. Already in 1950, an impactful report released by a librarian in Thuringia planned a program that would take the idea of "democratic and progressive" to an extreme.[20] Not only did the report urge the banning of fascist literature, it insisted upon libraries to abide by the following measures: "Works of authors who have appeared as anti-Soviet, nationalist, militant, chauvinistic, imperialist . . . as they do not contribute to the progressive cultural work . . . authors who express anti-Polish and anti-Soviet sentiments (for example Sinclair) . . . must be most strictly examined. . . . Literature that has lost its meaning for a new progressive consciousness . . . must be most strictly examined (for example [Jack] London)."[21] This document advised librarians to favor a collection of anti-imperialist, antiracial, and antinationalist literature. It preferred books that positively depicted the GDR, German-Soviet friendship, and class struggle, for example. However, in the field of belletristic, the document advised in favor of a "new progressive literature," one that promoted the humanistic and progressive literatures of all times and peoples. As a measure for raising the literary *niveau* of the reading public, the report argued for "the elimination of kitschy, decadent, tear-jerking, banal, immoral and purely sensational literature." Thus one already sees the problem of an overzealous presentation of the library as a "conscience of the nation": it easily became a forced conscience that would prescribe a particular political direction and could be manipulated for the sake of state power over public pedagogy.

There is no easy way to directly connect this report from Thuringia to the officially executed policy for the selection of literary works for libraries. However, one can see its impact on the formation of the literary canon—both German national and world literary—that emerges in the GDR.

In 1950, the Central Institute of Library Sciences came up with a list of "100 Titles for the Basic Acquisition of a Small Library."[22] The section on "Erzählung, Romane und Gedichte" (narration, novels, and poems) included a few German authors such as Becher, Fallada, Fontane, Goethe, Grimmelshausen, Seghers, and Zweig. Most of the authors listed belonged to the sphere of international literature, with Martin Anderson Nexø topping the list with four works. Mentioned among others were works by

Fadyev, Gorki, Pavlenko, Rolland, and Sholokhov. Andersen, Chekhov, Tolstoy, and Twain become part of "Jugendliteratur" (children's literature); Nexø, Gorki, and Smedley were included in recommended biographies; Marx and Engels, along with Lenin, Stalin, and Walter Ulbricht form the category "Politik, Wirtschaft und Geschichte" (politics, economics, and history). The majority of foreign works were from the Soviet Union. From German literature, important names such as Thomas Mann, Lion Feuchtwanger, Franz Kafka, Herman Hesse, Heinrich Mann, and even Bertolt Brecht were absent from the list. In a nation fast trying to distance itself from the literature of the West and still in search of voices that narrated its own story, a few Russian authors and a Danish icon become the necessary building blocks for public libraries. So impactful were Nexø, Gorki, and Sholokhov that questions about them were also included in exams for library professionals.[23]

However, no effort to create a new readership for a democratic and progressive world literature could have taken place without the necessary books being available. This particular niche was filled by the Leipzig branch of the publisher Reclam, and also by Volk und Welt, a publishing company dedicated completely to world literature.

The Reading Nation: World Literature in the Postwar GDR

After a period of conformation to the NS regime, Reclam emerged to reclaim its position in the German publishing scene, but its reemergence would be as a split personality, with one office in the West (Stuttgart), and the other one in the East (Leipzig). On March 14, 1946, Ernst Reclam received the license from the Soviet occupational forces to reopen the publication house in Leipzig,[24] but he left the city in 1950—a move that was reported in the centenary publication of the Leipzig-based Reclam as "illegal"[25]—and died in 1953. Reclam (Leipzig) was reincarnated as a publically owned publishing company (Volkseigener Verlag), and starting 1963, it became one of the state-run publishing companies with the Aufbau Verlag (Berlin and Weimar). In this new incarnation, the publishing house now turned to literature for the workers and the proletariat, that is, all the leftist and communist literature that was banned during the Nazi period.

The revival of the Universal-Bibliothek was one of the prime foci of the company. As a gesture of turning a new leaf—and, it must be added, a total silence over the history of the past two decades—the 1949 catalog of Universal-Bibliothek opened with two statements of praise by Arnold

Zweig and Gerhart Hauptmann, followed by a message from the publisher, strategically placed as a nod to the proletarian literature that was going to be primarily featured in the new regime:

> These confessions [by Zweig and Hauptmann] say what millions of Germans, whether workers or intellectuals, pupils or university students understand under the term Reclam: popular for every affordable little volume, which represent the factor of people's education that has become indispensable and self-understood since the founding of Reclam's Universal-Bibliothek in 1867. The classic works of world literature, the legacy of great thinkers, and contemporary national and foreign literature have ever since determined the face of Reclam. With the purpose of this universality, since the end of the war, the publishing house is keen to continue with the collection in the spirit of the demands of our time, through new editions of lively works of the past as well as through the inclusion of authors of our time, and through that to serve the cultural reconstruction of Germany.[26]

This blurb from the catalog appears as a strange mixture of partial silence over the history of the company during National Socialism and of partial urgency to look to the future in the face of a new historical reality. A list of works published by the Universal-Bibliothek (Leipzig) in 1952, covering the previous five years, gives strong clues to the reorientation of the publishing house. Prominently listed are works of the Danish author Nexø—who by this time had moved to Dresden and was an honorary citizen of the GDR—along with Dostoyevsky, Gogol, Gorki, Heine, and of course, Marx and Engels.[27] By 1955, Reclam Leipzig had been officially blessed by Walter Ulbricht, for whom the name Reclam was synonymous with the "popular, interesting, and inexpensive editions of Universal-Bibliothek" for "readers from around the world."[28] Ulbricht's statement did not just seem to refer to German migrants around the world. By 1957, Reclam had authorized booksellers in the capital cities of several socialist and communist republics, including Albania, Bulgaria, China, Czechoslovakia, Hungry, Poland, Romania, and the USSR;[29] in 1959 the list was expanded to include (North) Korea (Pyongyang), Vietnam (Hanoi), and a few major cities in the former Yugoslavia: Ljubljana, Zagreb, Sarajevo, and Belgrade.[30]

These circulation connections became part of the publication agenda as well. Mao-Tse Tung is first seen in a catalog from 1960,[31] the same year that the *Reclam-Buch* (1960) replaces so-called humanistic education ("humanitäre Bildung")—a key phrase in Universal-Bibliothek's marketing strategy since its inception (and until 1933)—with socialist upbringing ("sozialistische Erziehung"), which implied more than learning from books. Walter Ulbricht's thoughts on this new direction are expressed in his speech "Purpose of Socialist Upbringing" given at the Fifth Convention of the Socialist Unity Party (SED): "All-round development of the personality, education for solidarity and collective action. Education for love of work, education for militant activity, mediation of a high theoretical and general knowledge. Development of all the mental and physical abilities, that is, formation of socialist consciousness for the benefit of the people and the nation."[32] This message is fortified through the statistical presentation of developments in the GDR's investment in education (1951–1958), followed by a quote from Nikita Khrushchev, a statement from the Twenty-First Convention of the Communist Party of the Soviet Union: "The best school of education and the strictest teacher is life, our socialist reality. A bookish knowledge of the communist principles, detached from praxis, is no good."[33]

These citations served to frame the "practice" of a new form of socialist education through an engagement with literature, and both national and world literature were part of this enterprise. The *Reclam-Buch* (1960) published a special list of literary works to be used in the classroom from middle through high school. Among Russian authors, the recommended reading list included Pushkin's Robinhood-esque *Dubrowksi* (seventh grade), Tolstoy (eighth grade), Otrowski (ninth and tenth grade), Sholokhov (eleventh grade), and Gorki (twelfth grade). The list of non-Russian authors ranged from German and other classical authors—including Goethe, Schiller, and Shakespeare—to twentieth-century German authors such as Bertolt Brecht, Thomas and Heinrich Mann, and Anna Seghers.[34] Reclam was thus contributing to the construction of a world literary readership through a state-sponsored and -administered education program; it was also participating in the state's vision of such a program with the slogan, "Eine neue Zeit erfordert eine neue Schule" (figure 4-1).

In 1963, Reclam signed an agreement with the state-owned publishing house Volk und Wissen (people and knowledge) concerning a yearly contribution of the Universal-Bibliothek to the school system of the GDR through the publication of textbooks. This commitment came with formal and content-based changes: the number system was reorganized, the format was redesigned to fit the new GDR measurements for a pocketbook (10.3 × 16.5cm), and the covers were color coded to represent the new thematic groups: prose, poetry, drama, and social sciences; history and

Figure 4-1. "A New Time Requires a New School." Reclam catalog of February 1960 (Leipzig). (Courtesy of Deutsche Nationalbibliothek and Buch- und Schriftmuseum Leipzig, and Philipp Reclam jun. Verlag Stuttgart.)

culture; language, literature, and music; and biographies and documents. In addition, the Universal-Bibliothek's publication list was to eliminate titles with controversial content or content "unworthy" of reprint: "The new formation of 1963 was not to carry signs of Hesse's perception of world literature, but was to be inspired by the revolutionary spirituality of Friedrich Wolf."[35]

Friedrich Wolf (1888–1953) was a prolific German dramatist, essayist, and political activist. In August 1934, at the first Soviet Writers' Congress in Moscow, presided by Maxim Gorki, Wolf registered his opposition against Karl B. Radek (1885–1939), a prominent Marxist essayist, political author, and, for a short time, editor of the *Leipziger Volkszeitung* (1907).[36] In his speech, "Contemporary World Literature and the Tasks of Proletarian Art," Radek drew a very bleak picture of the Western bourgeoisie as well as revolutionary literature. In his own address, Wolf emphasized the differences between the political reality of the former USSR and other European nations, stating that a new revolutionary aesthetic was in fact on the rise.[37] It is not clear whether the "revolutionary spirituality" embraced by Reclam was based on Wolf's reaction to Radek's speech or Wolf's life work, which included many successful and well-known plays in which Wolf centralized class-struggles—a number of them performed even in the United States.

The source of this reorientation to Wolf notwithstanding, the shift from Hesse's idea of the pursuit of world literature as a goal unto itself to the new "revolutionary spirituality" was manifest not only in Reclam's agenda for world literature but in the GDR's own conceptualization of world literature for schools. In fact, the GDR could have easily been one of the only European countries with a dedicated program for educating school children in world literature.

In 1971 (around the time Plenzdorf's novel takes place), the Ministry for Public Education (Ministerium für Volksbildung) came up with a plan for education in the social sciences (Gesellschaftswissenschaft) for extended secondary school students (Erweiterte Oberschule) with a list of selected works of world literature from the nineteenth and the twentieth centuries. Stipulated in a document entitled *Lehrgang ausgewählter Werke der Weltliteratur des 19. und 20. Jahrhunderts*, the purpose of this plan was to instill international values in the pupils, familiarizing them with "writings of world literary rank" and conveying to them "world literary developments" in the nineteenth and twentieth centuries. The central purpose of this education in world literature at the school level was the "artistically created human image," in close alignment with the official pedagogical party line:

> At the center of the consideration of select works of world literature is the artistically created human image. The pupils are to understand how humanistic authors form—artistically and in diverse and original ways—their Weltanschauung and ideals, their experiences, insights, and assessments as well as their position vis-à-vis the struggle of the people against exploitation and for a meaningful existence. In close connection with the exploration of the ideal-aesthetic form of the writings, the pupils will enrich their literary-theoretical knowledge and their insights in various national literatures and in the developmental process of world literature. . . . The reception and acquisition of important works of world literature contributes to [the fact] that through decisions and contingencies of literary figures and of the authors, the pupils better understand the dialectic of class analysis in the epoch of transition from capitalism to socialism, and that [they] detect the connections between Weltanschauung and artistic mastery.[38]

While phrases such as "dialectic of class analysis" and the "transition from capitalism to socialism" are predictably in the service of state-sponsored ideology, it is the projected combination of literary and social interventionist comparison that makes the plan so interesting. Teachers were directed to incorporate these works into their teaching to expand the horizons of the students beyond the palate of German literature; in addition, they were asked to pay attention not merely to the social text of the narrative but to lay importance on the creative and literary aspects of the texts, to train students in "the interpretation of excerpts, scenes and poems, the exploration of artistic imagery, motives and plot lines, [drawing] comparisons, [and making] juxtapositions and summarizing observations."[39] Admittedly, the list for the nineteenth century was dominated by Russian authors such as Chekhov, Tolstoy, Dostoevsky, and Gorki, with a few works by Stendahl, Balzac, Flaubert, Zola, Scott, Dickens, Twain, Ibsen, Hauptmann, and Thomas Mann. The teaching directions underline a socialist framing of these texts, privileging the reading and interpretation of "works of bourgeois-humanist authors" of the nineteenth century through Russian and French literature, especially Stendhal, Tolstoy, and Gorki. The instructions further ask teachers to refer to earlier works by Gorki as an introduction to socialist literature around 1900 and the artistic representation of the working class.

There is no way to reconstruct the classroom execution of this document today. While the framing of the document is ideologically determined, there is little doubt that works chosen for students from grades seven through twelve were indeed those that had entered the world literary space, including that of Germany, through the medium of translation. The geographic and linguistic cultural diversity of the chosen works, especially from the twentieth century, is quite remarkable in this context. The recommended list of readings for the twentieth century does include a number of Russian and Soviet authors such as Alexander Serafimovich, Alexander Fadeyev (cofounder of the Union of Soviet writers), Chinghiz Aitmatov (the Kirghiz-Turkish author who wrote in Russian and Kirghiz), Aleksei Arbuzov, Vladimir Mayakovski, and of course the 1965 Nobel Laureate Mikhail Sholokhov. While this is not unpredictable, what is interesting is the representation of modern German-language literature and other non-Soviet literatures on the twentieth-century list. Among German authors, Johannes R. Becher becomes the sole East German on the list; others include German-Jewish authors such as Lion Feuchtwanger, the Austrian author Stephan Zweig, the Swiss author Friedrich Dürrenmatt, and from the nineteenth century Heinrich Mann and August Bebel. Within European literature, the list includes Romain Rolland, Bernard Shaw, Martin Andersen Nexø, Alberto Moravia, and García Lorca. Pablo Neruda is the only Latin American author on the list; Tagore is the only (South) Asian. The teaching directions to this section present Feuchtwanger's works as prime examples of antifascist literature, Shaw and Dreiser as examples of world literary realism, and Hemingway as the example of bourgeois humanistic realism. These themes would be extended in the study of poems by Mayakovski, Lorca, and Neruda.

While not all East German children went to the Gymnasium—the high school with special education in the sciences and humanities—choosing instead the vocational *Realschule*, the list is noteworthy in its effort to construct a world literary readership at an early stage of education. Given the literary politics of the GDR, which became rather programmatic and propagandistic after the Bitterfelder Weg (1965)—a movement to promote the writing worker ("schreibender Arbeiter"), under which the category of a professional author with no experience of work in factories or fields was considered bourgeois—the program comes across as impressive even in hindsight. The idea was not merely to educate students in world literature within the school but to create conditions whereby the appropriation of world literary treasures by the pupils becomes a life necessity ("Lebensbedürfnis") for them.[40]

No pedagogical plan, no creation of world literature as a *Lebensbedürfnis*, would actually succeed without a lifeline that granted access to the objects necessary for the readers' intellectual lives. While Reclam (Leipzig) provided inexpensive editions in the standard Universal-Bibliothek format, an entire publication program around world literary works for the general public was developed through a specialized publishing company, Volk und Welt. This would be the apt time to reveal that in the list of prescribed books of world literature, North America was represented by two US authors: Ernest Hemingway, with *Der alte Mann und das Meer* (*The Old Man and the Sea*), and J. D. Salinger, with *Der Fänger im Roggen*—Heinrich Böll and Irene Muehlon's translation of the *Catcher in the Rye*, which Edgar Wibeau discovers "outside of" the prescribed list of books. The translation was first published in Cologne by Kiepenheur und Witsch (in 1962), and the East German edition was published by Volk und Welt (in 1965).

In his introduction to the volume *Fenster zur Welt* (2003; Window to the world), the book historian Siegfried Lokatis comments: "One can only regret that in the Federal Republic there was no place for a publishing house with a cultural function of connecting people [with each other], whose program offered a clear focus on the entirety of world literature, which systematically explored the literature of Eastern Europe and the Soviet states through translations, whose special engagement was aimed at the authors of the Third World."[41] There is little exaggeration in Lokatis's words. From its establishment in 1947 to its end in 1989, Volk und Welt published 3,334 works (first editions) of 1,800 authors from about 76 nations.[42] Admittedly, in accordance with the larger cultural politics of the nation, Volk und Welt had a special predilection for works from the former Soviet Union and various other Eastern European nations, such as Poland, the former Yugoslavia, Hungary, and Romania. But the authors were not limited to these "friendly states." Volk und Welt's publication list included US authors (e.g., William Faulkner, Erskine Caldwell, Norman Mailer, Woody Allen, Saul Bellow, Truman Capote, John Steinbeck, and Toni Morrison), Central and Latin American authors (e.g., Miguel Ángel Asturias, Alejo Carpentier, Carlos Fuentes, Jorge Amado, Jorge Luis Borges, Pablo Neruda, and Octavio Paz), African authors (e.g., Nadine Gordimer, Naguib Mahfouz, Mehmod Darwish, Wole Soyinka, Mehmud Taymur, Ngugi wa' Thiongo, Mongo Beti, Chinua Achebe, and Pepetela),[43] British authors (e.g., Charles Dickens, Kingsley Amis, and Herbert Smith), and Asian authors, which included Indian writers (such as Rabindranath Tagore, Munshi Premchand, and S. H. Vatsyayana Agyeya); Indonesian writers (e.g., Pramodeya Ananta Toer), the Korean feminist author Kang Kyŏng-ae (Kong Gama); the Chinese author Mao Dun [Sheng Yanbing], and Japanese authors (e.g., Yasunari Kawabata and Kenzaburo Oe), as well as Turkish authors (e.g., Yeshar Kemal and Nazim Hikmet).

Why was Volk und Welt particularly successful in its vetting of authors from around the world? What gave its editorial direction this kind of freedom of expression and ideas? Most importantly, how was Volk und Welt framing world literature for its readership and providing them access to it? To answer these questions, it might be best to take a quick look at the history of Volk und Welt, followed by a brief, detailed discussion of *Bücherkarren* (bookcarts), the literary magazine (and marketing symbol) of Volk und Welt that also served as its seasonal catalog.

Volk und Welt was born as a post–World War II institution with an antifascist, pacifist disposition. It was established in 1947 by Michael Tschesno-Hell (1902–1980; editor-in-chief 1947–1950)—who came upon the idea at a Swiss Internship camp—initially as a publishing house for Soviet literature in German translation. *Neue deutsche Literatur*, the literary journal of the publishing house—edited by Willi Bredel as the flagship journal of the (East) German association of writers (Deutscher Schriftstellerverband, DSV)—was singularly beholden to the Soviet Union; the April 1953 issue was dedicated to Stalin and included a telegram from the German to the Soviet writers' association mourning Stalin's death.[44] However, the monograph publication of Volk und Welt under the leadership of Tschesno-Hell's successors—Bruno Peterson (1950–1954), Walter Czollek (1954–1972), and during the fifties the (executive) editor Marianne Dreifuß—established itself beyond the Soviet Union.[45]

The East German publishing industry went through a profiling (*Profilierung*) in 1960, whereby specific firms were also assigned specific roles in the publication of books according to subjects. This process happened parallel to the efforts to stabilize and strengthen the East German mark against foreign currencies. While there were other publishers such as Reclam and Insel in Leipzig that published works of both local and international authors, there was no publishing house that focused primarily on world literature, and Volk und Welt was able to fill that niche. As Lokatis observes in his essay on Volk und Welt, at a time when the East German cultural politics under Walter Ulbricht (cited by Karin's father in Braun's *Unvollendete Geschichte*) was strongly oriented toward Moscow—and when anyone from the West, especially West German migrants, were looked upon with suspicion—Volk und Welt was unusually West-oriented, with special connections to the world outside the Soviet bloc nations. The scholar Hans Mayer (who moved to West Germany) and the author Stephan Hermlin supported Volk und Welt with their Western connections; Marianne Dreifuß and Walter Czolleck had made first acquaintance in Shanghai while in exile; the five-member editorial board with Dr. Hans Petersen,

Roland Links, Leonhard Kossuth, Jutta Janke, and Christina Links had permission to travel to most countries around the world to scout the best works and their authors.

Volk und Welt also had an army of twenty-five editors and another dozen readers and fact checkers. And every leading editor had access to trained translators, external evaluators and editors, and qualified scholars who would serve as authors of prefaces and afterwords. The five editorial divisions were responsible for: (1) literatures of the Soviet Union (including Siberia and the Caucus mountains) and Eastern Europe, (2) literatures of people's democracies in countries as far flung as Mongolia and North Korea, (3) literatures of the two German states and Scandinavian countries, (4) Romance literatures, dominated primarily by French and Italian; while peninsular Spanish and Portuguese literatures were not well represented, significance was laid on literatures from their former colonies in Africa, Asia, and Latin America, (5) literatures of Great Britain, North America, Australia, Asian countries and Africa, as well as Asian and African writings in English.[46] Except for novels published under the series "ad-libitum," "Roman-Zeitung," or "Spektrum," the publication of shorter works was carried out under a magazine series called "Erkundungen" (explorations).[47]

There is little doubt, as Lokatis agrees, that the division of the world within the publishing house was resonant of the new postcolonial cartographies of the world marked by colonial historical burden on the one hand and the GDR's socialist ideology on the other. However, within these divisions and assignments there were important contributions for making less commonly available literatures accessible for general readers in German translations. *Bücherkarren*, the publishing house's official catalog and bimonthly literary magazine, played an important role in presenting international authors to its readers. Starting in August 1960 with issue no. 4, the catalog, which was earlier meant only for librarians and publishing houses, was turned into a literary magazine with essays on new publications, including brief biographies of authors, their major literary accomplishments, and the significance of the work in the creative trajectory of the author.[48] A few examples would suffice to illustrate the framing of the authors. The Cuban author Nicholas Guillén is presented alongside Jorge Amado and Pablo Neruda, as authors dedicated to democratic values of freedom and independence in Latin America. Guillén is also credited with bringing to the forefront the histories of "Negroes and Mulattos" in his work. Rabindranath Tagore is presented as the author who "was helped by farmers out of his ivory tower, and he did all he could as an individual to help them."[49] He is particularly praised for his letters about Russia ("Briefe über Rußland"), which he wrote during his visit to Moscow.[50] William Faulkner becomes the quintessential author to depict the polarization of blacks and whites and the unresolved past ("nicht-überwundene Vergangenheit") of the American South, whereas John Steinbeck, Erskine Caldwell, and Arthur Miller belong to the "other America" committed to class equality and political emancipation of the working class.[51] In an introduction to Frank London Brown, the first African-American author published by Volk und Welt, the magazine cites Alan Paton's review in the *Chicago Tribune*: "Of the courage, which is narrated in this novel, America should be proud. Even though it might shame white America and white people everywhere else."[52]

In the publication program for 1989, Volk und Welt released works of authors from thirty-six nations: sixty-nine from the USSR, twenty-nine from Eastern European socialist countries, thirty-nine from German-speaking countries, thirty from Italy, Spain, and France, thirteen from Scandinavia, thrity-four from the United States, the United Kingdom, and Australia, ten from Asia, eleven from Latin- and Central America, six from Africa, three from Greece, two from the Netherlands, and one translated from Yiddish.[53] The last years of the publishing company are reflected in a slow cultural shift in the publication agenda, as can be gathered from issues of *Bücherkarren*. The last available issue from 1988 announces the publication of a number of authors from the Soviet Union: Tatyana Tolstoya, Sergei Antonov, and Juri Trifonov,[54] as well as authors from "other socialist countries," such as Magda Szabó (Hungary), Ai Wu (China), Vasko Popa (Yugoslavia), and Nicolas Guillén (Cuba).[55] The solidarity with authors from Asian and African nations continues: Naguib Mahfouz,[56] and later Octavio Paz,[57] are celebrated for their Nobel Prize; in addition, Volk und Welt declares its solidarity with Salman Rushdie against the Fatwah.[58]

Volk und Welt's attempts to democratize public opinion, to make their readers aware of political inequalities in the world through literary works—even though the situation at home was no less problematic—were made possible due to, and in spite of, the cultural politics of the GDR. Thomas Reschke, long-time editor and translator of Russian works into German, believed that in its own way, the publishing houses even prepared the way for the events of 1989.[59] Reschke's thoughts find resonance with the East German mathematician and political activist Thomas Klein. In an interview about "The Unknown Reader," Klein states:

> As is generally known, the West Berliners felt walled in, but when I think about Volk und Welt, you would actually have to say that the GDR was a walled enclave itself. In this respect the publishing house

> offered a window to the world, and it was not a bad view you had there. Probably a lot of censorship, preselection, and abridgements will be discussed in this context, but on the whole the books of Volk und Welt made it possible for the inhabitants of the "reading nation" to have a very dignified view of foreign literature.[60]

Volk und Welt carried its legacy even into the last decade of the twentieth century. The publishing list was expanded with contemporary literatures from hitherto less published nations: from Canada, Alberto Manguel; from the United States, William Sapphire; and from Slovenia, the debated Slavoj Žižek.[61] However, with the Fall of the Berlin Wall, the necessity for having this special window to the world was lost in the euphoria of a new brand of freedom. Volk und Welt was finally liquidated in April 2001.

The Book Market: World Literature in Postwar West Germany

Indeed, it was a new brand of freedom of thought that was also promised by the United States to West Germany at the end of World War II.

While in the Soviet Occupation Zone and later in the GDR the value of socialist, progressive literature was on the rise, the nature of the concerns in the West were exactly the opposite. Along with the support of the German public libraries through the UNESCO commission, the Americans were also setting up new open American libraries—Amerika Gedankbibliotheken or America Häuser as they were known in West Germany. Precursors to these libraries were the Deutsche Freiheitsbibliothek (German freedom library) in Paris and the American Library of Nazi-Banned Books at the Brooklyn Jewish Center in New York, both established in 1934 as a gesture against the Nazi book burnings.[62] Through an order of the Allied Control Council from May 13, 1946, all materials belonging to any German libraries that contained any kind of Nazi propaganda were recalled.[63] While the official cultural program of the *Occupied Countries News Notes* (March 18, 1949) categorically stated that to force Germans into an American system of education was not part of the "fundamental principles"; the reorientation of West German occupied zones had already started taking place. The interest of the Americans was in a re-education of the entire nation. And through a program devised in collaboration with the Library of Congress, the circulation of American books in Germany was made possible.

The first Amerika Haus was founded on November 14, 1945, in Frankfurt. With its open-access shelving and a few reading programs, this library became a quintessential symbol of the United States. Dean Acheson, who led the program as the secretary of state, wrote, "The Public Library symbolizes the American philosophy of Freedom to learn, to study and to search after truth. This is the essence of a free society. This is the source of our freedom."[64] In addition to the libraries, the Americans also sponsored bookmobiles and translation services for university libraries. In fact, these libraries were to help Germans understand that "America was more than a nation of lady wrestlers, bloody strikes, and boogie-woogie fiends that Hitler had portrayed."[65] For West German readers, these libraries became a renewed source of world literature from the United States: "*Gone with the Wind*, with later novels of Hemingway, Faulker, and Thomas Wolfe, the poems of Emily Dickinson and Robert Lowell, or the plays of Eugene O'Neill and Thornton Wilder."[66]

However, to think that this symbol for American freedom stood forever would be a mistake. Already between 1951 and 1953, Joseph McCarthy, the Republican senator from Wisconsin, started promoting censorship measures. As Louise Robbins reports in her study about "Freedom to Read," the purpose of these libraries was to open "windows to the West." However, they were busy in making sure that any "windows to the communist East" were not by mistake opened on the American dime. McCarthy wanted thirty thousand books by communist authors—which had been "'publicly exposed' by his representatives Roy M. Cohn, chief counsel for the Permanent Subcommittee on Investigations, which McCarthy chaired, and the Committee consultant David Schine"—to be removed from all libraries in Germany.[67] The appearance of Howard Fast, author of *Citizen Tom Paine* and self-avowed communist, in front of the McCarthy Committee in February 1953, "alerted Amerika Häuser and the United States that McCarthy had taken aim at them and the directive that allowed latitude in book selection and presented the libraries from just being another propaganda organ."[68] Cohn and Schine were sent by McCarthy, and slowly any books by authors who had not shown up at McCarthy's trials were "stored" away. This did not go unnoticed in the German press. The famous German journalist Marion Gräfin Dönhoff reported:

> Once again libraries are being cleansed, books are being ripped from shelves . . . twenty years after May 9, 1933, when Dr. Goebbels, in the presence of Berlin's student body, threw the un-German, foreign, decomposing, and rotten literature to the flames . . . today on McCarthy's request books are being eradicated, pulped, burnt, locked away. . . . Fortunately, in America there are other forces at work next to McCarthy. President Eisenhower warned on June 26 in Los Angeles against

> the zealots and pointed out that freedom can neither be disposed [*verfügt*] law nor can it be brought about by censorship.[69]

The incident was followed by a media controversy in the United States when librarians became vocal against the program. Especially after Eisenhower's letter to the libraries in America, the *New York Times* ranked "Freedom to Read" as one of America's best state papers. While the controversy around the censorship slowly subsided both in the United States and in Germany, the aggressiveness with which literature from the Allied countries was promoted as a prominent aspect of world literature was criticized in the FRG—and not just in the context of originals available in libraries but also in translations sponsored by the Allied forces. A new magazine called *Freude an Büchern: Monatshefte für Weltliteratur* (Joy in books: Monthly magazine for world literaure, 1950–1954) prominently featured the debate on translated foreign literature in the early 1950s.[70]

With the pre- and post-Nazi magazine (*Die*) *Weltliteratur* no longer in existence, *Freude an Büchern* emerged as an important forum for world literary discussions after World War II in the German-speaking world. Founded by theater scholars Heinz Kindermann and Margeret Dietrich, the magazine was edited and published in Vienna and distributed through the Großbuchhandlung Carl Gabler in Munich. Contributors included new Austrian authors of the postwar generation—Ilse Aichinger, H. C. Artmann, and Ernst Jandl—as well as contemporary authors from continental Europe and the United States. The magazine featured discussions on both canonical and contemporary world literature. Excerpted texts by important European authors such as T. S. Eliot,[71] interviews with American authors such as Thornton Wilder,[72] and reports on non-Western literatures were often featured in the magazine.[73] The essential role of the magazine was to revive the culture of reading and discussions around books, which had been lost during the political events of the last decade and a half. In the inaugural issue, the program statement of the magazine underlined the role of books:

> Books are windows to the world. The hard-fought path of individual life is narrow, the horizon of every "I" necessarily limited. However, books, these messengers of spirit, which carry the inexhaustible wealth of knowledge, of fantasy, and formative reports through all peoples and ages, give a clear view of foreign life. They open the gates to the previously unimaginable. They have long-forgotten treasures or they break through the wall of impending paralysis and prepare the new,

> the upcoming. Their peculiar light illuminates anyone who is willing to open up his heart and to become an understanding person. Books build [*wölben*] bridges between countries and eras.[74]

The cultural bridge between countries, especially between the Allied Forces and the FRG, was also built through diplomatic state outfits. The United States Information Service sponsored the publication of a special brochure on the American novel from 1850–1951, included with the magazine's February 1951 issue. However, the magazine was not limited to a pro-American stance. The promotion of foreign literatures, especially literature from Allied countries in German translation, was questioned by Otto Flake (1880–1963), a prolific German novelist, essayist, and translator of works by Montaigne, Dumas, Balzac, and Diderot into German. In an essay entitled "Übersetzungswut" (translation rage), published in *Freude an Büchern*, Flake criticized the ferocity with which translated works were taking over the German literary landscape. Flake notes that following the introduction of the new German mark in 1948, a slew of foreign publishers started arriving in the FRG, pushing the translations of literary works into German. This translation wave ("Übersetzungswelle") had taken the shape of a storm tide ("Sturmflut"), and consequently the literary landscape around him is nothing else but a bad dream ("ein böser Traum").[75] Akin to Menzel in the nineteenth century, Flake claims that "the Germans are on a zeal to translate the good from all nations and to realize the Goethean concept of world literature; however, this time around they had become overzealous, something that had turned a few into (literary) lackeys."[76] Unlike Menzel, however, Flake insists that his perspectives are not offered in a nationalist spirit; he recognizes that in an era of intermingling and intermeshing between nations, translations are a matter of course. Furthermore, Germans, he states, have the need to catch up on world literature, as they were cut off from the world for over a decade.[77] He holds publishing houses—which should have a function to serve national writers as well—responsible for an unreflective promotion of foreign works, each one presented as a best seller. Flake describes the situation bitterly: apparently a number of German authors were forced to turn to translation as their prime source of income. And the resulting translations, he states, are neither valuable nor of high literary quality; rather, any work that grants a Western perspective is considered worthy of translation. It is this mass production, Flake complains, that is compromising the literary landscape of Germany.

Flake's thoughts were published in the light of an open letter to Theodor Heuss, the first president of the FRG, written by another prolific author and essayist, Wilhelm von Scholz (1874–1969). Scholz, who was officially loyal to the National Socialists and whose works were widely promoted during the NS-period, was declared a fellow traveller (*Mitläufer*) and managed to become the president of the (West) German writers' association in 1949. In his letter, Scholz "took a strong stance against the indiscriminate getting-out-of-hand of—often badly translated and primitive—foreign literature, and championed measures for the benefit of literature at home."[78] Scholz urged Heuss that "for each translation into German, one must be established from German into the respective foreign language."[79]

Given the significance of these ideas for the times, *Freude an Büchern* published a small debate on the topic, titled "Für und gegen Auslandsliteratur" (for and against foreign literature), as a supplement to Flake's essay. The first response was from Karl Friedrich Boree, secretary of the German Academy for Language and Literature in Darmstadt. Boree did not mince his words in his response to Scholz: "Until now I do not fear a sustainable alienation of the German spirit through the excessive inflow of foreign literature."[80] On the one hand, Boree mentions the revival of the German book market through the publication of new editions of German literary works, but on the other hand, he also stresses the fact that the "import of foreign books after 1945 was a cultural duty of German publishers."[81] He further notes that this import led to a popularity of foreign literature among readers, and now the "indiscriminate" import of any book, precisely because it originated elsewhere, is perhaps a result of this initial movement. Short statements from other contributors—all of them academics—demonstrate mixed sympathies to Scholz and the question of alienation or literally "overforeignization" of German literature through the import of foreign books. Without explicitly mentioning Scholz's own Nazi past, Rudolf Brunnberger, professor at the University of Vienna, recognized a deplorable state of affairs ("Mißstand") in the contemporary German literary landscape, while also warning against the cultural occupation of one country by another: "Political supremacy, and especially even to the extent of the occupation, almost always results in grotesque developments in the intellectual realm as well: one only need to recall the [system of] export[ation] that the Third Reich wanted to sustain in occupied Europe."[82]

The story of world literary circulation in the FRG, especially in the formative years and through the *Wirtschaftswunder* ("economic miracle") is a story of subsidized translation and book importation, both facilitated through a currency reform and cast as "a cultural duty." What develops in the next generations is a much more heterogeneous story, and Reclam's Universal-Bibliothek was a small part of it. As mentioned earlier, the two-state solution for Germany was reflected also in the splitting of Reclam, reflected also in the difference between the covers of Reclam catalogs for Leipzig (figure 4-1) and Stuttgart (figure 4-2).[83] On August 4, 1962, "Reclam" and "Universal-Bibliothek" were patented by Reclam Stuttgart. The new publishing house positioned itself as one focused on contemporary literature. Thus a new series of anthologies was launched with the first two volumes on contemporary French and Yugoslavian literatures, followed by anothologies on Italian (1964), American (Short Stories, 1964), Hungarian (1965), Irish (1965), Dutch (1966), Spanish (1968), and Danish (1968) writers. The non-Western agenda was still directed toward antiquity—in collaboration with UNESCO and under the rubric "UNESCO-Sammlung," Reclam Stuttgart also published collections such as *Chinese poets of the Tang period*, *Diwan of Jelaluddin Rumi*, *Nala and Damayanti* from the Mahabharata, and Japanese stories from the *Konjaku-Monogatarishu*.[84] As announced in their newsletter *Die Begegnung*, these were aimed to serve a further understanding between the Eastern and the Western worlds.

But Reclam was not the only publishing company in the FRG. There were many others: Insel, Suhrkamp, various outfits of Bertelsmann, and the Switzerland-based Manesse Verlag, who played a major role in the distribution of world literature in the postwar years. But it was not merely publication houses that played a role in world literary circulation. In the FRG, it was the Frankfurt Book Fair that became a node for world literary exchanges.

In September 1949, the (West) German Book Trade Association (Deutsche Buchhandelsverein) initiated a revival of the Frankfurt Book Fair. From the fifteenth through the seventeenth centuries, the Frankfurt Book Fair was claimed to be the biggest book fair in Germany and one of the largest in Europe, only to be taken over by the Leipzig Book Fair in the eighteenth century. The fame enjoyed by the Leipzig Book Fair for over a century was to come to an end in 1949. A new era of commercial publication, circulation, and distribution of books was about to begin, whereby decolonized nations of Asia and Africa and rising powers like China would play an important role. The Frankfurt Book Fair was to serve as an important hub for these transnational transactions of print culture, and by the end of the twentieth century it became the largest book fair in the world, the prime center for negotiation of translation rights, the place to showcase developing readerships in the world through a special "guest of honor"

Figure 4-2. Cover of a Reclam catalog, 1960/61 (Stuttgart). (Courtesy of Deutsche Nationalbibliothek and Buch- und Schriftmuseum Leipzig, and Reclam Verlag Stuttgart.)

status accorded to different countries, and more recently, the platform to think about new media and the future of the book. In short, Frankfurt was to become to the world of the late twentieth century what Timbuktu was to the African book market and what Baghdad was to the Afro-Asian book markets from the eleventh through the seventeenth centuries.

One year into the new beginnings of the Frankfurt Book Fair, Europe was still reeling from the effects of World War II and was ready to prepare for another ideological bifurcation through the advent of the Cold War. As a counter-statement to these growing divisions, the organizers of the Book Fair inaugurated the German Peace Prize (Der Deutsche Friedenspreis) in 1950.[85] The prize was established to recognize the outstanding contribution of an author, scholar, or an artist in promoting international cultural understanding. The first recipient of the prize was Max Tau, a German writer who lived in exile in Norway during the Third Reich. With the second recipient, Albert Schweitzer (1951), the ceremonial conferral of the prize was moved to the Paulskirche in Frankfurt—the seat of the Frankfurt National Assembly (Frankfurter Nationalversammlung, 1848). Since then, the impressive list of recipients has included the German-Jewish thinker Martin Buber (1953), the former president of India and translator (from Sanskrit into English) of the *Bhagavad-Gita*, Dr. Sarvapalli Radhakrishnan (1962), the first Senegalese president and anticolonial activist Leopold Senghor (1968), and the Jewish composer and conductor Yehudi Menuhin (1979). The list also reveals a number of novelists whose work has found recognition and readerships around the world: Hermann Hesse (1955), Octavio Paz (1984), Mario Vargas Llosa (1996), Chinua Achebe (2002), and Orhan Pamuk (2005), who was the second Turkish author to receive the award after Yesar Kemal (1997). Several of these were also Nobel Laureates in literature.

The Frankfurt Book Fair had become, and continues to be, a way station for bibliomigrancy, indeed for the "worlding" of literature in the post–World War II era. It was also marked by West Germany's own history of migration, initiated during the years of the *Wirtschaftswunder* under Konrad Adenauer in the 1950s. As I discuss in chapter 5, authors featured in the Frankfurt Book Fair—not the ones from East Germany, or even West German authors of migrant background and non-German heritages—would dominate conceptual associations with world literature in a united Germany. Discussions of world literature in the contemporary context are quick to point out the rise of migrant writings in Germany as part of the "new world literature." The story, however, is more complex than a quick assimilation of Germanophone literature with the more widely read Anglophone, Francophone, Hispanophone, or Lusophone writings. Unraveling the complexity of world literary circulation in a unified Germany into the twenty-first century is the task of chapter 5. For now, I will cast one last glance at the ideological bifurcation that formed and informed prospects of world literary circulation in the divided Germany.

Unfinished Histories

This chapter started with a discussion of Volker Braun's *Unvollendete Geschichte* and Ulrich Plenzdorf's *Die neuen Leiden des jungen W*. Both of these works squarely locate literary production and reception in the political and social text of a nation, in which ideological state participation was key to all aspects of public life, including the construction of world literature. In the case of West Germany, while the poisonous material was not necessarily identified by the state itself, there were other factors involved. Political forces elsewhere at play—across the Atlantic Ocean—were key to the control and distribution of texts, either couched in diplomacy or in outright censorship. Despite these tendencies, individuals and institutions found ways of translating, publishing, and disseminating world literature. The case of Volk und Welt is a prime example of this phenomenon. Regardless of "prescribed" literature, much was to be found, discovered, engaged with, and used as a way to obscure state politics and policies.

Whether or not Auerbach thought that the Western student was prepared or pedagogically trained to process literatures from "Islamic, Chinese, and Indian" worlds, whether or not Reclam decided to change its program from Hesse's humanistic ideal to a "revolutionary spirituality," the creation of readerships occurred because of, and sometimes at a distance from, market forces and dominant political ideologies. When seen from the current perspective, world literary creation does not appear as a choice between national memory and conscience. Texts circulated in East and West Germany, through Reclam and Volk und Welt, through the Leipzig and Frankfurt Book Fairs, attest to both the memory and the conscience of the divided German states.

Around the Fall of the Berlin Wall, along with other cultural institutions, the differences in the book industry and reading cultures of the two German states underwent comprehensive public scrutiny. As Martin Ahrends reported in *Die Zeit*, in an article tellingly entitled "Leseland BRDDR" (Reading nation FRGDR), the number of books published in the GDR was far larger than in the FRG, even if more book titles were published in the FRG. The GDR also excelled the FRG in its publication of literary works (*Belletristik*): 35 percent of total titles published every year in the GDR were literary works, as opposed to 18 percent in the FRG. More books were read in the GDR, even if the number of volumes sold in the FRG was much higher.[86] Ahrends's observations were based partially on Ursula E. E. Köhler's *Lesekultur der beiden deutschen Staaten* (1988), an authoritative comparison based on forty years of available data in the FRG and GDR. While Köhler did not isolate world literature as a separate category, statistics on reading preferences classified by genre showed that even in the late 1970s, the number of readers who preferred novels and short stories, for example, were 16.5 percent and 14.5 percent respectively in the GDR, almost double the numbers of readers in the FRG, 8.8 percent and 6.8 percent.[87] The number of library users in the GDR (35 percent of the population) exceeded those in the FRG (24.5 percent of the population).[88]

Public libraries in the GDR played a very important role in the creation of readership. The months following the Fall of the Berlin Wall were particularly eventful for East German libraries. On the one hand, the "Giftschrank" (poison cabinet)—a befitting epithet to the cabinets of books banned in the GDR—was opened up for public access, including the one in the Deutsche Bücherei.[89] On the other hand, the lack of financial investment in libraries of the GDR had left them far behind those in the FRG, both in infrastructural support and in modes of free access to information.[90] In addition, a different kind of "purging" of literature would take place in the GDR libraries. Books pertaining to Marxist and communist ideologies were either simply deacquisitioned or proactively dumped, creating a situation where the historical memory of a recently transformed nation was once again under erasure. Documents pertaining to the history of the GDR were decommissioned, and often sold or dumped in the trash.[91]

The book culture in the *Leseland* was fast changing. Books read by East Germans were disappearing from the bookstores, and booksellers had begun to cater to the tastes of their new readers. When Dieter E. Zimmer, one of the main editors of *Die Zeit* traveled to Leipzig to write an essay on the changing book industry in East Germany, he visited many bookstores.[92] At one of the stores, he witnessed a young man asking for a copy of Umberto Eco's *The Name of the Rose* in German translation, which was published by Volk und Welt. The new edition, the young man was told, was postponed by a year. Zimmer, who was next in line, asked for a book of poems by the Russian romantic poet Mihkail Lermontov (1814–1841), and the autobiography of GDR premier Erich Honecker (1912–1994). Lermontov—most probably the edition published by Universal-Bibliothek[93]—Zimmer was told, was unavailable at the time, and Honecker's *Aus meinem Leben* had sold out, because it had suddenly gained the status of a treasured object for bibliophiles.[94] The bookseller's comments succinctly capture the sentiment of the time: "I am also pissed about this . . . that they could just take it out of the consignment, as if they can cancel history."[95]

The coming together of German states might have enjoyed the grand closure culminating in the Fall of the Berlin Wall. But the history and the story of world literature in the two states are still entangled in mutual opposition, still left unfinished.

Reykjavik
Uppsala
Stockholm
Helsinki
Oslo
St. Petersberg
Amsterdam
The Hague
Copenhagen
Tallin
Lund
Moscow
Edinburgh
Riga
Dublin
Berlin
Aberystwyth
London
Prague
Kiev
Vienna
Paris
Bern
Zurich
Budapest
Chişinău
Astrakhan
Ulan Bator
Geneva
Zagreb
Belgrade
Boston
Cambridge
Bucharest
Milan
Sofia
Istanbul
Tbilisi
New York
Madrid
Rome
Tirana
Baku
Samarkand
Beijing
Centinje
Yerevan
Lisbon
Athens
Ankara
Patras
Valetta
Nicosia
Tokio
Calcutta
Kinshasa

CHAPTER 5

Libraries without Walls? World Literature in the Digital Century

Hear the legend from over there:
There was a thousandfold librarian,
who preserved the literary legacies
of those whose books had gone in flames back then.

—GÜNTER GRASS, *Transatlantic Elegy*, (1990)[1]

They only want to keep one book. A single book from the entire century should remain, which is to represent all the others from modernism, early modernism, late modernism, postmodernism, and post-postmodernism.

—KEMAL KURT, *Ja, sagt Molly* (1998)[2]

In the last lines of the poem "Transatlantische Elegie," the Nobel Laureate Günter Grass relies on the figure of a very special kind of librarian to convey a historical and cultural redress of Germany's Nazi past. The poem recounts a meeting with German emigrants whom Grass met during a social gathering in New York City in 1965. In the poem's earlier stanzas, his new acquaintances—Jewish and non-Jewish Germans who fled to the United States during the Third Reich—ask him questions about the land that they left behind: "How does it look over there?" they ask, "And your young people? Do they know? Do they want to?" . . . "Should one go back?"[3]

The poem made its way into an election campaign speech that Grass gave in the same year. The speech, "Was ist des Deutschen Vaterland?" (What is the German's Fatherland), owes its title to the nationalist poem "Des Deutschen Vaterland" (1813) by Ernst Moritz Arndt (1769–1860)—whose stringent criticism of world literature is discussed in chapter 2—a poem that strategically lists German-speaking regions: Prussia, Bavaria, Westphalia, Saxony, but also Austria and Switzerland as fragments that constitute the totality of an imagined "fatherland."[4] Starting with a recitation of the entire poem in his speech, Grass rearranges the memory of German cities and states in East and West Germany to highlight the artificiality of German geographical and ideological division. He admits to having learned the poem during his school years but quickly distances himself from its nationalist import, stating: "I certainly hope the memory banks of our newest voters are not being clogged with such multistanzaic nonsense." Instead, he mobilizes the last line of the poem—"Das ganze Deutschland soll es sein" (Let the whole Germany belong to thee!)—to imagine the possibilities of a functional peace, a mode of coexistence between the peoples of East and West Germany in a time of accelerated ideological bifurcation between the two nation-states.[5] There are two moments in the speech when Grass's conceptualization of the German fatherland emanates from a transnational and transcontinental perspective—literally and figuratively. Toward the second half of the speech, he admits to having outlined it in New York City; and at the end, he returns to Arndt's question by referencing German immigrants in the United States: "In New York, getting a sense for that province of German emigrants I'd like to see included in the German fatherland, I wrote this 'Transatlantic Elegy.'"[6] The speech, the memory of Arndt's poem, and the creation of Grass's poem all originate in a faraway geographical location. New York City becomes the site of reimagining the entire Germany ("das ganze Deutschland").

Grass's speech invokes the gravity of the historical moment of the Berlin Wall's construction and its immediate political consequences. Through the incorporation of Arndt's poem, he spotlights the civic construction of nationalism through cultural artefacts. The national "memory banks," as history witnessed, often outweighed the so-called *Lastenausgleich* ("equalizing the burden") between the official formula of "two states, one nation" during the existence of the Berlin Wall. Through a brief—albeit by no means undue—reference to the preservation of literary legacies, Grass draws our attention to histories of books that became sacrificial objects in the pogrom against free speech.

The process of coming to terms with Germany's past in a post-Wall world is still open for debate, as exemplified in Grass's autobiographical work *Beim Häuten der Zwiebel* (2006; *Peeling the Onion*). The acceptance of him being drafted into the SS during the National Socialist period calls upon us to question the nature of a "memory bank" of books that a "thousandfold librarian" wishes to preserve for the twenty-first century.

If Grass refers to *one* librarian that shall assure the existence of books in the future, the Turkish-German author Kemal Kurt, in his novel *Ja, sagt Molly*, narrates the story of the twentieth century through many librarians and books. Born in 1947 in Çorlu, Turkey, Kurt moved to Germany in

1972 and worked as an essayist, photographer, author of children's books, translator, and television writer. Kurt's novel bears the distinct marks of large-scale human migration and bibliomigrancy in the late twentieth century.

Kurt's novel begins on a rainy evening in a city with many names: "London, maybe, Paris or Berlin. Or also New York, Tokyo, Dublin, Istanbul, Toronto, Calcutta, Kinshasa, Ulan Bator, Samarkand, Astrakhan."[7] Having established his global locations, the narrator moves to look for a book of all books—"das totale Buch"—which would simultaneously serve as an "epitome and extract of all other books."[8] The "regressive method" suggested by the "blind librarian" whereby one has to look for book B in order to locate book A—the narrator writes referring to Borges's *The Library of Babel*—will not suffice. The opening scene brings the reader to the apartment of Leopold and Molly Bloom from Joyce's *Ulysses*. Molly, who is about to go to bed, finds Gregor Samsa (Kafka, *The Metamorphosis*) on the foot of her bed. At first astonished by Gregor's presence in her bedroom, Molly ends up inviting him to bed, and as she lies down, Gregor starts his erotic foreplay, slowly discovering her body as he discovers his own sexuality, symbolically denied to him in scene 2 of *The Metamorphosis*, when his mother and sister remove the framed picture of the lady in a fur boa (a reference to Leopold von Sacher-Masoch's *Venus in Fur*) from his room. Molly relents to his sexual advances with "*Ja, ich will Ja*,"[9] and thus the last sentence of Joyce's classic: "yes I said yes I will Yes"[10] becomes the opening line of the story of the twentieth century. And so the narrator begins the writing of that all-encompassing book, which narrates the twentieth century through conversations among characters from over 150 literary works written in about twenty languages. Kurt thus creates an archive of a multidirectional and multilingual modernism through a world literary inventory.

Grass and Kurt offer apt points of departure to think about world literature through the lived political realities of the late twentieth century. Throughout this book, I have discussed bibliomigrancy through mechanisms of translational and transnational exchanges—initiated and facilitated by colonialism, nurtured by well-organized oriental outfits, criticized by nationalists, banned through fascism, reshaped through political ideologies in a divided nation. In this chapter, I locate these translational exchanges through filters of migration. The story of world literature this chapter tries to tell is framed within two meanings of migration: (willing or forced) "physical" migration of human beings that becomes definitive to the social text of the late twentieth century, and the "digital" migration of books and libraries into a virtual space, one that has drastically changed modes of literary circulation beyond physical spaces.

The first half of this chapter seeks to demonstrate how in a post-Wall, reunified Germany, digital libraries themselves acquire the role of a memory bank, transform the media of future public and state memory, and, in turn, are transformed by the public sphere through the course of their existence. In the second half, I turn to the late twentieth century to examine the precarious position of German migration literature, written either by German-language authors with or without a migrant background, or non-German literature that centralizes migration into Germany. The borderlessness, transnationality, and cosmopolitanism embodied in this literature through registers of multilingualism is often celebrated within discussions of world literature, but—as I want to demonstrate—rather inadequately and sometimes even inaccurately.

No discussion of books or communities beyond borders in the German context can be complete without the iconography of the Berlin Wall, which becomes a signifying marker in the proposed two-pronged investigation. In fact, the Berlin Wall's compelling topography, the alluring mythography of its fall, and the fascinating cosmography of pre- and post-Wall European cultural politics create new contexts and grant new meanings to a "virtual" bibliograph of a very special kind of library and add new layers of meaning to world literature. The Fall of the Berlin Wall also challenges us to rethink the German polity—including migrants and East Germans—in the last decade of the twentieth century.

How do we imagine the relationship among world literature, migration, and digital media? Are the ever-expanding offerings of the worldwide web enough to assume the expansion of the world literary space? If yes, what are the essential features of this "virtual" world literary space? Who inhabits it? How do the inhabitants transform this space? What are some of the ways of measuring the transformation?

To approach these questions and to understand digital libraries as the figural reincarnation of a "thousandfold librarian," I will turn to a few recent positions on the transformation of libraries from a physical to a digital space. This will be useful to comprehend the construction of the European Library project (hereafter TEL) and its Internet portal, the European Digital Library (hereafter EDL), which provides access to the holdings of forty-eight "national libraries" across the continent of Europe.[11] However, instead of naively trying to establish a direct genealogy between the Fall of the Berlin Wall and a library without walls, the following discussion of TEL seeks to unravel the transnational construction, the cosmopolitan ambition, and the purportedly universal mission of digital libraries. The analysis proceeds in three steps. First, I situate TEL and the EDL in the recent history of the transformation of print cultures and libraries. Second, by elucidating several constitutive elements of TEL and the EDL, I evaluate TEL's politics of construction and self-representation. I use these elements to jump into a discussion of the contemporary understanding of world literature in Germany through filters of migration, in order to ask if and how current discussions actually take into account changing trajectories and modes of literary circulation. This chapter ends with a suturing of these two discussions through literature. I return to questions of accessibility, spatiality, and temporality in private and public libraries through a discussion of literary representations of nonvirtual libraries.

Virtual Bibliomigrancy: Transformation of Access

The virtual migration of books through technology demands an understanding of print culture's materiality as well as associated issues such as reading habits, reading strategies, and reader accessibility. Virtual bibliomigrancy is transforming access to the bibliograph—the catalogue of world literature—through a transformation of the physical space of the Bibliothek. As Robert Darnton reminisced in his essay "The Library in the New Age":

> To students in the 1950s, libraries looked like citadels of learning. Knowledge came packaged between hard covers, and a great library seemed to contain all of it. To climb the steps of the New York Public Library, past the stone lions guarding its entrance and into the monumental reading room on the third floor, was to enter a world that included everything known. In colleges everywhere the library stood at the center of the campus. It was the most important building, a temple set off by classical columns, where one read in silence: no noise, no food, no disturbances beyond a furtive glance at a potential date bent over a book in quiet contemplation.[12]

As knowledge now comes to us in the form of PDF files and other digital formats, the library comes to the laptop, and the image of the physical library building—as the citadel, a building with steps guarded by stone lions, a temple set off by classical columns, where the rituals of silent and solemn reading have taken place for centuries—is turning sepia. The part of the library most affected by this change is, of course, the rare book collection. In the same essay, Darnton asks the question, "Aren't rare book collections doomed to obsolescence now that everything will be available on the Internet?"[13]

James Cheng, one of Darnton's colleagues at the Harvard Libraries, provides one possible answer. Commenting on an agreement between Harvard College and the National Library of China to digitize one of the largest collections of rare Chinese books outside of China, Cheng stated: "We need to change the mind-set that rare materials must be kept behind closed doors," adding, "A library is not a museum."[14] While Darnton's architectural references allude to the iconic—even though diminishing—status of the library on the cultural-intellectual landscape of a university or a city, Cheng's pithy declaration is even more aggressively iconoclastic.

Cheng's brief statement immediately prompts a reevaluation of Michel Foucault's comparison of libraries with museums in his essay "Of Other Spaces." As discussed in the introduction to the book, among the heterotopias that Foucault mentions, the library and the museum categorically connect space with time. The accumulative instinct that Foucault ascribes to the nineteenth century allows for seeing libraries and museums as having intersecting, if not identical, functions. Libraries have long served as the sources of dissemination of knowledge, resources for learning and research, and physical depositories for the collection and accession of books and other "readable" objects. In addition, they have played the role of representative institutions for local, regional, and national cultural heritages: repositories, curio cabinets, and showcases of "national memory" in all its contested and contestable significations. Along with museums, they have also served as treasure chests of dubiously acquired objects: memorabilia and souvenirs of a nation's imperialist and colonialist past. Access to these objects for the general public has been through thematically organized exhibitions; alternatively, serious researchers have been able to gain access to them in rare books and special collections rooms. The transformation of print culture is changing that "look-but-not-touch policy," at least in the virtual space. Yet Cheng explicitly states that the digitization of library collections detaches the library from its function as a museum. The process of detachment, it can be argued, starts with the transformation of the meaning of "virtual space" that books and libraries now inhabit. Virtual space is no more a "conceptual" space—the opposite of physical and material space as Foucault imagined. Through advancement in electronic technology, digital space has created its own set of rules and regulations as well as terms and conditions about accessibility and inaccessibility.

Extant scholarship in the field of library and information studies engages with the infrastructural, technological, and organizational aspects of digital libraries. Gary Marchionini describes digital libraries as "logical extensions and augmentations of physical libraries," distinguished by a focus on the integration of services through "a holistic treatment of interface, location, time language, and system."[15] Donald Waters defines them as "organizations that provide the resources, including the specialized staff, to select, structure, offer intellectual access to, interpret, distribute, preserve the integrity of, and ensure the persistence over time of collections of digital works so that they are readily and economically available for use by a defined community or set of communities."[16]

This definition echoes ideas central to those of the Association of Research Libraries, which understands a digital library as "a group of entities—not a single entity—that uses technology to forge and maintain transparent links to the resources and services of multiple entities."[17] Christinger Tomer succinctly states that digital libraries are "little more than a loosely organized collection of digitized images and text."[18] In *Understanding Digital Libraries*, Michael Lesk compares digital libraries with H. G. Wells's dream of a "complete planetary memory for all mankind."[19]

While scholars in the humanities and cultural studies have recently tried to fathom the role and function of digital libraries, their understanding has largely been focused on changes in the habits of scholarship at US universities. In a 2009 issue of *Daedalus*, historian Anthony Grafton comments on the radical change in "the styles of great libraries," identifying "a strange kind of war . . . between styles of repository, reading, and research."[20] He starts his evaluation by outlining distinctions between established libraries such as those at Columbia, Harvard, and Yale "with their allegiance to old cultural traditions" and newer libraries such as those in Seattle and Salt Lake city that "scream their modernity" with "[g]leaming banks of computers";[21] he ends with the conclusion that "(physical) browsing remains a vital, irreplaceable form of research."[22] To be sure, Grafton does ask questions about—and provides a number of suggestions for—collaboration between university departments and libraries to "enable America to remain the land of the great democratic library for generations to come." However, his initial restraint concerning the entry of multinational capital into digitizing library resources infuses his evaluation with a profound sense of loss. Google and Starbucks therefore become part of the same equation, wooing students and scholars away from the library. In the same issue of *Daedalus*, classicist James J. O'Donnel comments on the "digital humanities," declaring at the very outset that "we speak seldom of the electrical, the automative, or the aeronautical humanities" and that the term someday will fall out of use.[23] While O'Donnel conveys more optimism in his evaluation of digital libraries, he aligns himself with Grafton in the dissociation of multinational capital and research libraries, asserting that:

> Access to resources, technical and human, that support scholarly ambition is a battle to be fought at the local level, but one to be supported by wise public funding nationally and internationally. . . . In the end, the work is ours. Do we have the right questions to ask? Do we have the right disciplinary alignments? Are we making the new (including the very products of cyberspace) a part of our own sphere of study and interpretation as responsibly and carefully as we maintain the old (and link the study of the old and the new)?[24]

If Grafton's and O'Donnell's insights are to be engaged with seriously, questions asked of digital libraries must go beyond just a pessimistic evaluation of multinational commerce's entry into the business of digital libraries. To this end, a romantic celebration of the past of older libraries, pitting them against new and modern libraries, will not suffice. Equally inadequate will be a reductive reading of digital libraries as mere "augmentations" of physical libraries or as tools and resources whose impact is mostly on academic research. The challenge lies in considering digital libraries as institutions with their own emerging set of rules of collection, classification, and cognition, and in extending the investigation of such questions to publicly funded mega-digital library projects. It would be productive, for example, to formulate questions of patrons—today also labeled end users—vis-à-vis political representation and self-representation, especially in the case of the so-called national libraries, which so far remain largely unarticulated. As books, audio, video, and other materials are digitized, Internet-based libraries become sites of virtual migration, not just of materials but also of users, the readers. Who has ownership claims over these materials? Furthermore, what are the implications of decoupling the library from the museum through the digitization of objects? If publics are at the center of these digitization projects, what discernible political purposes do they serve? Do they always promote or can they also impede access to materials? These questions inform the following discussion of virtual libraries such as TEL and the EDL.

TEL and the EDL: National Representation, Cosmopolitan Consumption

TEL is a *transnational* cultural institution, conceived, designed, and executed as an *international* conglomerate of multiple *national* institutions in the post-1989 era of pan-Europeanization through policies of the European

Union. If the Fall of the Berlin Wall serves as an important historical and political marker for TEL's origins, the progress made in the last twenty-five years in information technology facilitates its execution.

In 1987, representatives of eleven European "national" libraries—I will return to this term shortly—met for the first time in Lisbon to form the Foundation Conference of European National Librarians (CENL) with the following countries represented: Denmark, France, Germany, Greece, Luxembourg, the Netherlands, Norway, Portugal, Spain, the United Kingdom, and the Vatican City. As the CENL website reports:

> Topics on the agenda were the interconnection of computerized systems of the national libraries, acquisition policies, preservation and conservation, and financial issues of national libraries. The national librarians continued to meet annually *and the group grew steadily*. In 1991 CENL organized the first East-West conference with national libraries of Eastern Europe in Vienna in order to establish closer links and a defined partnership. It was a very successful meeting with concrete results leading to an ongoing dialogue. In 1998 CENL adopted its statutes and was transferred into a foundation under Dutch law.[25]

In 2001, the CENL and nine national member libraries became founding partners of the European Library, Gateway to Europe's Knowledge. The national libraries involved in the project were those of France, Italy, Germany, the Netherlands, Portugal, the United Kingdom, Finland, Slovenia, and Switzerland. Funded under the Fifth Framework Programme of the European Commission, TEL was conceived as a consortium to facilitate electronic access to the collections at participating libraries by users all over the world as a public service measure. In 2005, the European Commission released its "i2010" communiqué on the European Information Society, which was strongly endorsed by Jacques Chirac and five other heads of state in a letter to EC President José Manuel Barroso.[26] Vivienne Reding, the EC member responsible for Information Society and Media, used this letter to accelerate the European Library Project, stating that: "There is an emerging political will to make this happen. . . . He [Mr. Barroso] called for the Heads of State to support him in the European Commission's approach to safeguarding and adding value to Europe's cultural heritage, the mirror of our cultural diversity. But it is not going to happen automatically. It will require a real commitment of all involved, not least from the national libraries."[27] In response to Reding's speech and popular interest in the initiative, the EDL was launched in 2005. It had a budget of over two million euros, of which one million was contributed by the

European Commission's eContentplus program. The project started in September 2006 and was completed in February 2008; the specific steps taken included:

1. TEL-ME-MOR (2004–2006) brought in the national libraries of Poland, the Czech Republic, Hungary, Malta, Cyprus, Latvia, Lithuania, Estonia, and Slovakia.
2. The EDL project (2006–2008) worked toward integrating into TEL the bibliographic catalogues and digital collections of the national libraries of Belgium, Greece, Iceland, Ireland, Liechtenstein, Luxembourg, Norway, Spain, and Sweden.
3. TEL-plus (2007–2009) brought in the national libraries of Bulgaria and Romania by 2008.
4. FUMAGABA (2008–2009) enlarged TEL by adding the national libraries of Ukraine, Moldova, Georgia, Armenia, and Azerbaijan as well as of the former Yugoslav Republic—Macedonia, Albania, and Bosnia-Herzegovina.[28]

The European Digital Library 2.0, launched in 2008, was conceived as "a free service that gives users access to the resources of the 48 national libraries of Europe in 20 languages." A later version, EDL 2.2.0, was launched on October 19, 2009, at the Frankfurt Book Fair. It expands the language offerings by fifteen, with collections available in thirty-five languages. The European Library currently provides bibliographic access to 150 million entries across Europe.[29] New participating libraries include the National Library of Turkey in Ankara and the Russian collections in Moscow and St. Petersburg, among others. The grandiose future of the European Library Project is Europeana, a digital portal launched in 2008 that aims to double the number of accessible entries in the most technologically advanced, compact formats. Europeana includes "museums, archives, and other holders of cultural materials."[30]

To understand the nuances of self-constitution and self-representation through the European Library Project, it helps to juxtapose it with two other entities similar in scale but different in scope. Across the Atlantic Ocean, the US-based Universal Digital Library (also known as Ulib) went online in 2005.[31] With Carnegie Mellon University's Million Book Project serving as the prototype, Ulib is a collaborative of about fifty research libraries in Canada and the United States, the Bibliotheca Alexandrina in Egypt, and about thirty participating libraries in India and China. Its website incorporates the Gutenberg Project, the oldest digital library that was conceived by Michael Hart in 1971.[32] Financial and infrastructural support for the project comes from Carnegie Mellon, some participating libraries, UNESCO, the Library of Congress, and the governments of the United States, Canada, China, and India. The second example is the World Digital Library (WDL), supported by UNESCO and the James Madison Library at the Library of Congress.[33] Publically launched in April 2009, it provides bibliographic access to partner libraries from over forty UNESCO member countries; its financial sponsors include Google, Microsoft, and the Library of Congress, among others. The latest in this chain of institutions is the Digital Public Library of America (DPLA), launched in 2013,[34] which the historian Robert Darnton has recently discussed as a way out of commercialization and into democratization of knowledge.[35]

All these projects identify themselves as noncommercial service portals aimed at the digital preservation and collection of materials in literature, science, and many other fields. Their resources are digital or bibliographical (including books, posters, maps, sound recordings, and videos) and provide open access to the worldwide community of Internet users.

However, there are significant differences between these projects. Ulib necessitates, at least for now, literacy in English for access to its materials, which cover most European and some Asian languages; WDL is developing prototypes for multilingual usage; TEL requires literacy in English or the respective language of the participating European library for access to its materials, which range from Arabic to Sanskrit. Ulib identifies digital technology as the medium to conserve "all the significant literary, artistic, and scientific works of mankind" and aims at creating a library "which will foster creativity and free access to all human knowledge . . . without regard to nationality or socioeconomic background." WDL's principle objectives include promotion of "international and intercultural understanding" and "build[ing] capacity in partner institutions to narrow the digital divide within and between countries."[36] TEL, by contrast, "provides a vast virtual collection of material from all disciplines and offers visitors with interest a simple access to European cultural resources."[37]At Ulib, clusters of national, regional, and international libraries form the collaborative; the website categorically states that the Library of Congress is *not* the national library of the United States. DPLA, however, positions itself both as the "National Digital Public Library of America" and as a "World Digital Library." In its foundational phases, TEL operated with a clear definition of a national library: "A national library is the library specifically established by a country to store its information database. National libraries usually host the legal deposit and the bibliographic control centre of a nation" (figure 5-1).[38] This definition is not a convenient fiction

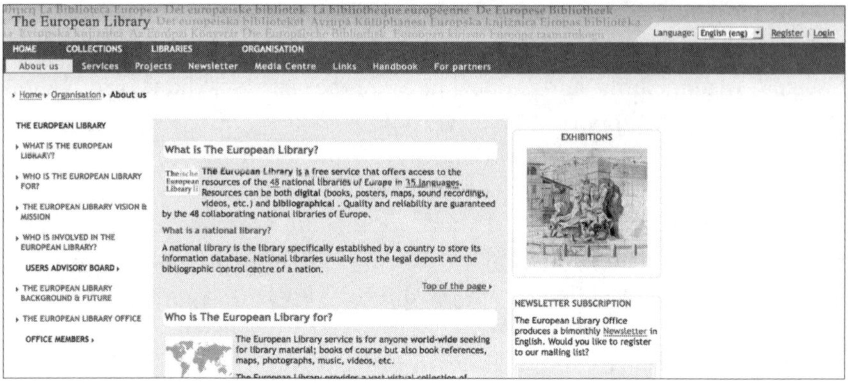

Figure 5-1. The European Library website, 2010.

adapted by TEL. As mentioned in its documents, it is an adaptation of the constitutional definition of a national library in most European countries, wherever it exists. While the network was expanded to include European research libraries in 2013,[39] the definition of a national library cannot be brushed off so easily. First, because it is at the core of TEL's construction and self-representation; second, because it draws attention—especially in the contracts—to internal discrepancies and uneven power structures between various European member nations; and third, because the very definition of "national" holdings of a European nation are immediately questionable due to Europe's colonial and imperial histories intertwined with other parts of the world. A few examples illustrate these three points.

The four contracts between member nations for various stages of TEL-ME-MOR, the EDL, TEL-plus, and FUMABAGA replicate the definition of "national libraries" in many ways. The revised 2006 EDL contract (the original was written in 2001) explains the value of Europe's national libraries as "world-class institutions with a vital role as holders of the national memory of the member states." Extending this definition, the document continues: "EDL creates a pan-European platform and is a strategic investment in European content enrichment." Among the functions it mentions are that EDL will "help European citizens, students, researchers, business users, and other users . . . to find and use digital content, irrespective of language and location." The project ascribes adjectives such as multicultural and multilingual to its "essential nature"; it lists as its service "aggregation of digital cultural objects and collections across borders"; and it explains the use of TEL as "a single access point" so "informed citizens in any country can utilize the resources . . . of his or her national library

. . . and other partner national libraries."[40] Two pages later, this fictitious end user, the European citizen, transforms briefly into a "worldwide end user" only to return to his or her original form as a "European citizen."[41] A search for the eternal recurrence of the European subject might be attributed to the following statement: "National Libraries are aware of the European identity of their collections alongside their national identity."[42] The section on "Community added value and contributions to EC policies" begins with "Building the European Library is an inherently European undertaking" and states "the EDL Project is also inherently European and not national."[43]

These inaugural formulations in the EDL's foundational document reveal three tendencies. First, in the post-Wall Europe of territorial expansion, regional integration, and financial collaboration, national-cultural particularities become the ultimate frontiers of collective difference. Second, such collective cultural difference manifests itself ideologically: in, through, and despite the new set of European cultural policies endorsed by member nation-states. And finally, the EU's attempts at regional cultural governance collide with member nations' historical conceptualization of cultural self-definition and self-representation. From TEL-ME-MOR and the EDL to FUMAGABA, the inherent differences in cultural and linguistic histories, political structures, and everyday operative realities between Western and the new Eastern European libraries subject to integration become painfully clear. The EDL as a model platform for "coordination of national initiatives" seems to need more groundwork in the context of post-1989 nation rebuilding. The subtlety of the section "Assessment of risks and potentials" is worthy of mention: "Risk in this project is increased by the following factors: 1) TEL Office has no track record of collaborating with the 8 target libraries on operational levels; 2) working personal relationships on operational levels between TEL Office and each target library still need to be set up; 3) some partners of the project might lack experience in international projects; 4) the potentially poor level of English spoken and written in the target libraries."[44] The solution provided in the section that follows is "good communication"—not specifying the language in which this good communication will take place, certainly not one of the many languages of the EU's new Eastern European members.

The geographical vicinity and cultural intersections of these Eastern European nation-states with Asia, or even their intertwined histories with Asian countries, is a fact that is subject to amnesia in all the TEL contracts but particularly noticeable in FUMAGABA. A resolution of this neglect cannot be expected in a working contract on libraries; however, it must be pointed out, owing to the primacy of the national paradigm used to define libraries. Insinuations of national memory, national heritage, European memory, European heritage, European cultural content, European citizens, and the European nature of these projects—all these factors seem to defy the grounds of cooperation and accessibility that TEL and other projects aim to achieve. To further underline the significance of this tension between "national" and "European" in the contracts, a brief comparison with a related theoretical discussion is in order.

In a coauthored 2007 study on *Cosmopolitan Europe*, Ulrich Beck and Edgar Grande evaluate the conditions of cosmopolitanism throughout the European Union. In the introductory chapter, they propose cosmopolitanism as a solution that overcomes the "European Malaise," which they attribute to the primacy of nationalism in European political history and to the neglect—if not entire eradication—of differences in European cultural politics. Highlighting the "dissolution of difference" as the mark of practiced universalism in Europe and declaring "nationalism" as an essential element of "first modernity," Beck and Grande propose the necessity of cosmopolitanism for Europe's contemporary and future existence. The recognition and mobilization of internal and external differences bereft of hierarchical orders or divisions—that is, in the service of egalitarianism among citizens and other residents—emerge as significant advantages of the cosmopolitanism that they identify for Europe. The promise of this premise is worked out in their evaluations of European history, national histories, and EU policies. In the last chapter, "Cosmopolitan Visions for Europe," they propose: "European Cosmopolitanism can no longer take its orientation from the principle of national self-determination and of nation building . . . but rather from the principle of regional cosmopolitanization."[45]

Thinking with Beck and Grande while investigating cultural manifestations of EU policies in pan-European cultural institutions, it is evident how principles of national self-determination and nation-building from the nineteenth century dominate the execution of regional cosmopolitanization. The politics of selective multiple affiliations remains a function of cultural and political representation of institutions. TEL, the EDL, and Europeana are not just products of innocent and enthusiastic conversations among cultural bureaucrats and technocrats. They are attestations of the EU's cultural policies in action, funded by public money to facilitate the transformation of EU publics in an information society. Yet while the digital divide and linguistic barriers still place the idea of equitable access to knowledge through virtual libraries in a distant future, universal ambition, a democratic mission, and worldwide reception are at the heart of these projects. In the case of TEL, the chase after these lofty principles comes to a screeching halt rather quickly. The definition of a national library draws our attention to basic principles of the organization, acquisition, collation, classification, location, and dissemination of resources.

A critique of national libraries also demands an internally differentiated understanding of any national library. The German context serves as an excellent example. At the 1987 CENL conference in Lisbon, two years before the fall of the Berlin Wall, "Germany" was represented by the Deutsche Nationalbibliothek in Frankfurt am Main. The Deutsche Bücherei in Leipzig, one of the most important centers for the documentation of German cultural history, especially print-cultural history, was not represented—not because it somehow did not contain documents befitting German national memory, but because it was located in the erstwhile GDR. Founded in 1913, the Deustche Bücherei's primary responsibility has been the collection, cataloging, and bibliographic indexing of all printed publications issued in Germany. Currently the collections exceed nineteen million units. In 1931, the Bücherei published the first *Deutsche Nationalbibliographie* in two series: (1) with lists of books published by members of the Deutsche Buchhandelsverein, and (2) books published by nonmembers. In 1942, the Nazis expanded the Bücherei's function for the first time by law. It was charged with collecting translations of German works into world languages and works on Germany published around the world. The Deutsche Bücherei remained the center for German print-cultural history until 1944, when it was shut down due to air raids. It reopened in 1945 when the second and last version of a united *Deutsche Nationalbibliographie* was published in Leipzig. However, with the division of Germany into two states on the horizon, it was clear that the Deutsche Bucherei would be the library of East Germany. As mentioned in the last chapter, in 1948, with American money and the collaboration of Frankfurt's Stadtbibliothek and Universitätsbibliothek, a new library was proposed as the future (West) German National Library, and the Deutsche Nationalbibliothek was born. Since then, two different national bibliographies were produced every other year until 1990. With Germany's reunification, the Deutsche Bücherei in Leipzig and the Deutsche Bibliothek in Frankfurt—which since 1970 has included the Deutsches Musikarchiv (Berlin)—were unified under the name Deutsche Nationalbibliothek.[46]

As this discussion demonstrates, history has more than once rendered questionable the notion of a single bibliographic control center—a single national library or a national memory bank in the German context. On the EDL website, this complex history is reduced to a set of factoids that indicate a teleological progression from 1913 to 1945 to 1990 to 2005, when the EDL was launched. The reduction, however, does not help to circumvent the historical circumstances that inform the selection of objects to be integrated into the European Library Project. Moreover, as members of the worldwide community—historically connected with Europe through imperialism and colonialism—become the target users of projects such as TEL, one cannot avoid questioning the clear geographical and geopolitical demarcation of cultural resources in insular terms—the very identification of cultural resources as European or belonging only to a specific European nation.

The competition between the state libraries of Berlin and Munich to acquire Sanskrit manuscripts in the early nineteenth century (discussed in chapter 1) as well as the large-scale acquisition of Arabic, Persian, and Urdu manuscripts and printed volumes by the Staatsbibliothek Berlin in the form of Bibliotheca Sprengeriana in the second half of the nineteenth century (discussed in chapter 2) suffice to illustrate these points. As Hartmut-Ortwin Feistel explains, important libraries were acquired, such as those of Sir Robert Chambers, judge of the British East India Company in Calcutta; Baron Heinrich Friedrich von Dietz, Prussian ambassador to the Ottoman Empire; Johan Gottfried Wettzstein, Prussian consul in Damascus; and many others.[47] Orientalist philologists encouraged these acquisitions and were strongly influenced by them. The role of the Deutsche Morgenländische Gesellschaft (German Oriental Society; see chapter 2) was indispensable for identifying these collections. Founded in 1845 with the goal of "supporting from all directions knowledge about Asia and countries in its close proximity as well as expanding participation in this endeavor to wider circles," it first collaborated with the Royal Library in Berlin and then started acquiring its own holdings.[48] The Staatsbibliothek's bibliographic control center is Germany, but that it is part of Germany's legal deposit is a claim best left open to interpretation.

The multiple contexts of print-cultural transformations, new media developments, public interactions with readable objects, and the blurry distinctions between the sacrosanct and the secularized must be understood in conjunction with the political formation of publics that are the end users of such products. A legal deposit, a bibliographic control center, an institution purloined through cultural history only to reemerge as a cultural icon, a historical building with national significance for a national or regional polity—these are the many meanings of a library that have been central to my critique of the European Library Project in this chapter. TEL and the EDL show the persistence of confining and limiting systems of nomination, categorization, and classification, even when the walls are metaphorically brought down. As a new definition of "virtual" spaces is rapidly transforming the collective cultural construction of libraries in the twenty-first century, the library's old functions still hold precedence over suspicion, neutralization, and inversion. The European Library Project and the European Digital Library may have the bold ambition of decoupling the museum from the library, but they are replicating to an extent the nineteenth-century obsession with ever-accumulating pasts, albeit now in virtual space. This inadequacy is not a consequence of myopic planning; libraries themselves cannot be disembedded from their convoluted histories of collection, acquisition, and accession. Yet the ideological implications of the library should not blind us to their spatial and temporal constitutions on the one hand, and ownership and accessibility on the other.

Ownership and accessibility indeed are the two key words that make digital libraries important circulatory portals for world literary artefacts, especially literary works from antiquity to the nineteenth century. PDF versions of translated classics of world literature in major European languages: *Kalila-wa-Dimna*, *Shahnameh*, and even Chinese texts read by Goethe—to name just a few—are available through Google Books or HathiTrust, which are part of a collaborative enterprise of many libraries around the world. However, through TEL and Europeana, sections of ancient manuscripts—if not entire manuscripts—are now being recirculated into the public realm, increasing accessibility and sometimes bringing hidden manuscripts for the first time to the public light.[49] Marked with a PD (public domain) sign, these manuscripts are being digitized by major national (and now research) libraries in Europe. It is true that in order to access these works or get a glimpse of these manuscripts, one needs access to the Internet. But when compared with the cost of travel from a non-European country to a European library—not to mention the financial requirements stipulated on Asian and African scholars for getting a visa to travel to Europe to gain access to printed volumes or manuscripts—Internet access is far more affordable. This is not to support the claim that digitization is the only or the most optimal solution. While digital access to manuscripts might inform the reader of the material history of a text, it does not help the reader in experiencing that material history; it is a mediated experience. So to a great extent, the "look-but-not touch" aspect that Cheng referred to is still in full force.

As for ownership, digital accessibility offers no simple solution other than diffusing the question. Despite the curious set of circumstances through which Sprenger accumulated his collection, it now belongs to the

Staatsbibliothek in Berlin. The kingdom of Awadh is long gone, and it would be precarious for the Indian, Egyptian, or Syrian governments to reclaim materials acquired by Sprenger. However, a future digitized access to *Bibliotheca Sprengeriana*—for it has not been done yet—would actually provide hundreds of scholars, but also singers and performers of verses of the fourteenth century Sufi Amir Khusro, access to his songs in manuscript form.

These are just a few examples. But in the very large collections of texts that were deemed world literary texts starting with the nineteenth century, these few examples serve well to demonstrate how digital libraries such as TEL are just beginning to provide new venues of world literary circulation. A world digital library can never be complete. However, through virtual bibliomigrancy, libraries could enhance borrowing privileges to a worldwide readership.

In his essay "World Literature and the Internet," Thomas O. Beebee refers to the Internet as the "'third revolution' in the fixation of linguistic and mental concepts, the first two being the invention of writing and development of movable type."[50] Beebee compares the development of the World Wide Web to the "ever-increasing rhythm of trade and commerce between European nations" during Goethe's time to prophesize the "profound impact" of the Internet on world literature, which he measures through the genre of "Internet Literature."[51] While the focus of my discussion has been digital libraries, as my analysis has shown, the "profound impact" of the digitization of libraries is yet to be seen.

Digitization, we should not forget, is a recent technological agent of access to world literature. Historical processes of decolonization around World War II and large-scale human migration in the second half of the twentieth century have recodified world literature. A new kind of migration of literature and books has impacted the conceptualization of world literature in Germany. This new world literature is even more self-consciously positioned in vectors of transnationalism, registers of cosmopolitanism, and vocabularies of multilingualism. As the digital migration of texts into the virtual sphere simultaneously exacerbates and mediates the tensions between nationally owned and transnationally shared materials, literary documentation of human migration challenges traditional notions of national literature based solely on the ethnicity of authors, as well as canonical notions of world literatures based on the best and the most representative works from the national literature. To understand the tensions between literatures of migration and world literature in the German context, it might be best to remind us of one of the first uses of the phrase "new world literature." A publishing firm first established by William Henry Heinemann

(1863–1920), a British publisher of German heritage, had something to do with it.

Beyond the Digital: Migration and Postcolonial World Literatures

"Thirty Years of a New World Literature" was the title of a short article in *The Bookseller* (1993) outlining the achievements of the Heinemann Educational Books' African Writers Series.[52] The author of the piece was Alan Hill, who served as the managing director of Heinemann at the time of the African Writers Series' inception in 1962. The article was published two weeks after the African Writers Series received the World Development Award for Business sponsored by the British Worldaware Organization. Queen Elizabeth II was the patron of this organization; Lord Grenfell, the chief of external relations of the World Bank, served as chair of the six-member jury. In his article, Hill mentions the profit-oriented mind-set of A. S. Frere, then chairman of Heinemann. Along with other publishing outfits, Frere was eager to tap into the African book market in the 1960s, "the frenetic era of nation-building" in postindependence African countries with a large demand for educational books—mostly textbooks and primarily in English. "For most of these companies," Hill writes, "African authors did not exist." Against this commercial backdrop Hill describes receiving, in 1957, a manuscript of a novel "from a student from Ibadan University."[53] This manuscript was *Things Fall Apart* (1958) by Chinua Achebe, who later became the first editor of the African Writers Series.

Hill's article can easily be read as a classic tale of the triumph of literature and art over commerce. Closer scrutiny reveals why it should be read differently. The sudden emergence of an African "masterpiece" as late as the 1950s—and in English, the language of the colonizer—today seems dubious. The purported nonexistence of African authors on a continent that is home to at least a few hundred languages and literary traditions would today be called a manifestation of sanctioned ignorance. Moreover, the characters involved in the recognition of the triumph—a Britain-based publisher, the Queen of England, a charity organization, the chair of the World Bank—all become part of a complex history of colonial mission, educational ambition, and corporate commission. The history of the African Writers Series and its cryptic role in the development of African literatures has been a topic of several scholarly discussions and debates.[54] The African Writers Series' geographical focus on West Africa, at least in the first decade of its existence, as well as its emphasis on English-language works written mostly by male authors has earned stringent criticism. After all, Heinemann "reminded" one of Africa through a particular "packaging" of the continent evident not merely in the editorial selection criteria but also on the dust jackets: invocations of "ethnicized" art reminiscent of Gauguin's Tahiti-period against a bright orange background.

William Heinemann was born in England of a German father, a naturalized British citizen, and a British mother.[55] He started his publishing career in 1879 as an apprentice of Nicholas Trübner, also a German native. Prior to his move to London to work for Longman, Trübner had extensive experience selling scholarly books in Götttingen, Hamburg, and Frankfurt and was considered to be the "literary intermediary between Europe and the East."[56] Heinemann's own list between 1890 and 1893 consisted of translations of German authors such as Heinrich Heine and Karl Emil Franzos,[57] but he soon moved to publishing authors from British colonies, most notably the novelist Rudyard Kipling[58] and the poet Sarojini Naidu.[59] Already in the early twentieth century, Heinemann was introducing the world to a "newer" world literature. The transformation of his company into a publisher of authors from former British colonies is not surprising, yet one cannot simply dismiss Heinemann's role in facilitating access to postindependence African writers. Between 1962 and 2003, Heinemann published some 350 titles by over 100 African authors.[60] For students at colleges and universities enrolled in courses in African literature, and to discerning readers who frequented bookstores and public libraries, Heinemann became synonymous with African writing both in the English originals and in translation. To think of Ngugi wa Thiong'o, Mweja Mwangi, Tayyeb al-Salih, and others was to think of Heinemann. Hill's claim for the production of a "new" world literature does not seem that far-fetched after all.

Contemporary German discussions of a new world literature might not bear any direct connection to the publisher Heinemann, but they are signposted between the new postcolonial literatures on the one hand, and literature of German authors of migrant background on the other.[61]

In her multiple contributions to translation studies and world literature, Doris Bachman-Medick centralizes the question of cultural difference and literature as a cultural text to highlight migration as one of the main sources for understanding difference.[62] The question of difference finds extension in Dieter Lamping's *Die Idee der Weltliteratur* (2010), especially in views on world literature and globalization.[63] For Lamping, bi- and multilingualism become central features of the contemporary world and therefore contemporary world literature. Along with authors such as Salman Rushdie, Assia Djebbar, Gloria Anzaldúa, Lamping appoints postcolonial literary critics such as Edward Said and Homi Bhabha as the spokespersons ("Fürsprecher") of world literature.[64] In *The Idea of World Literature* (2006), John Pizer examines canonicity with multiculturalism, arguing that cultural difference serves as a "dialectical filter" to imagine contemporary world literature.[65] The Syrian-German author Rafik Schami serves as a model for such a dialectical filter of difference. Pizer frames his thoughts through an engagement with Harald Weinrich: the renowned German critic and founder of the Chamisso Prize given to German-language authors of non-German heritages. Weinrich's recent ideas on globalization, technological commercialization, and world literature deserve a brief discussion, since his pioneering work on German migrant authors and the establishment of the Chamisso Prize play an important role in institutionalizing new world literatures in Germany.

In his essay "Chamisso, Chamisso Authors and Globalization," Weinrich touches upon major statements on world literature from the German-speaking world—Goethe, Marx and Engels, Auerbach—to propose that in the twenty-first century "it is no longer easy to distinguish sharply between world literature and Western literature."[66] Weinrich's proposal is thus not very dissimilar from that of Auerbach. However, while Auerbach prospectively anticipated the homogenization of literatures in the new world after World War II, Weinrich's retrospective analysis of new world literatures, fifty years after Auerbach, leads him to believe that such homogenization is already in place. Auerbach fears the arrival of Islamic, Chinese, or Russian Bolshevik literatures; Weinrich laments the establishment of world literature in English. Blaming the world literary market for the increasing domination of English, Weinrich claims that authors who choose to write in a language other than English are faced with impediments in entering the world literary space:

> All writers who lack the good fortune of growing up in a genuinely anglophone [*sic*] or a postcolonially anglophone [*sic*] land know it. It is a given that they will have a hard time with world literature. If, for instance, they have been driven from central or eastern Europe to Germany, they must come to terms with German as a "subglobal" language, which of course drastically curtails their prospects for entry into world literature. And yet, they are precisely the ones we particularly welcome as Chamisso authors, since their books spread "world" more than those of many indigenous authors. Or they have simply chosen wrong in settling on German for their literary language, far removed from English—the language of world literature—and its prevailing

discourses? If I am not mistaken, all non-anglophone [*sic*] authors pay this price, in the hard currency of lived time, for the label *world literature*, and so do all Chamisso authors.[67]

Weinrich's lament is located in the world of globalizing commerce, in which English gains supremacy. His concern for the challenges faced by non-Anglophone authors is genuine. Yet there are a number of problematic assumptions in Weinrich's rather romanticized version of Anglophone world literature. First, the very definition of a "genuinely Anglophone" land assumes the absence of any other languages in that country. English may be the dominant language of the United States, Canada, Australia, and New Zealand, but the assumption that English is the only language of literary production in these countries denies the very multilingual fabric of these nations, which survives along with, and sometimes in spite of, the dominance of English. Oral and printed literary production in many Native-American languages of the United States and Canada, not to mention literature produced in other immigrant languages such as French, German, Spanish, Italian, even Hindi, exists alongside literature in English. Not all literary production in these languages is necessarily translated; however, not all English literature produced in the US or Canada circulates in translation either. The same problem is true by extension of the so-called "postcolonially Anglophone" nations. With writers such as V. S. Naipaul and Salman Rushdie dominating his argument, Weinrich completely dismisses the fact that not every writer from India (or Anglophone Caribbean) writing in English is automatically part of the world literary space. In multilingual nations such as India, English is one of but not the only language of works in translation. There is a multilingual and multidirectional translational network spanning twenty-five officially recognized languages through which readers gain access to literary works. A different world of literature exists away from Germany, much larger than Eastern Europe and bigger than the German literary landscape. Weinrich's Auerbachian anxiety makes him believe that the promise of the Chamisso authors—not just in Germany but perhaps also elsewhere—has been largely diminished. He fails to note the important role that post–World War II migration into the so-called "genuinely Anglophone" countries has played in the transformation of literary languages—English, French, Spanish, and through the Chamisso authors, German—as also of the world literary space.

My criticism of Weinrich's ideas notwithstanding, the newness and the supremacy that is alluded to when considering English to be a world literary language is worthy of attention, especially when one looks at the latest publications in the German language that are aimed at a wider, nonuniversity-based, discerning readership.

The Berlin-based literary critic Sigrid Löffler's *Die neue Weltliteratur und ihre großen Erzähler* (2014), is the best example of the superiority accorded to Anglophone works within the contemporary German conceptualization of world literature. "A completely new non-Western literature has been created, which is mostly written by migrants and language-changers from former colonies and war zones," claims the dust-jacket of Löffler's book.[68] This new world literature, all of it, is for Löffler migration literature ("Migrationsliteratur"), where the "enigma of arrival"—Löffler states, drawing on V. S. Naipaul's famous work—and not necessarily the dilemma of departure, one should add, is its central feature.[69] This new world literature, representing the condition of nonnative speakers,[70] is "dynamic, rapidly growing, postethnic and transnational."[71] Mohsin Hamid, Teju Cole, Michael Ondatjee, Salman Rushdie, and J. M. Cotzee become representatives of this dynamic literature. They are the great narrators of the new world literature, but they are language changers: "Whatever their first language might have been: Urdu or Marathi, Bangla, Arabic, Amharic, Gikuyu, Swahili, Yoruba, or another one of the two thousand indigenous languages that are [spoken] in Africa, or the almost 800 languages that are spoken on the Indian subcontinent: for in the great narrative of their world-wandering almost all exchange their respective local language for the language of their former colonial masters."[72] There is no doubt that authors writing in languages other than their first have greatly enriched the world literary space. But to assume that great writing and great world-wandering requires changing languages is a huge fallacy. In a move slightly different from, but curiously close to Weinrich, Löffler acknowledges homogeneity but, unlike Weinrich, celebrates it. Consequently, authors writing in German, who might not have had clearly defined (former or current) colonial masters—such as Terézia Mora, Emine Sevgi Özdamar, Olga Matynova, or Sherko Fatah—are condescendingly mentioned as those that "meanwhile enrich German literature" but stay marginal to the new world literature.[73] They are not granted any more print space in the book than a mere mention.

This absence of German-language authors of non-German heritages in contemporary German discussions on world literature is palpable in physical book series such as *Die Zeit-Bibliothek der 100 Sachbücher* (1984) or electronic book series such as *100 Werke der Weltliteratur* (CD ROM, 2007). World literature in these book series is very much akin to Scherr's 1848 anthology *Bildersaal der Weltliteratur*: a collection of representative canonical masterpieces from various national literatures. More recent attempts to make world literature accessible to the general reading public through online seminars echo the very same idea. In the newspaper *Die Zeit*'s "*Weltliteratur*"—offered as part of the Zeit Akademie online learning site and available on DVD for 129 euros—world literature is primarily framed as literature "from Europe to America: from Camus to Hemingway," even if "Africa, Asia, North- and South America, and naturally . . . the European literary metropolis" are promised as part of the reader's discovery of world literature.[74] Led by Sandra Richter, professor at the University of Stuttgart, the seminar describes authors and novels selected for the program as "those who occupy a prominent position in their homelands and home cultures."[75]

In twenty-first-century Germany, where the idea of homeland and home culture has been radically challenged by authors of migrant backgrounds, the location of world literature in singular homelands and home cultures seems precariously outdated. Acknowledging the contributions of contemporary German-language authors of non-German heritages in the larger world literary space is not just a matter of inclusion or exclusion. As Azade Seyhan discusses in *Writing Outside the Nation* (2001), literatures of migration open doors to understand the "paranational alliances" of authors, which are formed at a critical distance from "both the home and the host culture."[76] As Leslie Adelson proposes in *The Turkish Turn in Contemporary German Literature* (2005), literatures of migration convolute our understanding of national literatures, not just through the differences but also through a "broad range of common ground, which can be thicker or thinner at some junctures."[77] As Yasemin Yildiz argues in *Beyond the Mother Tongue* (2012), authors with migrant backgrounds create a possibility of postmonolingualism "in which language and ethnicity may be fully delinked."[78]

While these scholars discuss literatures of migration with reference to national literatures, their arguments can pave the way to develop a new vocabulary for bibliomigrancy and contexts of minority literatures. At a distance from the current celebration or even denunciation of German migrant literature within world literary discussions in Germany, let me make three suggestions. First, a conceptualization of world literature that necessitates a unidirectional movement—*from* the point of origin *to* a point of arrival, or *from* the language of creation *to* a target language in which the work is translated—hardly suffices to think through the position and ambition of works that are marked by multiple spatial and linguistic origins. Second, declarations of the rise of a "completely new non-Western literature" that once again focuses on the old "empire writes back" paradigm is in today's world at best the harshest weapon for epistemic violence that neatly reestablishes the center-periphery paradigm while pretending to celebrate the subaltern south. And third, a negligence of transformations within national literary production—British, French, German, or US American—through various processes of forced or voluntary migrations will only compromise the capacity of what I have elsewhere discussed as the *Cosmopolitical Claims* (2007) of migrant authors. In other words, if the "elliptical relationship" between national and world literatures—as David Damrosch aptly formulates—is to be examined with some degree of sincerity, it must be understood that "national" and "world" literatures are dynamic categories: they are politically charged because they are historically determined and culturally conditioned.

As a counter example of Weinrich's comments on the compromised state of non-Anglophone authors I will end this chapter with a discussion of Kemal Kurt's *Ja, Sagt Molly*. Following Weinrich's definition he can be called a "Chamisso" author, although he never received the Chamisso prize. Leslie Adelson discusses this novel as the depiction of a "bloodthirsty and anxious affair" of fictional characters for survival in the twenty-first century, as "shelf space is at a premium and new rules of storage will soon prevail."[79] Tom Cheesman underlines the "sceptical cosmopolitanism of the republic of letters."[80] In the following discussion, however, I want to show that in the struggle for survival on the shelf-space of a library, Kurt invokes the empire of books (*Bücherreich*) as he challenges the world republic of letters. Kurt is thus able to show how the Borgesian "catalogue of catalogues" is anything but neutral.

A Library of World Literature

In search of the "total book," Kemal Kurt's novel *Ja, Sagt Molly* becomes the book of all books. As discussed earlier, the novel begins with the mention of multiple geographical locations, and, in the opening scene, Gregor Samsa tries to be intimate with Molly. As the reader tries to fathom whether the sexual intimacy between the human Molly and the vermin Gregor is the start of the rehumanization process for Gregor or a magical realist intercourse between species, the novel turns to Jimmy Herf and Congo Jake (Dos Passos, *Manhattan Transfer*). This transfer from Dublin to New York is punctuated in Kurt's novel by italicized insertions of important global events, telegraphically communicated as headlines of newspapers: the Boxer Uprising is crushed by interventionist forces,[81] Guglielmo Marconi succeeds in transatlantic wireless transmission of radio waves (*JSM*, 20), the financial crisis of 1929 hits the United States (*JSM*, 21), Einstein introduces the theory of relativity (*JSM*, 22), the plague spreads in India, and San Francisco experiences devastation through earthquake and fire (*JSM*, 23). In the midst of these moments of scientific discoveries and financial and natural disasters, Congo reads in the *New York Times* that the "Library of Babel" is full, and there is no room for any more books. Under the directorship of a blind librarian—the novel keeps it ambiguous whether the reference is to the blind librarian in Umberto Eco's *The Name of the Rose* or to Borges, the author of "The Library of Babel"—a commission of select librarians is making a decision about selecting that one book that will represent all forms of modernism (*JSM*, 24).

From this point on, Kurt's novel recreates the twentieth century through an engagement with its literary history. Disparate and unexpected conversations inhabit the novel: Hans Castorp (Thomas Mann, *The Magic Mountain*) experiences the violence of World War I with O-Lan (Pearl S. Buck, *The House of Earth*), who finds a copy of Flaubert's Madame Bovary in his pocket (*JSM*, 39); Clelia Oitana (Cesare Pavese, *The Beach*) tells Meuersault (Camus, *The Stranger*) that as a woman she finds herself alone in a library (*JSM*, 44); Zneno Cosini (Italo Svevo, *Zneno Cosini*) criticizes the Nobel Prize as "one named after the founder of the first weapon of mass destruction in the world" to Harry Haller (Hesse, *Steppenwolf*) as Hitler comes to power (*JSM*, 51); Martin Marco (Camilo José Cela, *The Hive*) discusses the expansion of libraries and the significance of books with William of Baskerville (Umberto Eco, *The Name of the Rose*) in the aftermath of World War II (*JSM*, 57); and between the Arab-Israeli Six-Day War and the assassination of Che Guevara, Saleem Sinai (Salman Rushdie, *Midnight's Children*), David Carvaggio (Michael Ondaatje, *The English Patient*), and Lord Jim (Joseph Conrad, *Lord Jim*) meet—where else?—in the House of Mr. Biswas (V. S. Naipaul, *A House for Mr. Biswas*), as Stevens (Kazuo Ishiguro, *Remains of the Day*), immaculately dressed, serves them tea (*JSM*, 70–71).

This is by no means an exhaustive reading of this complex and fascinating novel. Suffice it to say that throughout the rest of the narrative, a variety of actors converge and diverge to reflect on the state of literature and literary criticism as they present books and libraries as historically conditioned and politically charged. Punctuating these conversations is the slow foreplay between Molly and Gregor, which becomes more intense as the twentieth century ends. Toward the end of the novel, after the Fall of the Berlin Wall as violence against foreigners rises in Germany, Gregor fantasizes yet another transformation. He wants to be an oil beetle so he can turn Molly crazy by releasing Cantharidin (*JSM*, 127). Meanwhile a host of intoxicated characters: Rosario (Alejandro Carpentier, *The Kingdom of this World*), Lambert Strether (Henry James, *The Ambassadors*), Gora (Rabindranath Tagore, *Gora*), Babbitt (Sinclair Lewis, *Babbitt*), Sagoe (Wole Soyinka, *The Interpreters*), Piggy (William Golding, *Lord of the Flies*), Malte Laurids Brigge (Rainer Maria Rilke, *The Notebooks of Malte Laurids Brigge*), Querelle (Jean Genet, *Querelle*), and others join a procession (*JSM*, 125), shouting the slogan, "To the Library! To the Library!" (*JSM*, 129; Zur Bibliothek! Zur Bibliothek!). As former Czechoslovakia splits into Czech and Slovak Republics, and the World Trade Center bombing takes place in New York City, Gregor thinks of ancient Indian erotic texts, *Ananga Ranga* and *Kamasutra*, and discovers Molly's "Yoni" (*JSM*, 132–133). The entire history of the twentieth century and the sexual foreplay between Molly and Gregor reach their climax as the crowd of authors reaches Taksim Square, Istanbul, where the library burns.

What the European Digital Library Project aspires to do is accomplished by Kurt in his novel. The library depicted in Kurt's novel offers for consideration another dimension of difference through transformation, namely, the difference manifest in the spaces that hold and contain these novels, these "books." The bibliographic inventory of this *Bibliothek* at the millennial turn bears marks of human migration and signals the necessity to recognize the meanings of bibliomigrancy: the bearing across of books. The inventory of the *Bibliothek*, once outsourced, becomes a new resource. The conceptualization of a library—with or without walls—becomes space-based and space-bound: spatial and directional, locative and ablative.

The story of world literature, as mentioned at the beginning of this book, is not a single story. It consists of multiple stories of creation and innovation, interrogation through reformulation, and local disposition and worldly orientation. Much like libraries—and it does not have to be the perfect library of all libraries as in Borges—the order and system is coincidently interrupted with contesting narratives of disorder and purposeful disarrangement. As Benjamin makes us realize, dissemination becomes part of dispersion, and as Kurt reveals through his differential calculus of world literature, historical chronology is productively interrupted by the power of literary works. The thousandfold librarian is a virtual reality today, recoding the world literary catalog for the twenty-first century.

Epilogue

From Goethe's *Faust*, beleaguered in his claustrophobic study by his past, to Grass's future-oriented thousand-fold librarian, we have come a long way. We have been through many *Bibliotheken* (libraries) and met many bibliophiles and bibliophobes. We have seen the bibliograph of world literature undergo dramatic transformation—as part of major cultural historical shifts spanning a few decades, or within a few years under political pressure—underscoring my inaugural proposition that world literature is historically conditioned, culturally determined, and politically charged. We have traversed various trajectories of bibliomigrancy.

At the end of this book, we need to ask ourselves again, what are the advantages of refracting the term *world literature* through libraries and books? Let me offer a few summarizing thoughts.

World literature is not bound by a singular definition. It can be multiply defined: it is a philosophical ideal, a process of exchange, a pedagogical strategy, a mode of reading. It is neither a select set of representative texts from particular national or linguistic traditions (*Weltliteratur*) nor the sum total of all the literatures ever produced in the world (*Allerweltsliteratur*).

World literature is the literature of inhabitance, not inheritance. It is marked by creation and re-creation, coding and recoding, and interpretation and reinterpretation of literatures beyond their linguistic origins.

World literature is a mode of challenging the pedantic arrogance and collective narcissism evoked by national literatures. Contrary to Goethe's pronouncement, world literature does not render national literature meaningless.[1] Unlike Marx and Engles's prediction, world literature does not "arise" through a frictionless comingling of various national and local literatures.[2] World literature punctuates national literary production, it enriches national literature, and at times—just like in the case of the Nazis—it also becomes subservient to nationalist politics. In other words, world literature *upsets* but does not *annihilate* the national arrangement of literature.

World literature is a unit for the global comparative evaluation of aesthetic affinities among literary traditions; it is a way of putting to test the compound noun *Gemeingut* (shared property), not just in terms of formal similarities of aesthetic expression but also in terms of what is usurped, purloined, suppressed, and rejected through forces of history. If Auerbach's unsure stance on the possibility of world literature after World War II reveals anything, it is that every new world order creates new definitions of the shared and the unshared, of inheritance and inhabitance.[3]

World literature is a strategy of cosmopolitan affiliation to literature. As Hesse expressed it so succinctly, world literature is a way of slow familiarization with the thoughts, experiences, legends, and symbols of the world.[4] To this I would add that the engagement or the thoughts, experiences, or legends do not amount to a harmonious reconciliation with the world. Readers of world literature in the public sphere shape and inform this cosmopolitan affiliation by engaging with the inequities and inconsistencies of the world. The *Bücherfreude* (joy of books) and *Lesetrieb* (desire for reading) is a *step toward* creating and gaining access to a literary catalog of the world, not the end.

Finally, world literature is a system of classifying literature that decries its geolinguistic division. At the beginning of this book, I presented world literature as an ever-transforming literary catalog of the world, adding that the inventory, the bibliograph of world literature is anything but an alphabetically arranged bibliography. Visualizing the library as a space, let me offer a slightly different variation on the transnational arrangement: world literature is a conscious disarrangement of national literatures. World literature is a set of dispersed texts, in the original or in translation, that find new homes on shelves of national (literary) libraries, sometimes inserting themselves between works of "national" literature with whom they have aesthetic or formal affinities. World literature is a way of looking at the coexistence of books in many literary systems. Therefore, the "catalog of world literature," as Hesse also attests, is anything but neutral.

A print-cultural approach to world literature serves many purposes. First and foremost, such an approach helps us understand that world literature is not a randomly or accidently circulated and distributed body of texts. Literary works become part of networks through complex multiple processes of acquisition, collection, classification, and dissemination. Attention to these processes helps us to connect the materiality of a world literary text with the aesthetic and political issues that are read into the text, along with the space in which the text is read, which can be a public or private library or a politically organized state. The many libraries—physical, on paper (book series), and virtual (digital)—discussed in the period of two centuries that this book covers, serve as nodes in these networks. We have seen how the global network of libraries in the early nineteenth century created new possibilities to acquire manuscripts and printed books from Asia and Africa. Colonial/imperial libraries such as the Asiatick Society Library in Calcutta were connected—through the royal libraries of Awadh in Lucknow among others—to the Staatsbibliothek zu Berlin and the Bayerische Staatsbibliothek in Munich. We have seen the efforts toward the establishment of the German National Library in the late nineteenth century—which led to the foundation of the Deutsche Bücherei in Leipzig (1912)—and the splitting of the national spirit with the ideological and political division of Germany into two nation-states after World War II. While the Deutsche Bücherei in Leipzig oriented itself more toward Eastern European nations, the Amerika Häuser in several West German cities became symbols of freedom of speech, albeit marred by internal ideological pressures themselves.

Second, production, translation, and circulation—key terms in current debates on world literature—have concrete and complex material and political histories. An examination of global translation enterprises such as the Oriental Translation Fund—in tandem with scholarly societies such as the German Oriental Society—shows not only the institutionalization of world literature, such an examination gives an actual roadmap connecting far-flung libraries around the world from Alexandria to Singapore with centers of book production and world literary publication in London, Paris, Berlin, and Leipzig. Book series such as Reclam's Universal-Bibliothek, Diedrichs's Märchen series, GDR's Volk und Welt, and others exemplify concrete histories of translations, facilitating public access to world literature as well as the formation of small private libraries of world literature.

Third, the "medial" nature of the library, when subject to scrutiny, reveals the constantly moving boundaries between fact and fiction, history and memory, collection and dispersion, order and chaos. The silent order of the library unravels rather quickly to reveal the power structures and the uneven circulation and distribution of literature. From Nazi cultural officer Langenbucher to US Senator McCarthy, we have met many bibliophobes: suppressers of free speech, book-burners, and secretive censors who would purge libraries—public and private—of anything that did not fit their singular political vision of the world. In other words, an empirical study of world literature unmoors world literature from the constraints of a university classroom or specialized readers and places it in the larger public sphere.

Fourth, such an approach assists in challenging normative periodizations that turn world literature into a derivative discourse, into a unidirectional flow from Western centers to non-Western peripheries. We have met many bibliophiles: authors, translators, editors, publishers, librarians, government policy makers, intellectuals like Rolland and Tagore with dreams of a "world library," all of them striving toward the "coming of age of world literature" as Goethe hoped; at the same time partaking in and benefiting from international financial dependence, thereby contributing to the cosmopolitan consumption of world literature.

Finally, a print-cultural approach to world literature does more than merely replace Western with Eastern or Southern conceptualizations of world literature; it does help to decenter hegemonic Western positions, which, as we have seen, are not insulated from the non-West but are in fact formed precisely because of contact with non-Western parts of the world. Shaping this decentered approach are forms of *bibliomigrancy*, the physical and virtual migration of books from one geocultural space to another. Tracing bibliomigrancy initiates a difficult but necessary conversation comparing the dominant and the subservient, the colonizer and the colonized, but also the mainstream nationalist and the marginalized cosmopolitan. A print-cultural approach reveals the multicentric, multidimensional, and multilingual nature of world literature.

I started this book with a discussion of two authors as a way of featuring libraries as transactional spaces of the "worlding of literature." Let me end with an invitation to examine the non-neutrality of the catalog of world literature. There's no better place to demonstrate this than within literature itself.

One of the most claustrophobic images of a library in European novels from the twentieth century is offered by Elias Canetti, the German-language author of Sephardic-Jewish heritage who was born in Bulgaria and died in Zurich. In his novel *Die Blendung* (1936), translated into English as *Auto-da-fé* (1947), he takes his readers on a tour of the protagonist's library. The library takes up all four rooms in Peter Kien's spacious *fin-de-siècle* Viennese apartment on the top floor of 24 Ehrlich Straße. Kien, the readers are told, is the greatest living Sinologist and expert of several linguistic and literary traditions of the Orient. Unwilling to compromise his intellectual autonomy for financial gains, he regularly declines offers of employment from prestigious universities across Europe. In the pursuit of his collection and accumulation, he seeks to emulate Eratosthenes, the head librarian at Alexandria. Unlike Eratosthenes, however, Kien is not only the curator, cataloger, and organizer but also the sole and principle patron, with exclusive access to his twenty-five thousand volumes. His personal isolation manifests itself through the library's architectural insulation. The windows in all the rooms have been sealed shut and skylights have been installed, not only to assure maximum possible surface area for bookshelves and natural lighting respectively but also to ward off the "time-wasting and immoral habit" of watching what goes on in the street.[5] Organized by subject and language on the floor-to-ceiling shelves, the books are easily accessible with the movable ladder that glides on rails through all the rooms. The furniture in the apartment—before matrimony alters his existence—are Kien's large desk and chair and a divan in another room. In short, the entire library is designed to make sure that "no single superfluous article of furniture, no single superfluous person could lure him from his serious thoughts."[6] By giving the novel's readers partial access to Kien's library through description of its contents, Canetti promotes them to the status of visitors, only to demote them at once when they realize that their lack of access to the specialized knowledge of Sinology makes them as superfluous as people on the streets or, for that matter, as burdensome as Therese, who is promoted to the status of his wife and shortly thereafter demoted to her original position of housekeeper. The privileges of the library's upkeep are taken away from her.

Let us juxtapose this image with another literary representation of a library that stands in the leading commercial center of the German-speaking world, this time from Orhan Pamuk's *Kar* (2002; translated into English as *Snow* [2004]). Scoped by the narrator's probing eyes—also named Orhan—who has come to investigate the murder of the exiled Turkish poet Ka, the Stadtbücherei Frankfurt (city library) stands in sharp contrast to Kien's private library. The architectural description is sparse: the narrator characterizes it as "a modern and anonymous building."[7] The number of volumes, systems of cataloging, and the arrangement of books and other materials are perhaps too vast to explain and therefore remain unmentioned in the novel. Instead, the narrator chooses to comment on the multiple and heterogeneous body of users: "Inside were the types you always find in such libraries: housewives, old people with time to kill, unemployed men, one or two Turks and Arabs, students giggling over their homework assignments, and all other manner of stalwarts ranging from the ranks of the obese, the lame, the insane, and the mentally handicapped."[8] Everyone whom Kien considered superfluous and tempting is present in and an integral part of the Stadtbücherei. Unsurprisingly the library is Ka's public refuge from the isolation he experiences in his decrepit, tiny apartment in Frankfurt. This public space is his last stop before he is murdered on the street, so the readers enter it with Orhan for a forensic investigation. While Kien's library is a space where no time is wasted, Orhan, while opening copies of collections of poetry in the library's English section, "shed[s] tears for him [Ka] and for the years he'd wasted away in this library."[9] Unlike ancient Chinese scriptures, out-of-print editions, and scholarly commentaries by other distinguished scholars that Kien owns and has mastered, Ka's readings comprise poetry by W. H. Auden, Robert Browning, and Samuel Coleridge. Instead of bookplates that demonstrate the permanence of the Viennese native's propriety over Oriental knowledge, checkout slips with signatures of the exiled Turkish poet become identifiers of his temporary possession of volumes, indeed of his poetic borrowings. There is little to be owned in the exilic subject's life, one that is characterized by borrowed time, space, and, as the novel emphasizes, the materiality of intellectual stimulation.

The linguistic, national, and cultural differences between Canetti's *Die Blendung* and Pamuk's *Kar* are significant. The dust jacket on Kien's world is a map of early twentieth-century Vienna; folded in the jacket flaps is ancient Chinese and Japanese calligraphy that only Kien can decipher. Ka's world is covered with snow and the dust of several geographies. The dog-eared map of Kars—a small-town on the Turkish-Armenian border—carries smudges and fingerprints of many patrons of the Stadtbücherei.

The libraries depicted in these novels, when considered in tandem, offer for consideration another dimension of difference through transformation, namely, the difference manifest in the spaces that hold and contain these novels, these "books." Semiotically and symbolically, what offers itself in transformation is the house of books—the *Bibliothek*—as well as the virtual bibliographic space, a space that writes (*graph*) itself through books (*vivlion*). The bibliographs of these bibliotheks signal the necessity to rethink the meanings of bibliomigrancy and its effect on the bibliophiles and the bibliophobes. Thinking through this bibliomigrancy, I am suggesting, might assist us in a new understanding of world literature as a literary catalog of the world, as a collection of books that creates new shelf-space for itself in the libraries of "Others" in the readers' many "Elsewheres."

As books and libraries change in form and function, our understanding of their mediality will change. What I have perfomed in this book might be just one way of looking at world literature and print culture. Future readers and scholars will surely follow other paths. Because as the larger political world changes around us, so will our definition of world literature. The catalog of world literature will undergo transformation, because a literary catalog of the world is anything but neutral. As the literary catalog of the world changes, so does the reader. A reader of world literature is a "reader-in-translation," a reader who is recoded, re-identified time and again through engagement with someone else's literary inheritance. Translation interrupts our habits of reading. Access to world literature in translation helps us to think beyond our own literary inheritance; it inspires us to inhabit other worlds in translation.

World literature is anything but a detached engagement with the world. As Hermann Hesse put it, our love for books and our desire for reading will determine our relationship to world literature.

There might never be a Borgesian catalog of catalogs to serve as a key to all books in the world. But to understand our own pact with books, all we need to do is unpack someone else's library.

ACKNOWLEDGMENTS

I might have started alone on this journey of tracing movements of books. Over the years, as friends and well-wishers joined me, the caravan kept growing. I am deeply indebted to my fellow travelers for their inspiration, ideas, criticisms, challenges, and encouragement.

I want to start by thanking my undergraduate and graduate students at UW–Madison, with whom I formulated and tested my ideas in seminars on cosmopolitanism, world literature, print culture, and migration. Through their challenging questions and comments, my students turned the classroom into a real laboratory of ideas and have had an immeasurable impact on this book.

I am fortunate to be supported by a community of great scholars and colleagues at UW–Madison whose friendship immensely enriches my life. Klaus Berghahn and Caroline Levine, in many ways my first readers, nurtured this book from its first to the final draft, providing comments and criticisms with affection and encouragement. Susan Stanford Friedman asked the toughest questions and gave the best leads. These friends have also been—along with David Hildner, Ernesto Livorni, and Ellen Sapega—coconspirators of the World Literatures Research Workshop of UW–Madison. Jost Hermand offered a critical reading of the entire first draft of the manuscript and helped with sharpening some of my arguments by sharing his infinite knowledge of German cultural history.

Discussions and debates with many fellow practitioners and friends hugely benefited my project. Gerhard Bauer's supportive skepticism gave this book depth and focus in the initial stages of my writing. Djelal Kadir remains a model for multilingual comparisons and political readings of literature and supported me with his quintessential elegance and great generosity. Leslie Adelson, David Damrosch, César Domínguez, Randall Halle, Aamir Mufti, Lorraine Piroux, Azade Seyhan, Tania Roy, and Rebecca Walkowitz provided feedback, constructive criticism, and intellectual support at various stages of my working on this project. Their own work has been crucial to my project.

In addition, productive exchanges with William Banks, Sybille Baumbach, Sai Bhatawadekar, Alexander Beecroft, Russell Berman, Nina Berman, Elizabeth Bernhardt, Michael Camille, Maria Giulia Carone, Rosinka Chaudhuri, Adrian Daub, Daniel Elam, Matt Erlin, Søren Frank, Debjani Ganguly, Crister Garrett, Alys George, Kenneth George, Ela Gezen, Peter Goßens, Sabine Groß, Deniz Göktürk, Wail Hassan, Isabel Hofmeyr, Peter Höyng, Marko Juvan, David Kim, Cora Lee Kluge, Kader Konuk, Ingeborg Kongslien, Sarah Korpi, Svend Erik Larsen, Karolina May-Chu, Paulo de Medeiros, Doris Bachman Medick, Kamakshi Murti, Kirin Narayan, Adam Nelson, John Noyes, David Oels, Pamela Potter, Daniel Purdy, Sarah Reed, Sofia Samatar, Ken Seigneurie, Katrin Sieg, Karen Margrethe Simonsen, Rüdiger Singer, Suddhaseel Sen, Jola Skulj, Steve Smith, Lynne Tatlock, Paul Tenngart, Arlene Teraoka, Kirsten Thisted, Aarthi Vadde, and many others have proven invaluable for the book. In an unforgettable meeting in Delhi in 2009, Prakash Manu, the author of children's books, welcomed me with open arms in the office of the children's magazine *Nandan* and shared his knowledge on the Hindi series on world literature for children, which was immensely helpful in retracing steps of my own history of reading world literature.

I thank the hosts and lively audiences at universities and other venues who responded to portions of the book: Freie Universität, Berlin; Chicago Humanities Festival; University of Copenhagen; Cornell University; Justus-Liebig University, Giessen; Georg-August University, Göttingen; University of Hamburg; Center for Studies in Social Sciences, Kolkata; Bibliotheca Albertina, Leipzig; Leipzig University of Applied Sciences (HTWK); University of Leipzig; University of Lisbon; Institute for Slovenian Literature and Literary Studies, Ljubljana; University College London; University of California, Los Angeles; Lund University; Johannes Gutenberg University, Mainz; Middlebury College; University of Minnesota–Twin Cities; University of Santiago de Compostela; Southern Danish University, Odense; University of Oslo; University of Pittsburgh; Seminar in the History of the Book, Rutgers University; Stanford University; University of Utrecht; University of Virginia; and Washington University in St. Louis.

I am indebted to the late Helen Tartar, whose interest in the project resulted in my manuscript's finding its home with Fordham University Press. The professionalism and generosity of my editor, Thomas Lay, have been a source of great strength and confidence through the publication process. I am very grateful to the anonymous readers who evaluated the manuscript. Their astute readings, detailed comments and suggestions, and vitally useful criticism enriched this project and helped me to bring focus and clarity to the text.

Justin Court and David Korfhagen provided excellent editorial assistance during the preparation of this manuscript. Michael Koch's help during the copy-editing stages was indispensible for the book. I am grateful to all of them.

Preliminary research for the project was supported by seed funding from various sources at UW–Madison: the Center for European Studies; the DAAD Center for German and European Studies; the Center for Global Studies; the Department of German; the Graduate School; the Hamel Family Fund of the College of Letters and Science; International Division; the Institute for Research in the Humanities; and the Mellon Workshops of the Center for the Humanities. I am grateful to the Center for South Asia's Scholarly Activities Fund for their generous support of the book. Support for this research was also provided by the UW–Madison Office of the Vice Chancellor for Research and Graduate Education with funding from the Wisconsin Alumni Research Foundation. I thank all of these units.

I cannot understate the significance of the Alexander von Humboldt Foundation's Experienced Research Fellowship (2011–2012; Summer 2013) in the writing of this book. I am greatly thankful to my host institution, Leipziger Buchwissenschaft, University of Leipzig, and its director, Siegfried Lokatis. Exchanges with colleagues such as Thomas Keiderling and Ingrid Sonntag were invaluable for my training in the history of the German publishing landscape. Kristin Sprechert provided valuable help with preliminary research; Jan König became a great sounding board for ideas. I was fortunate to work at two fabulous libraries in Leipzig. At the German National Library's Buch- und Schriftmuseum, Carola Staniek and Katrin Teichmann provided resources and invaluable guidance when I hit roadblocks. I will always be grateful to Dr. Ulrich Johannes Schneider, Director, Bibliotheca Albertina, University of Leipzig for providing me with a working space in the library.

The help and guidance of a number of other librarians was indispensible for my project. I am very grateful to Todd Michelson-Ambelang, Michele Besant, Kevin Kurdylo, Mary Rader, and Laurie Wertmer, UW–Madison Libraries; Dr. Robert Giel and Siegfried Schmitt, Staatsbibliothek zu Berlin; Birgit Kienow and Marcel Lepper, Deutsches Literaturarchiv Marbach; Jarle Rui Aadna, Royal Library of Denmark, Copenhagen; Christiana Hergott, Goethe Schiller Archiv, Weimar; and Aubéry Escande, European Digital Library, The Hague. Special thanks to Stephan Koranyi, Philipp

Reclam jun. Verlag, for providing materials on the history of Reclam's *Universal-Bibliothek*.

I want to acknowledge the following journals, presses, and editors with whom I published articles that were reworked and incorporated into the book: "Bibliomigrancy: Book-Series and the Making of World Literature," in *The Routledge Companion to World Literature*, ed. Theo D'haen, David Damrosch, and Djelal Kadir, 283–296 (New York: Routledge, 2011); "Borrowing Privileges: Libraries and the Institutionalization of World Literature," *Modern Language Quarterly: A Journal of Literary History* 74, no. 2 (2013): 239–60; "Breaking Down the Walls: The European Library Project," in *The German Wall: Fall Out in Europe*, ed. Marc Silberman, 205–225 (New York: Palgrave Macmillan, 2011); and "Libraries," in *A New Vocabulary for Global Modernism*, ed. Eric Hayot and Rebecca Walkowitz (New York: Columbia University Press, 2016).

Tanya Buckingham and Constanza Bravoca at UW–Madison's Cartography Lab helped me with the creation of the maps depicting the circuits of bibliomigrancy. I also thank the following libraries and institutions for permission to reproduce images of their holdings as text figures in this book: Klassik Stiftung Weimar, Goethe-Schiller Archiv; Staatsbibliothek zu Berlin, Orientalische Handschriften Abteilung; Deutsche Nationalbibliothek and Buch- und Schriftmuseum Leipzig; and the European Digital Library. My special thanks to the Hermann Hesse-Stiftung, for permission to access unpublished letters of Hermann Hesse from the Deutsches Literaturarchiv, Marbach.

I am beholden to all of my dear friends: Anu Aneja and Neel Kohli, Puja Banta and Balu Nayar, Doris and Klaus Berghahn, Sunita and Naveen Bhatt, Nalan Erbil and Nurettin Erkan, Susan Howe and Antonio Rauti, Jan Leonhardt and André Kleinschmidt, Sayuri and Anshul Puri, Manfred Roth and Horst Winter, Serkan Arslan, Jan König, Simon May, Shefali Misra, Alfonso Moreno, Nicole Schulz, Hema Singh, Mark Skvarça, and Steve Smith supported me with their kind words, much needed distractions, and warmth and hospitality that spans three continents.

My dedication of this book to my aunts Radha Kumari and Nirupama Devi; my mother, Savitri Vishwanath; and the memory of my father, Balaji Vishwanath, is a very small gesture to acknowledge the constant love and encouragement that I have received, and continue to receive from my family. Gauri and Anu are the best sisters in the whole world! Shri Suryakirin Rai "Bahadur" Thapa takes excellent care of my family while asking me to focus on my work. Shri Jawaharlal Jetli, Maithili and Srinivas Aiyangar, Judy and Peter Ambelang, Kirin Narayan and Kenneth George, Somnath

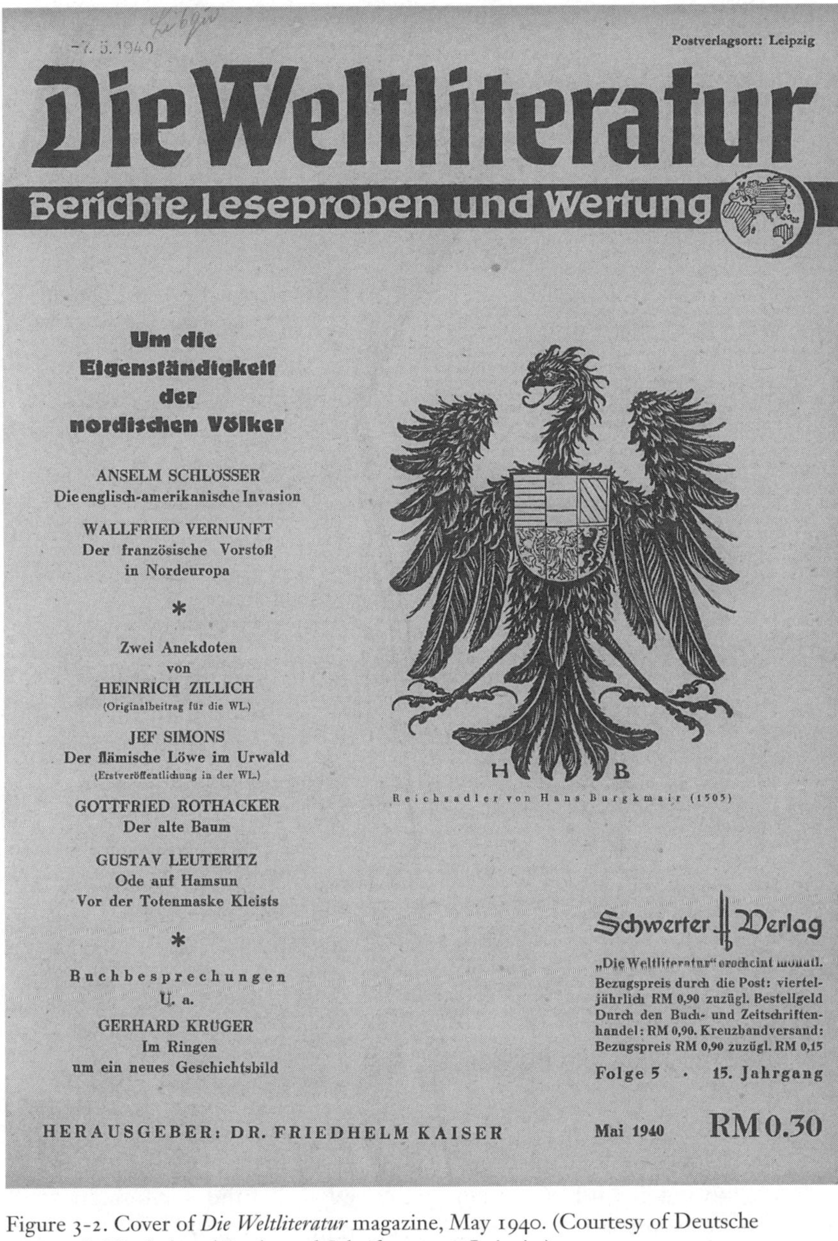

-7. 5. 1940

Postverlagsort: Leipzig

Die Weltliteratur

Berichte, Leseproben und Wertung

Um die Eigenständigkeit der nordischen Völker

ANSELM SCHLÖSSER
Die englisch-amerikanische Invasion

WALLFRIED VERNUNFT
Der französische Vorstoß
in Nordeuropa

*

Zwei Anekdoten
von
HEINRICH ZILLICH
(Originalbeitrag für die WL.)

JEF SIMONS
Der flämische Löwe im Urwald
(Erstveröffentlichung in der WL.)

GOTTFRIED ROTHACKER
Der alte Baum

GUSTAV LEUTERITZ
Ode auf Hamsun
Vor der Totenmaske Kleists

*

Buchbesprechungen
U. a.

GERHARD KRÜGER
Im Ringen
um ein neues Geschichtsbild

H B

Reichsadler von Hans Burgkmair (1505)

Schwerter Verlag

„Die Weltliteratur" erscheint monatl.
Bezugspreis durch die Post: vierteljährlich RM 0,90 zuzügl. Bestellgeld
Durch den Buch- und Zeitschriftenhandel: RM 0,90. Kreuzbandversand:
Bezugspreis RM 0,90 zuzügl. RM 0,15

Folge 5 · 15. Jahrgang

HERAUSGEBER: DR. FRIEDHELM KAISER

Mai 1940 RM 0.30

Figure 3-2. Cover of *Die Weltliteratur* magazine, May 1940. (Courtesy of Deutsche Nationalbibliothek and Buch- und Schriftmuseum Leipzig.)

Frankfurt
Amsterdam
Leipzig
Berlin
Moscow
Dublin
Warsaw
London
Prague
Budapest
Paris
Belgrade
Stuttgart
Bucharest
Sarajevo
Sofia
Rome
Madrid
Istanbul
Tirana
Athens
Haifa
Cairo
Madison
New Haven
New York
Washington DC
Havana
Mexico City
Guatemala City
Caracas
Lima
Rio de Janeiro
Santiago de Chile
Buenos Aires
Montevideo
Dakar
Ibadan
Douala
Campala
Luanda
Johannesberg
New Delhi
Varanasi
Calcutta
Beijing
Pyongyang
Songhwa
Tokyo
Shanghai
Hanoi
Jakarta
Canberra

53. "Was mir heute als Inbegriff der Weltliteratur erscheint, wird meinen Söhnen einst ebenso einseitig und ungenügend vorkommen, wie es meinem Vater oder Großvater belächelnswert erschienen wäre" (ibid., 43).

54. Ihde, *Handbuch der Reichsschrifttumskammer*, 1.

55. Ibid., 5.

56. Strothmann, *Nationalsozialistische Literaturpolitik*, 4.

57. Hitler and Nationalsozialistische Deutsche Arbeiter-Partei, "Rede auf dem 1. Nürnberger Parteitag."

58. Strothmann, *Nationalsozialistische Literaturpolitik*, 5.

59. "Die Reichskulturkammer ist heute judenrein. Es ist im Kulturleben unseres Volkes kein Jude mehr tätig. Ein Jude kann deshalb auch nicht Mitglied einer Kammer sein" (Goebbels, "Reichskulturkammer," 977).

60. "Für die Reichsschrifttumskammer seien Literaturpreise von insgesamt 250,000 RM pro Jahr. . . . Daneben ständen doch direkte Beihilfen an notleidende Schriftsteller in Höhe von 100,000 RM, zur unmittelbaren Werbung und Förderung des Schrifttums seien 500,000 RM zur Ausgabe gelangt" (ibid., 978).

61. Ihde, *Handbuch der Reichsschrifttumskammer*. For ordinances on book trade, see ibid., "Buchhandel" (95–129); for publishers see "Verlag" (135–192); for translations, see "Hinweise betr. Ausland, besetzte Gebiete, Übersetzungsschrifttum" (192–197); for lending libraries, see "Leihbücherei" (223–236); for authors, see "Schriftsteller" (249–254); for Book Clubs, see "Buchgemeinschaften" (166–168). The Reichsschrifttumskammer decided on everything from the format of signs on institutions affiliated with the Kammer ("Türplakette," 124) to cooking recipes on calendars, which were banned from being published starting April 1940 ("Kochrezepte," 153).

62. Ibid., 269–276.

63. Strothmann, *Nationalsozialistische Literaturpolitik*, 89–90. See also Bund Reichsdeutscher Buchhändler, "Vertrauliche Mitteilungen der Fachschaft Verlag der Gruppe Buchhandel in der Reichsschrifttumskammer."

64. "Die Reinung des Buchhandelsstandes von ungeeigneten Elementen [ist] eine der wesentlichen Voraussetzungen" (Strothmann, *Nationalsozialistische Literaturpolitik*, 130).

65. Ibid., 140.

66. "[nicht die] Wissens- sondern politische Willensbildung" (Rumpf, "Die Volksbüchereien," 227).

67. Studentowsky, "Partei und Volksbücherei," 289.

68. Reconstructed from Dähnhardt, "Richtlinien für Das Volksbüchreiwesen," 1–7.

69. See Dähnhardt, "Richtlinien für das Volksbüchreiwesen"; Hieronimi, "Ausländische Übersetzungsliteratur in den Volksbüchereien."

70. Langenbucher, *Weltliteratur; Romane, Erzählungen und Gedichte aller Zeiten und Völker*. All *Weltliteratur* excerpts from 1935–1939 are from the Wiking Verlag edition. On the history of the magazine, see also Thomik, *Nationalsozialismus als Ersatzreligion*. In extant scholarship, the editor of Habbel and Naumann's *Die Weltliteratur* is also supposed to be the editor of *Weltliteratur* published by Wiking Verlag in Berlin (1915–1925), although there are no records that he could have published the same magazine with different publishers in different cities, especially with Leipzig being so close to Berlin. Habbel was indeed the editor of Wiking Verlag, but the executive editor was Langenbucher; see Thomik, *Nationalsozialismus als Ersatzreligion*, 38–39. Thomik cites Kater, *Das "Ahnenerbe,"* to claim that the magazine was a continuation of *Die Weltliteratur* published under Franz Ludwig Habbel by Wiking Verlag in Berlin. He also supports his claim by citing Strothmann, *Nationalsozialistische Literaturpolitik*. Thomik's study does not mention the Regensburg- and Leipzig-based Habbel and Naumann's Die Welt-Literatur Verlag (1923–1924). Langenbucher himself advertises works that are published by Wiking Verlag yet are the same as those published by Habbel and Naumann. Thomik's claim that the southern market was goverened by Habbel and Naumann does not make sense, because they were based in Leipzig too.

71. Adam, *Lesen unter Hitler*, 47–49. Adam's book is an important contribution to best sellers and their readers during the Nazi era. The monograph briefly discusses the magazines *Weltliteratur* and *Die Weltliteratur* (155–156). However, the section on translated literature, "Fremde Erzählkunst: Bestseller aus dem Ausland" (223–248), does not discuss foreign literature in conjunction with the magazines; nor does Adam make any attempts to understand foreign literature as world literature.

72. This position was in addition to his responsibilities as director (*Schriftleiter*) of the magazine *Buch und Volk*, member of the overseeing board of the German book trade ancillaries ("Mitglied der Schriftleitung der Deutschen Buchhandlungshilfen"), head of the public relations office of the German book traders (Beauftragter für das Pressewesen des Bundes reichsdeutscher Buchhändler), and an observer of the film inspection board in Berlin (Beisitzer der Filmprüfstelle in Berlin). See Bähre, "Hellmuth Langenbucher (1905–1980)," 249–308.

73. See Langenbucher, "Die Kulturbedeutung des deutschen Buches"; "Kulturloser Buchhandel?"; "Bücher als Waffen im Kampf um die Deutsche Erneuerung"; "Mit dem Buch ins Volk"; "Das Volk lebt im Buch"; and "Der Soldat und das Buch."

74. "Wir bezeichnen als volkhafte Dichtung jede dichterische Aussage, die im Lebensraum des deutschen Volkes steht, die aus seiner Wirklichkeit,

aus dem Grunde seines Wesens, aus seinem Schicksal erwächst . . . die tiefe innere Verbindung des Dichters mit dem Leben seines Volkes ist eine selbstverständliche Voraussetzung, und das wieder bedeutet, daß nur Menschen unseres Blutes, Künder unseres Wesens, Gestalter unseres Schicksals, Bildner unseres Volkes zu sein vermögen" (Langenbucher, *Volkhafte Dichtung der Zeit*, 37).

75. "Damals galt es, die großen Linien einer neuen Wertung und Darstellung der Erscheinungen des literarischen Lebens herauszuarbeiten; es galt, eindeutig die undeutschen Erscheinungen einer vergangenen Zeit zu kennzeichnen, die sich eine ungebührliche Vormachtsstellung im geistigen Leben des deutschen Volkes angemaßt hatten; und es kam in erster Linie darauf an, einem allgemeinen Verständnis für jene Dichter den Weg zu bereiten, in deren Werk das Leben des deutschen Volkes in allen seinen Ausstrahlungen Bild und Sinnbild geworden ist. . . . Diese Entwicklung, der wir seit 1933 die unaufhaltsame fortschreitende und heute endgültig gewordene Säuberung des deutschen Kulturlebens von allen artfremden Verfälschungen verdanken, hat auch auf dem Gebiet des literarischen Lebens die klaren, gesunden Verhältnisse geschaffen, die jedem auf diesem Gebiet schöpferisch oder mittlerisch Tätigen erst wieder ein sinnvolles Arbeiten ermöglichen" (ibid., 11).

76. "Schicksal an der Memel," *Weltliteratur*, 1. The author of "Schicksal an der Memel," which becomes the short introduction to the novel excerpt, is not listed. It would be fair to assume that it is Langenbucher. Following the excerpt is a short piece by Langenbucher where he is indeed listed as the author.

77. Ibid., 1.

78. "Da erscheint zur rechten Stunde ein Buch, in dem das memeldeutsche Schicksal eine erschütternde Gestaltung gefunden hat, besonders erschütternd deshalb, weil wir aus jeder Zeile dieses Buches, das der Verfasser ein 'Roman' nennt, und mehr noch aus dem, was wir zwischen den Zeilen lesen, herausspüren, daß hier nur der nackte Bericht grausamer Tatsachen vorliegt. . . . Das ganze Buch ist eine ungeheure Anklage gegen das System von Versailles, das letzten Endes auch an dem unschuldigen Schicksal des Memellandes Schuldig ist" (ibid., 1).

79. Ibid., 2.

80. "Die Grenz- und Auslandsdeutschen sind unsere Brücke zu den übrigen Nationen und Rassen . . . haben wir sie für unsere Anschauungen gewonnen, dann wird es gelingen, auch die anderen Nationen und Rassen von der Größe und Entfaltungskraft der neuen Deutschland zu überzeugen. . . . Denn hier geht es um Werte, die weit über den Bereich des literarischen hinausgreifen ins Volkspolitische" (cited in Langenbucher, "Zwischen zwei Völkern," 15).

81. “Stücke von hohem literarischen Wert und gleich von großer Unterhaltungskraft,” Langenbucher, “Mitteilungen aus dem Verlag,” 64.

82. Belli, “Hauptströmungen der italienischen Dichtung in der Gegenwart.”

83. Payr, “Deutsch-Französische Begegnungen in dem Deutschen Roman 1937.”

84. “Mit diesen Ausgaben erfüllt die ‘Weltliteratur’ einen wesentlichen Teil ihrer Aufgabe. Sie bietet wirklich volkhaftes Geistesgut anderer Nationen und soll dadurch zum Verständnis völkischen Lebens anderer Art beitragen. Es ist natürlich, dass solche Literatur einer anderen Betrachtung bedarf, als Stücke der eigenen deutschen Dichtung. Sie ist nicht so ohne weiteres zugänglich, oft nicht sofort ‘ansprechend.’ Denn die ‘Weltliteratur’ kann ja aus fremdem Gut ebensowenig wie aus dem deutschen Schrifttum das aussuchen, was ein leichtes international gängiges Niveau hat, wie etwa die überall zu findenden Gesellschaftsromane. Sie will nur aus Quellen echter Dichtung schöpfen” (“Zu den Auslandsheften der Weltliteratur,” *Weltliteratur*, 129).

85. “Es mag sein, daß manche Menschen noch nicht den Zugang zu unserer Zeitschrift gewonnen haben, weil sie sich vor dem Begriff ‘Weltliteratur’ fürchten. Sie verwechseln diesen Begriff mit der Sache: ‘Allerweltsliteratur’ und glauben, es würde ihnen in dieser Zeitschrift ein Literatursalat vorgesetzt, der keine andere Wirkung haben könne, als ihnen den Magen zu verderben” (Langenbucher, “Weltliteratur?”).

86. “Wir pflegen Weltliteratur nicht als Allerweltsliteratur, um es noch einmal hervorzuheben, sondern als Dichtung, die charakteristischer Ausdruck des Volkes ist, aus dem sie herausgewachsen ist. Wir wollen keine literarische Weltsprache, sondern es ist uns darum zu tun, die Völker so kennenzulernen, wie sie wirklich sind, und dabei kann uns kein internationales literarisches Kauderwelsch helfen, sondern nur eine Dichtung, die aus dem Lebensboden ihres Volkes herauswächst. . . . Nur auf diese Art und Weise fördern wir das gegenseitige Verständnis zwischen den einzelnen Völkern. Der Name Goethes, mit dem sich für uns und für alle Welt verbinden: höchster geistiger Ausdruck unseres Volkes und sichtbarste, ewig gültige Leitung vor aller Welt, soll uns dabei Verpflichtung geben, unsere Arbeiten so zu durchführen, daß sie einem durch gegenseitige Achtung bestimmten Verhältnis der kulturellen Zusammenarbeit zwischen den Völkern dienlich sei” (ibid.).

87. Kaiser, *Die Weltliteratur: Berichte, Leseproben und Wertung*. The magazine claims to be in its fifteenth year of publication in 1940, thus linking itself directly to another magazine published between 1915 and 1922: *Die Welt-Literatur: Berichte, Leseproben und Wertung* (Dortmund und Leipzig: Schwerter Verlag). The cover of the 1940 magazine lists Leipzig as the “Postverlagsort” (place of publication); Schwerter Verlag is supposed to be housed

in Berlin. *Würffels Signete Lexikon deutschsprachiger Verlage* provides a very brief entry on the publishing house: "1942 an der Volkschaft-Verlag GmbH in Dortmund übergeben. Keine weitere Ermittlungen."

88. Strothmann, *Nationalsozialistische Literaturpolitik*, 335. Strothmann also states that in December 1940, Hans Ernst Schneider became the editor-in-chief (*Hauptschriftleiter*), and Hans W. Hagen became the official-in-charge for banning of books (*Verbotsreferent*) in Goebbel's office. The magazine's November 1940 issue with a focus on the Netherlands lists Schneider as the curator/special editor; Kaiser is listed as editor for the December 1940 issue. Hans W. Hagen did have an article in the December 1940 issue. See Hagen, "Gedanken zum kommenden Kriegsbuch."

89. Kater, *Das "Ahnenerbe,"* 132.

90. "In diesem Augenblick erfahren wir aufs neue, daß es auch im Bezirk des 'Literarischen' keinen Raum gibt, der außerhalb dieses einen stünde: die Entscheidung" (Kaiser, "Die Waffen des Geistes," 2).

91. "In diesem gewaltigen Strom soll auch der bescheidene Beitrag unserer Zeitschrift 'Die Weltliteratur' münden. Sie ist einst im Weltkrieg entstanden als eine preiswerte Lesezeitschrift, die nicht zuletzt für die Soldaten der Front Romane, Novellen, und Erzählungen brachte" (ibid.).

92. "Dabei ist die Aufgabe einer deutschen Zeitschrift eine doppelte: einmal aus deutscher Literatur zu würdigen und zu repräsentieren, was aus weltweitem Ansatz geschaffen wurde und 'Welt'-Format gefunden hat,—zum anderen aus der Literatur der Welt deutschen Lesern nahezubringen, was ihnen davon nützlich oder gar notwendig wird" (ibid.).

93. "Es sind die sogenanten 'Weltblätter' und ihre nicht wenig zahlreichen Trabanten, die den unseligen deutschen Hang pflegen, Ausländisches schon für gut und vornehm, die Beschäftigung mit ihm aber mindestens für 'geistig,' 'weltläufig' und großartig zu halten" (ibid.).

94. "Man wird daran merken, daß uns nichts ferner liegt, uns zu 'ausländern.' . . . Die 'Weltliteratur' gedenkt, an der Verwirklichung der 'Gespräche über die Grenzen,' wie alle große und bedeutsame Literatur sie anzuknüpfen vermag, mitzuarbeiten" (ibid., 2–3).

95. "daß es für uns keine andere 'literarische' Weltanschauung gibt als die politische Adolf Hitlers, nach der die gemeinsame Ordnung der Völker nur auf der Ordnung des Einzelvolkes nach seiner Eigenart beruhen kann. So wollen wir uns denn zu den Waffen des Geistes bekennen und sie ins Feld führen; so wollen wir, während unser Volk im Sturmschritt der Weltgeschichte marschiert, den Blick weit offen halten, wie es sich für uns nützlich zeigt und wie wir anderen unseren Blickwinkel zeigen mögen" (ibid., 3).

96. Graff, "Deutschheit und Weltliteratur," 26.

97. "Von Goethe ging der Begriff aus, den wir mit diesem Wort zu erfassen gewohnt waren: der Begriff und die Summe jener dichterischen Schöpfung aller Völker und Sprachen, die durch ihre menschliche Echtheit, ihre künstlerische Form und—nicht zuletzt—ihren nationalen Grundgehalt für die ganze Welt der Gebildeten gültig geworden sind" (ibid.).

98. "Hat diese Goethische Auffassung heute noch ihre Berechtigung? Ja: denn es ist die deutsche Auffassung schlechthin" (ibid.).

99. "Adolf Hitler hat einmal das schöne Bild von dem Baum gebraucht, der am weitesten seine Äste nach allen Seiten hin ausstreckt, weil er am tiefsten im Mutterboden der eigenen Erde wurzelt. Dieses Bild drückt am sinnfälligsten, was wir—in Goethes Sinne—trotz Kampf und Krieg unter 'Weltliteratur' begreifen" (ibid.).

100. "Um die Eigenständigkeit der nordischen Länder. Englische, amerikanische und französische Kulturpropaganda in Skandinavien / Kriegsvorbereitungen durch Bücher / Übersetzungsliteratur stärker als die eigene skandinavische Produktion" (Kaiser, introduction to Schlösser, "Die englisch-amerikanische Invasion," 70).

101. "Es gibt wohl kein Land in der Welt, in dem man mehr Kenntnis und feines Verständnis für nordische Kultur findet als Deutschland. Es gibt dort ein Gefühl für nordische Literaturschätze, das im Gemüt des Volkes liegt und das natürlich nicht durch das verändert wird, was politisch in Europa geschieht" (Gunnar Gunnarson, cited in ibid.).

102. "Demgegenüber muß man einschränkend feststellen, daß das gegenwärtig im Norden verbreitete amerikanische Schrifttum, ganz besonders das politische, seinem Charakter nach nicht auf völkischer Verwandtschaft basiert und keine schlechten Traditionen forsetzt, sondern überwiegend im Dienste der westlich-demokratischen Propaganda gegen Deutschland steht" (ibid., 71).

103. "Vielleicht wird eine neue politische Konstellation in Europa und in der Welt das gestörte Gleichgewicht auch ohne das Zutun des Nordens wiederherstellen und damit in Skandinavien eine kulturelle Gesundung herbeiführen" (ibid., 72).

104. Reichsschrifttumskammer, "Literarische Übersetzungen."

105. "Eine Anweisung vom 20.09.1939 forderte die Zeitungen auf, 'das Thema Übersetzungen am besten überhaupt nicht anzuschneiden'" (Strothmann, *Nationalsozialistische Literaturpolitik*, 195).

106. Ihde, *Handbuch der Reichsschrifttumskammer*, 197–204.

107. Strothmann, *Nationalsozialistische Literaturpolitik*, 195.

108. Ibid., 198.

109. Ihde, *Handbuch der Reichsschrifttumskammer*, 129.

110. Ibid., 133.

111. Strothmann, *Nationalsozialistische Literaturpolitik*, 201–202; Ihde, *Handbuch der Reichsschrifttumskammer*, 140.

112. Ihde, *Handbuch der Reichsschrifttumskammer*, 201–202.

113. Staatliche Landesfachstelle für Volksbüchereiwesen Sachsen, *Liste Verbotener Und Nicht Erwünschter Schriften*.

114. Reichsschrifttumskammer, *Jahresliste des schädlichen und unerwünschten Schrifttums*, 1939–1943.

115. Deutsche Bücherei, *Liste der in der Deutschen Bücherei unter Verschluß gestellten Druckschriften*, 1939–1943.

116. Bund Reichsdeutscher Buchhändler, *Vertrauliche Mitteilungen der Fachschaft Verlag Im Bund Reichsdeutscher Buchhändler*.

117. Reher, "Soziologische Streifzüge durch englische Romane"; Werder, "Nordamerikanische Romane."

118. "Der Sinn der Übersetzungsliteratur liegt darin, uns die anderen Völker in ihrer tiefsten und bezeichnendesten Eigenart zu zeigen und dafür ist neben anderen Kunstarten besonders die Literatur ein unmittelbarer Weg. Und gerade die Länder des Nordens sind uns dabei besonders nah, denn aus der rassischen und volkhaften Verwandtschaft oder gar Gleichheit müssen Verbindungen sich ergeben, die fester sind als zu anderen Völkern, Verständigungen, die notwendig sind im germanischen Raum. . . . Und es ist nicht nur für uns, sondern für diese größere Entscheidung von Bedeutung, wer für uns und wer gegen uns ist. Gewißlich ist es kein künstlerisches Argument mehr, aber man würde es wohl nicht verstehen, wenn ein Überfallener seinen Räuber zum Abendessen einlädt, und so wollen wir auch keine Feste für unsere Feinde; selbst wenn wir dadurch künstlerischer Werte entsagen, so ist uns die größere Aufgabe wichtiger als ein nicht lebenswichtiges Zugeständnis. . . . Wir lehnen alle Autoren, die gegen uns hetzen, ab" (Jessen, "Über nordländische Übersetzungsliteratur," 109).

119. "Es ist keine falsche Überheblichkeit, sondern nur dem schärfsten Bewußtsein für ausgeprägte Eigenständigkeit und einmalige Wertigkeit entsprungene Sicherheit, wenn wir feststellen, daß es schwer hält, bei Eskimos und Indianern einen Kalidasa, Ferdosi, Goethe, Dante, oder Shakespeare aufzufinden, Musiker vom Gipfelrang eines Johann Sebastian Bach, Beethoven, Bruckner oder Richard Wagner bei Negern nachzuweisen und einen Michelangelo, Dürer, Rembrandt oder Phidias unter Juden aufzuspüren. Es gibt nur eine indogermanische Symphonie, eine indogermanische Tragödie, ein indogermanisches Epos" (Wüst, "Indogermanische Bekenntnisse," 140).

120. "Für manchen Leser und Literaturfreund wird es in den letzten Jahren oft eine tiefe Enttäuschung gewesen sein, wenn ein Buchhandel das von ihm gewünschte Buch nicht bekommen konnte. 'Vergriffen,' so lautet oft die lakonische Antwort. [. . .] Trotz allen vollbringen Herstellung, Druck,

Bindereien, Verlag und Sortiment auch in dieser Zeit höchste Leistungen, zu denen sie der Dienst am deutschen Buch verpflichtet" (Lindener, "Ein Blick in den Buchhandel," 78).

121. Hesse, *Sämtliche Werke*, 527.

122. Ibid., 441–442.

123. "ein nicht deutscher Reichsangehöriger, sondern—Schweizer sei" (ibid., 530).

124. "Geschrieben wurde dieser Versuch einer Einführung in die Bücherwelt zu einer Zeit, in der das Beschaffen eines Buches leicht und wenig kostspielig war. Inzwischen hat Terror und Krieg mit der Bücherwelt, vor allem der deutschen, gründlich aufgeräumt, es ist beinah nichts übrig geblieben. Sehr vieles von dem Vernichteten wird für immer, oder doch für lange Zeit vernichtet sein. Als mein Büchlein zum ersten mal erschien, konnte jeder, der Lust dazu hatte, in jeder Buchhandlung die darin empfohlenen Bücher bestellen. Damit ist es für eine gute Weile zu Ende. Aber es sind wenigstens in unserem Lande öffentliche Bibliotheken erhalten geblieben, und es hat bei unseren Verlegern eine rege Tätigkeit im Herstellen von Neuausgaben eingesetzt. Zum größten Teil sind es allerdings nur Erstausgaben. Immerhin wird der ernstlich Suchende auch heute die Wege zu den ihm wichtig scheinenden Büchern finden" (Hesse, *Eine Bibliothek der Weltliteratur*, i).

125. "Es bilde sich eine allgemeine Weltliteratur, worin uns Deutschen eine ehrenvolle Rolle vorbehalten ist" (Meyer, *Die Weltliteratur im zwanzigsten Jahrhundert*," 12–13).

4. WINDOWS ON THE BERLIN WALL

1. Auerbach, "Philology and *Weltliteratur*," 7; hereafter cited in text as *PaW* and page number. Translation modified by the addition of "and its philology," a phrase that is present in the original but missing in the translation. "Auf diese Art ist unsere Vorstellung von der Weltliteratur und ihrer Philologie nicht minder menschlich und nicht minder humanistisch als die frühere; wie ja auch die Auffassung von Geschichte, die ihr zugrunde liegt, zwar nicht die glciche ist wie die einstige, aber doch aus ihr erwachsen und ohne sie undenkbar" (Auerbach, "Philologie der Weltliteratur," 43; hereafter cited in text as *PdW* and page number).

2. "'Book Burning': Where U.S. Officials Stand," *U.S. News and World Report*, June 26, 1953, 38. See also Robbins, "American Libraries and the Freedom to Read," 115.

3. "Es lag schon daran, daß die Literaten in unkonzentrierter Weise über alle möglichen Dinge schreiben, beinah so wie ihnen das einfiel, statt sich auf die wesentliche, aktuelle Frage zu einigen und lieber das *eine*, notwen-

dige Buch zu verfassen als so unübersichtlich viele. Außerdem, als gelernter Historiker mit statistischen Neigungen hatte er einen Widerwillen gegen die belletristische Darstellungsweise" (Braun, *Unvollendete Geschichte*, 39–40; italics in the original).

4. "Meine Meinung zu Büchern war: Alle Bücher kann kein Mensch lesen, nicht mal alle sehr guten. Folglich konzentrierte ich mich auf zwei. Sowieso sind meiner Meinung nach in jedem Buch fast *alle* Bücher. Ich weiß nicht, ob mich einer versteht. Ich meine, um ein Buch zu schreiben, muß einer ein paar tausend Stück andere gelesen haben. . . . Meine zwei Lieblingsbücher waren: Robinson Crusoe. . . . Das andere war von diesem Salinger. Ich hatte es durch puren Zufall in die Klauen gekriegt. . . . Ich meine: kein Mensch hatte es mir empfohlen oder so. . . . Meine Erfahrungen mit empfohlenen Büchern waren hervorragend mies" (Plenzdorf, *Die neuen Leiden des jungen W.*, 32–33).

5. Minor or passing references to Auerbach's essay are too many to list in one footnote. For the most direct engagement with the essay, see Yashin, "Euro(tro)pology Philology, World Literature, and the Legacy of Erich Auerbach"; Madsen, "World Literature and World Thoughts: Brandes/Auerbach"; Mufti, "Erich Auerbach and the Death and Life of World Literature."

6. Madsen, "World Literature and World Thoughts: Brandes/Auerbach," 55.

7. Mufti, "Erich Auerbach and the Death and Life of World Literature,"75.

8. This is an embarrassingly telegraphic recounting of the significance of Leipzig as *Buchstadt* (book city) of Germany. For the history of the movement of Germany's most important Book Fair from Frankfurt to Leipzig, see Fischer, *Die Abwanderung des Buchhandels von der Frankfurter Messe nach Leipzig*. For a history of the transformation of Leipzig as the *Buchstadt*, see Keiderling, *Aufstieg und Niedergang der Buchstadt Leipzig*. For Leipzig's book fair in relationship to Frankfurt, see Weidhaas, *Zur Geschichte der Frankfurter Buchmesse*. Weidhaas has written extensively on the Frankfurter Buchmesse, especially in his autobiographical account. See Weidhaas, *Und kam in die Welt der Büchermenschen*. The volume is full of his stereotypes about the world, from his first visit to the United States in 1974 to his most recent in India (2005), where he plans the India focus on the Book Fair. The "honest" but stereotypical, grandiose voice of someone who claims a position as powerful as the director of the world's most important book fair is already a sign of how the ownership of books from around the world was considered to be a prerogative of the capitalist West, whereby everything was available for sale, or, in the case of India, Turkey, and China, for material that could be turned into a marketable product.

9. Füssel, "Ein Frankfurter Phönix: Die Anfänge der Frankfurter Messe und Ihre frühe Internationalisierung."

10. Weidhaas, *Zur Geschichte der Frankfurter Buchmesse*, 144–145.

11. Weidhaas, *Und kam in die Welt der Büchermenschen*, 13–14.

12. Winckler, "Bibliotheken für neue Leser? Zur Literaturpolitik in der Sowjetisch Besetzten Zone und der frühen DDR," 92. See also Gantner, "Satzung für Volksbüchereien."

13. "alle Bücher, Broschüren, Zeitschriften, Alben und andere Literatur, enthaltend faschistische Propaganda, Rassentheorie, Literatur über gewaltsame Aneignung fremder Länder, ferner *aller Art Literatur, gegen die Sowjetunion und andere Vereinte Nationen gerichtet*" (Schuckov, "Ein Befehl Marschall Schukows"; italics added).

14. See Clay et al., "Befehl Nr. 4 des Alliierten Kontrollrates: Einziehung nationalsozialistischer und militaristischer Literatur." Section 1.a. of this order deletes Soviet Union and instead uses the phrase "gegen die Vereinten Nationen" ("against the United Nations").

15. "Die Hauptfrage der Volksbücherei besteht in der Hinführung des Volkes zur wertvollen klassischen und fortschrittlichen Literatur Deutschlands und der anderen Völker, um dadurch eine humane und demokratische Weltanschauung im deutschen Volke zu begründen" (Gantner, "Satzung für Volksbüchereien," 53).

16. "Die Volksbücherei muß heraus aus dem Dornröschenreich, in dem sie oft gestanden hat. Sie gehört in die pulsierenden Straßen unseres Lebens. Sie soll die Schätze der Literatur vor uns ausbreiten, die Werke unserer Klassiker und der Weltliteratur neben die Bücher über Gegenwartspolitik vor uns stellen. Sie soll uns zur Stellungnahme zu den geistigen und politischen Problemen unserer Zeit auffordern, das Material dazu bereitstellen und dieses nicht wie in einem Heiligschrein weit ab von der Wirklichkeit des täglichen Lebens verbergen" (Schröter, "Vom Zusammenbruch zu neuen Aufgaben,"10).

17. "Die Bibliothek . . . soll nicht nur das Gedächtnis der Nation . . . sondern auch dem Bewußtsein der Nation dienen" (Adler, "Büchereiarbeit und ihre Aufgaben," 71).

18. Deutschland (DDR). Deutsche Verwaltung für Volksbildung in der sowjetischen Besatzungszone, *Liste der auszusondernden Literatur*, 1. This agency became the Volksbildungsministerium der DDR in 1949.

19. "Die Büchereigesetz des Land Sachens," cited in Korn, "Die Bedeutung des Büchereigesetzes," 12–13.

20. *Der Bibliothekar*, "Der Thüringer Landesausschuß für Bibliotheksfragen."

21. "Für Autoren . . . die antipolnische und anti-sowjetische Meinung äußerten (zum Beispiel Sinclair) . . . sind daher genauestens zu überprüfen. . . .

Literatur, die in ihrer Bedeutung für die Bildung eines neuen fortschrittlichen Bewußtseins verloren hat, ist . . . genauestens zu überprüfen (zum Beispiel [Jack] London)" (cited in Winckler, "Bibliotheken für neue Leser? Zur Literaturpolitik in der Sowjetisch Besetzten Zone und der frühen DDR," 98).

22. *Der Bibliothekar*, "100-Titel-Liste für den Grundbestand der kleinsten Büchereien." See also Schröter, "Zur Kritik der Bücherbestände"; and Günnel, "10 Jahre allgemeine öffentliche Bibliotheken der DDR."

23. Winckler, *Kulturelle Erneuerung und gesellschaftlicher Auftrag*, 30–31.

24. Bode, *Reclam: Daten, Bilder und Dokumente zur Verlagsgeschichte; 1828–2003*, 114.

25. Marquardt, "1950: Dr. Ernst Reclam verläßt im Mai illegal die DDR," 516.

26. "Diese Bekenntnisse sprechen das aus, was Millionen von Deutschen, ob Arbeiter oder Intellektuelle, Schüler oder Studenten unter dem Begriff Reclam verstehen: volkstümliche, für jeden erschwingliche Bändchen, die seit der Gründung von 'Reclams Universal-Bibliothek' im Jahre 1867 einen unentbehrlichen, selbstverständlich gewordenen Faktor der Volksbildung darstellen. Die klassischen Werke der Weltliteratur, die Vermächtnisse großer Denker und die zeitgenössiche Literarur des In- und Auslandes haben seit je das Gesicht der 'Universal-Bibliothek' bestimmt. Im Sinne dieser Universalität ist der Verlag seit Kriegesende bestrebt, die Sammlung durch Neuauflagen lebendiger Werke der Vergangenheit sowie durch Aufnahme von Autoren unserer Zeit im Geiste der Forderung des Tages weiterzuführen und damit dem kulturellen Neuaufbau Deutschlands zu dienen" ("Reclam Katalog 1949," 2; repr. in "Reclam Katalog 1953," 3). All catalog citations for Reclam Leipzig and Stuttgart refer to the archival materials from "Sammlung Verlagskataloge 1946–1989," Deutsches Buch- und Schrift Museum, Deutsche Nationalbibliothek, Leipzig.

27. Reclam, *Reclams Universal-Bibliothek: Neuauflagen und Neuerscheinungen seit 1945*, 2–8.

28. "Mit dem Namen Reclam verbinden heute Leser in aller Welt den Begriff für die volkstümlichen, interessanten, und preiswerten Ausgaben der Universal-Bibliothek" (Ulbricht, "Reclam Katalog 1955," 2).

29. *Reclam Katalog 1957*, 90.

30. *Reclam Katalog 1959*, 93–94.

31. *Reclam Katalog 1960*, 28.

32. "Allseitige Entwicklung der Persönlichkeit, Erziehung zur Solidarität und kollektivem Handeln. Erziehung zur Liebe zur Arbeit, Erziehung zur kämpferischen Aktivität, Vermittlung einer hohen theoretischen und Allgemeinbildung. Entfaltung aller geistigen und körperlichen Fähigkeiten, das heißt Bildung des sozialistischen Bewußtseins zum Wohle des Volkes und

der Nation" (Ulbricht, "Das Ziel der sozialistischen Erziehung: Auf dem V. Parteitag der SED," 2).

33. "Die beste Schule der Erziehung und der strengste Lehrmeister ist das Leben, unsere sozialistische Wirklichkeit. Ein von der Praxis losgelöstes Buchwissen über kommunistische Leitsätze taugt nichts" (Khruschchow, "Das Ziel der sozialistischen Erziehung: Auf Dem XXI. Parteitag Der KPdSU," 2).

34. "Lesestoffe für den Literaturunterricht im Schuljahr 1959–60," *Das Reclam-Buch*, 14:12–13.

35. "Inhaltlich soll diese 'Neuformung 1963 nicht das Zeichen Hesse-scher Auffassung von Weltliteratur' tragen, sondern von der revolutionären Geistigkeit eines Friedrich Wolf inspiriert sein,'" (Bode, *Reclam: Daten, Bilder und Dokumente zur Verlagsgeschichte; 1828–2003*, 141).

36. A detailed discussion of Wolf and Radek is beyond the scope of this chapter. See Radek, "Karl Radek: Contemporary World Literature and the Tasks of Proletarian Art (August 1934)." Radek does not provide a comprehensive understanding of world literature, although he illustrates his critique by providing many examples from various national literatures.

37. Wolf, "Faschistische und Antifaschistische Dramaturgie im Westen." See also Pollatschek, *Friedrich Wolf: eine Biographie*, 207; and Schiller, "Vom 'Mamlock' zum 'Beaumarchais': Friedrich Wolf im Exil 1933 bis 1940."

38. "Im Mittelpunkt der Betrachtung ausgewählter Werke der Weltliteratur steht das künstlerisch gestalte Menschenbild. Die Schüler erfassen, wie humanistische Schriftsteller ihre Weltanschauung und ihre Ideale, ihre Erlebnisse, Erfahrungen und Wertungen sowie ihre Stellung zum Kampf des Volkes gegen Ausbeutung und für ein sinnerfülltes Dasein künstlerisch und in origineller Weise gestaltet haben. . . . Die Aufnahme und Aneignung bedeutender Werke der Weltliteartur trägt dazu bei, daß die Schüler an den Entscheidungen und Bewährungen der literarischen Gestalten sowie der Schriftsteller die Dialektik der Klassenauseinandersetzungen in der Epoche des Übergangs vom Kapitalismus zum Sozialismus besser verstehen und Zusammenhänge zwischen Weltanschauung und künstlerischer Meisterschaft erkennen" (ibid., 5).

39. "Bei der Gestaltung des fakultativen Unterrichts ist besonderer Wert auf die schöpferische Arbeit am litearischen Texte zu legen. Dazu gehören die selbstständige Interpretation von Ausschnitten, Szenen und Gedichten, das Erschließen der künstlerischen Bilder, der Motive und Handlungslinien, Vergleiche, Gegenüberstellungen und zusammenfassende Betrachtungen" (ibid., 6).

40. This program for creating a pedagogical plan for readers of world literature underwent an expansion in 1982. The goals and aims of this expan-

sion were in continuation with the internationalization of education and the efforts to develop an aesthetic experience and understanding of works of the foremost rung from the body of world literature. However, the reading list in the 1980s included many more works from the former Soviet Union. See ibid.

41. "Man kann nur bedauern, daß in der Bundesrepublik kein Platz für einen Verlag von völkerverbindender Kulturfunktion war, dessen Program einen übersichtlichen Focus der gesamten Weltliteratur bot, der die Literatur Osteuropas und der Länder der Sowjetunion systematisch durch Übersetzungen erschloß, dessen besonderes Engagement den Autoren der dritten Welt galt" (Lokatis, "Nimm den Elefanten–Konturen einer Verlagsgeschichte," 25).

42. Barck and Lokatis, "Stichworte zum Verlagsalltag."

43. Gerlach, "Zur Literatur aus Lateinamerika und Afrika."

44. Deutscher Schriftsteller-Verband, "Telegramm: An den Sowjetischen Schriftsteller-Verband."

45. Lokatis, "Nimm den Elefanten–Konturen einer Verlagsgeschichte," 17.

46. Ibid., 28–29.

47. Hinze, "50 Bände Erkundungen." Some issues of *Erkundungen* focused on specific nations and featured around 15–20 authors from that nation.

48. See also Tschörtner, "Der Bücherkarren–Eine Literaturzeitschrift als Werbeblatt."

49. "Aber die Bauern halfen ihm aus seinem Elfenbeinturm heraus, und er tat alles, was er als einzelner tun konnte, den Bauern zu helfen" (Ruben, "Rabindranath Tagore: Indiens grosser Humanist," 5).

50. Ibid., 6.

51. Schultz, "Früchte des Zorns: Zur Literatur des anderen Amerika."

52. "Auf den Mut, von dem dieser Roman berichtet, sollte Amerika stolz sein. Er mag freilich auch die weißen Amerikaner beschämen und die weißen anderswo auch" (*Der Bücherkarren*, "Frank London Brown," 3).

53. Buder, "Bilanz in Zahlen."

54. Moegelin, "Blick in den Themenplan 1989: 1. Neuerscheinungen der Sowjetliteratur."

55. Jähn, "Blick in den Themenplan 1989: 2. Aus anderen sozialischtischen Ländern."

56. Neue Zürcher Zeitung, "Der Dieb und die Hunde: Nobelpreis für Nagib Machfus." The article contains a citation from *Neue Zürcher Zeitung* followed by a discussion of Mahfouz's novel published by Volk und Welt. No other author is listed.

57. Brang, "Nobelpreiz für Octavio Paz."

58. Volkert, "Der Autor von Weltrang: Salman Rushdie."

59. Reschke, "Bücher haben die Wende von 1989 mit vorbereitet."

60. "Bekanntlich fühlten sich die Westberliner eingemauert, aber wenn ich über Volk und Welt nachdenke, müsste man eigentlich sagen, daß die DDR selbst eine eingemauerte Enklave war. Insofern bot der Verlag ein Fenster zur Welt, und es war gar kein schlechter Blick, den man da hatte. Vermutlich wird in diesem Zusammenhang viel von Zensur, von Vorauswahl und von Kürzungen die Rede sein, insgesamt ermöglichen die Bücher von Volk und Welt den Bewohnern des 'Leselandes' eine sehr gediegene Sicht auf die Literatur des Auslands" (Klein, "XY–Der unbekannte Leser: Prägung durch Bücher," 385).

61. For a full list see Barck and Lokatis, "Bibliographie des Verlags Volk und Welt (1990–2001)."

62. Merveldt, "Books Cannot Be Killed by Fire."

63. Lemke, "Kultur und Bibliothekspolitik der Besatzungsmächte: USA," 329.

64. Bjorklund, "Research and Evaluation Programs of the U.S. Information Agency and the Overseas Information-Center Libraries," 407.

65. Mahoney, "Windows to the West," 1583.

66. Kühnelt-Leddihn, "America Houses in Europe," 609.

67. Robbins, "American Libraries and the Freedom to Read," 115.

68. Ibid., 120.

69. "Wieder werden Bücher gesäubert, werden Bücher aus den Regalen gerissen . . . 20 Jahre, nachdem Dr. Goebbels am 9. Mai 1933 im Beisein der Berliner Studentenschaft die undeutsche, volksfremde, zersetzende Fäulnisliteratur den Flammen eines Scheiterhaufens übergab. . . . Heute werden entsprechend den Wünschen McCarthys Bücher ausgemerzt, eingestampft, verbrannt, weggeschlossen. . . . Glücklicherweise sind in Amerika neben McCarthy noch andere Kräfte am Werk. Präsident Eisenhower hat am 26. Juni in Los Angeles vor den Eiferern gewarnt und darauf hingewiesen, daß die Freiheit weder durch Gesetz verfügt noch durch Zensur hervorgebracht werden kann" (Dönhoff, *Die Bundesrepublik in der Ära Adenauer: Kritik und Perspektiven*, cited in Lemke, "Kultur und Bibliothekspolitik der Besatzungsmächte: USA," 333).

70. "Freude an Büchern," accessed July 16, 2014, http://www.onb.ac.at/oe-literaturzeitschriften/Freude_an_Buechern/Freude_an_Buechern.htm.

71. Eliot, "Das Drama der Ideen."

72. Wagner, "Ein 'Abendländer in der neuen Welt': Gespräch mit Thornton Wilder."

73. Closs, "Indien und Europa."

74. "Bücher sind Fenster in die Welt. Der schwer umkämpfte Weg des Einzellebens ist schmal, der Horizont jeden Ichs notwendig begrenzt. Die

Bücher aber, diese Boten des Geistes, die das unerschöpfliche Gut des Erkennens, der Phantasie und des gestaltenden Berichtens durch Völker und Jahrhunderte tragen, geben den Blick frei für fremdes Leben. Sie öffnen die Tore zum bisher Ungeahnten. Sie heben längst vergessene Schätze oder sie durchbrechen den Wall drohender Erstarrung und bereiten das Neue, das Kommende vor. Ihr seltsamer Glanz leuchtet jedem, der bereit ist, sein Herz zu erschließen und zum Verstehenden zu werden. Bücher wölben Brücken zwischen Ländern und Epochen" ("Vorwort," *Freude an Büchern*, 5).

75. Flake, "Die Übersetzungswut," 169.

76. "Die Deutschen sind auf ihren Eifer, das Gute aus allen Nationen herbeizutragen und damit der von Goethe verlangten Weltliteratur zu dienen, sehr stolz. Nur birgt jeder Eifer eine Gefahr—sobald er zum Übereifer wird. Dem Eifer zu dienen, hat manchen schon zum Lakaien gemacht" (ibid., 169).

77. "Ich möchte um keinen Preis ins Nationalistische geraten. Übersetzungen sind in diesem Zeitalter der Verfluchtung selbstverständlich. Und bei den Deutschen kam nach dem Krieg hinzu, daß sie nachholen mußten" (ibid., 169).

78. "Wilhelm von Scholz richtete kürzlich einen vieldiskutieren Brief an Bundespräsidenten Dr. Heuss, in dem er scharf gegen das wahllose Überhandnehmen von—oft schlecht übersetzter und niveauloser—Auslandsliteratur Stellung nahm und für Maßnahmen zugunsten der heimischen Literatur eintrat" (cited in "Für und Gegen Auslandsliteratur"). This letter could neither be located through the Wilhelm Scholz archives at the Literaturarchiv Marbach nor through the Theodor Heuss Archiv, Stuttgart. *Freude an Büchern* did not publish this letter.

79. "Für jede Übersetzung ins Deutsche eine aus dem Deutschen in die entsprechende Fremdsprache nachgewiesen werden muß" (Heidecke, "Zu einem 'Offenen Brief' von Wilhelm v. Scholz"). In his scathing commentary on the letter, Heidecke criticizes Scholz for coming out of hibernation to protect the writers' capitalist interests in West Germany, and points out that the crisis of German literature that Scholz mentions in his letter is a crisis of West German literature; such an alienation or overforeignization is not palpable in the GDR.

80. "Eine nachhaltige Überfremdung des deutschen Geistes durch das übermäßige Einströmen fremder Literatur befürchte ich bis jetzt noch nicht" (Boree, "Für und gegen Auslandsliteratur," 177).

81. "Der Import ausländischer Werke war nach 1945 eine kulturelle Pflicht der deutschen Verleger" (ibid.).

82. "Politische Überlegenheit, und zumal gar im Ausmaß der Besetzung, führt im geistigen Bereich fast immer zu grotesken Entwicklungen: man erinnere sich dazu nur des Exports, den das Dritte Reich im besetzten Europa

aufrechtzuerhalten vermochte" (Brunnberger, "Für und gegen Auslandsliteratur," 178).

83. *Reclam Katalog 1956*, 12–15; *Reclam Katalog 1958*, 14–19; *Reclam Katalog 1960*, 17–21.

84. Debon, *Chinesische Dichter der Tang-Zeit* (UB 8910), Jalal al-Din Rumi, *Aus dem Diwan* (UB 8911), Wezler, *Nala und Damayanti; eine Episode aus dem Mahabharata* (UB 8938), and Minamoto, *Erzählungen des alten Japan aus dem Konjaku-Monogatari* (UB 8960).

85. Börsenverein des Deutschen Buchhandels e.V., "Der Friedenspreis des Deutschen Buchhandels," accessed August 20, 2014, http://www.friedenspreis-des-deutschen-buchhandels.de/445652/.

86. "In der Bundesrepublik wurden weit mehr Buchtitel produziert, insgesamt aber weniger Bücher als in der DDR (pro Kopf der Bevölkerung). Der DDR-Buchmarkt war weit 'einheitlicher' als der bundesdeutsche. Dabei erschienen in der Bundesrepublik mehr Sachbücher als in der DDR; entsprechend war der Anteil der belletristischen Produktion (BRD: 18 Prozent, DDR: 35 Prozent). . . . In der BRD werden mehr Bücher gekauft, in der DDR mehr Bücher gelesen" (Martin Ahrends, "Leseland BRDDR?," *Die Zeit*, June 29, 1990, accessed August 14, 2015, http://www.zeit.de/1990/27/leseland-brddr).

87. See Table 30 in Köhler, *Lesekultur in beiden deutschen Staaten: 40 Jahre-ein Vergleich: Geschichte, Theorie, Empirie*, 2558.

88. See Table 25 in ibid., 2538.

89. See Kahlefendt, "Abgestempelt und Weggesperrt."

90. See Birgit Dankert, "Bücher Statt Apfelsinen," *Die Zeit*, April 27, 1990, accessed August 15, 2015, http://www.zeit.de/1990/18/buecher-statt-apfelsinen.

91. Bernhard Heimrich, "Um Dokumente der Revolution Bitten Bibliotheken Vergebens: Ein Pappkarton in Dresden," *Frankfurter Allgemeine Zeitung*, March 31, 1990, 16.

92. Dieter Zimmer, "Lermontows Werke, Honeckers Leben," *Die Zeit*, February 23, 1990, accessed August 15, 2015, http://www.zeit.de/1990/09/lermontows-werke-honeckers-leben.

93. Lermontov, *Einsam tret ich auf den Weg, den leeren*.

94. "Der vor mir an der Reihe ist, fragt nach Ecos 'Namen der Rose,' den es schon einmal gegeben hat. Es war doch eine Nachauflage angekündigt? 'Richtig,' sagt der junge Mann. 'Aber die ist auf 1991 verschoben.' Ich bin an der Reihe und frage erstens nach der neuen Lermontow-Ausgabe und zweitens nach Honeckers Leben. Er verschwindet im Durchgang zur Hauptversorgungseinrichtung und kommt kurz darauf zurück: Lermontow sei nicht mehr da, und Honecker schon gar nicht—der sei inzwischen fast eine bibliophile Kostbarkeit" (Zimmer, "Lermontows Werke, Honeckers Leben").

95. "Ich bin auch sauer drüber, . . . daß sie den einfach aus dem Sortiment genommen haben, als könnten sie die Geschichte rückgängig machen" (ibid.).

5. LIBRARIES WITHOUT WALLS?

1. Grass, "What Is the German's Fatherland," 90; Grass, "Was ist des Deutschen Vaterland?," 121: "Hört die Legende von drüben: / Es war ein tausendfältiger Bibliothekar, / Der die Nachlässe jener verwahrte, / deren Bücher gebrannt hatten, damals."

2. "Nur ein Buch wollen sie aufbewahren. Ein einziges Buch aus dem ganzen Jahrhundert soll übrigbleiben, das alle anderen aus der Moderne, der Frühmoderne, der Spätmoderne, der Postmoderne, und der Postpostmoderne vertreten soll" (Kurt, *Ja, sagt Molly: Roman*, 24).

3. Grass, "What Is the German's Fatherland," 89; for the German, see Grass, "Was ist des Deutschen Vaterland?," 110.

4. For a discussion of Arndt with special reference to "Germania" in relation to Europe, see Pundt, *Arndt and the Nationalist Awakening in Germany*. A more recent study, Erhart and Koch, *Ernst Moritz Arndt (1769–1860): Deutscher Nationalismus–Europa–transatlantische Perspektiven* situates Arndt in contemporary discussions on nationalism and transnationalism.

5. Grass, "What Is the German's Fatherland," 78; Grass, "Was ist des Deutschen Vaterland?," 110. The speech is neither bipartisan nor ideologically unbiased. To give one example, Grass juxtaposes Walter Ulbricht with Willy Brandt and accentuates the significance of the East German workers' uprising on June 17, 1953, to underline the "Stalinist" dimensions of the GDR.

6. Ibid., 88; 119.

7. "Eine Stadt mit vielen Namen: London vielleicht, Paris oder Berlin. Oder auch New York, Tokio, Dublin, Istanbul, Toronto, Kalkutta, Kinshasa, Ulan Bator, Samarkand, Astrachan" (Kurt, *Ja, sagt Molly: Roman*, 10).

8. "Für *das totale Buch, das Inbegriff und Auszug aller ist*, kommt lediglich die eine wohl Allerweltsgeschichte in Frage" (ibid., 11; italics in the original).

9. Ibid., 10; italics in the original.

10. Joyce, *Ulysses*, 933.

11. European Digital Library Project, "European Digital Library Project," site discontinued, last accessed March 29, 2010.

12. Robert Darnton, "The Library in the New Age," *New York Review of Books*, June 12, 2008, accessed August 15, 2015, http://www.nybooks.com.ezproxy.library.wisc.edu/articles/archives/2008/jun/12/the-library-in-the-new-age/.

13. Ibid.

14. Rachel Lee Harris, "Rare Chinese Books," *New York Times*, October 12, 2009, accessed August 15, 2015, http://www.nytimes.com/2009/10/12/books/12arts-RARECHINESEB_BRF.html.

15. Gary Marchionini, "Overview of Digital Libraries," School of Information and Library Science, University of North Carolina, 1999, accessed August 15, 2015, http://www.sils.unc.edu/~march/overview_slides/index.html. See also Marchionini and Fox, "Progress Toward Digital Libraries."

16. Donald Waters, "What Are Digital Libraries?," *CLIR Issues*, no. 4, July–August, 1998, accessed August 18, 2014, http://www.clir.org/pubs/issues/issues04.html#dlf

17. Association of Research Libraries, "Appendix II: Definition and Purposes of a Digital Library," May 17–19, 1995, accessed August 12, 2014, http://old.arl.org/resources/pubs/mmproceedings/126mmappen2~print.shtml.

18. Tomer, "Digital Libraries in Public Libraries," 884.

19. Lesk, *Understanding Digital Libraries*, xxviii.

20. Grafton, "Apocalypse in the Stacks? The Research Library in the Age of Google," 87.

21. Ibid., 88.

22. Ibid., 98.

23. O'Donnell, "Engaging the Humanities."

24. Ibid., 104.

25. "About CENL," Conference of European National Librarians, accessed July 29, 2014, http://www.cenl.org/about-cenl.

26. European Commission, "i2010—A European Information Society for Growth and Employment," {SEC(2005) 717}, accessed July 29, 2014, http://eur-lex.europa.eu/LexUriServ/LexUriServ.do?uri=COM:2005:0229:FIN:EN:PDF. See also European Commission, "Digital Agenda for Europe," accessed August 12, 2014, https://ec.europa.eu/digital-agenda/.

27. European Commission, "EDL: The European Digital Library," 13.

28. Adapted from "FUMAGABA Project," The European Library, accessed August 27, 2015, http://www.theeuropeanlibrary.org/confluence/display/wiki/FUMAGABA+project.

29. European Commission, "The European Library: Connecting Knowledge," accessed August 18, 2014, http://www.theeuropeanlibrary.org/tel4/.

30. European Commission, "Europeana: About Us," Europeana: Think Culture, accessed July 29, 2014, http://www.europeana.eu/portal/aboutus.html.

31. "The Universal Digital Library: Million Book Collection," Carnegie Mellon University, accessed July 29, 2014, http://www.ulib.org/.

32. "Project Gutenberg," accessed July 29, 2014, https://archive.org/details/gutenberg.

33. "World Digital Library: Mission," accessed July 29, 2014, http://www.wdl.org/en/about/.

34. Robert Darnton, "The National Digital Public Library Is Launched!" *New York Review of Books*, April 25, 2013, accessed July 21, 2016, http://www.nybooks.com.ezproxy.library.wisc.edu/articles/archives/2013/apr/25/national-digital-public-library-launched/.

35. Robert Darnton and Charles Simic, "A World Digital Library Is Coming True!" *New York Review of Books*, May 22, 2014, accessed July 21, 2016, http://www.nybooks.com.ezproxy.library.wisc.edu/articles/archives/2014/may/22/world-digital-library-coming-true/.

36. "World Digital Library—Mission," accessed July 29, 2014, http://www.wdl.org/en/about/.

37. European Commission, "EDL: The European Digital Library," 10.

38. European Commission, "What Is the European Library?," European Digital Library Project, accessed March 29, 2010, http://www.theeuropeanlibrary.org/portal/organisation/cooperation/archive/edlproject/. This particular definition of National Libraries is not cited in the current edition of the European Library website. See European Commission, "About: The European Library," accessed August 18, 2014, http://www.theeuropeanlibrary.org/tel4/aboutus.

39. Savinije, "The European Library: Annual Reports and Accounts 2013," 6. See also European Commission, "Commission Recommendation on the Digitisation and Online Accessibility of Cultural Material and Digital Preservation," accessed July 29, 2014, https://ec.europa.eu/digital-single-market/news/commission-recommendation-digitisation-and-online-accessibility-cultural-material-and-digital.

40. European Commission, "EDL: The European Digital Library," 2–3.

41. Ibid., 5.

42. Ibid., 7.

43. Ibid., 13.

44. Adapted from "FUMAGABA Project," 6.

45. Beck and Grande, *Cosmopolitan Europe*, 257.

46. Deutsche Nationalbibliothek, "Chronik," accessed August 12, 2014, http://www.dnb.de/DE/Wir/Geschichte/geschichte_node.html. For a recent history of the German national libraries, see Deutsche Bibliothek (Frankfurt am Main) and Ansorge, *Die Deutsche Bibliothek: Leipzig, Frankfurt am Main, Berlin*. Olson, *The Odyssey of a German National Library: A Short History of the Bayerische Staatsbibliothek, the Staatsbibliothek zu Berlin, the Deutsche Bücherei, and the Deutsche Bibliothek* declares: "A single German National Library is unnecessary and unrealistic now and in the future" (104). Olson thus echoes the bittersweet moment of unification of German libraries as characterized by Kaltwasser, "German Libraries Reunited," 18.

47. Hartmut-Ortwin Feistel, "A Brief History of the Oriental and East Asian Collections Staatsbibliothek zu Berlin," Staatsbibliothek zu Berlin,

September 18, 2000, accessed August 15, 2015, http://staatsbibliothek-berlin.de/fileadmin/user_upload/zentrale_Seiten/orientabteilung/pdf/history.pdf.

48. "Die Kenntnis Asiens und der damit in näherem Zusammenhange stehenden Länder nach allen Beziehungen zu fördern und die Theilnahme daran in weitern Kreisen zu verbreiten" ("Zielsetzung," Deutsche Morgenländische Gesellschaft, accessed March 29, 2010, http://www.dmg-web.de/?page=1).

49. See, for example, Ibn-Al Mokaff, "Kitab Kalila wa Dimna, histoire de Kalila et Dimna; version d'Ibn al-Mokaffa; exemplaire divisé en 16 chapitres," Europeana, accessed August 14, 2014, http://www.europeana.eu/portal/record/9200103/BibliographicResource_3000094705838.html.

50. Beebee, "World Literature and the Internet," 305.

51. Ibid., 304.

52. Hill, "Thirty Years of a New World Literature."

53. Ibid., 58.

54. See Mpe, "The Role of the Heinemann African Writers Series in the Devolpment and Promotion of African Literature"; Cantalupo and Chakava, "Publishing Ngugi: The Challenge, the Risk and the Reward."

55. St. John, *William Heinemann*, 4.

56. Ibid., 5.

57. Ibid., 11.

58. Ibid., 21.

59. Ibid., 126–128.

60. Currey, *Africa Writes Back: The African Writers Series & the Launch of African Literature*, 301–310.

61. At the risk of glossing over the rich history of migration into (West) Germany, let me provide a few notes, especially for the nonspecialist readers. As is well known, starting in 1955, the Federal Republic of Germany signed labor contracts with Italy, Greece, and Spain, and then with Turkey to bring guest workers to fill the 650,000 vacant positions in private and public factories and other infrastructural construction projects. The choice of the word *Gastarbeiter* (guest worker) served well to allude to their impermanence, not to mention to avoid the use of *Fremdarbeiter* (foreign worker) a term that carried the historical burden of use by National Socialist party officials. Coming from smaller towns and villages in their home countries, with little or absolutely no knowledge of German, these workers often lived in cramped quarters and were employed mostly as assembly line workers. One fifth of these workers were women, working for Siemens, Krupp, Grundig, and other companies on assembly lines for electronic equipment. When the one-millionth guest worker, a Turkish citizen named Ismail Bahadir arrived in Berlin in 1969, no one could imagine that one day Turkish-German authors such as

Emine Sevgi Özdamar and Aras Ören would be winning major national literary prizes, that Fatih Akin and Yüksel Yavuz would represent German cinema in the international film industry, that Cem Özdemir would be the cochair of the political party the Greens, or that someone with a name like Mesut Özil would be on the German national football team and would be nominated for the Golden Ball at the 2010 FIFA World Cup. For detailed discussions see Seyhan, *Writing Outside the Nation*; Adelson, *The Turkish Turn in Contemporary German Literature: Toward a New Critical Grammar of Migration*; Chin, *The Guest Worker Question in Postwar Germany*; Cheesman, *Novels of Turkish German Settlement: Cosmopolite Fictions*; and Mani, *Cosmopolitical Claims*.

62. Bachmann-Medick, "Multikultur oder kulturelle Differenzen?"; Bachmann-Medick, "Introduction: The Translational Turn."

63. Lamping, *Die Idee der Weltliteratur: ein Konzept Goethes und seine Karriere*, 130–135.

64. Ibid., 131.

65. Pizer, *The Idea of World Literature*, 115–137.

66. Weinrich, "Chamisso, Chamisso Authors, and Globalization," 1344.

67. Ibid., 1345.

68. "Eine völlig neue nicht-westliche Literatur ist entstanden, die zumeist von Migranten und Sprachwechslern von ehemaligen Kolonien und Kriegsregionen geschrieben wird" (Löffler, *Die neue Weltliteratur und ihre großen Erzähler*, dust-jacket).

69. Ibid., 9.

70. The term Löffler uses is *Nicht-Muttersprachlichkeit*, the condition of nonnative speech, which can only find an awkward and approximate translation into English (ibid., 15).

71. "Diese neue Weltliteratur ist eine dynamische, rasant wachsende, postethnische und transnationale Literatur" (ibid., 17).

72. "Was auch immer ihre Muttersprache gewesen sein mag, Urdu oder Marathi, Bangla, Arabisch, Amharisch, Gikuyu, Swahili, Yoruba, oder eine andere der zweitausend indigenen Sprachen, die in Afrika, oder der fast achthundert Sprachen, die auf dem indischen Subkontinent gesprochen werden: Für die große Erzählung ihrer Weltwanderung wechseln fast alle aus ihrer Lokalsprache in die Sprache der einstigen Kolonialherren" (ibid., 15).

73. "[eine] wachsende Gruppe von Schriftstellern migrantischer Herkunft, die inzwischen die deutsche Literatur bereichern—wie etwa Terézia Mora, Emine Sevgi Özdamar, Olga Martynova, Sherko Fatah" (ibid., 17).

74. "Von Europa bis Amerika. Von Camus bis Hemingway: Es geht nach Afrika, Asien, Nord- und Südamerika—und natürlich in die europäischen Literaturmetropolen" (*Die Zeit* and Richter, "Weltliteratur"), ZEIT Akademie, accessed June 29, 2015, https://www.zeitakademie.de/seminare/die-schoenen-kuenste/weltliteratur.

75. "Autoren und Romane, die in ihren Heimatländern und Heimatkulturen eine herausragende Stellung einnehmen" (ibid.).

76. Seyhan, *Writing Outside the Nation*, 10.

77. Adelson, *The Turkish Turn in Contemporary German Literature: Toward a New Critical Grammar of Migration*, 20.

78. Yildiz, *Beyond the Mother Tongue*, 201.

79. Adelson, *The Turkish Turn in Contemporary German Literature: Toward a New Critical Grammar of Migration*, 171.

80. Cheesman, *Novels of Turkish German Settlement: Cosmopolite Fictions*, 53–58.

81. Kurt, *Ja, sagt Molly: Roman*, 18. Hereafter cited in text as *JSM* and page number.

EPILOGUE

1. Eckermann, *Conversations with Goethe*, 94.
2. Marx and Engels, "The Manifesto of the Communist Party," 73.
3. Auerbach, "Philology and Weltliteratur," 2–3.
4. Hesse, *Eine Bibliothek der Weltliteratur*, 3.
5. Canetti, *Auto-Da-Fé*, 23; Canetti, *Die Blendung*, 21.
6. Ibid.
7. Pamuk, *Snow*, 252.
8. Ibid.
9. Ibid.

BIBLIOGRAPHY

Adam, Christian. *Lesen unter Hitler: Autoren, Bestseller, Leser im Dritten Reich*. Berlin: Galiani, 2010.

Adelson, Leslie A. *The Turkish Turn in Contemporary German Literature: Toward a New Critical Grammar of Migration*. New York: Palgrave Macmillan, 2005.

Adler, Ernst. "Büchereiarbeit und ihre Aufgaben." *Bibliothekar* 1, no. 2 (1946): 70–75.

Adler, Hans. "Weltliteratur-Nationalliteratur-Volksliteratur: Johann Gottfried Herders Vermittlungsversuch als Kulturpolitische Idee." In *Nationen und Kulturen: Zum 250. Geburtstag Johann Gottfried Herders*, edited by Regine Otto, 271–284. Würzburg: Königshausen und Neumann, 1996.

Agnew, Vanessa. *Enlightenment Orpheus: The Power of Music in Other Wolds*. Oxford: Oxford University Press, 2008.

Ali, Tariq. *Shadows of the Pomegranate Tree*. London and New York: Verso, 1993.

Allén, Sture, Kjell Epsmark, and Frank Michael-Kirch. *Der Nobelpreis für Literatur: Eine Einführung*. Stockholm: Schwedische Akademie, 2011.

Allen, William Francis, Charles Pickard Ware, and Lucy McKim Garrison, eds. *Slave Songs of the United States*. Chapel Hill: University of North Carolina at Chapel Hill Library, 2011.

American Book Trade Manual. "International Statistics of Book and Periodical Production," 11–19. New York: R. R. Bowker, 1915.

Aneesh, A. *Virtual Migration: The Programming of Globalization*. Durham, NC: Duke University Press, 2006.

Apter, Emily S. *Against World Literature: On the Politics of Untranslatability*. London and New York: Verso, 2013.

Arndt, Ernst Moritz. "Lasset Euch nicht Verführen, oder, Die Weltliteratur." In *Schriften für und an seine lieben Deutschen, zum ersten Mal gesammelt und durch Neues vermehrt*, 303–332. Leipzig: Weidmann'sche Buchhandlung, 1845.

Arnold, Paul Josef. *Die Welt-Literatur: Die besten Romane und Novellen aller Zeiten und Völker. Reihe VI. Orientalische Erzählungen*. 2 vols. Regensburg and Leipzig: Habbel und Naumann, 1923.

Auerbach, Berthold. "Weltliteratur und Humanität." *Das Magazin für die Literatur des In- und Auslandes: kritisches Organ der Weltliteratur* 50, no. 1 (1881): 1–2.

Auerbach, Erich. "Philologie der Weltliteratur." In *Weltliteratur: Festgabe für Fritz Strich zum 70. Geburtstag*, edited by Walter Muschg and Emil Staiger, 39–51. Bern: Francke Verlag, 1952.

———. "Philology and Weltliteratur." Translated by Maire Said and Edward Said. *The Centennial Review* 13, no. 1 (1969): 1–17.

Aurich, Ursula. *China im Spiegel der deutschen Literatur des 18. Jahrhunderts.* Berlin: E. Ebering, 1935.

Bachmann-Medick, Doris. "Introduction: The Translational Turn." *Translation Studies* 2, no. 1 (2009): 2–16.

———. "Multikultur oder kulturelle Differenzen? Neue Konzepte von Weltliteratur und Übersetzung in postkolonialer Perspektive." *Deutsche Vierteljahrsschrift für Literaturwissenschaft und Geistesgeschichte* 68, no. 4 (1994): 585–612.

Bähre, Ralf. "Hellmuth Langenbucher (1905–1980): Beschreibung einer literaturpolitischen Karriere." In *Archiv für Geschichte des Buchwesens*, edited by Monika Estermann, Reinhard Wittmann, Börsenverein des deutschen Buchhandels, and Historische Kommission, 47:249–308. Frankfurt am Main: Buchhändler-Vereinigung, 1997.

Barck, Simone, and Siegfried Lokatis, eds. "Bibliographie des Verlags Volk und Welt (1990–2001)." In *Fenster zur Welt: Eine Geschichte des DDR-Verlages Volk und Welt*, 400–422. Berlin: Links, 2003.

———, eds. "Stichworte zum Verlagsalltag." In *Fenster zur Welt: Eine Geschichte des DDR-Verlages Volk und Welt*, 397. Berlin: Links, 2003.

Bartels, Adolf, ed. *Einführung in die Weltliteratur (von den ältesten Zeiten bis zur Gegenwart) im Anschluss an das Leben und Schaffen Goethes*. Munich: G. D. W. Callwey, 1913.

Baumgartner, Alexander, ed. *Geschichte der Weltliteratur 1: Die Literatur Westasiens und der Nilländer*. Freiburg im Breisgau and Munich [u.a.]: Herder, 1901.

———, ed. *Geschichte der Weltliteratur 2: Die Literaturen Indiens und Ostasiens.* Freiburg im Breisgau and Munich [u.a.]: Herder, 1897.

———, ed. *Geschichte der Weltliteratur 3: Die griechische und lateinische Literatur des klassischen Altertums*. Freiburg im Breisgau and Munich [u.a.]: Herder, 1900.

———, ed. *Geschichte der Weltliteratur 4: Die lateinische und griechische Literatur der christlichen Völker*. Freiburg im Breisgau and Munich [u.a.]: Herder, 1900.

Beck, Ulrich, and Edgar Grande. *Cosmopolitan Europe*. Translated by Ciaran Cronin. Cambridge, England: Polity, 2006.

Beebee, Thomas O. "World Literature and the Internet." In *The Routledge Companion to World Literature*, edited by Theo D'haen, David Damrosch, and Djelal Kadir, 297–306. Milton Park, England, and New York: Routledge, 2012.

Beecroft, Alexander. *An Ecology of World Literature: From Antiquity to the Present Day*, London and New York: Verso, 2015.

Begegnung (Reclam Stuttgart). "Die 'Begegnung.'" No. 1 (1964): 20.

Beil, Else. *Zur Entwicklung des Begriffs der Weltliteratur*. Leipzig: Voigtländer, 1915.

Belli, Adriano. "Hauptströmungen der italienischen Dichtung in der Gegenwart." *Weltliteratur: Romane, Erzählungen und Gedichte aller Zeiten und Völker* 30 (March 1938): 29–30.

Benjamin, Walter. "Bücher und Lektüre des Kindes." In *Medienästhetische Schriften*, edited by Detlev Schöttker, 186–194. Frankfurt am Main: Suhrkamp, 2002.

———. "Dienstmädchenromane des vorigen Jahrhunderts." In *Medienästhetische Schriften*, edited by Detlev Schöttker, 156–157. Frankfurt am Main: Suhrkamp, 2002.

———. "Ich packe meine Bibliothek aus." In *Gesammelte Schriften*, edited by Tillman Rexroth, 4.1:388–396. Frankfurt am Main: Suhrkamp, 1991.

———. "Nr. 13: Bücher und Dirnen." In *Medienästhetische Schriften*, edited by Detlev Schöttker, 155. Frankfurt am Main: Suhrkamp, 2002.

———. "Unpacking My Library." In *Illuminations*, edited by Hannah Arendt, translated by Harry Zohn, 59–67. New York: Schocken Books, 2007.

———. "Was die Deutschen lasen, während ihre Klassiker schrieben." In *Medienästhetische Schriften*, edited by Detlev Schöttker, 183–185. Frankfurt am Main: Suhrkamp, 2002.

Berghahn, Klaus. "Das schwierige Geschäft der Aufklärung." In *Aufklärung: Ein literaturwissenschaftliches Studienbuch*, edited by Hans-Friedrich Wessels, 30–66. Königstein im Taunus: Athenäum, 1984.

Berington, Simon, and Johann Bernhard Nack. *Geschichte des Gaudentio di Lucca: oder merkwürdige Nachricht seiner sonderbahren Reise durch die Sandwüsteneyen des innern Africa nach Mezzoranien: nebst der Einwohner Ursprung, Religion, Regierungsart*. Frankfurt am Main [u.a.]: Duren, 1751.

Berman, Antoine. *The Experience of the Foreign: Culture and Translation in Romantic Germany*. Translated by S. Heyvaert. Albany: State University of New York Press, 1992.

Berman, Nina. *Orientalismus, Kolonialismus und Moderne: Zum Bild des Orients in der deutschen Kultur um 1900*. Stuttgart: Metzler, 1997.

Bernofsky, Susan. *Foreign Words: Translator-Authors in the Age of Goethe*. Detroit, MI: Wayne State University Press, 2005.

Bertz, Eduard. *Spemanns goldenes Buch der Weltliteratur*. Berlin: Spemann, 1912.

Bhavabhuti. *Malati und Madhava: Ein indisches Drama*. Translated by Ludwig Fritze. Leipzig: Reclam, 1883.

Der Bibliothekar: Zeitschrift für die Bücherei-Praxis. "100-Titel-Liste für den Grundbestand der kleinsten Büchereien." Vol. 4, no. 4 (1950): 229–231.

———. "Der Thüringer Landesausschuß für Bibliotheksfragen." Vol. 4, no. 7 (1950): 365–369.

Biedermann, Woldemar. *Goethe-Forschungen*. Frankfurt am Main: Literarische Anstalt Rötten und Loening, 1879.

———. *Goethe-Forschungen: Anderweite Folge*. Leipzig: F. W. v. Biedermann, 1899.

Bjorklund, Edith Marie. "Research and Evaluation Programs of the US Information Agency and the Overseas Information-Center Libraries." *Library Quarterly* 38, no. 4 (October 1, 1968): 406–421.

Blätter für Literarische Unterhaltung. "Chinesische Erzählungen. Herausgegeben durch Abel Rémusat, und deutsch mitgetheilt von . . . r. Drei Bändchen. Mit drei Kupfern: Leipzig, Ponthieu, Michelsen u. Comp., 1827." No. 167 (July 19, 1828): 665–666.

———. "Chinesische Erzählungen. Herausgegeben durch Abel Rémusat, und deutsch mitgetheilt von . . . r. Drei Bändchen. Mit drei Kupfern: Leipzig, Ponthieu, Michelsen u. Comp., 1827. (Fortsetzung I)." No. 168 (July 21, 1828): 669–670.

———. "Chinesische Erzählungen. Herausgegeben durch Abel Rémusat, und deutsch mitgetheilt von . . . r. Drei Bändchen. Mit drei Kupfern: Leipzig, Ponthieu, Michelsen u. Comp., 1827. (Fortsetzung II)." No. 169 (July 22, 1828): 673–675.

———. "Weltliteratur: Cooper's neuster Roman." No. 179 (August 4, 1827): 713–714.

———. "Weltliteratur: Cooper's neuster Roman (Fortsetzung)." No. 180 (August 6, 1827): 717–719.

Bloom, Harold. *The Western Canon: The Books and School of the Ages*. New York: Harcourt Brace, 1994.

———. *Where Shall Wisdom Be Found?* New York: Riverhead Books, 2004.

Bode, Dietrich. *Reclam: Daten, Bilder und Dokumente zur Verlagsgeschichte; 1828–2003*. Stuttgart: Reclam, 2003.

Bopp, Franz. *Indralokagamanam: Ardschuna's Reise zu Indra's Himmel, nebst anderen Episoden des Maha-Bharata*. Berlin: Königliche Akademie der Wissenschaften, 1824.

Boree, Karl Friedrich. "Für und gegen Auslandsliteratur." *Freude an Büchern: Monatshefte für Weltliteratur* 4, no. 4 (1953): 177.

Borges, Jorge Luis. "The Library of Babel." In *Collected Fictions*, translated by Andrew Hurley, 112–118. New York: Viking, 1998.

Boxberger, Robert. "Mitteilungen von Zeitgenossen über Goethe." *Goethe Jahrbuch* 1 (1880): 313–58.

Brang, Heidi. "Nobelpreiz für Octavio Paz." *Der Bücherkarren: Internationale Literatur im Verlag Volk und Welt Berlin* 1 (1991): 15.

Braun, Volker. *Unvollendete Geschichte*. Frankfurt am Main: Suhrkamp, 1977.

Brockhaus, Heinrich Eduard, and Thomas Keiderling. *Die Firma F. A. Brockhaus von der Begründung bis zum hundertjährigen Jubiläum; 1805–1905. F. A. Brockhaus: 1905–2005*. Mannheim: Bibliographisches Institut und F. A. Brockhaus, 2005.

Brockhaus, Hermann. *Ueber den Druck sanskritischer Werke mit lateinischen Buchstaben: Ein Vorschlag*. Leipzig: F. A. Brockhaus, 1841.

Brunnberger, Rudolf. "Für und Gegen Auslandsliteratur." *Freude an Büchern: Monatshefte für Weltliteratur* 4, no. 4 (1953): 178.

Der Bücherkarren: Internationale Literatur im Verlag Volk und Welt Berlin. "Frank London Brown." No. 3 (1964): 3–4.

———. "Nicolas Guillén." No. 3 (1951): 16.

———. "William Faulkner." No. 2 (1963): 5.

Die Bücherei: Zeitschrift der Reichsstelle für das Volksbüchereiwesen. "Liste der unerwünschten Bücher." Vol. 6, no. 2 (1935): 279–281.

Buder, Horst. "Bilanz in Zahlen." *Der Bücherkarren: Internationale Literatur im Verlag Volk und Welt Berlin* 6 (1989): 10.

Bund Reichsdeutscher Buchhändler. *Vertrauliche Mitteilungen der Fachschaft Verlag Im Bund Reichsdeutscher Buchhändler*. Leipzig: Geschäftsstelle der Fachschaft Verlag, 1935.

Busse, Carl. *Geschichte der Weltliteratur: in zwei Bänden*. Bielefeld and Leipzig: Velhagen und Klasing, 1910.

Calderón de la Barca, Pedro. *Das Leben ein Traum. Schauspiel in fünf Akten*. Translated by Joseph Schreyvogel. Stuttgart: Afrika World Press 1868.

Canetti, Elias. *Auto-Da-Fé*. Translated by C. V. Wedgewood. New York: Farrar, Straus and Giroux, 1984.

———. *Die Blendung*. Frankfurt am Main: Fischer, 2005.

Cantalupo, Charles, and Henry Chakava, eds. *Publishing Ngugi: The Challenge, the Risk and the Reward*. Trenton, NJ: Africa World Press, 1995.

Casanova, Pascale. *The World Republic of Letters*. Translated by M. B. DeBevoise. Cambridge and London: Harvard University Press, 2007.

Casson, Lionel. *Libraries in the Ancient World*. New Haven, CT: Yale University Press, 2001.

Chaghatai, Muhammad Ikram. "Dr. Aloys Sprenger and the Delhi College." In *The Delhi College: Traditional Elites, the Colonial State, and Education Before 1857*, edited by Margrit Pernau, 105–124. New Delhi: Oxford University Press, 2006.

Chartier, Roger. *The Order of Books: Readers, Authors, and Libraries in Europe Between the Fourteenth and Eighteenth Centuries*. Translated by Lydia G. Cochrane. Stanford, CA: Stanford University Press, 1994.

Cheah, Pheng. "What Is a World? On World Literature as World-Making Activity." *Daedalus* 137, no. 3 (2008): 26–38.

Cheesman, Tom. *Novels of Turkish German Settlement: Cosmopolite Fictions*. Rochester, NY: Camden House, 2007.

Chen, Chuan. "Die chinesische schöne Literatur im deutschen Schrifttum." Kiel: Christian-Albrechts-Universität, 1933.

Chin, Rita C. K. *The Guest Worker Question in Postwar Germany*. Cambridge and New York: Cambridge University Press, 2007.

Clay, D., M. I. Dratwin, L. Koeltz, and B. H. Robertson. "Befehl Nr. 4 des Alliierten Kontrollrates: Einziehung nationalsozialistischer und militaristischer Literatur." *Der Volksbibliothekar: Zeitschrift für den Volksbücherei-Praxis* 1, no. 1 (October 1946): 15.

Closs, A. "Indien und Europa." *Freude an Büchern: Monatshefte für Weltliteratur* 4, no. 1 (1953): 38–39.

Cohen, Ralph. "Introduction: Literary History in a Global Age." *New Literary History* 39, no. 3 (July 1, 2008): vii–xx.

Cooppan, Vilashini. "The Ethics of World Literature: Reading Others, Reading Otherwise." In *Teaching World Literature*, edited by David Damrosch, 34–43. New York: Modern Language Association of America, 2009.

Cramer, Wilhelm, Heinrich Eduard Brockhaus, and Friedrich Brockhaus. *Ueber Die Verhältnisse Der Buchhandlung F. A. Brockhaus in Leipzig Zu Herrn Hofrath Dr. J. P. Eckermann in Weimar in Beziehung Auf Das Werk "Gespräche Mit Goethe in Den Letzen Jahren Seines Lebens."* Leipzig: F. A. Brockhaus, 1846.

Currey, James. *Africa Writes Back: The African Writers Series and the Launch of African Literature*. Athens: Ohio University Press, 2008.

D'haen, Theo. *The Routledge Concise History of World Literature*. London and New York: Routledge, 2012.

D'haen, Theo, David Damrosch, and Djelal Kadir, eds. *The Routledge Companion to World Literature*. Milton Park, England, and New York: Routledge, 2012.

D'haen, Theo, César Domínguez, and Mads Rosendahl Thomsen, eds. *World Literature: A Reader*. London and New York: Routledge, 2012.

Dähnhardt, Dr. "Richtlinien für das Volksbüchreiwesen." *Die Bücherei: Zeitschrift der Reichsstelle für das Volksbüchereiwesen* 5, no. 1 (1938): 1–7.

Damrosch, David. "Toward a History of World Literature." *New Literary History* 39, no. 3 (2008): 481–96.

———. *What Is World Literature?* Princeton, NJ: Princeton University Press, 2003.

Damrosch, David, ed. *Teaching World Literature*. New York: Modern Language Association of America, 2009.

Damrosch, David, and Gayatri Chakravorty Spivak. "Comparative Literature/World Literature: A Discussion with Gayatri Chakravorty Spivak and David Damrosch." *Comparative Literature Studies* 48, no. 4 (2011): 455–485.

Darnton, Robert. "What Is the History of Books." In *The Case for Books: Past, Present, and Future*, 175–206. New York: Public Affairs, 2009.

De Ferrari, Guillermina. "Utopías Críticas: La Literatura Mundial Según América Latina." *1616: Anuario de Literatura Comparada*, no. 2 (2012): 15–32.

Debon, Günther. "Goethe erklärt in Heidelberg einen chinesischen Roman." In *Goethe und China, China und Goethe: Bericht des Heidelberger Symposions*, edited by Günther Debon and Adrian Hsia, 51–64. Bern and New York: Peter Lang, 1985.

Debon, Günther, trans. *Chinesische Dichter der Tang-Zeit*. Stuttgart: Reclam, 1964.

Decker, Jan. *Eckermann, oder, Die Geburt der Psychoanalyse: Theatermonolog*. Bucha bei Jena: Quartus-Verlag, 2012.

Deutsche Bibliothek, and Kathrin Ansorge. *Die Deutsche Bibliothek: Leipzig, Frankfurt am Main, Berlin*. Frankfurt am Main: Deutsche Bibliothek, 2004.

Deutsche Bücherei. *Liste der in der Deutschen Bücherei unter Verschluß gestellten Druckschriften im Auftrag des Reichsministeriums für Volksaufklärung und Propaganda bearbeitet von der Deutschen Bücherei*. Leipzig: Deutsche Bücherei, 1939.

Deutscher Schriftstellerverband. "Telegramm: An den Sowjetischen Schriftsteller-Verband." *Neue Deutsche Literatur* 1, no. 4 (1953): 3.

Deutschland (DDR). Deutsche Verwaltung für Volksbildung in der sowjetischen Besatzungszone. *Liste der auszusondernden Literatur*. Berlin: Deutscher Zentralverlag, 1946.

Dietmann, Carl Gottlob, and Johann G. Haymann. *Das Königreich Frankreich: nebst den Besitzthümern dieser Krone in Afrika, Asien und Amerika*. Dresden [u.a.]: Addresscomtoir, 1765.

Dirr, Adolf, ed. *Kaukasische Märchen*. Jena: E. Diederichs, 1920.

Djain, Jean-Michel. "Le Mundaneum, google de papier." *Le Monde Magazine* 14 (December 19, 2009): 46–51.

Domínguez, César. "Circulation in Premodern World Literature: Historical Context, Agency, and Physicality." *Primerjalna Književnost* 35, no. 1 (2012): 35–46.

Dönhoff, Marion. *Die Bundesrepublik in der Ära Adenauer: Kritik und Perspektiven*. Reinbek bei Hamburg: Rowohlt, 1963.

Dostoevsky, Fyodor. *Aparadh aur Dand*. Translated by Vadim Kozinov. Moscow: Raduga Publishers, 1985.

Dow, Alexander. *Die Geschichte von Hindostan, aus dem Persischen von Alexander Dow, und nach der 2. verb. englischen Ausg. ins Deutsche übers.* Leipzig: Junius, 1772.

———. *The History of Hindostan.* London: T. Becket and P. A. de Hondt, 1772.

Eckermann, Johann Peter. *Conversations with Goethe.* Translated by Gisela C. O'Brien. New York: Ungar, 1964.

———. *Gespräche mit Goethe in den letzten Jahren seines Lebens.* Berlin and Weimar: Aufbau-Verlag, 1982.

Eco, Umberto. *Der Name der Rose: Roman.* Translated by Burkhart Kroeber. Berlin: Volk und Welt, 1989.

Eliot, T. S. "Das Drama der Ideen." Translated by Paul Ellmer. *Freude an Büchern: Monatshefte für Weltliteratur* 4, no. 1 (1953): 74.

Engel, Eduard. *Gutes Deutsch: Ein Führer durch Falsch und Richtig.* Leipzig: Hesse und Becker, 1918.

———. *Übersetzungsseuche in Deutschland.* Leipzig: Friedrich, 1881.

———. *Was bleibt? Die Weltliteratur: Mit 25 Bildnissen und einer Handschrift.* Leipzig: Koehler und Amelang, 1928.

Enk, Michael. "Zur neusten Literatur von Ludlof Wienbarg." *Jahrbücher der Literatur* 72 (1835): 197–209.

Eppelsheimer, Hanns W. *Handbuch der Weltliteratur von den Anfängen bis zur Gegenwart.* Frankfurt am Main: V. Klostermann, 1960.

Erhart, Walter, and Arne Koch, eds. *Ernst Moritz Arndt (1769–1860): Deutscher Nationalismus—Europa—transatlantische Perspektiven.* Tübingen: Niemeyer, 2007.

Espmark, Kjell. *Der Nobelpreis für Literatur: Prinzipien und Bewertungen hinter den Entscheidungen.* Translated by Ruprecht Volz and Fritz Paul. Göttingen: Vandenhoeck und Ruprecht, 1988.

European Commission. "EDL: The European Digital Library." Document, 2005. ECP-2005-CULT-38074.

Fabian, Bernhard, eds. "Handbuch der historischen Buchbestände in Deutschland, Österreich und Europa (Fabian-Handbuch): Herzogin Anna Amalia Bibliothek." In *Handbuch der historischen Buchbestände in Deutschland.* Hildesheim: Olms Neue Medien, 2003. http://fabian.sub.uni-goettingen.de/fabian?Herzogin_Anna_Amalia_Bibliothek.

Febvre, Lucien, and Henri-Jean Martin. *The Coming of the Book: The Impact of Printing 1450–1800.* Translated by David Gerard. London: NLB, 1976.

Fischer, U. C. "Goethe's 'Chinese-German Book of Seasons and Hours' and 'Worldliterature.'" *United College Journal,* no. 6 (1967): 27–34.

Fischer, Walter. *Die Abwanderung des Buchhandels von der Frankfurter Messe nach Leipzig.* Frankfurt am Main: Bottrop, 1934.

Flake, Otto. "Die Übersetzungswut." *Freude an Büchern: Monatshefte für Weltliteratur* 4, no. 4 (1953): 169–170.

Foucault, Michel. "Of Other Spaces." Translated by Jay Miskowiec. *Diacritics* 16, no. 1 (April 1, 1986): 22–27.

Frank, Othmar. "Über den Wissenschaftlichen Gehalt der Sanskrit Literatur." *Vjasa: über Philosophie, Mythologie, Literatur und Sprache der Hindu* 1, no. 1 (1826): 1–25.

———. "Vorrede." *Vjasa: über Philosophie, Mythologie, Literatur und Sprache der Hindu* 1, no. 1 (1826): iii–x.

Freude an Büchern: Monatshefte für Weltliteratur. "Vorwort." Vol. 1, no. 1 (1950): 5.

Fück, Johann. *Die Arabischen Studien in Europa: bis in den Anfang des 20. Jahrhunderts*. Leipzig: Otto Harrassowitz, 1955.

Füssel, Stephan. "Ein Frankfurter Phönix: Die Anfänge der Frankfurter Messe und ihre frühe Internationalisierung." In *50 Jahre Frankfurter Buchmesse 1949–1999*, edited by Stephan Füssel, 12–25. Frankfurt am Main: Suhrkamp, 1999.

Gantner, Elizabeth. "Satzung für Volksbüchereien." *Der Volksbibliothekar: Zeitschrift für den Volksbücherei-Praxis*, no. 1 (1946): 53–55.

George, Andrew R., trans. *The Epic of Gilgamesh: The Babylonian Epic Poem and Other Texts in Akkadian and Sumerian*. London and New York: Penguin Books, 2003.

Gerhard, Heinz. *Kameraden an der Memel: Roman*. Berlin: Brunnen-Verlag, 1935.

Gerlach, Carola. "Zur Literatur aus Lateinamerika und Afrika." *Der Bücherkarren: Internationale Literatur im Verlag Volk und Welt Berlin* 1 (1958): 14–15.

Goebbels, Joseph. "Reichskulturkammer." *Börsenblatt für den deutschen Buchhandel* 268 (November 18, 1935): 977–978.

Goethe, Johann Wolfgang von. "Chinesisches." In *Goethe Berliner Ausgabe*, 18:135–138. Berlin: Aufbau-Verlag, 1965.

———. *Faust: Eine Tragödie*. In *Goethe Berliner Ausgabe*, 8. Berlin: Aufbau-Verlag, 1965. Translated by Walter Arndt as *Faust: A Tragedy: Interpretive Notes, Contexts, Modern Criticism*. New York: W. W. Norton, 2001

———. "Ferneres über Weltliteratur." In *Goethe Berliner Ausgabe*, 18:429–431. Berlin: Aufbau-Verlag, 1965.

———. "Gesellschaft für Ausländische schöne Literatur in Berlin." In *Goethe Berliner Ausgabe*, 18:426–428. Berlin: Aufbau-Verlag, 1965.

———. "Indische Dichtungen." In *Goethe Berliner Ausgabe*, 18:130–132. Berlin: Aufbau-Verlag, 1965.

———. "Sakontala." In *Goethe Berliner Ausgabe*, 3:381. Berlin: Aufbau-Verlag, 1965.

———. "Tausendundeine Nacht." In *Goethe Berliner Ausgabe*, 18:139. Berlin: Aufbau-Verlag, 1965.

———. "'Touti-Nameh,' Übersetzt von Professor Iken, mit Anmerkungen und Zugaben von Professor Kosegarten." In *Goethe Berliner Ausgabe*, 18:133–135. Berlin: Aufbau-Verlag, 1965.

Goßens, Peter. *Weltliteratur: Modelle transnationaler Literaturwahrnehmung im 19. Jahrhundert*. Stuttgart: Metzler, 2011.

Götz von Olenhusen, Albrecht. "Das Genie und die Geschäfte: Der Konflikt Dr. Johann Peter Eckermanns (Weimar) mit dem Verlag F. A. Brockhaus (Leipzig) über 'Goethes Gespräche mit Eckermann'; zum Autor-Verleger-Verhältnis im 19. Jahrhundert." *UFITA Archiv für Urheber- und Medienrecht* 3 (2010): 747–794.

Götze, Alfred, Walther Mitzka, and Karl Trübner, eds. *Trübners Deutsches Wörterbuch*. Berlin: de Gruyter, 1943.

Graff, Lieutenant Sigmund. "Deutschheit und Weltliteratur." *Weltliteratur: Berichte, Leseproben und Wertung* 3 (March 1940): 26.

Grafton, Anthony. "Apocalypse in the Stacks? The Research Library in the Age of Google." *Daedalus* 138, no. 1 (2009): 87–98.

Grass, Günter. *Beim Häuten der Zwiebel*. Göttingen: Steidl, 2006.

———. *Peeling the Onion*. Translated by Michael Henry Heim. Orlando, FL: Harcourt, 2007.

———. "Was ist des Deutschen Vaterland?" In *Deutscher Lastenausgleich: wider das dumpfe Einheitsgebot: Reden und Gespräche*, 108–121. Frankfurt am Main: Luchterhand, 1990.

———. "What Is the German's Fatherland?" In *Two States—One Nation?*, translated by Krishna Winston and Arthur S. Wensinger, 76–89. San Diego, CA: Harcourt Brace Jovanovich, 1990.

Grimm, Jacob, and Wilhelm Grimm. *Deutsches Wörterbuch von Jacob und Wilhelm Grimm*. München: Deutscher Taschenbuch Verlag, 1984.

Günnel, Peter. "10 Jahre allgemeine öffentliche Bibliotheken der DDR." *Der Bibliothekar: Zeitschrift für die Bücherei-Praxis* 13, no. 10 (1959): 1041–1045.

Gutzkow, Karl. *Maha Guru: Geschichte eines Gottes*. Stuttgart and Tübingen: Cotta, 1833.

———. "Über Goethe im Wendepunkte zweier Jahrhunderte." In *Gutzkows Werke: Aufsätze zur Literaturgeschichte*, edited by Reinhold Gensel, 10:23–94. Berlin, Leipzig: Deutsches Verlagshaus Bong, 1910.

Hagen, Hans W. "Gedanken zum kommenden Kriegsbuch." *Die Weltliteratur: Berichte, Leseproben und Wertung*, no. 12 (December 1940): 230–231.

Halm, Karl. *Denkschrift über die Verhandlungen zwischen der Direction der k. Hof- und Staatsbibliothek zu München und Dr. A. Sprenger über den Ankauf der Sprenger'schen Bibliotheca Orientalis*. Heidelberg: Goerg Mohr, 1857.

Hambruch, Paul, ed. *Südseemärchen aus Australien, New-Guinea, Fidji, Karolinen, Samoa, Tonga, Hawaii, New-Seeland u.a.* Jena: E. Diederichs, 1916.

Harris, Michael H. *History of Libraries in the Western World*. Metuchen, NJ: Scarecrow Press, 1995.

Heidecke, Manfred. "Zu einem 'Offenen Brief' von Wilhelm v. Scholz." *Die neue deutsche Literatur* 1, no. 5 (May 1953): 209–211.

Heilbron, Johan. "Structure and Dynamics of the World System of Translation," 1–7. New York: UNESCO, 2010.

Heine, Heinrich. "Al Mansor." In *Düsseldorfer Heine-Ausgabe*, edited by Manfred Windfuhr, 5:7–68. Hamburg: Hoffmann und Campe, 1973.

———. "Concerning the History of Religion and Philosophy in Germany." In *The Romantic School and Other Essays*, edited by Jost Hermand and Robert C. Holub, translated by Helen Mustard, 33:128–144. The German Library. New York: Continuum, 1985.

———. "Deutschland: Ein Wintermärchen." In *Düsseldorfer Heine-Ausgabe*, edited by Manfred Windfuhr, 4:91–160. Hamburg: Hoffmann und Campe, 1973.

———. "Germany: A Winter's Tale." In *Heinrich Heine: Poetry and Prose*, edited by Jost Hermand and Robert C. Holub, translated by Aaron Kramer, 32:231–297. The German Library. New York: Continuum, 1982.

———. "Die Harzreise." In *Düsseldorfer Heine-Ausgabe*, edited by Manfred Windfuhr, 6:81–138. Hamburg: Hoffmann und Campe, 1973.

———. "Moses Moser (Nr. 91, 21. Januar 1824)." In *Heine-Säkularausgabe*, edited by Nationale Forschungs- und Gedenkstätten der Klassischen Deutschen Literatur (DDR) and Centre national de la recherche scientifique (France), 20:136–137. Berlin, Paris: Akademie-Verlag und Editions du CNRS, 1970.

———. "Moses Moser (Nr. 96, 25. Februar 1824)." In *Heine-Säkularausgabe*, edited by Nationale Forschungs- und Gedenkstätten der Klassischen Deutschen Literatur (DDR) and Centre national de la recherche scientifique (France), 20:144. Berlin and Paris: Akademie-Verlag und Editions du CNRS, 1970.

———. "Oestliche Poeten." In *Düsseldorfer Heine-Ausgabe*, edited by Manfred Windfuhr, 6:165–66. Hamburg: Hoffmann und Campe, 1973.

———. "Reise von München nach Genua." In *Düsseldorfer Heine-Ausgabe*, edited by Manfred Windfuhr, 7.1:61–62. Hamburg: Hoffmann und Campe, 1973.

———. "Zur Geschichte der Religion und Philosophie in Deutschland." In *Düsseldorfer Heine-Ausgabe*, edited by Manfred Windfuhr, 8.1:9–120. Hamburg: Hoffmann und Campe, 1973.

———. "The Romantic School." In *The Romantic School and Other Essays*, edited by Jost Hermand and Robert C. Holub, translated by Helen Mustard, 33:1–127. The German Library. New York: Continuum, 1985.

———. "Die romantische Schule." In *Düsseldorfer Heine-Ausgabe*, edited by Manfred Windfuhr, 8.1:121–244. Hamburg: Hoffmann und Campe, 1973.

———. "Der Tannhäuser." In *Düsseldorfer Heine-Ausgabe*, edited by Manfred Windfuhr, 2:53–59. Hamburg: Hoffmann und Campe, 1973.

———. "Tannhauser (III)." In *Heinrich Heine: Poetry and Prose*, edited by Jost Hermand and Robert C. Holub, translated by Aaron Kramer, 32:27–41. The German Library. New York: Continuum, 1982.

———. "Welthülfsliteratur." In *Düsseldorfer Heine-Ausgabe*, edited by Manfred Windfuhr, 7.1:507. Hamburg: Hoffmann und Campe, 1973.

Hertel, Johannes, ed. *Indische Märchen*. Jena: E. Diederichs, 1921.

Hesse, Hermann. *Eine Bibliothek der Weltliteratur*. Leipzig: Reclam, 1929.

———. *Eine Bibliothek der Weltliteratur*. New York: Ungar, 1931.

———. *Eine Bibliothek der Weltliteratur*. Stuttgart: Reclam, 2003.

———. *Eine Bibliothek der Weltliteratur*. Stuttgart: Reclam, 2011.

———. *Eine Bibliothek der Weltliteratur: Mit den Aufsätzen "Magie des buches" und "Lieblingslektüre."* Vol. 15, Vom Dauernden in der Zeit. Zürich: Werner Classen, 1946.

———. *Sämtliche Werke*. Edited by Volker Michels. Vol. 15. Frankfurt am Main: Suhrkamp, 2004.

———. *Siddhartha: Eine indische Dichtung*. Frankfurt am Main: Suhrkamp, 1974.

Hesse, Hermann, ed. "Geleitwort." In *Das Meisterbuch*, 352–355. Berlin: Deutsche Bibliothek, 1913.

Hieronimi, Martin. "Ausländische Übersetzungsliteratur in den Volksbüchereien." *Die Bücherei: Zeitschrift der Reichsstelle für das Volksbüchereiwesen* 6, no. 5 (1939): 279–297.

Hill, Alan. "Thirty Years of a New World Literature." *The Bookseller*, no. 4543 (January 15, 1993): 58–59.

Hinze, Michael. "50 Bände Erkundungen." In *Fenster zur Welt: Eine Geschichte des DDR-Verlages Volk und Welt*, edited by Simone Barck and Siegfried Lokatis, 212–214. Berlin: Links, 2003.

Hitler, Adolf, and Nationalsozialistische Deutsche Arbeiter-Partei. "Rede auf dem 1. Nürnberger Parteitag." In *Nürnberg 1933 eine Sammlung der wichtigsten Reden auf dem Parteitag der Nationalsozialistischen deutschen Arbeiter-Partei vom 30. August bis 3. September 1933. Mit 22 Abbildungen*, 1–9. Berlin: Zentralverlag, 1933.

Holtermann, Karl, ed. *Kurze Geschichte der Weltliteratur: Mit 82 Bildern*. Freiburg (im Breisgau): Herder, 1912.

Homer. *Homers Werke 1. Homers Ilias*. Translated by Johannes Heinrich Voss. Reclams Universal-Bibliothek 251–253. Leipzig: Reclam, 1871.

———. *Homers Werke 2. Homers Odyssee*. Translated by Johannes Heinrich Voss. Reclams Universal-Bibliothek 281–283. Leipzig: Reclam, 1871.

Honecker, Erich. *Aus Meinem Leben*. 14th ed. Berlin: Dietz, 1989.

Houben, Heinrich Hubert. *J. P. Eckermann: sein Leben für Goethe; nach seinen neu aufgefundenen Tagebüchern und Briefen*. Vol. 1. Leipzig: Haessel, 1925.

Ibsen, Henrik. *Die Stützen der Gesellschaft: Schauspiel in vier Aufzügen*. Translated by Wilhelm Lange. Leipzig: Reclam, 1877.

Ihde, Wilhelm, ed. *Handbuch der Reichsschrifttumskammer*. Leipzig: Verlag des Börsenvereins der Deutschen Buchhändler zu Leipzig, 1942.

Jäger, Georg. "Reclams Universal-Bibliothek bis zum Ersten Weltkrieg: Erfolgsfaktoren der Programmpolitik." In *Reclam 125 Jahre Universal-Bibliothek, 1867–1992: Verlags- und kulturgeschichtliche Aufsätze*, edited by Dietrich Bode, 29–45. Stuttgart: Reclam, 1992.

Jähn, Karl-Heinz. "Blick in den Themenplan 1989: 2. Aus anderen sozialischtischen Ländern." *Der Bücherkarren: internationale Literatur im Verlag Volk und Welt Berlin*, no. 7 (1988): 15.

Jahresbericht der Deutschen morgenländischen Gesellschaft für das Jahr 1845. "Beilage 1." No. 1 (1845): 131.

Jalāl al-Dīn Rūmī. *Aus dem Diwan*. Translated by Annemarie Schimmel. Stuttgart: Reclam, 1964.

Jessen, Heinrich. "Über nordländische Übersetzungsliteratur." *Die Weltliteratur: Berichte, Leseproben und Wertung*, no. 4 (April 1941): 109–110.

Joyce, James. *Ulysses*. London and New York: Penguin Books, 2000.

Kadir, Djelal. *Memos from the Besieged City: Lifelines for Cultural Sustainability*. Stanford, CA: Stanford University Press, 2011.

———. "World Literature: The Allophone, the Differential, and the Common." *MLQ* 74, no. 2 (2013): 293–306.

Kahlefendt, Nils. "Abgestempelt und Weggesperrt." In *Hundert: Das Jubiläumsmagazin der deutschen Nationalbibliothek*. Vol. 3. Frankfurt am Main and Leipzig: Deutsche Nationalbibliothek, 2012.

Kaiser, Friedhelm. "Die Waffen des Geistes: Zur neuen Folge der 'Weltliteratur.'" *Die Weltliteratur: Berichte, Leseproben und Wertung* 1, no. 2 (February 1940): 2–3.

Kalidasa. *Malavika und Agnimitra: Ein indisches Schauspiel von Kalidasa*. Translated by Ludwig Fritze. Reclams Universal-Bibliothek 1598. Leipzig: Reclam, 1881.

———. *Sakuntala: Drama in sieben Akten*. Translated by Hermann Camillo Kellner. Leipzig: Reclam, 1890.

———. *Sakuntala: Schauspiel in 5 Aufzügen. Frei nach Kalidasa's altindischem Drama*. Translated by Alfred von Wolzogen. Leipzig: Reclam, 1880.

———. *Urvasi: Ein indisches Schauspiel*. Translated by Ludwig Fritze. Leipzig: Reclam, 1881.

Kaltwasser, Franz Georg. "German Libraries Reunited." Translated by D. L. Paisey. *Times Literary Supplement*, September 25, 1992, 18.

Kanowsky, Walter. "Heine als Benutzer der Bibliotheken in Bonn und Göttingen." *Heine Jahrbuch*, no. 12 (1973): 128–153.

Kant, Immanuel. "Über die Buchmacherey." In *Kleinere Schriften zur Geschichtsphilosophie, Ethik und Politik*, edited by Karl Vorländer, 213–215. Leipzig: F. Meiner, 1913.

Kater, Michael H. *Das "Ahnenerbe": Die Forschungs- und Lehrgemeinschaft in der SS. Organisationsgeschichte von 1935–1945*. Heidelberg: Deutsche Verlags-Anstalt, 1966.

Kehlmann, Daniel. *Measuring the World*. Translated by Carol Brown Janeway. New York: Vintage Books, 2007.

———. *Die Vermessung der Welt: Roman*. Reinbek: Rowohlt, 2005.

Keiderling, Thomas. *Aufstieg und Niedergang der Buchstadt Leipzig*. Beucha, Germany: Sax-Verlag, 2012.

Keudell, Elise, ed. *Goethe als Benutzer der Weimarer Bibliothek: Ein Verzeichnis der von ihm entliehenen Werke*. Weimar: Böhlau, 1931.

Khruschchow, Nikita S. "Das Ziel der sozialistischen Erziehung: Auf dem XXI. Parteitag der KPdSU." In *Das Reclam-Buch*, 14:2. Leipzig: Reclam, 1960.

Klein, J. Stefan, ed. *Die Welt-Literatur: Die besten Romane und Novellen aller Zeiten und Völker. Reihe V. Ungarische Erzähler. Herausgegeben und übertragen von Stefan J. Klein*. Regensburg and Leipzig: Habbel und Naumann, 1923.

Klein, Thomas. "XY–Der unbekannte Leser: Prägung durch Bücher." In *Fenster zur Welt: Eine Geschichte des DDR-Verlages Volk und Welt*, edited by Simone Barck and Siegfried Lokatis, 385–391. Berlin: Links, 2003.

Kleine digitale Bibliothek. *100 Werke der Weltliteratur, die jeder haben muss: CD-ROM*. Kleine digitale Bibliothek 29. Berlin: Directmedia Publishing, 2007.

Knuth, Rebecca. *Libricide: The Regime-Sponsored Destruction of Books and Libraries in the Twentieth Century*. Westport, CT: Praeger, 2003.

Koch, Ebba. "The Madrasa of Ghaziu'd-Din Khan at Delhi." In *The Delhi College: Traditional Elites, the Colonial State, and Education Before 1857*, edited by Margrit Pernau, 35–39. New Delhi: Oxford University Press, 2006.

Koch-Grünberg, Theodor, ed. *Indianermärchen aus Südamerika*. Jena: E. Diederichs, 1920.

Köhler, Ursula E. E. *Lesekultur in beiden deutschen Staaten: 40 Jahre—ein Vergleich: Geschichte, Theorie, Empirie*. Vol. 2. Frankfurt am Main: Verlag der Buchhändler-Vereinigung, 1990.

Kontje, Todd Curtis. *German Orientalisms*. Ann Arbor: University of Michigan Press, 2004.

Konuk, Kader. *East West Mimesis: Auerbach in Turkey*. Stanford, CA: Stanford University Press, 2010.

Korn, Ilse. "Die Bedeutung des Büchereigesetzes." *Der Volksbibliothekar: Zeitschrift für den Volksbücherei-Praxis* 3, no. 1 (1949): 8–13.

Kosenina, Alexander. *Der gelehrte Narr: Gelehrtensatire seit der Aufklärung*. Göttingen: Wallstein, 2003.

Kretschmer, Paul, ed. *Neugriechische Märchen*. Jena: E. Diederichs, 1917.

Krickeberg, Walter, ed. *Indianermärchen aus Nordamerika*. Jena: E. Diederichs, 1924.

Kühnelt-Leddihn, Erik von. "America Houses in Europe." *Commonwealth*, September 25, 1953, 609.

Kurio, Hars. *Arabische Handschriften Der "Bibliotheca Orientalis Sprengeriana" in Der Staatsbibliothek Preussischer Kulturbesitz, Berlin: Histor. u. Quantitative Unters. an d. Sammlung d. Islamhistorikers Sprenger (1813–1893), d. Abt. Geschichte, Geographie u. Ḥadiṯ*. Freiburg im Breisgau: Schwarz, 1981.

Kurt, Kemal. *Ja, sagt Molly: Roman*. Berlin: Hitit, 1998.

Lamping, Dieter. *Die Idee der Weltliteratur: Ein Konzept Goethes und seine Karriere*. Stuttgart: Kröner, 2010.

Lamping, Dieter, and Frank Zipfel. *Was sollen Komparatisten lesen?* Berlin: Erich Schmidt, 2005.

Langenbucher, Hellmuth. "Bücher als Waffen im Kampf um die deutsche Erneuerung." *Börsenblatt für den deutschen Buchhandel* 102, no. 184 (1935): 530.

———. "Die Kulturbedeutung des deutschen Buches." *Börsenblatt für den deutschen Buchhandel* 101, no. 7 (1934): 21.

———. "Kulturloser Buchhandel?" *Börsenblatt für den deutschen Buchhandel* 101, no. 154 (1934): 598.

———. "Mit dem Buch ins Volk." *Börsenblatt für den deutschen Buchhandel* 102, no. 236 (1935): 844.

———. "Mitteilungen aus dem Verlag." *Weltliteratur; Romane, Erzählungen und Gedichte aller Zeiten und Völker*. No. 4 (January 1936): 64.

———. "Der Soldat und das Buch." *Börsenblatt für den deutschen Buchhandel* 106, no. 283 (1939): 745–746.

———. "Das Volk lebt im Buch." *Börsenblatt für den deutschen Buchhandel* 103, no. 249 (1935): 925.

———. *Volkhafte Dichtung der Zeit: Mit der Grundliste guter deutscher Romane der Reichsstelle zur Förderung des deutschen Schrifttum*. Berlin: Junker und Dünnhaupt Verlag, 1935.

———. "Weltliteratur?" *Weltliteratur: Romane, Erzählungen und Gedichte aller Zeiten und Völker*. No. 25 (Oktober 1937): 385.

———. "Zwischen zwei Völkern." *Weltliteratur; Romane, Erzählungen und Gedichte aller Zeiten und Völker*. No. 1 (October 1935): 15–16.

Langenbucher, Hellmuth, ed. *Weltliteratur: Romane, Erzählungen, und Gedichte aller Zeiten und Völker*. Berlin: Wiking Verlag, 1935.

Lehmann, Joseph. "Magazin für die Literatur des Auslandes." *Magazin für die Literatur des Auslandes*, 1832.

Lehmstedt, Mark, and Andreas Herzog, eds. *Das bewegte Buch: Buchwesen und soziale, nationale und kulturelle Bewegungen um 1900*. Vol. 12. Schriften und Zeugnisse zur Buchgeschichte. Wiesbaden: Harrassowitz, 1999.

Lehrgang ausgewählter Werke der Weltliteratur des 19. und 20. Jahrhunderts: Pläne für den fakultativen gesellschaftswissenschaftlichen Unterricht in der erweiterten Oberschule Berlin, April 1971. Berlin: Volk und Wissen, 1971.

Lemke, Antje Bultmann. "Kultur und Bibliothekspolitik der Besatzungsmächte: USA." In *Die Entwicklung des Bibliothekswesens in Deutschland 1945–1965*, edited by Peter Vodosek and Joachim-Felix Leonhard, 19:327–337. Wolfenbütteler Schriften zur Geschichte des Buchwesens. Wiesbaden: Harrassowitz Verlag, 1993.

Lermontov, Michail J. *Einsam tret ich auf den Weg, den leeren: Gedichte russisch und deutsch*. Translated by Vera Feyerherd. Universal-Bibliothek. Leipzig: Reclam, 1985.

Lesk, Michael. *Understanding Digital Libraries*. Amsterdam: Elsevier, 2005.

Leskien, August, and Paul Zaunert, eds. *Balkanmärchen aus Albanien, Bulgarien, Serbien und Kroatien*. Jena: Eugen Diedrichs, 1915.

Leutritz, Gustav. "Ode auf Hamsun." *Die Weltliteratur: Berichte, Leseproben und Wertung*, no. 5 (May 1940): 71.

Levine, Caroline. "The Great Unwritten: World Literature and the Effacement of Orality." *MLQ* 74, no. 2 (2013): 217–237.

Levine, Caroline, and B. Venkat Mani. "What Counts as World Literature?" *MLQ* 74, no. 2 (2013): 141–149.

Lewandowski, J. D. "Unpacking: Walter Benjamin and His Library." *Libraries and Culture* 34, no. 2 (1999): 151–157.

Lindener, Gottfried. "Ein Blick in den Buchhandel." *Die Weltliteratur: Berichte, Leseproben und Wertung*, nos. 4–5 (May 1943): 78.

Literarisches Conversations-Blatt. "Betrachtungen über Bücher und Büchervermehrung." No. 273 (November 27, 1822): 1089–1091.

Löffler, Sigrid. *Die neue Weltliteratur und ihre großen Erzähler*. Munich: Beck, 2014.

Lokatis, Siegfried. "Nimm den Elefanten–Konturen einer Verlagsgeschichte." In *Fenster zur Welt: Eine Geschichte des DDR-Verlages Volk und Welt*, edited by Simone Barck and Siegfried Lokatis, 15–30. Berlin: Links, 2003.

Longfellow, Henry Wadsworth. *Hiawatha*. Translated by Carl Hermann Simon. Leipzig: Reclam, 1870.

Löwis, August von, ed. *Russische Volksmärchen*. Translated by August von Löwis. Jena: E. Diederichs, 1914.

Macaulay, Thomas Babbington. "Mr. (Lord) Macaulay's Great Minute (English versus Sanscrit and Arabic) 2nd February 1835." In *Sketches of Some*

Distinguished Anglo-Indians: (second Series) Including Lord Macaulay's Great Minute on Education in India; with Anglo-Indian Anecdotes and Incidents., edited by W. F. B. Laurie and Thomas Babbington Macaulay, 170–185. London: W. H. Allen and Co., 1888.
Macy, John. *The Story of the World's Literature*. Garden City, NY: Garden City Publishing, 1932.
Madsen, Peter. "World Literature and World Thoughts: Brandes/Auerbach." In *Debating World Literature*, edited by Christopher Prendergast and Benedict Anderson, 54–75. London and New York: Verso, 2004.
Das Magazin für die Literatur des In- und Auslandes: Kritisches Organ der Weltliteratur. "Vorwort." Vol. 50, no. 1 (1881): 1.
Mahoney, Haynes R. "Windows to the West." *Library Journal* 75, no. 1 (1950): 1582–1586.
Mani, B. Venkat. *Cosmopolitical Claims: Turkish-German Literatures from Nadolny to Pamuk*. Iowa City: University of Iowa Press, 2007.
Mann, Thomas. "Tonio Kröger." In *Death in Venice and Other Tales*, translated by Joachim Neugroschel, 161–228. New York: Viking, 1998.
———. "Tonio Kröger." In *Tonio Kröger und Mario und der Zauberer: Ein tragisches Reiseerlebnis*, 7–73. Frankfurt am Main: Fischer, 2011.
Mantl, Norbert. *Aloys Sprenger: Der Orientalist und Islamhistoriker aus Nassreith im Tirol: Zum 100. Todestag am 19. Dezember 1993*. Nassereith, Austria: Selbstverlag der Gemeinde Nassereith, 1993.
Marchand, Suzanne L. *German Orientalism in the Age of Empire: Religion, Race, and Scholarship*. Washington, DC, Cambridge, and New York: German Historical Institute and Cambridge University Press, 2009.
Marchionini, Gary, and Edward A. Fox. "Progress Toward Digital Libraries: Augmentation through Integration." *Information Processing and Management* 35, no. 3 (January 1999): 219–225.
Marquardt, Hans. "1950: Dr. Ernst Reclam verläßt im Mai illegal die DDR." In *Hundert 100 Jahre Reclams Universal-Bibliothek: 1867–1967; Beiträge zur Verlagsgeschichte*, edited by Hans Marquardt. Leipzig: Reclam, 1967.
Marx, Karl. "Letter to Laura Lafargue." In *Karl Marx Friedrich Engels Gesamtausgabe*, edited by Hans-Peter Harstick. Vol. 32. Berlin: Akademie-Verlag, 1999.
Marx, Karl, and Friedrich Engels. *Das kommunistische Manifest: Eine moderne Edition*. Hamburg: Argument, 1999.
———. "The Manifesto of the Communist Party." In *Political Writings*, edited by David Fernbach, 1:62–98. New York: Vintage Books, 1974.
McGetchin, Douglas T. *Indology, Indomania, and Orientalism: Ancient India's Rebirth in Modern Germany*. Madison, NJ: Fairleigh Dickinson University Press, 2009.

Meinhof, Carl, ed. *Afrikanische Märchen. Herausgegeben von C. Meinhof.* Jena: E. Diedrichs, 1917.

Melas, Natalie. *All the Difference in the World: Postcoloniality and the Ends of Comparison*. Stanford, CA: Stanford University Press, 2007.

Menzel, Wolfgang. "Einfluß der fremden Literatur." In *Die deutsche Literatur: 2. Vermehrte Auflage, Teil 1*, 67–85. Stuttgart: Hallberg'sche Verlagshandlung, 1828.

———. "Influence of Foreign Literature." In *German Literature*, translated by Thomas Gordon, 1:59–76. Oxford: D. A. Talboys, 1840.

———. "Mass of Literature." In *German Literature*, translated by Thomas Gordon, 1:1–33. Oxford: D. A. Talboys, London, 1840.

———. "Die Masse der Literatur." In *Die deutsche Literatur: 2. Vermehrte Auflage, Theil 1*, 1:1–38. Stuttgart: Hallberg'sche Verlagshandlung, 1836.

———. "Die neue Gallomanie." In *Die deutsche Literatur: 2. Vermehrte Auflage, Theil 4*, 319–346. Stuttgart: Hallberg'sche Verlagshandlung, 1836.

———. "The New Gallo-Mania." In *German Literature*, translated by Thomas Gordon, 4:288–311. Oxford: D. A. Talboys, 1840.

Merveldt, Nikola von. "Books Cannot Be Killed by Fire: The German Freedom Library and the American Library of Nazi-Banned Books as Agents of Cultural Memory." *Library Trends* 55, no. 3 (Winter 2007): 523–535.

Meyer, Richard M. *Die Weltliteratur im zwanzigsten Jahrhundert vom deutschen Standpunkt aus betrachtet*. Stuttgart and Berlin: Deutsche Verlags-Anstalt, 1913.

———. *Die Weltliteratur im zwanzigsten Jahrhundert: Vom deutschen Standpunkt aus betrachtet*. Stuttgart and Berlin: Deutsche Verlags-Anstalt, 1922.

Meylan, Jean-Pierre. "Der Plan einer 'Weltbibliothek' von Romain Rolland und seinem Schweizer Verleger und Mäzen Emil Roniger, 1922–1926." *Librarium* 53, no. 1 (2010): 3–13.

Miksa, Francis. *The Development of Classification at the Library of Congress. Occasional Papers, Number 164*. Champaign: Graduate School of Library and Information Science, Publications Office, University of Illinois, 1984.

Minamoto. *Erzählungen des alten Japan aus dem Konjaku-Monogatari*. Translated by Horst Hammitzsch and Ingrid Schuster. Stuttgart: Reclam, 1965.

Moegelin, Sabine. "Blick in den Themenplan 1989: 1. Neuerscheinungen der Sowjetliteratur." *Der Bücherkarren: Internationale Literatur im Verlag Volk und Welt Berlin* 8 (1988): 14–15.

Molière. *Die Schule der Ehemänner: Lustspiel in drei Aufzügen*. Translated by Emilie Schroeder. Leipzig: Reclam, 1870.

Mommsen, Katharina. "Goethe und China in ihren Wechselbeziehungen." In *Goethe und China, China und Goethe: Bericht des Heidelberger Symposions*, edited by Günther Debon and Adrian Hsia. Bern and New York: Peter Lang, 1985.

Moreto, Agustín. *Donna Diana: Lutspiel in drei Aufzugen*. Translated by Joseph Schreyvogel. Leipzig: Reclam, 1867.

Moretti, Franco. "Conjectures on World Literature." *New Left Review*, no. 1 (2000): 54–68.

———. "Goethe's Faust as a Modern Epic." In *Faust: A Tragedy: Interpretive Notes, Contexts, Modern Criticism*, edited by Walter Arndt and Cyrus Hamlin, 611–634. New York: W. W. Norton, 2001.

Mpe, P. "The Role of the Heinemann African Writers Series in the Development and Promotion of African Literature." *African Studies* 58, no. 1 (1999): 105–122.

Mufti, Aamir. "Erich Auerbach and the Death and Life of World Literature." In *The Routledge Companion to World Literature*, edited by Theo D'haen, David Damrosch, and Djelal Kadir, 71–80. Milton Park, England, and New York: Routledge, 2012.

———. *Forget English! World Literatures and Orientalisms*. Cambridge, MA: Harvard University Press, 2016.

Müller, Friedrich Max. "Aus einem Briefe von Dr. Max Müller." *Zeitschrift der deutschen Morgenländischen Gesellschaft*, no. 3 (1849): 120–121.

Mundt, Theodor. *Geschichte der Literatur der Gegenwart*. Berlin: M. Simion, 1842.

Murti, Kamakshi P. *India the Seductive and Seduced "Other" of German Orientalism*. Westport, CT: Greenwood Press, 2001.

Narang, Gopi Chand. *Amira Khusaro ka Hindavi Kavya: Springara Sangraha ki Barlina Prati sahita*. New Delhi: Simanta Prakasana, 1990.

Naschér, Eduard. *Handbuch der Geschichte der Weltliteratur*. Berlin: Bard, 1900.

Nationalsozialistische Deutsche Arbeiter-Partei, and Reichsparteitag. *Nürnberg 1933 eine Sammlung der wichtigsten Reden auf dem Parteitag der Nationalsozialistischen deutschen Arbeiter-Partei vom 30. August bis 3. September 1933. Mit 22 Abbildungen*. Berlin: Zentralverlag, 1933.

Neue Zürcher Zeitung. "Der Dieb und die Hunde: Nobelpreis für Nagib Machfus." *Der Bücherkarren: Internationale Literatur im Verlag Volk und Welt Berlin*, no. 7 (1988): 13.

O'Donnell, James J. "Engaging the Humanities: The Digital Humanities." *Daedalus* 138, no. 1 (Winter 2009): 99–104.

Olson, Michael P. *The Odyssey of a German National Library: A Short History of the Bayerische Staatsbibliothek, the Staatsbibliothek zu Berlin, the Deutsche Bücherei, and the Deutsche Bibliothek*. Wiesbaden: Harrassowitz, 1996.

Oriental Translation Fund. *Oriental Translation Fund, Report of the Proceedings of the Second General Meeting of the Subscribers to the Oriental Translation Fund: With the Prospectus, Report of the Committee and Regulations*. London: J. L. Cox, 1829.

———. *Report of the Proceedings of the First General Meeting of the Subscribers to the Oriental Translation Fund: With the Prospectus, Report of the Committee, and Regulations*. London: J. L. Cox, 1828.

———. *Report of the Proceedings of the Third General Meeting of the Subscribers to the Oriental Translation Fund: With the Prospectus, Report of the Committee, and Regulations*. London: J. L. Cox, 1830.

Pamuk, Orhan. *Benim Adım Kırmızı*. Istanbul: Iletişim, 1998.

———. "Dünya Edebiyati." In *Öteki renkler: seccme yazılar ve bir hikaaye*, 203–204. Istanbul: İletişim, 1999.

———. *Kar*. Istanbul: İletişim, 2002.

———. *My Name Is Red*. Translated by Erdağ M. Göknar. New York: Alfred A. Knopf, 2001.

———. *The New Life*. Translated by Güneli Gün. New York: Vintage International, 1998.

———. *Other Colors: Essays and a Story*. Translated by Maureen Freely. New York: Alfred A. Knopf, 2007.

———. *Snow*. Translated by Maureen Freely. New York: Alfred A. Knopf, 2004.

———. *Yeni Hayat*. Istanbul: İletişim, 1994.

Patterson, Maureen L. P. "The South Asian P. L. 480 Library Program, 1962–1968." *Journal of Asian Studies* 28, no. 4 (1969): 743–754.

Payr, Bernhard. "Deutsch-französische Begegnungen in dem deutschen Roman 1937." *Weltliteratur: Romane, Erzählungen und Gedichte aller Zeiten und Völker* 31 (April 1938).

Pernau, Margrit. "Entangled Translations: The History of Delhi College." In *The Delhi College: Traditional Elites, the Colonial State, and Education Before 1857*, edited by Margrit Pernau, 1–34. New Delhi: Oxford University Press, 2006.

Piper, Andrew. *Dreaming in Books: The Making of the Bibliographic Imagination in the Romantic Age*. Chicago: University of Chicago Press, 2009.

Piroux, Lorraine. *Moins que livres: essai sur l'illisibilité, du livre des Lumières à la boîte de Cornell*. Québec: Éditions Nota bene, 2010.

Pizer, John David. *The Idea of World Literature: History and Pedagogical Practice*. Baton Rouge: Louisiana State University Press, 2006.

Plenzdorf, Ulrich. *Die neuen Leiden des jungen W*. Frankfurt am Main: Suhrkamp, 1976.

Pollatschek, Walther. *Friedrich Wolf: Eine Biographie*. Berlin: Aufbau-Verlag, 1963.

Pollock, Sheldon I. *The Language of the Gods in the World of Men: Sanskrit, Culture, and Power in Premodern India*. Berkeley: University of California Press, 2006.

Prawer, S. S. *Karl Marx and World Literature*. Oxford: Clarendon Press, 1976.

Procházka, Stephen. "Aloys Sprenger: Orientalist." In *Österreichisches biographisches Lexikon 1815–1950*, 13:49. Vienna: Verlag der Österreichischen Akadamie der Wissenschaften, 2007.

Publishers Weekly: The American Book-Trade Journal. "International Statistics of Book Production 1927." January 21, 1928, 241–253.

Puchner, Martin, ed. *The Norton Anthology of World Literature*. New York: W. W. Norton, 2012.

Pundt, Alfred G. *Arndt and the Nationalist Awakening in Germany*. New York: Columbia University Press, 1935.

Pushkin, Aleksandr Sergeevich. *Der Gefangene Im Kaukasus. Frei Nach Dem Russischen . . . von A. Seubert. [In Verse.]*. Translated by Adolf Friedrich Seubert. Leipzig: Reclam, 1873.

———. *Onegin. Roman in Versen. Frei aus dem Russischen des Alexander Puschkin*. Translated by Adolf Friedrich Seubert. Leipzig: Reclam, 1900.

Racine, Jean. *Phädra: Trauerspiel in fünf Aufzügen*. Translated by Friedrich von Schiller. Leipzig: Reclam, 1868.

Raddatz, Fritz J. *Die Zeit-Bibliothek der 100 Sachbücher*. Frankfurt am Main: Suhrkamp, 1984.

Radek, Karl. "Karl Radek: Contemporary World Literature and the Tasks of Proletarian Art (August 1934)." Marxist Internet Archive, 2004. http://www.marxists.org/archive/radek/1934/sovietwritercongress.htm.

Ramanujan, A. K. "Three Hundred Ramayanas." In *Many Ramayanas: The Diversity of a Narrative Tradition in South Asia*, edited by Paula Richman, 22–48. Berkeley: University of California Press, 1991.

Rausse, Hubert. *Die Welt-Literatur: Spanische Novellen. Die Welt-Literatur: Die besten Romane und Novellen aller Zeiten und Völker 1*. Regensburg and Leipzig: Verlag der Weltliteratur / Habbel und Naumann, 1923.

Reclam. "Lesestoffe für den Literaturunterricht im Schuljahr 1959–60." In *Das Reclam-Buch*, 14:12–13. Leipzig: Reclam, 1960.

———. *Reclam Katalog 1904*. Leipzig: Philipp Reclam jun., 1904. Deutsches Buch- und Schrift Museum, Leipzig, Archiv Verlagsgeschichte.

———. *Reclam Katalog 1949*. Leipzig: Philipp Reclam jun., 1949. Deutsches Buch- und Schrift Museum, Leipzig, Archiv Verlagsgeschichte.

———. *Reclam Katalog 1953*. Leipzig: Philipp Reclam jun., 1953. Deutsches Buch- und Schrift Museum, Leipzig, Archiv Verlagsgeschichte.

———. *Reclam Katalog 1956*. Leipzig: Philipp Reclam jun., 1956. Deutsches Buch- und Schrift Museum, Leipzig, Archiv Verlagsgeschichte.

———. *Reclam Katalog 1957*. Leipzig: Philipp Reclam jun., 1957. Deutsches Buch- und Schrift Museum, Leipzig, Archiv Verlagsgeschichte.

———. *Reclam Katalog 1958*. Leipzig: Philipp Reclam jun., 1958. Deutsches Buch- und Schrift Museum, Leipzig, Archiv Verlagsgeschichte.

———. *Reclam Katalog 1959*. Leipzig: Philipp Reclam jun., 1959. Deutsches Buch- und Schrift Museum, Leipzig, Archiv Verlagsgeschichte.

———. *Reclam Katalog 1960*. Stuttgart: Philipp Reclam jun., 1960. Deutsches Buch- und Schrift Museum, Leipzig, Archiv Verlagsgeschichte.

———. *Reclams Universal-Bibliothek: Neuauflagen und Neuerscheinungen seit 1945*. Leipzig: Philipp Reclam jun., 1952. Deutsches Buch- und Schrift Museum, Leipzig, Archiv Verlagsgeschichte.

Reclam, Ernst. "Brief an Hermann Hesse: 8. Juli 1929," July 8, 1929. Deutsches Literaturarchiv, Marbach.

Reher, Werner. "Soziologische Streifzüge durch englische Romane." *Die Weltliteratur: Berichte, Leseproben und Wertung*, no. 7 (July 1941): 180–183.

Reichsschrifttumskammer. *Jahresliste des schädlichen und unerwünschten Schrifttums*. Leipzig: Ernst Hedrich Nachs Verlag, 1939.

———. "Literarische Übersetzungen." *Börsenblatt für den deutschen Buchhandel*, no. 122 (May 28, 1938): 498.

Reschke, Thomas. "Bücher haben die Wende von 1989 mit vorbereitet." In *Fenster zur Welt: Eine Geschichte des DDR-Verlages Volk und Welt*, edited by Simone Barck and Siegfried Lokatis, 15–30. Berlin: Links, 2003.

Rice, Yael. "A Persian Mahabharata: The 1598–1599 Razmnama." *Manoa* 22, no. 1 (2010): 125–131.

Robbins, Louise. "American Libraries and the Freedom to Read." In *Bibliotheken, Bücher und andere Medien in der Zeit des Kalten Krieges*, edited by Peter Vodosek and Wolfgang Schmidt, 115–131. Wiesbaden: Harrassowitz, 2005.

———. *The Dismissal of Miss Ruth Brown: Civil Rights, Censorship, and the American Library*. Norman: University of Oklahoma Press, 2000.

Roth, R. "Nachricht über etliche indische Handschriften und Drucke." *Zeitschrift der deutschen Morgenländischen Gesellschaft*, no. 1 (1847): 199–201.

Ruben, Walter. "Rabindranath Tagore: Indiens grosser Humanist." *Der Bücherkarren: internationale Literatur im Verlag Volk und Welt Berlin*, no. 1 (1961): 5–6.

Rumpf, Walter. "Die Volksbüchereien." In *Die Welt des Buches, eine Kunde vom Buch*, edited by Hellmuth Langenbucher, 224–234. Ebenhausen bei München: Wilhelm Langewiesche-Brandt, 1938.

Ruppert, Hans, and Goethe-Nationalmuseum. *Goethes Bibliothek: Katalog*. Weimar: Arion Verlag, 1958.

Said, Edward W. *Orientalism*. New York: Vintage Books, 1994.

Salinger, J. D. *Der Fänger im Roggen: Roman*. Translated by Heinrich Böll and Irene Muehlon. Cologne: Kiepenheuer und Witsch, 1962; repr. Volk und Welt, 1965.

Savinije, Bas. "The European Library: Annual Reports and Accounts 2013." The Hague: The European Library, 2013.

Scherr, Johannes. *Bildersaal der Weltliteratur aus dem Literaturschatz der Morgenländer, der Alten, etc. ausgewählt, systematisch geordnet*. Stuttgart: A. Becher, 1848.

Schiller, Dieter. "Vom 'Mamlock' zum 'Beaumarchais': Friedrich Wolf im Exil 1933 bis 1940." In *Friedrich Wolf 2003: Zum 50. Todestag Friedrich Wolfs: Beiträge zu den Friedrich-Wolf-Kulturtagen 2003 in Berlin, Lehnitz und Potsdam*, edited by Thomas Naumann, 61–75. Lehnitz: Friedrich-Wolf-Gesellschaft, 2003.

Schimmel, Annemarie. *German Contributions to the Study of Indo-Pakistani Linguistics*. Hamburg: German-Pakistan Forum, 1981.

Schlegel, August Wilhelm von. *Bhagavad-Gita, id est Thespesion melos sive almi Krishnae et Arjunae colloquium de rebus divinis, Bharateae episodium*. Bonn, 1823.

———. "German Oriental Literature: Professor Schlegel's Prospectus." *Asiatic Journal and Monthly Register for British India and Its Dependencies* 17 (January 1824): 52–53.

Schlösser, Anselm. "Die englisch-amerikanische Invasion." *Die Weltliteratur: Berichte, Leseproben und Wertung*, no. 5 (May 1940): 70–74.

Schröter, Erich. "Vom Zusammenbruch zu neuen Aufgaben." *Der Volksbibliothekar Zeitschrift für den Volksbücherei-Praxis* 1, no. 1 (1947, 1946): 5–13.

———. "Zur Kritik der Bücherbestände." *Der Bibliothekar: Zeitschrift für die Bücherei-Praxis* 4, no. 8 (1950): 402–406.

Schuckov, G. "Ein Befehl Marschall Schukows." *Der Volksbibliothekar: Zeitschrift für den Volksbücherei-Praxis* 1, no. 1 (October 1946): 14.

Schultz, Klaus. "Früchte des Zorns: Zur Literatur des anderen Amerika." *Der Bücherkarren: Internationale Literatur im Verlag Volk und Welt Berlin*, no. 3 (1964): 3–4.

Schulz, Gerd. "Das Klassikerjahr 1867 und die Gründung von Reclams Universal-Bibliothek." In *Reclam 125 Jahre Universal-Bibliothek, 1867–1992: Verlags- und kulturgeschichtliche Aufsätze*, edited by Dietrich Bode, 11–28. Stuttgart: Reclam, 1992.

Schwabe, Johann Joachim. *Allgemeine Historie der Reisen zu Wasser und Lande; oder Sammlung aller Reisebeschreibungen, welche bis itzo in verschiedenen Sprachen von allen Völkern herausgegeben worden: Worinnen der wirkliche Zustand aller Nationen vorgestellet, und das Merkwürdigste, Nützlichste und Wahrhaftigste in Europa, Asia, Africa und America enthalten ist; Mit nöthigen Landkarten und mancherley Abbildungen 9*. Leipzig: Arkstee und Merkus, 1751.

Seyhan, Azade. *Writing Outside the Nation*. Princeton, NJ: Princeton University Press, 2001.

Sontag, Susan. "Literature Is Freedom." In *At the Same Time: Essays and Speeches*, edited by Paolo Dilonardo and Anne Jump, 192–209. New York: Farrar, Straus, and Giroux, 2007.

Spivak, Gayatri Chakravorty. *A Critique of Postcolonial Reason: Toward a History of the Vanishing Present*. Cambridge, MA: Harvard University Press, 1999.

———. *Death of a Discipline*. New York: Columbia University Press, 2003.

———. "The Stakes of a World Literature." In *An Aesthetic Education in the Era of Globalization*, 455–466. Cambridge, MA: Harvard University Press, 2012.

Sprenger, Aloys. *A Catalogue of the Arabic, Persian and Hindu'sta'ny Manuscripts, of the Libraries of the King of Oudh, Compiled under the Orders of the Government of India. Vol. 1, Containing Persian and Hindu'sta'ny Poetry*. Calcutta: J. Thomas, 1854.

———. *A Catalogue of the Bibliotheca Orientalis Sprengeriana*. Giessen: W. Keller, 1857.

———. *Dr. Halm und die Bibliotheca Sprengeriana*. Heidelberg: N. Adlon, 1857.

———. "Literaturbericht aus Ostindien." *Zeitschrift der deutschen Morgenländischen Gesellschaft*, no. 3 (1849): 344–357.

———. "Über eine Handschrift des ersten Bandes des Kitáb Tabaqát al-Kabyr vom Sekretär des Wáqidy." *Zeitschrift der deutschen Morgenländischen Gesellschaft*, no. 3 (1849): 450–455.

St. John, John Richard. *William Heinemann: A Century of Publishing, 1890–1990*. London: Heinemann, 1990.

Staatliche Landesfachstelle für Volksbüchereiwesen Sachsen. *Liste Verbotener Und Nicht Erwünschter Schriften*. Dresden: Staatliche Landesfachstelle für Volksbüchereiwesen Sachsen, 1934

Steinmetz, George. *The Devil's Handwriting: Precoloniality and the German Colonial State in Qingdao, Samoa, and Southwest Africa*. Chicago: University of Chicago Press, 2007.

Stephen, Leslie. *Hours in a Library*. London: Folio Society, 1991.

Strich, Fritz. *Goethe and World Literature*. Translated by C. A. M. Sym. London: Routledge and K. Paul, 1949.

———. *Goethe und die Weltliteratur*. Bern: A. Francke, 1946.

Strothmann, Dietrich. *Nationalsozialistische Literaturpolitik: Ein Beitrag zur Publizistik im Dritten Reich. 2. Auflage*. Bonn: H. Bouvier, 1963.

Studentowsky, Werner. "Partei und Volksbücherei." *Die Bücherei: Zeitschrift der Reichsstelle für das Volksbüchereiwesen* 7/8, no. 4 (1937): 289–294.

Summarische Beschreibung der ganzen Welt: von den vier Theilen der Erden Asia, Europa, Afrika und Amerika; was in der ganzen Welt an allen Orten und

Enden für merkwürdige Sachen zu sehen und zu finden; wie auch von den vier Elementen, woher die Winde kommen, von Erdbeben, Finsternissen, Sonn und Mond, von allen Geschöpfen Gottes, und wie alle Creaturen erschaffen. Augsburg: n.p., 1750.

Tagore, Rabindranath. "Shakuntala." In *Rabindranath Tagore: Selected Writings on Literature and Language*, edited by Sukanta Chaudhuri and Sisir Kumar Das, translated by Sukanta Chaudhuri, 237–251. New Delhi and New York: Oxford University Press, 2001.

Tatlock, Lynne. "The Book Trade and 'Reading Nation' in the Long Nineteenth Century." In *Publishing Culture and the "Reading Nation": German Book History in the Long Nineteenth Century*, edited by Lynne Tatlock, 1–21. Rochester, NY: Camden House, 2010.

Taylor, William. "Analysis of the McKenzie Manuscripts Deposited at the Madras College Library." *Journal of the Asiatic Society*, no. 75 (March 1838): 173–192.

Thapar, Romila. "Orientalism, German Romanticism, and the Image of Sakuntala." In *Śakuntalā: Texts, Readings, Histories*, 197–217. London: Anthem Press, 2002.

———. *Somanatha, the Many Voices of a History*. New Delhi and New York: Penguin, Viking, 2004.

Thomik, Josef. *Nationalsozialismus als Ersatzreligion: Die Zeitschriften "Weltliteratur" und "Die Weltliteratur" (1935/1944) als Träger nationalsozialistischer Ideologie: Zugleich ein Beitrag zur Affäre Schneider/Schwerte*. Edited by Josef Schreier. Aachen: Einhard, 2009.

Thomsen, Mads Rosendahl. *Mapping World Literature: International Canonization and Transnational Literatures*. London and New York: Continuum, 2008.

Tomer, Christinger. "Digital Libraries in Public Libraries." Edited by Miriam A. Drake. *Encyclopedia of Library and Information Science*. New York: Marcel Dekker, 2003: 884–891.

Tschörtner, Heinz-Dieter. "Der Bücherkarren–Eine Literaturzeitschrift als Werbeblatt." In *Fenster zur Welt: Eine Geschichte des DDR-Verlages Volk und Welt*, edited by Simone Barck and Siegfried Lokatis, 15–30. Berlin: Links, 2003.

Tsu, Jing. "National Literature and World Literature." In *The Routledge Companion to World Literature*, edited by Theo D'haen, David Damrosch, and Djelal Kadir, 158–168. Milton Park, England, and New York: Routledge, 2012.

Turgenev, Ivan Sergeevich. *Ein König Lear der Steppe . . . Aus dem Russischen von W. Lange*. Translated by Wilhelm Lange. Leipzig: Reclam, 1876.

———. *Väter und Söhne . . . Aus dem Russischen von W. Lange. Zweite Auflage, mit einem Nachwort des Verfassers*. Translated by Wilhelm Lange. Leipzig: Reclam, 1876.

Ulbricht, Walter. "Reclam Katalog 1955." Leipzig: Reclam, 1955.

———. "Das Ziel der sozialistischen Erziehung: Auf dem V. Parteitag der SED." In *Das Reclam-Buch* 14. Leipzig: Reclam, 1960.

Varma, Maha Devi. "Sahitya, Sanskriti aur Shaasan." In *Sambhaashana*, 38–43. Allahabad: Sahitya Bhavana, 1975.

Veigl, Franz Xavier. *Gründliche Nachrichten über die Verfassung der Landschaft von Maynas, in Süd-Amerika, bis zum Jahre 1768*. Nürnberg: Johann Eberhard Zeh, 1798.

Verhandlungen der ersten Versammlung deutscher und ausländischer Orientalisten in Dresden den 1. 2. 3. und 4. Oktober 1844. Leipzig: W. Engelmann, 1845.

Virgil. *Vergils Aeneide*. Translated by Johann Heinrich Voss. Leipzig: Reclam, 1870.

Volkert, Hans-Joachim. "Der Autor von Weltrang: Salman Rushdie." *Der Bücherkarren: Internationale Literatur im Verlag Volk und Welt Berlin*, no. 4 (1990): 5.

Vorstand des Allgemeinen Deutschen Schriftsteller Verbandes. "Eine deutsche Reichsbibliothek." *Das Magazin für die Literatur des In- und Auslandes: Kritisches Organ der Weltliteratur* 50, no. 21 (1881): 323–324.

Wagner, Georg. "Ein 'Abendländer in der neuen Welt': Gespräch mit Thornton Wilder." *Freude an Büchern: Monatshefte für Weltliteratur* 4, no. 3 (1953): 128–138.

Wagner-Dittmar, Christine. "Goethe und die chinesische Literatur." In *Studien zu Goethes Alterswerken*, edited by Erich Trunz, 122–228. Frankfurt am Main: Athenäum-Verlag, 1971.

Walkowitz, Rebecca L. *Born Translated: The Contemporary Novel in an Age of World Literature*. New York: Columbia University Press, 2015.

———. "The Location of Literature: The Transnational Book and the Migrant Writer." *Contemporary Literature* 47, no. 4 (2006): 527–545.

Wallace, R. G, and F. L. Rhode. *Denkwürdigkeiten Indiens enthaltend eine kurze geographische Beschreibung von Ost-Indien; nebst einer gedrängten Geschichte Hindostans von den frühesten Zeitaltern bis zu Ende der Marquis Hastingischen Verwaltung im Jahre 1823*. Frankfurt am Mein: Wilmans, 1826.

Walser, Martin. *In Goethes Hand: Szenen aus dem 19. Jahrhundert*. Frankfurt am Main: Suhrkamp, 1982.

Weber, Jürgen. "Herzogin Anna Amalia Bibliothek: Bestandbeschreibung 2.11." In Fabian, *Handbuch der historischen Buchbestände in Deutschland, Österreich und Europa: Herzogin Anna Amalia Bibliothek*, 2003. http://fabian.sub.uni-goettingen.de/fabian?Herzogin_Anna_Amalia_Bibliothek.

Weidhaas, Peter. *Und kam in die Welt der Büchermenschen: Erinnerungen.* Berlin: Links, 2007.

———. *Zur Geschichte der Frankfurter Buchmesse.* Frankfurt am Main: Suhrkamp, 2003.

Weinrich, Harald. "Chamisso, Chamisso Authors, and Globalization." Translated by Marshall Brown and Jane K. Brown. *PMLA* 119, no. 5 (October 1, 2004): 1336–1346.

Wellek, René, and Austin Warren. *Theory of Literature.* New York: Harcourt, Brace, 1949.

Die Welt-Literatur: Die besten Romane und Novellen aller Zeiten und Völker. "'Die Sammlung': Neue Folge der Weltliteratur." No. 21 (1924): 45–46.

———. "E. T. A. Hoffmann: Einführung." No. 37 (1916): 1.

———. "François Gayot de Pitaval: Einführung." No. 14 (1917): 1.

———. "Schickt die 'Welt-Literatur' ins Feld: Sie bringt die besten Romane und Novellen aller Zeiten und Völker." No. 13 (1916): 12.

———. "Die 'Welt-Literatur' als Geschenk für Soldaten und Offiziere." No. 13 (1916): 12.

Die Welt-Literatur: Jede Woche ein Werk: Die besten Romane und Novellen aller Zeiten und Völker. "Ankündigung 1." No. 52 (1919): 17.

———. "Ankündigung 2." No. 11 (1921): 9.

———. "Anzeige 1." No. 14 (1917): 6.

———. "Anzeige 2." No. 24 (1917): 10.

———. "Lob für Die Welt-Literatur 1." No. 36 (1917): 10.

———. "Lob für Die Welt-Literatur 2." No. 12 (1920): 12.

Weltliteratur: Romane, Erzählungen und Gedichte aller Zeiten und Völker. "Benito Mussolini." No. 30 (March 1938).

———. "Deutsche Dichtung in Österreich 1." No. 32 (May 1938).

———. "Deutsche Dichtung in Österreich 2." No. 33 (June 1938).

———. "Norwegische Literatur." No. 2 (November 1935).

———. "Polnische Literatur." No. 6 (March 1936).

———. "Schiksal an der Memel." No. 1 (October 1935): 1–2.

———. "Sudetendeutsche Dichtung." No. 35 (August 1938).

———. "Südslavisches Schrifttum." No. 9 (June 1936).

———. "Ungarische Dichtung." No. 18 (March 1937).

———. "Zu den Auslandsheften der Weltliteratur." No. 9 (June 1936): 129.

Werder, Peter von. "Nordamerikanische Romane." *Die Weltliteratur: Berichte, Leseproben und Wertung*, nos. 3–4 (April 1944): 32–36.

Werner, Meike. "Modern Jena as a Model of Cultural Regeneration in Wilhelmine Germany." *Journal of the History of Ideas* 74, no. 2 (2013): 267–288.

———. *Moderne in der Provinz: Kulturelle Experimente im Fin de Siècle Jena.* Göttingen: Wallstein, 2003.

Wezler, Albrecht, trans. *Nala und Damayanti; eine Episode aus dem Mahbharata*. Stuttgart: Philipp Reclam, 1965.

Whitmire, Ethelene. *Regina Anderson Andrews: Harlem Renaissance Librarian*. Urbana: University of Illinois Press, 2014.

Wiegler, Paul. *Geschichte der fremdsprachigen Weltliteratur*. Munich: E. Heimeran, 1933.

———. *Geschichte der Weltliteratur: Dichtung fremder Völker*. Berlin: Ullstein, 1920.

Wienbarg, Ludolf. "Goethe und die Weltliteratur." *Literarische und kritische Blätter der Börsen-Halle*, no. 1011 (March 2, 1835): 204–207.

Wilhelm, Richard, ed. *Chinesische Volksmärchen*. Translated by Richard Wilhelm. Jena: E. Diederichs, 1914.

Winckler, Lutz. "Bibliotheken für neue Leser? Zur Literaturpolitik in der Sowjetisch Besetzten Zone und der frühen DDR." In *Dialektik des Anfangs: Spiele des Lachens, Literaturpolitik in Bibliotheken: Über Texte von Heiner Müller, Franz Fühmann, Stefan Heym*, edited by Paul Gerhard Klussmann and Heinrich Mohr, 91–108. Bonn: Bouvier Verlag, 1986.

———. *Kulturelle Erneuerung und gesellschaftlicher Auftrag: Zur Bestandspolitik der öffentlichen Bibliotheken und Betriebsbüchereien in der SBZ und DDR 1945 bis 1951*. Tübingen: M. Niemeyer, 1987.

Wolf, Friedrich. "Faschistische und Antifaschistische Dramaturgie im Westen." In *Aufsätze 1919–1944*, edited by Else Wolf and Walther Pollatschek, 335–361. Berlin: Aufbau-Verlag, 1967.

Wright, Alex. *Cataloging the World: Paul Otlet and the Birth of the Information Age*. Oxford and New York: Oxford University Press, 2014.

Würffel, Reinhard. "Schwerter Verlag." *Würffels Signete-Lexikon über 4500 deutschsprachige Verlage, 11000 Signete*. Berlin: Grotesk-Verlag, 2010.

Wüst, Walther. "Indogermanische Bekenntnisse." *Die Weltliteratur: Berichte, Leseproben und Wertung* 7 (July 1942): 134–142.

Yashin, Veli N. "Euro(tro)pology Philology, World Literature, and the Legacy of Erich Auerbach." *Yearbook of Comparative Literature* 57 (May 2011): 269–290.

Yildiz, Yasemin. *Beyond the Mother Tongue: The Postmonolingual Condition*. New York: Fordham University Press, 2013.

Zaunert, Paul, ed. *Deutsche Märchen seit Grimm*. Jena: E. Diederichs, 1922.

Zeco, Munevera. "Research Notes: The National and University Library of Bosnia and Herzegovina during the Current War." Translated by William B. Tomljanovich. *Library Quarterly* 66, no. 3 (1996): 294–301.

Zeitschrift der deutschen Morgenländischen Gesellschaft. "A. Sprengers neuste Leistungen." No. 3 (1849): 359–360.

———. "Eine orientalische Bibliothek in Rhodus." No. 3 (1849): 120.

INDEX